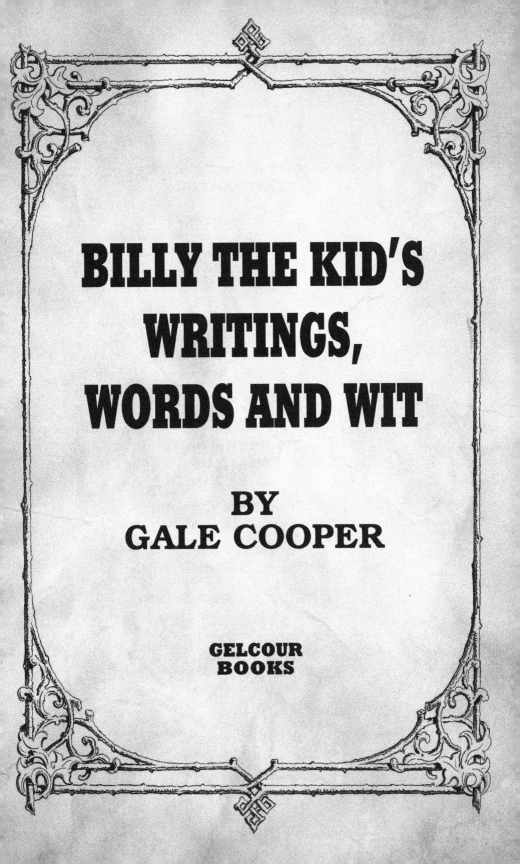

BILLY THE KID'S WRITINGS, WORDS AND WIT

BY
GALE COOPER

GELCOUR
BOOKS

ISBN: 978-1-949626-04-9 HARDCOVER
ISBN: 978-1-949626-05-6 PAPERBACK
Library of Congress Control Number: 2018954304

FIRST EDITION © 2011 Gale Cooper
SECOND EDITION © 2017 Gale Cooper

GELCOUR BOOKS
2270D Wyoming Boulevard NE, Suite 217
Albuquerque, NM 87112

WEBSITE:
GaleCooperBillyTheKidBooks.com

YOUTUBE:
Gale Cooper's Real Billy The Kid

ORDERING THIS BOOK:
Amazon.com, BarnesandNoble.com, bookstores

Printed in the United States of America
on acid free paper

OTHER BILLY THE KID BOOKS
BY GALE COOPER:

*BILLY AND PAULITA: THE SAGA OF BILLY THE KID,
PAULITA MAXWELL, AND THE SANTA FE RING*

*THE LOST PARDON OF BILLY THE KID:
AN ANALYSIS FACTORING IN THE SANTA FE RING,
GOVERNOR LEW WALLACE'S DILEMMA,
AND A TERRITORY IN REBELLION*

*THE SANTA FE RING VERSUS BILLY THE KID:
THE MAKING OF AN AMERICAN MONSTER*

*BILLY THE KID'S PRETENDERS
BRUSHY BILL & JOHN MILLER*

*CRACKING THE BILLY THE KID CASE HOAX:
THE STRANGE PLOT TO EXHUME BILLY THE KID,
CONVICT SHERIFF PAT GARRETT OF MURDER,
AND BECOME PRESIDENT OF THE UNITED STATES*

*BLANDINA SEGALE,
THE NUN WHO RODE ON BILLY THE KID:
SLEUTHING A FOISTED FRONTIER FABLE*

*THE COLD CASE BILLY THE KID MEGAHOAX:
A RASCALLY REPLAY OF BILLY THE KID CASE'S
FORENSIC FLIMFLAM AND BRUSHY BILL'S
BILLY THE KID BAMBOOZLE*

**For William Henry Bonney:
a rebel with a cause**

"I am not afraid to die like a man fighting."

W.H. Bonney

(Letter to Governor Lew Wallace,
Thursday, March 20, 1879)

Contents

INTRODUCTION

BILLY BONNEY'S HISTORY

SPEAKING THROUGH TIME

WORLD FOR THE WORDS

WORDS OF FRIENDS AND FOES

NINETEENTH CENTURY HANDWRITING

BILLY BONNEY'S WRITING STYLE

ANONYMOUS REGULATOR MANIFESTO LETTER

DEPOSITION TO ATTORNEY ANGEL

BILL OF SALE TO HENRY HOYT

GOVERNOR WALLACE'S AMNESTY PROCLAMATION

BILLY'S FIRST LETTER TO LEW WALLACE

BILLY-WALLACE MEETING

BILLY'S LETTER FLURRY TO WALLACE AND WILSON

WALLACE INTERVIEWS BILLY

THE "BILLIE" LETTER FRAGMENT

WALLACE'S OMINOUS LETTER TO CARL SCHURZ

BILLY'S LOST GRAND JURY TESTIMONY

BILLY'S COURT OF INQUIRY TESTIMONY

HUNTED BILLY'S LETTER TO WALLACE

JAILED BILLY'S LETTERS TO LEW WALLACE

BILLY'S MESILLA HANGING TRIAL

BILLY'S JAIL LETTER TO EDGAR CAYPLESS

BILLY'S BALCONY SPEECH

BILLY'S IRONIC WIT

AFTERMATH

REFERENCES AND RESOURCES

OLD-TIMER'S FOREWORD

I'm the old-timer who commenced jawing fer this here author's Billy the Kid novel called *Billy and Paulita*; bout Billy being a freedom fighter, not no outlaw. And me being fictional ain't stopped me from kicking the horse into a gallop fer her Billy books ever since; since she's busier then a one-armed monkey with fleas in helping Billy Bonney's repatation - which was basically amazing fer a teenager; which is when he got his repatation.

Not that I bring luck. After that novel, her books fought varmints messing with Billy's history. *Billy the Kid's Pretenders* took on long-in-the-tooth liars saying they was Billy in the 1900's. And her *MegaHoax: The Strange Plot to Exhume Billy the Kid and Become President* stopped modern politicos hijacking Billy's history fer pocket-lining. Basically she's been collecting big ol' enemies as good as Billy did in his day; and that's not lucky.

Anyways, bad-mouthing Billy - in his day called Billy the Kid only by his enemies (they was called the Santa Fe Ring) - sure as heck gets you this here author snapping at your heels.

Anyways, this here book is this here author's fight against calling Billy "illiterate." Fact is, he spelled good and wrote a better hand then Governor Lew Wallace, who he was mostly writing to.

The bonus of this book is that the author figered out that an old letter that Lew Wallace hung onto was by Billy too; and she put it in here with all her ideas bout how great it is.

Another bonus is her showing Billy's fight with that Santa Fe Ring which makes Billy's words make sense. Also thrown in is this author's fight with today's Santa Fe Ring and with lily-livered historians who's been keeping Billy's repatation down.

So this here book's pretty much like bringing Billy Bonney back to life, with him letter-writing and talking - like in his depositioning and his court testifying and his interviewing with newsmen - which was all smarter then a tree-full of owls; and brave too, cause he was risking his life doing all that. But he was the kind who'd die standing up - and he did.

And he did it all with a laugh, cause basically he was happy to be alive, foxy enough to stay alive, and knew that most everything is funny if you think of it that way.

Vern Blanton Johnson, Jr.
Lincoln, Lincoln County, New Mexico

AUTHOR'S PREFACE

Reading 40,000 pages of archival documents and books for my *Billy and Paulita* novel, left me impressed by Billy Bonney. And his own writings, words, and wit helped me to extrapolate his personality for that docufiction. To his admiring compatriots, Billy was a freedom fighter they called "Kid." To corrupt Santa Fe Ring politicians, who killed him as the last rebel of the lost Lincoln County War, he was the outlaw: "Billy the Kid."

Billy had the last say because he left his words in a deposition, letters, court testimony, and newspaper interviews. And authenticated here is another letter, with intriguing implications.

Billy's words are of a teenager unintimidated by authority; audaciously bargaining for clemency with a governor, or testifying against murderers and the military for his own anti-Ring agenda.

Despite his limited education, his articulate and literate early letters are in fine Spencerian penmanship. Later, in custody, he apologized for script imperfections caused by wearing handcuffs.

Speaking first through time at eighteen, and in an 1878 deposition to an attorney sent by President Rutherford B. Hayes to investigate the Santa Fe Ring-linked murder of John Henry Tunstall, Billy displays meticulous detail and roguish brashness. Only Ring corruption prevented the convictions he sought.

Billy's Grand Jury testimonies, in 1878 and 1879, could also have hanged Ringmen, if not for corruption that blocked verdicts.

In 1879, besides Billy's gubernatorial testimony for amnesty, he testified in a Court of Inquiry against the commander whose illegal intervention in the Lincoln County War brought defeat to Billy's side. But corruption prevailed again, exonerating that man.

Nevertheless, unremitting injustice dimmed neither Billy's spirit nor humor. After his capture in 1880, to interviewing newspapermen, he merely quipped and joked. For example, about his alleged killings, he said that over two hundred men died in the Lincoln County War, but he had not killed all of them.

Billy's marveling contemporary friends - whose own late-in-life memoirs complement his writings, words, and wit - undo negative propaganda of his Santa Fe Ring enemies, and by his subsequent pretenders, hoaxers, and cautious historians.

Gale Cooper
Sandia Park, New Mexico

Editorial Methodology

Editorial methodology for the text to follow is presented here.

REPETITION OF INFORMATION

- For reference, some facts are repeated throughout the book.

PRESENTATION OF ORIGINAL WRITINGS

- Original writings are in italics; and retain spacing, underlinings, cross-outs, blanks, idiosyncrasies, and errors.
- Period newspaper articles are in distinguishing fonts.
- Reproductions of all original Billy the Kid writings are in Appendixes 1-11, which are referenced in the preceding text.
- Original documents sometimes have tiny, bracketed, archival dates on their top right corner.

COMMENTARY ON ORIGINAL WRITINGS

- Author's input within original texts is in brackets or boldface.

RETAINED ERRORS IN ORIGINAL WRITINGS

- Misspelled words appear without use of [sic].
- Some misspelled or omitted personal names, for historical clarity, are corrected in brackets.
- Grammatical errors remain.
- Missing periods, common with Billy Bonney, are not added.
- Missing capitalizations at sentence's start, or capitalizations used for emphasis, are retained.
- Spaces left by a writer (indicating unknown information, like a first name) are retained.
- Cross-outs or underlinings are retained as per the writer.

ATTRIBUTIONS OF ORIGINAL WRITINGS

- In Figure labels
- In Appendices 1-11
- In Annotated Bibliograph

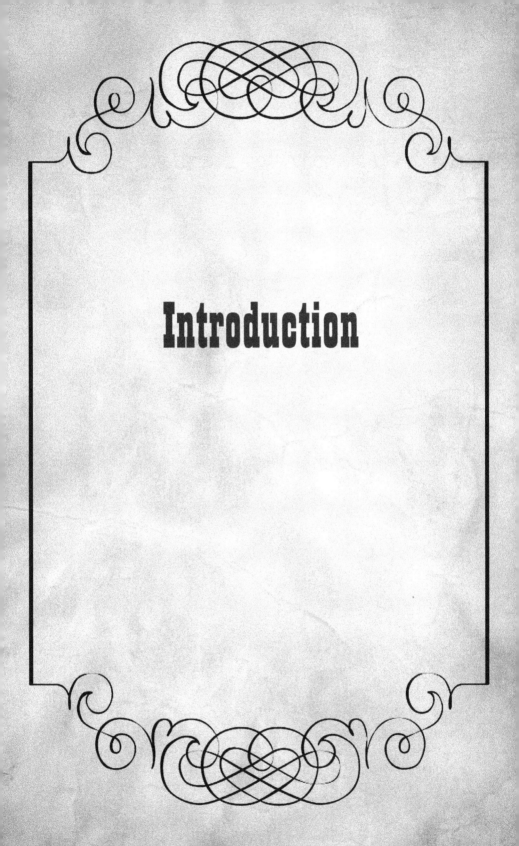

Introduction

OUTLAW VERSUS FREEDOM FIGHTER

Revolutionary uprisings yield heroes and villains because historians may be the second oldest profession, pandering to victors. One such victim is Billy Bonney, made infamous by his enemies as "Billy the Kid;" and still lurching between personas of illiterate homicidal outlaw or literate freedom fighter.

As Billy's revisionist historian, my focus is on New Mexico Territory's robber barons, who killed him to conceal their crimes; until his glaring fame exposed them as the monstrous Santa Fe Ring: spawned in his lifetime and continuing to ours. Fittingly, Billy's own writings and words vindicate him from old mythology and historians' conservatism, while exposing the political rapacity and hypocrisy of foes that set his fate.

Billy Bonney's life spanned the heyday of America's dream of a limitless Frontier. In that vast southwest, where skydome met horizon's perimeter of mountainous desert plains, lived townspeople impassioned by liberties won in their recent Civil War and founding Revolutionary War. Waning of Frontier optimism came not from barbed wire's segmenting open range, not from railroads' ending cattle drives and cowboys, but from emergence of two Americas: one a power elite, the other its increasingly disenfranchised majority - tyranny's formula.

Billy lived at this tipping point.

And he, with others, fought the Lincoln County War; believing that only sixty men - Hispanic, Anglo, and African-American - could stop a political machine. They almost did, in five days, before illegal military intervention in the service of Santa Fe Ring domination, defeated them on the sixth.

Billy Bonney further threatened Ring domination by his atypical multiculturalism, which, in racist times, united Anglos and Hispanics; the latter often land-grab victims after their lost Mexican-American War. Its 1848 Treaty of Guadalupe Hidalgo ceded northern Mexico - five hundred twenty-five thousand square miles - to the United States. Though promised protection, stranded Mexicans became prey to Anglo attorneys using Congressional demand for title proof to steal their holdings. Those profits transmogrified into the Santa Fe Ring.

Ultimately, Billy Bonney's fatal bullet, from a New Mexico Territory lawman's gun, was released from Washington, D.C. Could Billy, the downtrodden people's hero, have instigated another uprising? That bullet was the Ring's answer.

A CHARMING DANGEROUS BOY

For a teenaged homeless drifter, Billy Bonney made a near inconceivable impact on his times. To friends he was "a wonder": brilliant, charismatic, romantic, wild, dangerous, respected, and feared.

At 5 feet 8 inches - above average for his day - he was a lithe 140 pounds: a fair, handsome, beardless youth, pictured in his tintype with thick hair curling; wearing winter layers and the photographer's narrow-brimmed prop hat, rather than his usual Mexican sombrero. Sneering, he displays his right hand cocked at a gunman's, high-holstered, revolver butt; and his left hand flaunts his upright Winchester '73 carbine and pinky-ring shiner, used in poker cheating.

Because he was unforgettable, the Lincoln County insurrection against the Santa Fe Ring is still remembered. And his traitorous ambush murder in the mansion bedroom of his young lover's brother made his death a Greek tragedy.

Knowing he was spectacular, Billy's contemporaries, both friends and foes, saved his words. Also saved are his anti-Ring deposition and some court testimonies, and his letters seeking gubernatorial pardon for his wartime killings.

Billy himself knew he was special. His jaunty audacity came from intelligence, preternatural physicality, fearlessness, and joie de vivre; flaunted in dancing and singing, jailbreaking, shooting, rebelling, thieving, killing, and terrifying adversaries.

Middle class in early years, literate through home and brief public schooling, by 14½ Billy was abruptly homeless after his mother's death and his step-father's abandonment. Already bi-lingual in Spanish, he then survived, for the rest of his life, by wits alone - on both sides of the law and in two cultures.

By eighteen, even among past Civil War soldiers or outlaws drifting into New Mexico Territory, Billy was respected as rough; though affectionately called "Kid." Possibly he even invigorated the Lincoln County War's timid attorney leader.

And a year after that war was lost, that county's local Ring boss made a peace overture to teenaged Billy. Did that measure the boy's power? Billy had already been present at, or active in, each wartime gunfire death of a Ringmen.

Billy Bonney's first killing was at seventeen, in Arizona: shooting a bullying, but unarmed, blacksmith. He escaped, but the Coroner's Jury called it unjustified homicide; thus, a likely trial verdict of first degree murder. So, from that August 1877 day, till his last, a hangman's noose hung over him like the sword of Damocles. Death's reminder just toughened him early.

Eight more fatal shootings made his life-tally. Five of those, in Lincoln County War fighting, were unprovable as his; while four by him are certain - two being his deputy guards during his jailbreak sixteen days before his scheduled hanging.

Billy, by reputation, was a romancer. Scorning class, he aimed low and high, but favored beauty. Sallie Chisum, stunning blond niece of cattle king, John Chisum, according to her 1878 diary, got wooing presents of a fancy beaded tobacco pouch and two candy hearts from *"Willie"* Bonney - ever creative with his name for alias or impact.

But Billy Bonney's true-love was Paulita Maxwell. His appeal to that young heiress and her aristocratic mother, Luz Beaubien Maxwell, seems merely to have been himself - the defiantly shabby youth of his tintype, taken in their family-owned town of Fort Sumner. When Billy was killed in their family mansion by Sheriff Pat Garrett, Paulita was rumored to be pregnant with his child. She would have heard the fatal shot, and the immediate, unnecessary, second one.

And the Maxwell family's Navajo servant, Deluvina, lovingly laid wildflowers on Billy's nearby grave for forty years.

Paulita herself was rushed into marriage after Billy's death; and she divorced after five years. Never remarrying, she is buried in Fort Sumner forty paces from where Billy lies.

So when Billy Bonney communicated - in his varied productions now archived in Indiana, New Mexico, Texas, and Washington, D.C. - he was someone to be reckoned with. And he knew it.

SANTA FE RING AND BILLY'S WORDS

Billy Bonney's words make most sense in their political context of his participation in rebellion against the Santa Fe Ring from 1877 to his murder in 1881. That big-money political and law enforcement cabal had precipitated not only 1878's Lincoln County War against it, but also other grass-roots uprisings throughout New Mexico Territory from that decade's start.

In 1876, the Territory's eastern county of Grant (containing Silver City), after years of the Ring's draconian political abuse, published a "Declaration of Independence" and tried, unsuccessfully, to secede and join contiguous Arizona Territory.

In 1877, in the north, flared the Colfax County War, eerily mirroring the next year's Lincoln County War, by a murdered idealistic leader and defeat through military intervention.

By late 1878, with the Lincoln County War lost, as an admonition for incoming governor, Lew Wallace, Santa Fe Ring players were listed in a notebook by an attorney, Frank Warner Angel: a Washington, D.C. - sent investigator of the Lincoln County "troubles." Lew Wallace himself came by appointment of President Rutherford B. Hayes, after the corrupt Ring-partisan governor was ousted by Angel's incriminating reports.

And an attorney-judge named Ira Leonard - Governor Lew Wallace's associate and eventually Billy's ally and lawyer - wrote to Wallace on May 20, 1879: *"the Santa Fe ring ... has been so long an incubus on the government of this territory."*

Back then, the name "Thomas Benton Catron" would have been recognized by all as the Ring's head and as the Territorial U.S. Attorney, ruling by favor and fear. With 1912 statehood, Catron was appointed a senator - after handing out an astounding one million dollars in apparent bribes.

AN HISTORIAN AND THE SANTA FE RING

Scholarly presentation of the Santa Fe Ring appears in D.W. Meinig's 1998 *The Shaping of America.* He wrote:

In the 1870's anticipation of railroad connections to the East began to alter the prospects [in New Mexico] for profits and position. Slowly forming over the years, the "Santa Fe Ring" now emerged into full notoriety: "it was essentially a set of lawyers, politicians, and businessmen who united to run the territory and to make money of this particular region. Although located on the frontier, the ring reflected the corporative, monopolistic, and multiple enterprise tendencies of all American business after the Civil War. Its uniqueness lay in the fact that, rather than dealing with some manufactured item, they regarded land as their first medium of currency." "Land" meant litigation, and "down the trail from the states came ... an amazing number of lawyers" who, "still stumbling over their Spanish, would build their own political and economic empire out of the tangled heritage of land grants." And so, somewhat belatedly, a general repetition of the California situation got under way, and with the same general results: "eventually over 80 per cent of the Spanish grants went to American lawyers and settlers." Important differences were the presence in New Mexico of a much greater number of Hispanic peasants and communities well rooted on the land, the considerable resistance and violence generated by this American assault, and the sullen resentment created in an increasingly constricted and impoverished people who felt they had been cheated out of much of their lands.

Only by comprehending the ruthless might and limitless gluttony of the Santa Fe Ring, can one comprehend the courage of Billy Bonney's and his contemporaries' fight against it; and appreciate Billy's resulting words as his triumph in spirit, if not in fact.

RING FIGHTER MARY McPHERSON

Fittingly, vehement modern exposure of the Santa Fe Ring began in the 1980's by Norman Cleaveland, a descendant of the newspaper-owning Morleys of Cimarron, in Colfax County where the 1877, anti-Ring fight had been fought and lost.

Cleaveland's great-grandmother, Mary McPherson was an unsung crusader in that war period. Her persistent letter writing documented Ring oppression and foreshadowed, by names and deeds, the coming Lincoln County War of 1878.

From April to August of 1877, she sent to President Rutherford B. Hayes and Secretary of the Interior Carl Schurz a hundred and forty-one pages of letters; affidavits; petitions; newspaper articles; itemized requests for removal of Ring-partisan Governor Samuel Beach Axtell and District Judge Warren Bristol; documentation of Ring-instigated military intervention against civilians; documentation of the Ring murder of its local opposition leader Methodist Reverend F.J. Tolby; and identification of the Santa Fe Ring's primary members as U.S. Attorney Thomas Benton Catron, Congressional Delegate Stephen Benton Elkins, and Chief Justice Henry Waldo.

Colfax County Ring-complicit military was at Fort Union; whose commander, Colonel Nathan Augustus Monroe Dudley, was transferred in April of 1878 to command Fort Stanton. After Dudley intervened illegally in the 1878 Lincoln County War, his rigged military Court of Inquiry in 1879 was headed by his good friend from Fort Union, Colonel Galusha Pennypacker, as its chief judge. Of course, Dudley was absolved.

In April of 1877, Mary McPherson and a Washington, D.C. based attorney, W.B. Matchett, sent their charges against the Ring collusion of officials in New Mexico Territory to President Hayes, with enclosed explanatory letter, newspaper articles about Santa Fe Ring atrocities, a petition to remove Judge Warren Bristol, and affidavits about the Ring.

All these communications put a lie to President Hayes or Secretary of the Interior Carl Schurz being ignorant of the existence of the Santa Fe Ring. Furthermore, that information puts the lie to later Ring propaganda, continuing to the present, that the cabal never even existed.

Mary McPherson sent the following to Washington, D.C.:

Charges, against
S.B. Axtell, Governor of New Mexico:

First. – His refusal to execute properly the laws of the Territory by removing their Courts, and refusing to return the same upon petition.

Second . – His neglect to listen to the petitions of the people of the Territory, to either visit them or interest himself in, or redress their grievances.

Third . – His denial of justice in his refusal to give them a speedy trial by a jury of their peers, and within the District where the pretended crimes with which they stand charged were alleged to have been committed.

Fourth. His collusion with the "Rings," having for their direct object the reduction of the private Grants to public domain by a class legislation ...

* * * * * * *

To the President:
The undersigned in behalf of the people of the Territory of New Mexico herewith present the following *charges* with evidence in support thereof against the persons named herein and ask your early consideration of the same:

They charge the United States District Attorney, Thomas B. Catron; Associate Justice Warren Bristol; Henry L. Waldo, Chief Justice; Samuel B. Axtell, Governor, and others of the said Territory, to them unknown, as having conspired together to corrupt and defraud justice and defeat the ends thereof, both by fraudulent and illegal practices in their respective Districts and offices; and by procuring the passage of insidious legislative enactments tending to dismemberment, confusion, and centralization of power and designed to protect infamy, legalize crime, deprive its citizens of personal liberty, and the right of trial by jury; compass the revenues of the Territory and the property of its citizens for purposes of private gain ...

And they therefore respectfully request their removal from office:

It is in evidence that for several years these parties have been in collusion in a general plan having for its aim the centralizing of power, the reduction of large and valuable private Grants of land within the Territory to their personal use and benefit, by corrupt Territorial and Congressional enactments, and by passage of bills of attainment & de facto laws depriving the citizens of due process of law, legalizing crime and then punishing the criminal, and thereby making the Court a vehicle to compass their covert and vindictive designs, thus rendering its edicts a farce and bringing its judicial character into distrust and contempt.

To accomplish these purposes this Ring so formed appear to have paused at nothing however difficult or questionable. This course has kept back the prosperity of the Territory and its people in a continued state of disquiet and insecurity both of persons and property – An inside view of this matter may be better obtained by a glance at its origin:

Among the possessions acquired by the Treaty of 1848 with Mexico, were large private Grants of land, both to individuals and corporations – (about 150 in number) – which excited at once the cupidity and avarice of the of the unscrupulous adventurer and the wily politician.

The failure of the U.S. Government to afford the relief guaranteed by the Treaty and by the Confirmatory Act of 1860, June the 21ˢᵗ left matters in an unsettled state as to titles, which fact was soon taken advantage of by the settlers and caused difficulties to arise between them and the holders of the Grants. Upon the influence of population these difficulties were increased and under the constant pressure they were compelled to take sides against the Grants.

The Ring perceiving their opportunity, forced themselves into power, and began a system of corrupt and compulsory legislation, oppressive in its exactions upon the grantees and those who sided with them, to worry them into submission, or by fraudulently depreciating their titles, compel them either to abandon their grants entirely, or sell at a sacrifice and quit the Territory. Many did this, - some did not. Under this compulsion the Ring or their friends became the purchasers ...

Another convenient system of iniquity is that relating to Indictments: They are obtained with the greatest possible ease *imaginable – and in <u>any numbers required for the emergency</u> – and for the <u>same offence</u> – in some cases <u>several indictments</u> for the same offence.*

That Colfax County made the most diligent opposition to the attempts of the Ring to deprive them of their rights and subject them to their schemes. (In fact this is the only county that saved itself from their rapacity.)

Failing in this, the pretext soon came, upon the assassination of a Methodist Missionary, named Tolby, - a worthy man, - who at the first sympathized with the Ring, but, upon maturer reflection, abandoned them, when they hired two assassins to deliberately murder him, after they (the Ring) had publicly warned him to leave the country, - which he failed to do ...

Mary McPherson enclosed the following article about the murder of Ring opponent, Reverend F.J. Tolby - mirroring the murder of Attorney Alexander McSween the next year:

"The Territory of Elkins."
Assassination of Supposed Sun Correspondent.
The Murder of the Rev. F.J. Tolby in New Mexico.
A Probate Judge Accused of Complicity in the Crime.
Indignation Meeting.

Santa Fe, N.M. Nov. 26, 1876. The political revolution which has taken place and is still in progress in this Territory is mainly attributed to the exposures of the Santa Fe Ring which have appeared in the Sun, and which have created great consternation among our corrupt officials, the Sun having a wide circulation in this region. By means of libel suits, and still more effectual measures, the Ring has succeeded in intimidating the local press, with one or two exceptions; and so long as the courts are constituted as they are at present, it is absolutely unsafe for any man to actively oppose the corrupt scheme of the Ring. The nature of the means taken to harass those who show rebellious spirit has already been described in this correspondence and events of recent occurrence, which will form the subject of this letter, will give the reader an idea of the difficulties which are encountered by those who are striving to effect a reform in the administration in our territorial affairs.

On the 14th of September last, the Rev. F.J. Tolby, a minister of the gospel, generally respected and beloved, was brutally murdered on the highway while passing through a lonely canyon. The murder was involved in mystery for a time. Mr. Tolby was an active bold and outspoken man, who took much interest in public affairs and did not hesitate to express his opinion. He was not known to have an enemy in the world, save members of the Ring whom he had vigorously and publicly denounced for their offence against society.

It is said that a few days before his death Mr. Tolby had a warm discussion with Judge Palen of the first Judicial District, one of the chiefs of the Ring, who tried to intimidate him without effect, for the preacher boldly announced his intention of writing of the Ring rascalities for the eastern press, and up to the time of his murder he exerted all his influence against the rogues in office.

It was known that Mr. Tolby had threatened to make exposures through the press, and in some quarters he was suspected of having written the letter to the Sun which excited such commotion in the Federal Ring. These, and other circumstances, excited suspicion from the first that he had fallen a victim to the malevolence of the Ring, or of some of its members, but for a long time no direct proof of it could be obtained. At last, however, the actual murderers were hunted down, and when it was found that they implicated the principal members of the Colfax County branch of the Ring as the instigators of the crime, the indignation of the people knew no bounds. At one time it was feared that every one of the politicians named in the connection with the murder would be strung up by the neck without the intervention of judge or jury; but calmer counsel prevailed and acting upon information gained from the murderers and other sources, warrants were issued for the arrest of the accused parties.

The persons charged by the murderers as the planners and accessories to the murder, are the recognized strikers of the Ring in Colfax County. Some of them were lately elected to office through the influence of the Ring ... and the feeling against all persons who are supposed to be connected in any way to the operation of Elkins & Co. is bitter in the extreme ...

If a new election for Delegate to Congress could be held for tomorrow, Elkins would be defeated by such a tremendous majority that not even the tools of the Santa Fe Ring would not dare attempt the job of counting him in.

Mary McPherson enclosed the following *"Petition to Remove Judge Bristol."*

We the undersigned citizens of the Third Judicial District of the Territory of New Mexico, without regard to party, would respectfully request and petition for the removal of Judge Warren Bristol from the office of Judge of the District and Territory aforesaid, <u>for the following special and general reasons</u>.

1ˢᵗ. We charge that Warren Bristol has been guilty of secretly making known his opinions to attorneys engaged on the side of a cause pending before him, and informing them as to the nature and character of his decisions, several days before delivering them judicially from the bench.

2ⁿᵈ. We charge that in consequence of his secretly making known his opinions that great advantage thereby resulted to the parties employing said attorneys, and great loss and injury to the opposite party.

3ʳᵈ. We charge that Warren Bristol in an important mining suit, in which Amartin W. Bremen and Silas Tidwell were plaintiff, and Robert B. Wilson made defendant, secretly advised with an attorney of said plaintiffs, and informed and advised him as to the proper steps he should pursue in conducting the cause during the very time that the subject matter of his secret advice was under consideration by said Warren Bristol, as judge.

4ᵗʰ. We charge Warren Bristol with writing out a full and complete form for relocating a mine for one of the plaintiffs aforesaid, while the title to said mine was then a matter before his court for adjudication.

5ᵗʰ. We charge that Judge Bristol imprisoned an honorable and worthy citizen of Grant County for contempt, during the pleasure of the court, for no other reason than that he availed himself of information communicated to him by his counsel, which had been prematurely and secretly revealed by the said Judge Bristol.

6ᵗʰ. We charge that Judge Bristol during the July term of court 1875, held in Grant County, did in open court publicly confer that he had been guilty of revealing a secret opinion to one of the attorneys employed by said Bremen and Tidwell, but rendered no valid excuse for such injudicial conduct.

7th. We charge Judge Bristol with granting a writ of restitution to the plaintiff in a suit of ejectment after an appeal had been allowed and perfected to the Supreme Court, in the absence of any statutory provision authorizing such to issue.

8th. We charge that Judge Bristol acting as Judge aforesaid, actually refused in an important murder trial, after the prisoners arraignment at the first term to grant continuance, although proper affidavits were filed according to law, for the procurement of absent material witnesses, and forced the prisoner to trial which resulted in his conviction and execution.

9th. We charge that Judge Bristol in another important murder trial absolutely refused to the prisoner the right of compulsory process to procure witnesses in his behalf.

10th. We charge that Judge Bristol as Judge aforesaid, willfully refused in two other important murder trials to allow the defendants to exercise their right to the full number of peremptory challenges to jurors, given by the statute in such cases although his attention was repeatedly called to the statutory provision allowing the defendant the right to ten preemptory charges.

11th. We charge that the said Judge Bristol made a false accusation from the bench against the grand jurymen of Grant County, N.M. and that they, in proper justification of themselves, were forced to state publicly and in print that such accusation was false, and furthermore, that said public statement of the grand jurymen aforesaid has not, and cannot be denied by the said Judge Bristol.

12th. **We charge that Judge Bristol is guilty of manifest partiality, while acting in the trial of causes.** [Author's boldface]

13th. And generally we charge that Judge Bristol, as judge aforesaid, frequently consults and advises with attorneys about causes coming and pending before his court for adjudication, who are interested in the results of the suits as feed attorneys.

14th. We charge that Judge Bristol frequently makes rulings in important causes involving large amounts of property and the liberty of citizens, without proper thought and investigation, and that consequent to this, he constantly changes his rulings *during the progress of important trials, and* **orders his clerk to expunge the record, in order to hide his indolence and ignorance, and thus deprives parties litigante of the proper recorded history of the causes.** [Author's boldface]

15th. We charge that Judge Bristol is ignorant of the fundamental rules and principles of law with which every tyro should be conversant, and that he is indolent and not disposed to study, thus causing a universal feeling among the people of insecurity to life, liberty and property.

16th. We charge that Judge Bristol appointed a man clerk of his court, whom he knew all the time to be lewdly and publicly living with a kept mistress, and notwithstanding he is still so living, continues to retain him as clerk of his court.

17th. We aver that all of the foregoing statements and specifications can be substantiated on oath, by good, respectable citizens of this Territory irrespective of party predilection.

There follows about 250 signatures among which are many of the most influential men in that section of the territory.

Another enclosed article concerned the Ring in action:

At It Again

The latest advices from New Mexico are to the effect that the "ring" are at their old tricks ...

One of our correspondents says: "People here are in constant fear and nobody dares to raise his voice against the terrible anarchy we are undergoing in this country. These gentlemen and their organ at Santa Fe, (The *New Mexican*) seem to have an absolute power in everything in New Mexico. They run our legislature and make this ignorant people pass such laws as will gratify their rapacious ambition. They control the courts to such an extent that respectable citizens regard them as a public calamity. They have juries appointed, who, instead of bringing peace to the community, will cause but alarm to the people. As a general think thieves and murderers are turned loose."

The lawyers of New Mexico, with the exception of a very few honorable exceptions, are members of this corrupt ring ... A defendant who has been prosecuted by the ringites has but little chance of being defended, and even if he does succeed in obtaining the services of an attorney, the rulings of the courts are always against him.

Enclosed also were multiple affidavits about Santa Fe Ring corruption. An example is as follows:

I, John L. Taylor, a resident of San Miguel Co., N.M. do voluntarily make the following statements.

I have resided in said Territory and in said County for the past twenty-two (22) years – Am well informed as to the political history of the Territory. I have been credibly informed by various persons, all well known to me, that during the first candidacy of Stephen B. Elkins for Representative in the U.S. Congress from this Territory, many persons in San Miguel and Moro Counties were arrested, charged with illegal trading with the Comanche Tribe of Indians. Many of these persons were known to me. They were placed under bonds, and when they appeared for trial at Santa Fe, they were released – as I am informed by them and verily believe – upon the payment of fees to prosecuting Attorney, and the agreement upon their part to cast their Ballots for said S.B. Elkins. The above-mentioned transactions took place about four years ago.

John L. Taylor

Letters from Mary McPherson and W.B. Matchett about the Ring also were sent to Secretary of the Interior Carl Schurz.

Washington, May 5th '77

To the Honor
    The Secretary of the Interior,
                Sir – Accompanying
please find <u>copy</u> of charges, &c., against S.B. Axtell, Governor, and other New Mexican Officials, filed with the President in April last, which, together with the papers in evidence, we desire made a part thereof, in the proceedings now instituted in your Department against the said Governor James B. Axtell.

Very respectfully
Your obedient sevts,
W.B. Matchett
M.E. McPherson
In behalf of the citizens of New Mexico

Enclosed to President Rutherford B. Hayes from Mary McPherson's son-in-law, William R. Morley, were writings called "Extracts." In the 1890's, Morley was murdered, possibly by the Ring; the crime never solved. He wrote as follows:

Cimarron, March 6ᵗʰ 1877

. . . . . I was astonished beyond measure at your proceedings, and have fears as to the result: at the same time I will not throw a straw in your way, but will do what I can to help matters ...

Efforts have been made to get the Court back here, but failed. The Ring will not permit it, and say that the objects for which the Court was taken away have not been accomplished: Now you know what the objects were – to defeat the Tolby investigation, and to punish Colfax County for presuming to interfere in such matters ... The election of Hayes leads many to think that the old regime will hold over [sic - the corruption of President Grant]*, and that other Tolby affairs will happen. The people are badly discouraged, and many talk of leaving the county, as their only protection against the machinations of their enemies in power. New Mexico today is ruled by five of the Ring, supported as they have been by Federal authority; and the use of troops. If you can affect any removals, you will certainly do good. Four or five men run this Territory, and run it with unparalleled desperation ... The removal of one or two, even, of these officials would remedy the great evil; provided men were in their places who could not be controlled by the Ring ... If the office of Chief Justice alone could be filled by a new man with good motives and principles, a short time would defeat the rest. The Governor* [Axtell]*, Chief Justice* [Waldo]*, and U.S. Attorney* [Catron] *control New Mexico ... If you could remove any of these men, do so by all means. But to get evidence of the facts which you and all of us are convinced, can only be done in one way, viz: If a secret agent were to come here* duly authorized*, he could get them – get evidence to astonish the world! But people are afraid to tell what they know in affidavits until they feel sure it will not pass into the hands of the enemy to be used against themselves ... But secrecy is all important -* publicity is *dangerous in the extreme. You must be cautious also what you do, or it will react on us here ... Remember that Elkins, Catron, and Waldo were all in the Rebel cause down and about Westport, Missouri, and all red hot Democrats up to their appointment for office, since when, they were radical of radicals ...*

Effect one removal, - the Governor or Chief Justice, and if a Governor could be appointed who knew the circumstances here, it would be best, - any good, square man would do ... a removal or two would restore confidence ... but as it is now people are disheartened. Grant, the other American County, is likely to secede and join Arizona, to get away from the Ring.

W.R. Morley
Vice Prest & Executive Officer
Max. [Maxwell] Land Grant & R'wy Co.

* * * * * * *

These communications by Mary McPherson were all stonewalled in Washington, D.C. So giving up on the President and Secretary of Interior, she tried the Attorney General.

But at that office, on an internal cover sheet attached to her letter, *"Attorney General"* is crossed out and replaced with *"Secretary of the Interior"* - routed back to Carl Schurz. McPherson was in a purposeful, bureaucratic, endless loop of cover-up by futility. She had written:

Washington D.C.
Aug 23 1877

To the President
   Please place before the Attorney General for immediate action "The Charges vs. New Mexican Officials" now on file, as evidence in the case of Gov Axtell of New Mexico.

Respectfully
Mary E. McPherson

RING FIGHTER FRANK SPRINGER

Anti-Ring attorney, Frank Springer, a Cimarron resident, co-owned the *Cimarron News and Press* with William Morley, Mary McPherson's son-in-law, and opposed Thomas Benton Catron and Stephen Benton Elkins. From 1872 to 1873, Elkins was president of the Maxwell Land Grant and Railway Company (before becoming a Territorial Delegate to Congress in 1874). Catron was that company's legal counsel. So Frank Springer had fought the Santa Fe Ring from its earliest days.

After the Colfax County War, and a month before the one in Lincoln County began, Springer supported removal of Ring-partisan Governor Samuel Beach Axtell to President Hayes and Secretary of the Interior Carl Schurz. Springer wrote:

FRANK SPRINGER,
ATTORNEY AND COUNSELOR AT LAW,
Cimarron, New Mexico, June 10, 1878

Hon Carl Schurz,
Secretary of the Interior
Sir:
I endorse herewith, directed to the President charges against S.B. Axtell, Governor of New Mexico, supported by affidavits verifying the facts stated.
As one whose life was jeopardized by the action of Mr. Axtell, whether through malevolence, stupidity, or blind partisanship matters little. I submit the facts and request you to present them to the President.
Very respectfully
Frank Springer

* * * * * * *

This was Frank Springer's letter to President Hayes:

To His Excellency, the President of the United States:
The undersigned, a citizen of the County of Colfax, Territory of New Mexico, begs to call your attention to the official conduct of Samuel B. Axtell, Governor of

New Mexico, which show that said **Axtell has by false pretense and representation procured the use of United States troops, and employed them in the County of Colfax in a manner directly calculated to produce confusion and bloodshed,** [Author's boldface] *and to create disturbance of the public peace in a time of quiet.*

That under pretence of a desire to arrest a certain person for some pretended offence, not disclosed, said Axtell planned and conspired by falsehood and treachery to induce a number of peaceable citizens to assemble in a place and under circumstances where under the instructions given by said Axtell for the occasion it was almost certain that most of them would be killed. That had not the plot of said Axtell been discovered in time, it is very probable that it would have resulted in the death of the undersigned, and several other law abiding citizens assembled for a peaceful purpose upon the strength of an invitation to meet the governor. And it is the belief of the undersigned that it was expected by said Axtell that such would be the result of the sending of U.S. troops to said Colfax County.

That the real object of said Axtell was not merely the arrest of a certain person is indicated by the fact that when afterwards arrested by the military this person was at once released and that said Axtell – while Governor of New Mexico – afterwards made an appointment with the person and traveled with him in a friendly way in the stage coach.

The undersigned respectfully submits that whether through ignorance or corrupt motive, the action of said Axtell is to keep many parts of the territory in a state of turmoil and confusion when intelligent and non partisan action on the part of the executive might end much of the difficulty. His use of the military force of the United States has been partisan in every instance and the undersigned submits that no person capable of forming such a letter of instructions as the one set forth in the accompanying affidavit is fit to be entrusted with any power whatever, and respectfully asks that he be removed from his position.

Very respectfully
Your obedient Servant
Frank Springer

Billy Bonney's
History

Twenty-One Years to Live

Billy Bonney's biographic panorama sets the stage for understanding his motivations, bravery, optimism; and the historical import of his writings, words, and wit.

Like others who die early, Billy retained romanticized youth, even in the distorting prism of history told by enemies, which transmogrified the Lincoln County War freedom fight against the Santa Fe Ring to mere rampage and outlawry - a version parroted by tellers of his tale to this day.

LIFE PATH TO A BULLET

At a quarter to midnight, in summer heat of New Mexico Territory full-mooned brightness, the 21 year old, homeless youth, Billy Bonney, in trusting stockinged feet, unknowingly walked his last minutes of life to the Fort Sumner, porticoed mansion of the fabulously wealthy Maxwell family.

The ending day, July 14, 1881, was the third anniversary of the Lincoln County War's start. That Territorial war, a grass-roots, multicultural uprising against governing, corrupt, robber barons, and lost by Billy's side, had ultimately left him the most hunted outlaw in the country; though, to himself, he remained a soldier: the last of the Regulators; the sole war participant, out of two-hundred, to be tried and sentenced to hang; and the betrayed victim of an anticipated, but unfulfilled, gubernatorial pardon.

Only his enemies, a minority in the Territory - but with power of politicians and press - called him "Billy the Kid," made synonymous by them with "desperado."

Now, that late July night, Billy, a fugitive wanted nationally dead or alive, planned to cut a dinner steak from the side of beef hanging - in generosity of Fort Sumner's patrón to his townspeople - on the Maxwell family mansion's north porch; but first to stop at its south-east corner bedroom, to check with the town's owner, the patrón, Peter Maxwell; having been directed there by a traitor who would remain forever undiscovered.

Asleep in the mansion that night was Billy's secret lover, Peter Maxwell's pretty and vivacious sister, Paulita, seventeen, and just pregnant with Billy's child.

In the mansion also was a never-emancipated Navajo slave, Deluvina, purchased, as a child, by Peter's and Paulita's deceased father - rich erstwhile frontiersman from Illinois, Lucien Bonaparte Maxwell, when the family still lived in Cimarron: the town Lucien built on his almost two million acre, Mexican land grant, encompassing northern New Mexico Territory and southern Colorado.

That was before Lucien Maxwell had been cheated out of it by the law partners who represented him in its sale: Thomas Benton Catron and Stephen Benton Elkins, founders and master-minds of the robber baron Santa Fe Ring.

As Billy knew, that power elite - a corrupt collusion of politicians, attorneys, law enforcement, and big money - still controlled New Mexico Territory. Not only the Lincoln County War of 1878 been fought against that Ring; but also the revolutionary uprising of the suppressed Colfax County War, a year earlier and in the northern part of the Territory. Even Grant County, to the west, in 1876, had threatened secession from the Territory and annexation to Arizona to escape Santa Fe Ring clutches.

Billy also knew that two months had passed since his scheduled hanging date of May 13th; evaded by his jailbreak on April 28th. Pursuit was inevitable by Lincoln County Sheriff and Deputy U.S. Marshal Pat Garrett, who had captured him on December 22, 1880 at Stinking Springs for his hanging trial; and whose Lincoln courthouse-jail Billy had escaped after killing his two deputies. Garrett would shoot him on sight.

When first tracking Billy, Pat Garrett had even killed the boy's friends and fellow Regulators, Tom O'Folliard and Charlie Bowdre - only by accident, missing Billy in those ambushes.

In fact, at the December 22, 1880 Stinking Springs capture of Billy and his companions, Garrett mortally shot Charlie Bowdre; mistaking him for Billy because of that man's fateful donning of the boy's sombrero when exiting their rock-walled, line cabin hide-out that dawning day.

To be near Paulita Maxwell, Billy had made this reckless choice to return to Fort Sumner instead of fleeing to Old Mexico with his fluent bilingual skills. But he trusted the Maxwell family's protection as well as the townspeople's, known by him since late 1877. And defiance came naturally to Billy, after his taunting death so many times.

Billy was a second son, born illegitimately in New York City as Henry McCarty, on November 23, 1859.

Raised in Indianapolis, Indiana, he became "Henry Antrim" after his mother's New Mexico Territory marriage to William Henry Harrison Antrim when Billy was 13½; the family having moved with Billy's brother, Josie, to Silver City at Antrim's impetus for its mining opportunities.

Billy lived there with lower middle class status attained by added income of his mother's laundry business.

In Silver City, he was likely schooled by a succession of teachers (Dr. Webster, Miss Pratt, and Mary Richardson) to write Spencerian-style penmanship.

There, he probably also became bi-lingual, since Silver City had a considerable Hispanic population; and, thereafter, he amicably bridged Anglo and Hispanic sub-cultures in those racist times.

Billy's mother's tuberculosis death in 1874, a year and a half after their Silver City move, left him a homeless victim of his stepfather's avarice, and relying for income on thievery, as well as butcher shop and hotel work; until, the following year, he was arrested for laundry and revolver theft by Silver City's sheriff, Harvey Whitehill.

Incarcerated, Billy faced thirty-nine lashes and ten years hard labor, Territorial law making no provision for juveniles.

Desperation at his dire fate and the beating's fatality risk must have energized his escape - through the jail's chimney - yielding necessary relocation across the western border.

Billy ended up in the Arizona Territory town of Bonita, adjacent to Fort Grant. There, a fugitive from the law, but still calling himself Henry Antrim - his Silver City name - he again combined work - as a cook at a small hotel - with illegality: stealing blankets, saddles, and horses.

In 1877, jailed in Fort Grant with his older accomplice, John Mackie, he escaped the guardhouse by wriggling through the roof's ventilation space. But he stayed in Bonita, the rustling charges having been dropped through a technicality.

Six months hence, his life again was wrenched drastically. On August 17, 1877, at Bonita's Atkin's Cantina, Billy's heated argument with a bullying blacksmith, named Frank "Windy" Cahill, escalated to Billy's fatally shooting that unknowingly unarmed man, likely in self-defense during a outmatched fight.

Billy escaped on a stolen race horse.

The Coroner's Jury stayed in sympathy with unarmed Cahill, declaring Henry Antrim, in absentia, guilty of unjustified homicide: with hanging for first degree murder being the likely outcome if there had been a trial.

But Billy was back in New Mexico Territory, shielded by a new identity as William Henry Bonney - Billy Bonney - "Bonney" possibly being his mother's maiden name. All his subsequent writings would use it. It would be on his tombstone.

Not yet 18, by the next month, September of 1877, Billy, choosing outlawry, joined the Santa Fe Ring-affiliated rustler gang of Jessie Evans; and was even involved in a stagecoach hold-up with Evans and his boys.

But weeks later, by October of '77, Billy abandoned criminality and hired on as a Lincoln County ranch hand for a wealthy, idealistic Englishmen: John Henry Tunstall, who was investing his family's fortune in a store and grazing land.

Lincoln County was, at the time, the largest county in the United States - bigger than combination of Massachusetts, Connecticut, Vermont, Rhode Island, and Delaware - and constituted the south-east quarter of New Mexico Territory.

Tunstall, by making financial inroads in this vast domain, became a Santa Fe Ring mercantile and ranching competitor.

Soon, Billy was affectionately nick-named "Kid" by Tunstall's older workers; and seemed on the way to future stability, and even prosperity, since one of Tunstall's business associates was the Territory's cattle king, John Chisum.

Billy's popularity also soared among locals, grounded in his charismatic combination of high spirits, intelligence, sharp-shooting skills, singing, dancing, romancing, and probable ingratiating search for missed fatherly love.

In partnership with one of John Tunstall's employees, a handsome half-Chickasaw named Fred Tecumseh Waite, Billy was given, by Tunstall, a Peñasco River ranch under the Homestead Act - probably one of Billy's proudest moments; since he later used it as a personal identifier in a deposition.

But in under five months, Billy's destiny repeated its pattern of sudden loss, with the horrific, February 18, 1878, Santa Fe Ring murder/mutilation of John Tunstall in an ambush involving Billy and other ranch hands.

The reactive slide of outraged anti-Ring citizens into violence and mayhem culminated cataclysmically, five months later, in July's Lincoln County War.

By that time, the Civil War had already ruined the life of a man almost ten years older than Billy: Patrick "Pat" Floyd Garrett. Born to an Alabama plantation family, and relocated to a Claiborne Parrish, Louisiana, plantation when still a boy, young Garrett was even willed a slave by his grandfather.

Garrett's family lost everything in the "great War;" and he, like so many of his generation, became a westward wanderer, ending up in Texas.

There, he may have abandoned a common-law wife and child and possibly murdered a black man, before becoming a buffalo hunter, from 1876 to 1878, with two partners; and, initially, with a 19 year old kid named Joe Briscoe. Garrett shot that kid point-blank, one irritable day in their hunting camp; but successfully claimed self-defense.

On the Texas buffalo range, Pat Garrett never met fellow buffalo hunter, John William Poe. Later Garrett's, Poe's, and Billy's histories would merge on that July 14, 1881 night.

By early 1878, Pat Garrett, dramatically tall at 6'4", had settled in New Mexico Territory's town of Fort Sumner; and had met there the transient youth named Billy Bonney, as both gambled at local Hargrove's or Beaver Smith's Saloons. Of different generations, their only bonds were mutual recognition and townspeople's nicknames: "Big Casino" and "Little Casino," given for their avid poker playing and height discrepancies.

The original Fort Sumner, built in typical lay-out of military buildings rimming an almost square parade ground, yielded the town's name. It was built by the United States government in 1865 on desert flatlands, east of the north to south flowing Pecos River, for soldiers guarding a concentration camp named Bosque Redondo, and holding captive 3,500 Navajos and 400 Apaches. The Native Americans' starvation on that arid land became a governmental embarrassment; and, in 1868, surviving Navajos were sent back to their homeland; the Apaches already having escaped.

In 1870, that fort complex, with surrounding thousands of acres, was bought by frontiersman, Lucien Bonaparte Maxwell, by then one of the Territory's richest men.

To the fort's buildings around the parade ground, he moved, from Cimarron, his family, including his wife, Luz Beaubien; daughters; only son, Peter; and loyal Cimarron employees. He converted fort structures into residences and businesses; and refurbished its huge officers' quarters as his mansion.

Retained a quarter mile from the town was the half acre military cemetery for his family. It eventually received Billy's body also; to lie beside Pat Garrett's earlier victims resulting from his hunting of the boy: Billy's Lincoln County War Regulator pals, Tom O'Folliard and Charlie Bowdre.

For his new town, Lucien Maxwell planted a peach orchard and crops; and ranched primarily sheep - up to 50,000 head. Dying in 1875, he left Fort Sumner to the care of his wife and his son, Peter; who eventually became the family's ruin through gaming, alcoholism, and financial mismanagement.

But when Pat Garrett and Billy Bonney gambled there, Fort Sumner was still thriving.

Before Lucien Maxwell bought Fort Sumner, his great wealth arose from his almost 2 million acre, gold-rich Maxwell Land Grant, then by his selling it; though he was cheated out of its full value by his negotiating attorneys, Thomas Benton Catron and Steven Benton Elkins, who immediately resold it to foreign investors for twice the original amount.

That Catron-Elkins profit and technique arguably marked the start of the Santa Fe Ring's ongoing land grab schemes to disenfranchise primarily Hispanic land grant owners - as had been the father of Lucien Maxwell's wife, Luz Beaubien, from whom the Land Grant had been inherited.

The Santa Fe Ring recruited, as needed, by favor or fear, the Territorial Governor, Samuel Beach Axtell; other public officials and law enforcement officers; and the local military.

Those robber barons, Thomas Benton Catron and Stephen Benton Elkins, profited immensely, in land, railroads, banks, and mines. Catron would eventually own six million acres - more than any man in United States history.

And, during the Lincoln County War period, Thomas Benton Catron held the Territory's highest legal post: U.S. Attorney; using it to perpetrate and cover up crimes in the service of greed and cronyism.

Pat Garrett and Billy Bonney led separate lives, though connected to Fort Sumner's Gutierrez sisters: Juanita, Apolinaria, and Celsa. Billy befriended Celsa, married to her cousin, Saval Gutierrez, a Maxwell sheep herder.

Garrett married Juanita, who died shortly thereafter of a possible miscarriage. Two years later, he married Apolinaria, with whom he would father eight children. It was a double marriage with his Fort Sumner friend, Maxwell's foreman, Barney Mason; who, a few years later, became Garrett's spy assisting in Billy's 1880 capture at Stinking Springs; and possibly assisting in Billy's ambush killing the next year.

Pat Garrett, when arriving in New Mexico Territory from Texas in 1878, lacked financial security. Initially, for Peter Maxwell, he drove a wagon. Then he worked with a local hog raiser, Thomas "Kip" McKinney. A bartending job in Fort Sumner's Hargrove's Saloon gave little improvement in finances or self-esteem.

Then came 1880 and the opportunity of Pat Garrett's life. Huge Lincoln County needed a new sheriff for its November election, one compatible with Santa Fe Ring interests in that period still seething with anti-Ring resentment from the Lincoln County War and its aftermath.

To qualify, Garrett moved with his wife, Apolinaria, to that county's town of Roswell; adding, as a boarder, an unemployed journalist named Ashmun "Ash" Upson, who would eventually be the ghost-writer for Garrett's 1882 book on "Billy the Kid."

There is no indication that Pat Garrett knew Lincoln County War issues, or was tempted by corrupt Ring affiliation. But the town of Lincoln had been the epicenter of Santa Fe Ring mercantile and political abuses. There, "the House," a giant two-story store run by local Ring bosses, Lawrence Murphy and James Dolan, had bled cash-poor Mexicans and white homesteaders with exorbitant credit on goods.

Their business extended back to 1874 with a Fort Stanton suttler's store, coupled with illegal whiskey production and counterfeiting; and was first run by an Emil Fritz and the same Lawrence Murphy, with James Dolan as clerk.

Historically, that Ring-affiliated business used thuggery to maintain its growing economic hold. Back in 1875, when a rancher named Robert Casey won a local election against Lawrence Murphy, he was shot dead the same day. And the anti-Ring, Mexican, community leader, Juan Patrón, was likewise shot soon afterward by another Dolan partner, John Riley; though Patrón survived as a limping cripple.

The seeds of the future Lincoln County uprising were sown in late 1876 with the arrival of the sweet-tempered, wealthy, English merchant named John Henry Tunstall; who was persuaded to settle in Lincoln by a local attorney, Alexander McSween, a Ring opponent, but once legal counsel to Murphy's and Dolan's House business, and privy to its improprieties.

By 1877, John Tunstall had built, just a quarter mile east of the Murphy-Dolan House, and on Lincoln's single street, a large store with a bank. And he purchased land for two cattle ranches. All that constituted direct competition with the Santa Fe Ring; though Tunstall probably underestimated the danger.

John Tunstall also hoped to wrest from the House its lucrative beef and flour traderships to Fort Stanton and the nearby Mescalero Indian Reservation; and he even exposed, in a local newspaper, Lincoln County's Ring-partisan Sheriff, William Brady, for using taxpayer money to pay for Ring cattle.

So John Tunstall became next for Ring elimination, with Alexander McSween a close second.

The Ringmen preferred to kill with guise of legality. So they entangled John Tunstall in a fabricated web. Its thread began with Tunstall's friend, Attorney Alexander McSween, who had retained an important House connection: representation of the estate of its founding partner, Emil Fritz, who had died intestate in 1874, and had two siblings, Charles Fritz and Emilie Scholand, living in the Territory.

The Ring chose, as a hook for legal harassment, Emil Fritz's $10,000, life insurance policy, which McSween was attempting to collect from its dishonestly evasive, New York City company.

That collection was eventually achieved by McSween's hired New York law firm, which subtracted about $3,000 from the total for their services. And McSween took, from the remainder, his own legal fees of about $700.

But Alexander McSween had an agenda beyond financial: the determination to end the House's hegemony. Knowing that Murphy and Dolan, verging on bankruptcy from Tunstall competition, would wrangle for themselves the remaining Fritz insurance policy money from the local heirs, McSween dug in strategically, and delayed turn-over of the remaining insurance policy money, citing other possible heirs in Germany.

Then McSween left on business to St. Louis with his wife and with John Tunstall's business associate, cattle king, John Chisum, then also president of the bank in Tunstall's store.

The Ring used Alexander McSween's departure to pounce: declaring him an absconding embezzler of the collected, Emil Fritz, insurance money. Colluding Ring head, U.S. Attorney Thomas Benton Catron, issued arrest warrants for McSween.

Captured, McSween was transported to Mesilla; and indicted for embezzling and breach of contract by Ring judge, Warren Bristol (later Billy's hanging judge).

McSween avoided likely assassination, if incarcerated in Lincoln's underground pit jail, by intervention of an honest deputy sheriff from his arrest site in Las Vegas, New Mexico - courageous Adolph Barrier - who kept him in personal custody.

But Judge Warren Bristol had set a trap. When he indicted McSween, he did two things. First, he set his bail at $8,000; but granted its approval only to Ringman, District Attorney William Rynerson, who refused all bondsmen. That meant McSween could be taken into possibly fatal custody at any time by Lincoln County Sheriff William Brady - not coincidentally the leader of John Tunstall's murder posse, fourteen days later.

Bristol's second stipulation was the clincher. He attached McSween's personal property to the sum of $10,000 - falsely deemed the amount of embezzled money - to satisfy any judgment against him at his April Grand Jury trial.

The snare was that Judge Bristol also falsely declared that John Tunstall was in partnership with McSween, and attached his property also. Tunstall was the Ring's real target.

Sheriff Brady and his deputies were to do the attaching: an aggressive inventory of property in both men's residences, Tunstall's store, and Tunstall's Feliz River ranch - based on that untrue allegation of their "partnership."

Hoped for was provocation of a violent response from Tunstall and his employees - including hot-headed Billy - to achieve Tunstall's "justifiable" killing in a confrontation.

John Tunstall, however, merely said that one man's life was worth more than all he owned. But he protectively transferred his fine horses from Lincoln to his Feliz River ranch, confident that they were immune to the attachment.

Lacking any other excuse, on February 18, 1878, Sheriff Brady used that stock movement - from the Feliz Ranch back to Lincoln - to send his posse (illegally including Ring-thug outlaw, Jessie Evans, and his boys) to pursue Tunstall and his ranch hands, including Billy, on the fifty mile return trail.

In the ensuing ambush, probably by Jessie Evans and his boys - Frank Baker, William "Buck" Morton, and Tom Hill - John Tunstall, becoming separated from his fleeing men, was murdered; and his hidden body, along with that of his sadistically slain horse, was mutilated.

Tunstall's martyrdom and its aftermath, exploded into the Lincoln County War through escalating Ring outrages.

The first was Sheriff Brady's protection of Tunstall's killers by blocking service of murder warrants - which included ones for James Dolan and Jessie Evans, and other Brady possemen.

Those warrants, issued by Lincoln County Justice of the Peace John "Squire" Wilson, had been given, for service, to Tunstall employees, Billy Bonney and Fred Waite, whom Wilson appointed as Deputy Constables under Town Constable Atanacio Martinez.

But illegally, Sheriff Brady briefly jailed Billy, Waite, and Martinez in Lincoln's pit jail to prevent their arresting James Dolan and others; and, at the same time, confiscated Billy's Winchester '73 carbine. It was clear that, by then, volatile Billy, who had been verbally threatening to Brady's deputies doing attachment inventories, was feared by the Ringmen.

Justice of the Peace Wilson, emerging as an anti-Ring partisan, next deputized Tunstall's foreman, Dick Brewer, who, in turn, declared Tunstall's men, including Billy, his posse to arrest the murderers under those warrants.

Meanwhile, recognizing his extreme risk of assassination by the Ring, Attorney Alexander McSween, accompanied by Deputy Sheriff Adolph Barrier, went into hiding - often in the Hispanic town of San Patricio, or at South Spring River Ranch: the Pecos River area spread of John Chisum.

By March of 1878, a month after Tunstall's killing, Dick Brewer's posse had captured two of John Tunstall's murderers: William "Buck" Morton and Frank Baker. Both were fatally shot by Brewer's possemen on the way to the Lincoln jail while allegedly attempting escape. Billy was in the firing group.

At that point, including Frank "Windy" Cahill, Billy was now involved in three murders.

Then the Ring acted again. Ring-partisan Governor Samuel Beach Axtell, by official proclamation, illegally removed John Wilson's Justice of the Peace title - and retroactively canceled all his powers and appointments, thus, outlawing Dick Brewer's posse. And Axtell declared Sheriff William Brady to be Lincoln County's only acceptable law enforcer.

Enraged, Tunstall's men named themselves "Regulators" after Revolutionary War era vigilantes. Those Regulators included Billy; Fred Waite; John Middleton; Jim "Frenchie" French; Josiah "Doc" Scurlock; cousins, George and Frank Coe; Charlie Bowdre; and a John Chisum cattle detective, Frank MacNab. Dick Brewer was chosen as their leader.

And the Regulators went on a rampage.

On April 1, 1878, anticipating Alexander McSween's death risk at Sheriff William Brady's hand upon return to Lincoln for his Grand Jury embezzlement trial that month, some Regulators with carbines, and Billy with only a revolver, ambushed Brady and his three deputies from behind an adobe wall of the Tunstall store's corral as those lawmen walked past on Lincoln's single street.

Brady and Deputy George Hindman died instantly. Recklessly, Billy, along with Regulator Jim "Frenchie" French, ran out to retrieve his confiscated Winchester carbine from Brady's body; and both youths got leg wounds from firing surviving deputy, Jacob Basil "Billy" Matthews.

Three days later, occurred a Regulator debacle as their leader, Dick Brewer, in search of stolen Tunstall stock and its rustlers, led Billy, Tom Middleton, Fred Waite, Frank Coe, George Coe, and Charlie Bowdre to Blazer's Mill - a privately owned lumber and grist mill complex and way station, surrounded by the Mescalero Indian Reservation. There, accidentally, they encountered Ringman bounty-hunter and Tunstall murder posseman, Andrew "Buckshot" Roberts, for whom they had a warrant.

When "Buckshot" Roberts offered armed resistance, aiming poorly, Charlie Bowdre shot him in the belly. But Roberts, pumping his Winchester carbine, struck Charlie Bowdre's belt buckle. That ricocheting bullet wrenched George Coe's extended revolver, mutilating his trigger finger. John Middleton, shot in the chest by Roberts, survived. Next, Roberts, taking cover, killed Dick Brewer. Later Roberts died from his abdominal wound. Billy had not fired a shot.

But Billy's murder involvement now totaled six men; though only Frank "Windy" Cahill was his certain victim.

Attorney Alexander McSween's exoneration at the April, 1878 Grand Jury merely energized his attacks on the Santa Fe Ring. And Tunstall's men, the Regulators, including Billy, became McSween's protective entourage.

McSween took aggressive action. Knowing that a foreign citizen's murder could elicit a Washington investigation, he informed the British ambassador and President Rutherford B. Hayes about Tunstall's murder; and accused United States officials - meaning the Santa Fe Ring - of being complicit.

Of course, a formal ambassadorial complaint to Hayes followed; and energetic intelligent Attorney Frank Warner Angel was sent by the Departments of the Interior and Justice to New Mexico Territory as the investigator.

Using transcriptionists, Frank Warner Angel took over a hundred depositions under oath, among them from volunteer William Bonney. Becoming Billy's first recorded words, that transcribed deposition ended with his first known signature, attesting to his having read and approved the document.

Thus, Billy, risking his life by testimony exposing murderous Ring members, began a pattern which he would continue to the end of his days.

In Lincoln County, public optimism of Santa Fe Ring overthrow further grew when its County Commissioners appointed a McSween-sympathizing sheriff to replace dead William Brady: a local rancher named John Copeland.

Optimism was short-lived. On April 28, 1878, the new Regulator leader, Frank MacNab (replacing murdered Dick Brewer), was killed in an ambush near Lincoln by Ring-instigated Dolan men and Seven Rivers men.

Worse followed for the McSween side. By May 28th, because Sheriff John Copeland had forgotten a requirement of a newly instated sheriff to post a tax collecting bond, Governor Samuel Beach Axtell, by another questionable proclamation, removed him; and reinstated Ring power by appointing, as sheriff, George Peppin, a former Sheriff Brady deputy, who had been present at the Brady ambush the month before.

Boding even worse for eventual justice in Lincoln County, was Alexander McSween's unawareness that Santa Fe Ring influence extended to Washington, D.C.

Attorney Frank Warner Angel, after documenting illegal acts of Governor Axtell, U.S. Attorney Catron, and Sheriff Brady's posse - all linked to the Tunstall murder - concluded shockingly, in his secret October 1878 report, possibly under duress, that no U.S. officials had been involved in that crime.

Nevertheless, as possible fallout of Angel's investigation, Thomas Benton Catron resigned as U.S. Attorney. And Governor Axtell was removed mid-term and replaced by Civil War Major General Lew Wallace on October 1, 1878.

But months before those Regulator achievements - and tempering their impact - on July 19, 1878, Alexander McSween was killed by the Ring faction in the Lincoln County War.

War's fervor had mounted from that February's Tunstall murder; with Regulators, and oppressed Mexicans and Spaniards, calling themselves "McSweens" and identifying that stubbornly idealistic attorney as their leader.

Billy's affiliation with local firebrand youth, Yginio Salazar, and Billy's closeness to Hispanic residents of nearby San Patricio and Picacho, arguably strengthened the zeal that brought them into a McSween alliance for a Lincoln uprising.

By April 30th, McSweens were skirmishing with Ring partisans, known as "Murphy-Dolans;" though Lawrence Murphy was, by then, dying of alcoholism.

Of necessity, McSween had again gone into hiding, often in nearby San Patricio. Ominously and illegally, Sheriff George Peppin even brought troops from Fort Stanton to that town to hunt him; though that probable assassination attempt failed.

A final straw for the populace was Sheriff Peppin's retaliatory massacre of San Patricio's inhabitants on July 3rd; assisted by notorious John Kinney's Mesilla rustler gang.

Only 10 days after that San Patricio massacre, on July 14th, the Lincoln County War began. Alexander McSween, with about sixty men - the original Regulators, along with Hispanic residents of San Patricio and Picacho - rode into the mile long town of Lincoln to take a stand; though most of its residents had already fled, leaving Sheriff George Peppin, his deputies, and Ring loyalist possemen to fight. Fatefully, Justice of the Peace John "Squire" Wilson had remained.

Reflecting Alexander McSween's optimism at peaceful victory by ousting James Dolan's Ring faction from the town, was the fact that, in his big double-winged house, had remained his wife; her sister with her five young children; and that sister's attorney husband's law intern, Harvey Morris - the sister's husband, David Shield, being away on business.

McSween's men took strategic positions in houses throughout the east-to-west oriented town, which was bordered by high hills to the south and the Bonito River to the north.

When Seven Rivers and John Kinney's men arrived to join James Dolan and Sheriff Peppin with his possemen, Billy; his friends, Yginio Salazar and Tom O'Folliard; and San Patricio men - José Chávez y Chávez, Ignacio Gonzales, Florencio Chávez, Francisco Zamora, and Vincente Romero - raced to McSween's house, joining the single guard there, Jim "Frenchie" French.

Though the Peppin-Dolan men attained the south hills, they were kept at bay by McSweens for five days. Victory by default appeared eminent for Billy's side.

But Attorney Alexander McSween's underestimation of Ring influence included nearby Fort Stanton's new commander, Colonel Nathan Augustus Monroe Dudley as a partisan. Further lulling McSween was that, the month before, the Posse Comitatus Act had been enacted in Washington, D.C., making illegal military intervention in civilian disputes.

But in the days of mutual gunfire, a fort soldier, cavalryman Private Berry Robinson, sent to Lincoln by Commander Dudley for fact-finding, had almost been hit. Without basis, McSween was blamed for attempted murder of a soldier, setting the stage for military intervention.

And, by the 18th, James Dolan informed Commander Dudley that women and children were at risk at the home of Ring partisan resident, Saturnino Baca.

So the next day, the 19th, risking Posse Comitatus Act violation, but armed with the trumped-up excuses, Colonel Dudley marched on Lincoln with sixty troops - white infantry, black 9th Cavalry, and white officers - two ambulances; a mountain howitzer cannon; and a Gatling gun: a machine gun which was the country's most awesome weapon of war.

Panicked by that military might, McSween's men - except for those trapped in his besieged house, including Billy - fled north to safety across the nearby Bonito River.

Commander Dudley personally informed McSween that, if any of his soldiers were shot, he would raze his house to the ground with his cannon and Gatling gun.

Furthermore, Dudley left three soldiers at the McSween property, and provided three more to accompany Sheriff Peppin. Though they did not participate in shooting, these troops impeded defensive shooting by McSween's men and functioned as Peppin's guards as he patrolled the town's street.

In addition, Dudley forced Justice of the Peace "Squire" Wilson, by veiled death threat of double ironing at Fort Stanton, to write out arrest warrants for Alexander McSween and his men as Private Berry Robinson's assailants.

With those inhibitory advantages, on that July 19th, Sheriff George Peppin's men soon took strategic positions and set fire to the west wing of the McSween's besieged house, while Commander Dudley cautiously kept his non-participating soldiers encamped at the east side of town.

Evacuated from the house while the fire raged, were only McSween's wife, Susan; her sister, Elizabeth Shield; and Elizabeth's children. The trapped men were slated to die.

By nightfall, the McSween house conflagration - worsened by an exploding gunpowder keg inside - left the desperate inmates marooned in the remaining east wing.

At about 9 PM, escape from the house was made into the amassed, fire-lit, shooting adversaries. In Billy's group was law intern, Harvey Morris, whom he saw killed by their attackers.

And, before Billy and others crossed the Bonito River to rescue by waiting Regulators, Billy witnessed Commander Dudley's secret and illegal intervention: three white soldiers had been among the burning building's assailants; and had fired at least one volley at Billy and his escaping fellows from the rear corner of Tunstall's adjacent property. Arguably those soldiers had killed Harvey Morris.

And shot dead were Alexander McSween, Francisco Zamora, and Vincente Romero. Billy's friend, Yginio Salazar, shot also, survived. The war was lost.

Symbolizing Billy's dreadful trauma, that night, starving, yard chickens consumed the eyeballs of McSween's corpse. Again had occurred murder and mutilation in Lincoln County.

Though most Regulators fled the Territory, Billy stayed. With Tom O'Folliard and Charlie Bowdre - relocated to Fort Sumner with his wife Manuela - Billy continued the war effort by guerilla rustling attacks on Thomas Benton Catron's brother-in-law, Edgar Walz, and on the man Billy most blamed: John Chisum, who had traitorously refused make-or-break aid of his eighty cowboys to both John Tunstall and Alexander McSween; and had reneged on his promise to pay Tunstall's men for services - an agreement preceding Tunstall's murder.

Billy used non-Ring outlets for his stolen horses and cattle: Pat Coghlan in the western part of the Territory; and Dan Dedrick, a counterfeiter and rustler at Bosque Grande, a ranch 12 miles south of Fort Sumner. Dedrick, with his two brothers, Mose and Sam, also owned a livery stable in White Oaks, a town about 45 miles northwest of Lincoln.

Billy also sold rustled horses in Tascosa, Texas, where he wrote a subsequently famous, bill of sale to a Dr. Henry Hoyt for a flashy sorrel horse, which may have been Sheriff Brady's.

Billy also gambled along a circuit, from Fort Sumner to Las Vegas, to get additional money while he bided his time.

Lincoln County's next hope was Lew Wallace, replacing removed Governor Samuel Beach Axtell on October 1st. Wallace was a son of an Indiana governor; a Civil War Major General; the attorney prosecutor in the Abraham Lincoln murder trial; an author of a best-selling historical novel, *The Fair God*; and was then writing *Ben-Hur: A Tale of the Christ*. Elitist wealthy Wallace had desired an ambassadorship to exotic Turkey, not this Territorial backwater.

A month after arrival, to address continuing tensions of the Lincoln County "troubles," Governor Wallace posted an "Amnesty Proclamation" for Lincoln County War participants; though it excluded anyone already indicted. Billy, indicted in the 1878 Grand Jury for the murders of Sheriff William Brady, Deputy George Hindman, and Andrew "Buckshot" Roberts was, thus, unprotected by that decree.

Also enhancing local hope was Attorney Huston Chapman, brought to Lincoln by McSween's brave widow, Susan, for legal action against Commander Nathan Augustus Monroe Dudley for the murder of her husband and arson of her home.

In that atmosphere of dangerous scrutiny, James Dolan, still the local Ring boss, made peace overtures, first to Susan McSween, then to Billy, demonstrating that teenager's perceived threat. Billy's bi-lingual closeness to the Hispanic population had arguably brought men into the Lincoln County War - and could do so again in any other uprising.

The Billy-Dolan peace meeting was fatefully set for February 18, 1879, the first year anniversary of John Henry Tunstall's murder. It ended in calamity.

That night, as James Dolan; Billy; Jessie Evans with gang member, Billy Campbell; and Billy's fellow Regulators, Tom O'Folliard and Josiah "Doc" Scurlock walked Lincoln's dark street after the meeting, they accidentally encountered Attorney Huston Chapman, walking alone. Dolan and Campbell fired at close range, killing this hated opponent of Commander Dudley, then setting fire to his clothing. Again was murder and mutilation in Lincoln County.

And, as Billy had previously witnessed the criminality of shooting soldiers in the Lincoln County War, he had now witnessed the next Ring-perpetrated atrocity.

Attorney Huston Chapman's murder forced Governor Lew Wallace to come finally to Lincoln - and to put aside his self-serving months of renovating his Palace of the Governors residence and his writing of *Ben-Hur*.

In Lincoln, Lew Wallace's quixotic plan for quelling the unrest was elimination of outlaws and rustlers. That action, irrelevant to political roots of the "troubles," indicated that Wallace had expended no effort in comprehending the oppression of the citizens, or its Santa Fe Ring implications - though he never exhibited Ring alliances.

But Billy had long been known to Lew Wallace; in fact, from Wallace's first month in the Territory. As William Bonney "the Kid," Billy was number fourteen on a list of almost forty "outlaws" - mostly Regulators - prepared for Wallace by U.S. Marshal John Sherman in Santa Fe.

And, when Wallace arrived in Lincoln, Ring-partisans may have again accused Billy of being a dangerous outlaw - the murders of lawmen Brady and Hindman being dramatic proof. So Wallace, with a predilection for melodrama, apparently focused on Billy as the desperado causing "the troubles," put an astronomical reward of $1000 on the his head, and mobilized Fort Stanton troops to apprehend him.

Informed by his loyalists about Governor Wallace's pursuit, Billy took the audacious approach of not fleeing the Territory, but writing to him to negotiate exoneration!

That subsequently famous epistle, written about March 13, 1879, in Billy's most meticulous Spencerian script and on fine stationery, offered his eye-witness testimony against Attorney Chapman's murderers in exchange for gubernatorial annulling his Lincoln County War indictments.

That deal was Billy's calculated risk for negating Ring power over himself, while landing a blow against Ring murderers. The plan may have even represented a larger scheme of McSween partisans for their own agenda of convicting James Dolan and his minions; as well as assisting Billy, a local hero of the Lincoln County War. That possibility gains credence from the newly authenticated letter fragment from Billy discussed later; and apparently sent to Lew Wallace, arguably that same month of March.

Billy's March 13th letter was effective. It achieved a March 17, 1879 night-time meeting in Justice of the Peace "Squire" Wilson's Lincoln house with Governor Wallace, already in town interviewing citizens about "outlawry."

From that meeting, with "Squire" Wilson as witness, Billy apparently believed that a promise of annulling his indictments in exchange for his Chapman testimony had been established; though crafty attorney Wallace possibly had merely tricked the scorned "desperado" by ambiguous verbal and written responses lacking confirmation of an agreement.

But believing in a pardon promise, on March 20th, in a flurry of back-and-forth letters with Lew Wallace and "Squire" Wilson, Billy proceeded with the testimony plan, adding feigned arrest as cover to prevent his Santa Fe Ring assassination before his April Grand Jury testimony.

For that incarceration, Billy was kept in the home of the Lincoln jailor, Juan Patrón, Billy's friend and a McSween sympathizer. Billy wore shackles for the sham.

And, while awaiting the Grand Jury the following month, Billy even joined other trusting citizens in providing Governor Wallace with information about Territorial rustlers and hide-outs - by direct interview and by letter. The newly authenticated letter fragment indicates that Billy and Wallace even discussed some more relevant Lincoln County War issues in addition to general outlawry.

Concomitantly, Alexander McSween's intrepid widow, Susan, retained Attorney Huston Chapman's associate, Attorney Ira Leonard, to continue her murder and arson case against Commander N.A.M. Dudley.

But proactively, to undermine her courtroom credibility, Dudley obtained defamatory affidavits about her from Ring partisans. Dudley also requested a Court of Inquiry into his conduct on July 19, 1878, knowing that being cleared by a military court would serve well when later facing the same indictments before a civilian court's jury.

Dudley must also have known that military court vindication was inevitable, though he already had two prior Court Martials. For one, a year before the Lincoln County War, he had even been represented by Santa Fe Ring head, Thomas Benton Catron himself! And for the upcoming Court of Inquiry, Catron's friend, Henry Waldo, one of the Territory's best trial lawyers, would represent him. And the Presiding Judge would be Dudley's good friend: Colonel Galusha Pennypacker, from Fort Union, where they had both served.

But, annoyingly, Governor Lew Wallace planned to testify against Dudley, probably unaware of those Ring machinations.

In April, Billy's Grand Jury testimony about Attorney Huston Chapman's murder yielded James Dolan's and Billy Campbell's indictments for murder, and accessory to murder for Jessie Evans. And, while in his sham, Patrón house arrest, Billy may have also testified in other Grand Jury cases, since 200 indictments were handed down, all against the Ring side.

Though testifying in the Dudley Court of Inquiry, starting in May, was not in Billy's clemency deal, he volunteered; staying incarcerated and probably awaiting Wallace's amnesty.

Billy testified in Fort Stanton at the Court of Inquiry on May 28th and 29th of 1879. His words are preserved as part of that entire transcript. In his precise way, unfazed by Attorney Henry Waldo's bullying, Billy devastatingly reported white soldiers' firing a volley at them - "volley" and "white" meant officers shooting in unison under orders. That meant Commander Dudley was guilty of treason (ordering firing on American citizens in violation of the Posse Comitatus Act). Billy was now fighting the Ring in his own way.

Billy had fulfilled his Wallace pact in spades. And, had the Dudley Court of Inquiry been fair, Dudley would have progressed to Court Martial - even to a treason hanging. But neither Lew Wallace nor the Inquiry Court were fair.

Governor Wallace, trounced by Attorney Waldo during his disjointed and unprepared testimony in the Court of Inquiry, returned to Santa Fe humiliated; and apparently washed his hands of Lincoln County - and Billy.

The Ring succeeded in protecting its members. James Dolan and others indicted in the Grand Jury were given venue changes out of Lincoln County; and their cases were ultimately dismissed by Judge Warren Bristol. And the Court of Inquiry exonerated Dudley.

So, still in sham custody in Lincoln, Billy was totally vulnerable. Seeking his speedy hanging - more convinced of his risk to them after his devastating testimonies - Ring partisans, District Attorney William Rynerson and Judge Bristol, changed the venue of his murder trials for Andrew "Buckshot" Roberts, Sheriff William Brady, and Deputy George Hindman from sympathetic Lincoln County to Mesilla, in Dona Aña County, where Lincoln County War issues were unknown.

And, guaranteeing that no one missed the message that Ring opposition could be fatal, on the night of April 25th, an assassination attempt had been made on Attorney Ira Leonard, before his Dudley prosecutions began: a grim near re-enactment of Attorney Huston Chapman's end, and a reinforcement of intimidation to all.

By mid-June, without pardon, Billy, anticipating transfer and hanging trial in Mesilla, departed his Patrón house arrest.

Billy had achieved two things: Ring enmity at the highest levels and friendship with Ira Leonard, who would continue to press Governor Wallace for his pardon; and would represent Billy initially in his 1881, Mesilla, hanging trial.

Loose again, Billy stubbornly stayed in the Territory, optimistically awaiting his indictments' annulling; but aware of his death risk. And he returned to Fort Sumner and secret assignations with young Paulita Maxwell.

Meanwhile, Billy had gained a "reputation" as a gunman. So, on January 3, 1880, when he was leaving Hargrove's Saloon in Fort Sumner, an ambitious Texan stranger and possible bounty-hunter, Joe Grant, attempted to shoot him in the back. Grant's borrowed gun misfired; and Billy retaliated fatally. Obvious self-defense, it was not legally pursued.

So, by 1880, Billy was involved with seven murders, only two - "Windy" Cahill and Joe Grant - certain by his own hand.

By then, Billy may have heard mythology of his killing a man for every year of his life. The Ring was setting its trap.

Besides homicidal maniac and rustler, Billy would be declared a counterfeiter, which brought in the limitless power and financing of the Treasury Department's Secret Service. Billy would become one of its first political murders.

James Dolan initiated Secret Service intervention by reporting receipt of a counterfeit $100 bill in his Lincoln store.

By September 11, 1880, Secret Service Special Operative Azariah Wild was on his way to Lincoln. Dolan's counterfeit bill would be linked to Billy, though it actually was passed by a youth who worked with the real counterfeiter, Dan Dedrick: Billy Wilson and Tom Pickett. He also occasionally rustled with Billy and his regulars: Tom O'Folliard, Charlie Bowdre, and a "Dirty Dave" Rudabaugh.

Gullible Operative Azariah Wild was soon led to believe by James Dolan and other Ringmen - including Thomas Benton Catron's brother-in-law, Edgar Walz - that Billy was part of the country's largest counterfeiting and rustling gang.

In late December of 1880, the *New York Sun* ran a Ring-inspired story about Billy Bonney as: "Outlaws of New Mexico. The Exploits of a Band Headed by a New York Youth. The Mountain Fastness of the Kid and his Followers - War Against a Gang of Cattle Thieves, Murderers, and Counterfeiters." In it, Billy was that "Kid." His national fame was starting.

The Santa Fe Ring's plan for framing Billy, however, almost backfired because of loyal Attorney Ira Leonard, whom Azariah Wild interviewed. Leonard assured Wild that Billy would testify against the counterfeiters. On October 8th, Wild wrote in his daily report, mailed to his Chief, James Brooks, that he could arrange Billy's pardon in exchange for that testimony.

But Wild also told James Dolan his plan, resulting in Dolan's convincing him that Billy was the *gang's leader*!

So, in his October 14, 1880 report, Azariah Wild recorded his plan to arrest Billy in their meeting about his testifying.

By then, Billy was cautious. He held up the stagecoach carrying Operative Wild's mail, read that report, and avoided apprehension by avoiding that get-together.

The next Ring plan was to promote for election a Lincoln County sheriff willing to arrest Billy. Ring-partisan George Peppin, having quit, had been replaced by McSween-side sympathizer, George Kimbrell. Kimbrell had even deputized a John Chisum rustling spy: Robert M. Gilbert, who had been one of the citizens, in March through June of 1879, giving Governor Lew Wallace information about cattle thievery.

The Ring chose erstwhile buffalo hunter, Pat Garrett, and convinced Azariah Wild that Sheriff George Kimbrell was protecting "the Kid." So Wild backed Garrett and paid for spies to create dragnet posses to capture Billy and his "gang;" while, for the upcoming November election, Garrett was advertised as a law-and-order man to Lincoln County's new gold-rush settlers in White Oaks, ignorant of Lincoln County War issues, but representing a third of the county's population.

In the November 2, 1880 sheriff's election, Garrett got 358 votes to Kimbrell's 141. Azariah Wild, had Garrett immediately deputized for 1880, as well as giving him Territorial power for Billy's capture by making him a Deputy U.S. Marshall.

Billy, not knowing all that, would have erroneously believed that Garrett had no law enforcement power until becoming sheriff on January 1, 1881 and that his authority was limited to Lincoln County. So Billy thought Fort Sumner was safe.

Also ignorant of his publicized "outlawry," Billy continued to sell stolen horses at the Dedrick brothers' White Oaks livery.

On November 22, 1880, a White Oaks posse ambushed Billy, Tom O'Folliard, Billy Wilson, Tom Pickett, and "Dirty" Dave Rudabaugh at nearby Coyote Spring; killing two of their horses before they all escaped.

Five days later, that same posse besieged them 45 miles northeast of White Oaks at the way station ranch of "Whiskey" Jim Greathouse; killing their leader, Jim Carlyle, in friendly fire, but blaming it on Billy, who escaped with his group.

That murder accusation prompted another of Billy's letters to Lew Wallace. Over a year had passed from their pardon negotiations. It would be Billy's last letter to the governor before his final four sent from jail. On December 12th, Billy wrote its two double-sided pages, denying his outlawry and the Carlyle murder. Wallace never responded.

Instead, ten days later, on December 22nd, Wallace placed a column notice in the Las Vegas *Gazette* for "Billy the Kid: $500 Reward." Wallace's betrayal was complete.

Dreadful days were about to begin for Billy, unaware that Pat Garrett had assembled posses to ride after him; using mostly Texans, since Billy's loyalist New Mexicans refused.

The first Garrett ambush occurred on December 19, 1880, when Billy, Tom O'Folliard, Charlie Bowdre, Billy Wilson, Tom Pickett, and Dave Rudabaugh rode into Fort Sumner on its snow-stormed night. O'Folliard was killed; the rest escaped.

Billy and the others, attempting to flee the Territory in the continuing storm, stopped, on December 21st, at a Maxwell sheep herders', rock-walled, line cabin at Stinking Springs, on their way to Texas.

There, at dawn on the 22nd, Garrett and his posse ambushed them; killing Charlie Bowdre, mistaken for Billy by wearing his sombrero. The rest surrendered. That was Garrett's greatest moment - until actually killing Billy about 6 months and 22 days later.

Pat Garrett transported his prisoners by train, via Las Vegas, New Mexico, to the Santa Fe jail. There, Billy waited from December 27th to March 28th for completion of the railroad to the Mesilla trial site - so fearful was the Ring of his rescue - and a measure of his popularity as a freedom fighter.

In fact, Billy almost escaped anyway by tunneling out with fellow prisoners; though probably betrayed by one of them.

From his cell, Billy wrote again to Governor Lew Wallace: four insistent letters for the pardon. On March 4, 1881, he stated: *"I have done everything that I promised you I would, and you have done nothing that you promised me."*

Wallace never answered, yet intriguingly saved them for the rest of his life, along with Billy's other letters; as well as his notes on Billy's March 1879 interview; though he retained no other letters from the Territory's common citizens.

Billy's Mesilla murder trial, under Ringman judge, Warren Bristol, began on March 30, 1881. He was represented by Attorney Ira Leonard for Case Number 411, the murder of Andrew Roberts: "The United States versus Charles Bowdre, Josiah Scurlock, Henry Brown, William Bonney alias Henry Antrim alias the Kid, John Middleton, Frederick Waite, Jim French, and George Coe."

Surprising everyone, Attorney Leonard got the Roberts indictment quashed based on a technicality that the plaintiff, the federal government, had no jurisdiction over Blazer's Mill, the murder site; since private property, like it, was under *Territorial jurisdiction.* The fact that the property was surrounded by the federally controlled Mescalero Reservation was irrelevant. The argument was correct. Judge Bristol had no choice but to move on to Billy's next indictment.

It seemed possible that Billy could win. Left only were the Brady and Hindman indictments; and not only had Billy been firing in a group, he had only a revolver, lacking accurate range. Second degree, rather than first degree murder, was arguable. Hanging might not be inevitable.

But, suddenly, Attorney Ira Leonard withdrew from his representation. A Ring death threat is a possibility. For Billy, that loss was a major and traumatic set-back.

Replacing Ira Leonard, were court appointed attorneys, Albert Jennings Fountain and John D. Bail. Fountain, though not a Ringman, was also a local newspaper owner vehemently opposed to outlawry; and he believed that Billy was the outlaw and murderer of his unjust reputation.

On April 8th and 9th of 1881, occurred Billy's trial for the Sheriff William Brady group murder. Billy's Spanish-speaking jury, not granted a translator, heard only witnesses against him, including James Dolan himself.

After prejudicial instructions by Judge Warren Bristol (with a translator), making Billy's mere presence at the Brady killing the same as committing the murder as a sole assailant, the jury found Billy guilty of first degree murder; its only punishment being hanging.

On April 13th, Bristol set the hanging date for the next month, May 13th; insuring insufficient time for an appeal.

Nevertheless, hoping for one, Billy wrote, on April 15th, from the Mesilla jail, to Attorney Edgar Caypless, whom he had engaged earlier to pursue the theft of his bay racing mare by Pat Garrett's posseman, Frank Stewart, after the Stinking Springs capture. To Edgar Caypless, Billy expressed urgent need to recover her for resale, to get money for a defense attorney. Ever the perfectionist, Billy apologized in that letter because handcuffs had ruined his penmanship! (Caypless did win the replevin suit, but after Billy's death. And the sale of the mare merely paid Caypless's own fee.)

For hanging, Billy was transported back to Lincoln. There, ironically, the newly refurbished courthouse-jail, in which he was incarcerated under Sheriff Pat Garrett, was the resold Murphy-Dolan House.

James Dolan had repositioned himself, first mortgaging the House to Thomas Benton Catron, then buying the vacated Tunstall store for himself. Catron, in turn, sold the building to the county, which converted it into its new courthouse, with a second floor jail.

And Governor Lew Wallace, seventeen days after Billy's sentence, made sure to send Sheriff Garrett his own death warrant, requesting report of the successful completion of Billy's hanging.

By heavily guarded wagon, Billy was delivered to the Lincoln courthouse-jail on April 21, 1881. Sheriff Garrett had taken precautions against rescue or escape. For Billy's 24 hour guard, he had deputized a White Oaks man, James Bell, and a Seven Rivers man, Robert Olinger. Garrett also shackled Billy at wrists and ankles, and secured him to a ring in the plank floor - all to guarantee his death.

But on April 27th, Garrett left for three days to collect White Oaks taxes. The next day, Billy escaped. An unknown accomplice may have left Billy a revolver in the outdoor privy; though Garrett later claimed weapon theft from the armory.

A likely prospect for providing an outhouse gun was the building's caretaker, Gottfried Gauss, who had been John Tunstall's loyal cook; even present when Tunstall and his men rode from the Feliz River ranch to the fatal ambush.

So, with a revolver, Billy shot Deputy Bell, as the man fled down the jail's narrow stairway. That gun was never found.

Deputy Robert Olinger, across the street at the Wortley Hotel, taking lunch with other jail prisoners, either heard the shot, or was told. He ran back, and Billy, waiting at an eastward-facing jail window, vindictively shot him with his own Whitney double-barrel shotgun.

While Lincolnites watched without interference, Billy then broke his leg chain with a miner's pick. And taking more weapons from the armory, he escaped on a stolen pony.

Billy had now been involved in the murder of nine men; James Bell and Robert Olinger, adding to Frank "Windy" Cahill and Joe Grant, as his only provable killings.

Of the dead, Billy would have claimed being a posseman with William "Buck" Morton and Frank Baker, would have denied shooting at Andrew "Buckshot" Roberts, would have called Frank Cahill and Joe Grant self-defense, and would have seen James Bell's death as necessary to save himself.

Only Robert Olinger, hated for murdering his friend, John Jones; and present on the enemy side in each confrontation - from the John Tunstall murder posse to the Frank MacNab ambush, to the war in Lincoln - would have been killed fiercely. Billy's rage was so great, that, after the shooting, he even smashed apart the man's shotgun, delaying his own escape.

That count of nine murdered men - with only four certain as his victims - remained as Billy's final tally.

Within days of the escape, on May 3, 1881, Governor Lew Wallace repeated his personal reward notice of $500 for Billy the Kid; but in the *Daily New Mexican*. In addition, again with his own money, he ordered wanted posters for "the Kid."

Even before learning of the escape, in a newspaper interview, Wallace announced his adamant refusal to pardon Billy to a J.H. Koogler, owner of the Las Vegas *Gazette*.

Billy's escape route was northward, across the Capitan Mountains, to the Las Tablas home of his friend, Yginio Salazar. Next was southward to John Meadows's small ranch. But instead of continuing to Old Mexico, Billy reversed to Fort Sumner, Paulita Maxwell, and hiding in its sheep camps.

Though speculation, elopement of Billy and Paulita was possible. Paulita's oldest sister, Virginia, had chosen that option in Cimarron, in the Maxwell Land Grant; leaving for New York with the local Indian Agent, Captain A.S.B. Keyes, in 1870, the year her father sold the two million acres.

By July 14, 1881, though he was unsuspecting, Billy had traitors among Fort Sumner residents. And Barney Mason, Pat Garrett's friend and Secret Service Operative Azariah Wild's paid informant, though no longer Peter Maxwell's foreman, had spies reporting Billy in the town's vicinity.

Garrett's two deputies for that final pursuit, John William Poe and Thomas "Kip" McKinney, did not know Billy. Poe, a buffalo hunter, a past Deputy U.S. Marshall in Texas, a cattle detective, and a recent White Oaks settler, had met Garrett during the Azariah Wild-assisted, tracking of "the Kid gang." McKinney knew Garrett from their hog farming days.

That final plans for ambushing Billy were uncertain, is indicated by dissent between Garrett and Poe. Garrett was pessimistic about Billy's being in Fort Sumner. Poe tipped the balance to staying. As a stranger, he did reconnaissance in the town during the day of July 14th; Garrett and McKinney staying a few miles away. Poe also interviewed Sunnyside postmaster, Milnor Rudolph, seven miles to the north.

When Poe joined Garrett and McKinney that night, he was convinced Billy was near; and the ambush was planned. Its location being Peter Maxwell's bedroom necessitated both Maxwell's involvement, and concealment of that treachery; given townspeople's affection for Billy.

Also, someone, who has remained unknown, must have told Billy to go to that bedroom late at night to meet with Maxwell. And possibly another traitor called Billy into town.

While John William Poe and "Kip" McKinney went to the vicinity of the Maxwell mansion, Pat Garrett checked the nearby peach orchard. There he saw distant shadowed figures - possibly Billy with Paulita - before he went to Maxwell's bedroom to await the ambush.

Poe and McKinney remained outside on the porch, presumably to prevent Billy's escape if the ambush failed.

Billy began his near-midnight death walk across Fort Sumner's 300 yard, almost square parade ground, within the town's perimeter. He had exited the converted barracks house of his friends, Celsa and Saval Gutierrez, carrying their butcher knife to cut a dinner steak from a side of beef on the Maxwell mansion's north porch.

The moon was unusual. Rising at about 10 PM to the southeast, almost full, through the night it hovered along the horizon, looking giant and mimicking daylight.

Approaching the mansion, which occupied much of the west side of the parade ground, Billy went first toward Peter Maxwell's presumably curtained, darkened bedroom.

Maxwell was in bed as a decoy. Beside it, Pat Garrett lurked with his blued, Colt .44, single action revolver, with a 7½ inch barrel and serial number 55093.

Though strangers in town would have been common, Billy, as the most hunted man in the country, reacted with caution to John William Poe on the porch, and asked in Spanish - presumably as a disguise - who he was, while drawing his gun.

Poe supposed him to be a Maxwell worker or guest.

Then Billy entered Maxwell's darkened bedroom.

Immediately, sensing someone in shadows, Billy asked, in Spanish, who it was. Garrett recognized his voice. Possibly Billy hesitated to shoot, guessing Pat by his hunched size.

In seconds, Poe, McKinney, and townspeople heard the first shot. It was Garrett's. Garrett then fired again, though wild. But Billy was already dead.

As Peter Maxwell ran out in panic, Poe, thinking he was Billy escaping, almost shot him.

Then Garrett exited.

Uncertainty that Billy was dead, made Peter Maxwell send in family servant, Deluvina with a candle. She would have been the first to see the deceased boy, 21 years, 7 months, and 7 days old. Then Garrett checked.

Anguished townspeople were permitted to take Billy's body across the parade ground to their carpenter's shop for a candlelit vigil and burial dressing. He was laid out on the carpenter's workbench.

The following morning, a Coroner's Jury of six men met. Their foreman, Sunnyside postmaster Milnor Rudolph, a Ring partisan and no fancier of Billy, had a son, Charlie, who had ridden in one of Garrett's pre-Stinking Springs posses.

The jurymen identified the body, interviewed the eye-witness, Peter Maxwell, and declared the killing of Billy Bonney by Sheriff and Deputy U.S. Marshal Pat Garrett to be justifiable homicide. The case was closed.

Billy was buried by townspeople in the northwest corner of the Maxwell family's cemetery, beside Charlie Bowdre and Tom O'Folliard. One gravedigger was Billy's local friend, Paco Anaya, who later wrote a memoir: *I Buried Billy.*

By that burial day, Lew Wallace had already departed his backwater governorship early for his originally desired, exotic destination: Constantinople, as the Ambassador to Turkey. His *Ben-Hur*, released that year, was already a bestseller.

But Lew Wallace had also carefully stored Billy's letters in his Crawfordsville, Indiana, home before going abroad.

Years later, in long newspaper articles, dated 1900 and 1902, Lew Wallace presented his nascent "romance of Billy the Kid," in which the boy was "the most notorious outlaw the far West has ever produced."

Wallace's fascination with Billy had apparently been there all along, not for mercy; but as possible fodder for another historical novel.

Only Lew Wallace's unexpected death by cancer, three years after his 1902 article on Billy the Kid, put an end to his mythologizing of the Old West, with denigration of Billy Bonney as its ultimate outlaw.

But Wallace's adoring and literary wife, Susan, completing her husband's autobiography after his passing, made sure to include one of her husband's fantasies: that Territorial Governor Wallace had been the main object of desperado, serial killer, Billy the Kid's murderous obsession all along.

Ironically, the real Billy Bonney was destined to far surpass Lew Wallace's fleeting fame; though, arguably, the unfulfilled gubernatorial pardon catapulted Billy's fate: a tragedy of political intrigue, willing sacrifice, and doomed love, more magnificent than any storyteller's imaginings.

And Lew Wallace's carefully preserved hoard of the boy's writings would eventually let Billy speak.

Speaking Through Time

WHAT THE WORDS ARE

Billy Bonney himself left many recorded words; and his contemporaries published his quotes or provided their context. But many of Billy's words are lost. They include Grand Jury testimonies in 1878 and 1879, letters he referenced to Governor Lew Wallace, letters known to rancher John Meadows, and a pardon bargain letter to Secret Service Operative Azariah Wild for exchanging testimony against counterfeiters for a pardon. And there may be more awaiting discovery.

SUMMARIZING BILLY'S KNOWN WORDS

Billy Bonney's known words were in the service of justice: first for his murdered boss John Tunstall; then against other Santa Fe Ring crimes while he sought clemency for himself. Clearly, Billy believed he could prevail - though homeless and penniless - against politicians, military brass, and a cattle king.

For posterity exist the following by Billy Bonney:

- Deposition to Attorney Frank Warner Angel
- One bill of sale to Henry Hoyt for a horse
- Two amnesty negotiation letters to Governor Wallace
- One amnesty negotiation letter to "Squire" Wilson
- Interview notes recorded by Governor Wallace
- One newly authenticated interview follow-up letter
- Testimony in the Dudley Court of Inquiry
- One pre-capture letter to Governor Wallace
- Four clemency plea jail letters to Governor Wallace
- One letter to Attorney Edgar Caypless to sell his horse to appeal his hanging sentence

DEPOSITION TO ATTORNEY ANGEL

Billy Bonney's first recorded words are his June 8, 1878, court reporter transcribed and personally signed deposition to a federal investigator for the Departments of Justice and the Interior named Attorney Frank Warner Angel. It documents circumstances of the February 18, 1878 murder of John Henry Tunstall; which Billy knew as a ranch hand and an eye-witness of the ambush, though not the actual shooting.

HOYT BILL OF SALE

After the Lincoln County War's defeat, Billy Bonney became a petty rustler/gadfly harassing Ringmen. One location Billy used for stock disposal was Tascosa, Texas; where, on October 24, 1878, he wrote, and had legally witnessed, a bill of sale for an expensive horse to a Henry Hoyt.

TWO LETTER AMNESTY DEAL TO WALLACE

In early 1879, Billy Bonney commenced his famous letter writing to Governor Lew Wallace about annulment of his Lincoln County War murder indictments in exchange for his Grand Jury testimony against Santa Fe Ring murderers of Attorney Huston Chapman: James Dolan, Billy Campbell, and Jessie Evans. These two letters are dated March 13(?), 1879 and March 20, 1879.

ONE "SQUIRE" WILSON LETTER

For his Governor Lew Wallace amnesty negotiation, on March 20, 1879, Billy Bonney also wrote a letter to his friend and McSween-side partisan, Lincoln County Justice of the Peace John "Squire" Wilson. Wilson had hosted in his Lincoln house, and possibly arranged, Billy's March 17, 1879 face-to-face meeting with the governor. Wilson then became the go-between in the governor's ongoing arrangements for Billy's feigned arrest in protective preparation for giving his April Grand Jury testimony in Lincoln for the clemency deal.

GOVERNOR LEW WALLACE'S INTERVIEW NOTES

On March 23, 1879, during Billy Bonney's amnesty deal's feigned imprisonment at jailor Juan Patrón's house, he, like other Lincoln County citizens, provided Governor Lew Wallace with an interview about local outlawry. It was written down by Wallace. That interview's shared information, however, was not part of their clemency bargain.

NEWLY AUTHENTICATED LETTER

A letter fragment, newly authenticated in this book, appears to be the immediate follow-up to the March 23, 1879 Billy-Wallace interview on local outlawry; thus, postulated as having been written on March 24, 1879.

APRIL 1879 GRAND JURY TESTIMONY

For his agreement with Governor Lew Wallace about annulling his Lincoln County War indictments, Billy Bonney, while in feigned incarceration, testified in Lincoln's April 1879 Grand Jury against the murderers of Attorney Huston Chapman; though those court transcripts are lost. Possibly Billy provided testimony for other cases too, since two hundred indictments, primarily against Santa Fe Ring partisans, were achieved.

DUDLEY COURT OF INQUIRY TESTIMONY

Remaining in feigned imprisonment in Juan Patrón's Lincoln house, on his own initiative, Billy Bonney testified, on May 28 and 29, 1879, against Commander N.A.M. Dudley in the Fort Stanton Court of Inquiry for possible Court Martial.

ONE PRE-CAPTURE LETTER TO LEW WALLACE

On December 12, 1880, Billy Bonney wrote to Governor Lew Wallace - ten days before the Stinking Springs capture - denying being a gang leader or killing White Oaks posseman Jim Carlyle at the Greathouse Ranch fourteen days earlier.

FOUR SANTA FE JAIL LETTERS TO LEW WALLACE

From his Santa Fe jail incarceration, awaiting railroad completion for his transport to Mesilla, Billy Bonney wrote four clemency plea letters to Governor Wallace - whose Palace of the Governors office was only blocks away - dated January 1st, March 2nd, March 4th, and March 27th of 1881. The last was a day before Billy's being taken to his Mesilla hanging trial.

ONE LETTER TO ATTORNEY CAYPLESS

On April 15, 1881, two days after being sentenced to hang the next month, on May 13th, Billy Bonney wrote to his attorney, Edgar Caypless, whom he had previously engaged for a replevin law suit to reclaim his racing mare - stolen by a posseman at the Stinking Springs capture. Billy expressed urgent need to get her back for resale to pay an attorney for appeal of his hanging sentence. It is Billy's last known writing before his being killed by Pat Garrett on July 14, 1881.

SUMMARIZING CONTEMPORARIES' WORDS

Additional Billy Bonney quotations come from newspaper articles. He was famous by 1880, and was interviewed by reporters from the time of his Stinking Springs capture to his receiving his hanging sentence in Mesilla.

Billy's contemporaries, both friend and foe, also referenced him. Friends were Henry Hoyt; Gottfried Gauss; Attorney Ira Leonard; the Coe cousins, and Frank and George; Paco Anaya, and John Meadows. And a roving cowboy named "Teddy Blue" Abbott, who never met him but passed through the Territory, confirmed Billy's reputation for Hispanic affinity as well as his burgeoning notoriety by the early date of 1878.

And Billy's foes who preserved his words or their context were Governor Lew Wallace; Secret Service Operative Azariah Wild; Sheriff and Deputy U.S. Marshal Pat Garrett; Garrett's posseman Jim East; and Garrett's deputies John William Poe and Thomas "Kip" McKinney.

All these contemporaries, friend and foe, varying in motives and veracity, helped seal Billy's fame.

WHERE THE WORDS ARE

Billy Bonney's words are stored in historical collections; none are known to be in private hands.

INDIANA HISTORICAL COLLECTIONS

Indiana became the repository of Lew Wallace's papers because he was its native son: with birth and death in Crawfordsville - and national and international achievements in military service, politics, law, and literature in between.

Lew Wallace was an avid archivist of his own papers, whose thousands of pages encompass letters (with copies of those he himself sent), his book manuscripts - including the renowned *Ben-Hur: A Tale of the Christ* - and his press clippings. In 1881, Wallace, departing his New Mexico Territory governorship, even controversially took with him most of his administration's internal documents. Within that hoard were the Billy the Kid letters, noteworthy in being the only Territorial papers not by officials or high-ranking individuals. By 1900, Wallace was on lecture tours and giving newspaper interviews about his exploits; and his collection of Billy's letters was clearly referenced for an Old West theme - and possibly contemplated as a never-written historical novel.

Later, Wallace's son, Henry; grandson, Lew Wallace Jr.; and great-grandson, William N. Wallace, participated in preservation and eventual public placement of the collection.

In 1940, the bulk of Lew Wallace's papers - along with those of his wife Susan - were acquired from Lew Wallace Jr. by the great-grandsons of wealthy Civil War Colonel Eli Lilly, who founded the Eli Lilly pharmaceutical company in 1876 - when Billy Bonney was just entering history as an Arizona horse thief. Both of Eli Lilly's great-grandsons served as presidents of the family company.

Eli Lilly's great-grandson, Josiah Kirby Lilly Jr., a bibliophile who ultimately amassed 20,000 rare books and 17,000 manuscripts, housed the literary portion of Lew Wallace's papers in his custom-built Lilly Library at Indiana University's Bloomington campus.

Josiah Kirby Lilly Jr.'s brother, Eli Lilly Jr., in December of 1940, donated the rest of the Lew Wallace papers - military, political, and miscellaneous - to the Indiana Historical Society, then located in the State Library in Indianapolis.

In 1999, the Eli Lilly Jr. part of the Lew Wallace Collection was moved from the State Library to the magnificent, privately endowed, Indiana Historical Society building. There, the Billy the Kid letters are specially stored in a high-security vault.

NEW MEXICO HISTORICAL COLLECTIONS

Two Billy the Kid letters to Lew Wallace had been retained by the Wallace family: the March 13(?), 1879 first letter and the March 2, 1881 Santa Fe jail letter.

Those were acquired in the 1980's by the private, New Mexico Lincoln County Heritage Trust museum from great-grandson, William N. Wallace. In 2009, when the state acquired those Heritage Trust holdings, those two letters went to their current archiving at the Fray Angélico Chávez Historical Library in Santa Fe.

PANHANDLE-PLAINS HISTORICAL MUSEUM

The Hoyt Bill of Sale was probably donated by Dr. Henry Hoyt himself to the Panhandle-Plains Historical Museum in Canyon, Texas; where it is currently archived. However, the museum lacks documentation of the date of contribution or certainty that it was included in Hoyt's larger donation.

WASHINGTON, D.C. NATIONAL ARCHIVES

The Washington, D.C. National Archives Old Military Records Division has the complete transcript of the 1879 Court of Inquiry for Commander Nathan Augustus Monroe Dudley.

The National Archives also stores the reports by Washington, D.C. appointed Attorney Frank Warner Angel concerning his Lincoln County investigations. The reports include his October 4, 1878 *In the Matter of the Examination of the Causes and Circumstances of the Death of John H. Tunstall a British Subject* (including Billy Bonney's deposition), and

In the Matter of the Lincoln County Troubles. Dated October 3, 1878, is Angel's *In the Matter of the Investigation of the Charges Against S.B. Axtell Governor of New Mexico.* And Angel's October 2, 1878 report is: *Examination of Charges Against F. C. Godfroy, Indian Agent, Mescalero, N. M.*

Accompanying Angel's reports are his letters to Secretary of the Interior Carl Schurz, documenting attempts by Santa Fe Ring partisans to influence, or to interfere with, his New Mexico Territory investigations.

Attorney Angel also provided incoming governor, Lew Wallace, with a personally prepared notebook listing Territorial individuals along with their Santa Fe Ring affiliations. Only that notebook's copy is in the Indiana Historical Society, since the original "disappeared" as a possible example of the thoroughness of Santa Fe Ring expurgations, extending into the 20th century, of any incriminating documents.

World for the Words

Recreating Billy Bonney's World

Historians need hard data. But history of Billy Bonney and the Lincoln County War period is plagued by self-protective Santa Fe Ring cover-ups and records expurgations.

To compensate for that lost information, for my docufiction novel *Billy and Paulita*, I constructed its virtual world using extrapolation from intensive historical research.

To add flavor to Billy's and his contemporaries' actual words which are presented later in this book, excerpts from *Billy and Paulita* appear in this section, along with known facts about the particular protagonists.

Portrayed are the three men to, or about whom, were directed the preponderance of Billy Bonney's words: Investigator Attorney Frank Warner Angel, New Mexico Territory Governor Lew Wallace, and Fort Stanton Commander Nathan Augustus Monroe Dudley - words that came in the form of a deposition, letters, and court testimony. Those three men, though dissimilar in circumstances and nature, are linked by virtue of moral failure: abandoning Billy Bonney and the Lincoln County citizens to corrupt Santa Fe Ring oppression.

The failure of those three men yielded Billy's fate; and is summarized in *Billy and Paulita* by the character Fred Waite - John Tunstall's ranch hand and Billy's erstwhile partner in a planned Peñasco River ranch. Waite says prophetically to Billy: "Lincoln County is a moral proving ground. Evil here's so powerful it breaks people where they're weakest."

Billy Bonney's historical words in relation to Angel, Wallace, and Dudley mark the test of honesty which each of them failed.

ATTORNEY FRANK WARNER ANGEL

Frank Warner Angel was a 33 year old, astute attorney from New York City when he was appointed by President Rutherford B. Hayes, in 1878, as an Investigator for the Washington, D.C., Departments of Justice and the Interior to investigate the multi-faceted Lincoln County "troubles."

The "troubles" included - besides the February 18, 1878 murder of British citizen and merchant-rancher John Henry Tunstall - improprieties involving land grants as well as questionable billings and dealings by the local Mescalero Apache Indian Reservation Agent.

From May to October of 1878, energetic Attorney Angel collected a prodigious amount evidence consisting of documents and sworn depositions, among which was Billy Bonney's. Angel, thus, became the first high-ranking official to encounter the boy, who, at the time, was only eighteen.

Central to Attorney Angel's investigation was potential prosecution of Territorial public officials: like Governor Samuel Beach Axtell and U.S. Attorney Thomas Benton Catron. In addition, since one of the crimes was murder of a foreign citizen - John Tunstall - large financial reparations to the family would have resulted if culpability was proved.

The question remains, however, as to whether the motivation of those in Washington, D.C. who sent Angel was exposé or cover-up of the Territorial officials' crimes.

Billy Bonney's deposition, on June 8, 1878, to Frank Warner Angel was a transcribed, long, earnest, sworn statement - with his verifying signature - about his presence at the ambush-murder of John Tunstall, and about events that led up to that assassination by Sheriff William Brady's posse.

Billy, by then a Regulator, probably believed his words would go right to President Hayes: heady power for a teenager.

Billy also knew he was risking his life to come into Lincoln for that deposition - probably in its courthouse. By June 8th, the Regulator's Santa Fe Ring enemies were prevailing by blocking arrests of Tunstall's murderers and by illegal gubernatorial proclamations. Worse, Billy already had three outstanding murder indictments. Since that March, he had been involved in Regulator killings of Lincoln's Sheriff William Brady and Deputy George Hindman; Tunstall's murderers, Frank Baker and William "Buck" Morton; and bounty hunter, Andrew "Buckshot" Roberts. Adding risk was that Ring spy and collaborator, Saturnino Baca, lived right in town.

But Billy knew that at stake was finally getting indictments against the United States officials behind John Tunstall's killing, and tipping the power balance from the Ring to the oppressed people. Billy, as well as Lincoln citizens, must have felt optimistic that justice was at hand.

Attorney Frank Warner Angel produced reports addressing each of his investigative assignments. Dated October 2, 1878 was his *Examination of Charges against F. C. Godfroy, Indian Agent, Mescalero, N. M.* Dated October 3, 1878, was his *In the Matter of the Investigation of the Charges Against S.B. Axtell Governor of New Mexico.* Though the reports found wrong-doings that led to removal of Godfroy and Axtell, both men were expendable to Santa Fe Ring interests.

John Tunstall's murder was a different matter. Angel's reports on that were his October 4, 1878 *In the Matter of the Examination of the Causes and Circumstances of the Death of John H. Tunstall a British Subject,* and *In the Matter of the Lincoln County Troubles* - which included Billy's June 8, 1878 deposition.

By October of 1878, Angel's shocking conclusion, ignoring obvious culpability detailed in depositions like Billy's, denied involvement of any United States officials in that killing. Historians are left only with that documented peculiarity, not its cause. But soon after his reports were submitted, Angel received reward: appointment as assistant to the District Attorney for the Eastern District of New York.

Meanwhile, Ring head Thomas Benton Catron had taken precautions in the face of Angel's investigation of himself: stonewalling presentation of any requested documents. Eventually, Angel's report on Catron, including that man's deposition, was "lost" at the Washington, D.C. level. Nevertheless, defensively, by that October, Catron resigned as U.S. Attorney; though continuing as Ring head, amassing his ill-gotten fortune, and ultimately becoming a state senator.

So, thanks to Attorney Angel's apparent yielding to corrupt influence, Billy's first foray seeking Ring retribution was a failure that left him an identified opponent.

Possibly it was no coincidence in that same October, with the arrival of Lew Wallace as the new governor replacing Governor Samuel Beach Axtell, that Billy's name was number fourteen on a list of "outlaws" provided to Wallace by U.S. Marshal John Sherman in Santa Fe. The remainder of that list of almost forty names featured other Regulators.

But Frank Warner Angel, apparently had enough conscience to seek justice as his personal agenda. That October, he presented to Governor Wallace a notebook in which he listed powerful Territorial people along with their Santa Fe Ring affiliations: the real fruit of his Territorial investigations. If Wallace read that notebook, it should have enhanced Billy's credibility when the boy contacted him six months later. And it should have prepared Wallace for making substantive reforms to end the Territorial turmoil by addressing Ring corruption.

But there is no sign that Wallace read Angel's notebook. Instead, Wallace concluded idiosyncratically, by the next year, that the Lincoln County "troubles" resulted from "outlawry and rustling." And though not a Ring sympathizer or participant, Wallace primarily used Ring-biased sources for information; and, ultimately, his acts during his administration served to protect Ringmen, leaving them to regroup for the future.

So Frank Warner Angel, initially welcomed with hope by Billy Bonney and the beleaguered Lincoln County populace, destroyed the opportunity to implicate United States officials in the murder of John Henry Tunstall, and to topple Thomas Benton Catron and his Ring.

And, because his investigation, conducted in a time of extreme crisis, yielded no relief to the citizens, Angel indirectly made inevitable the Lincoln County War's desperate uprising, which took place when he was still in New Mexico Territory.

Angel had arrived with a chance to end the Santa Fe Ring. He failed; instead insuring its unimpeded growth, and, one could say, started Billy Bonney's trajectory to his fatal bullet.

FICTIONALIZING INVESTIGATING ATTORNEY FRANK WARNER ANGEL

Why did Attorney Frank Warner Angel, intelligent, diligent, and honorable, cover-up the existence and crimes of the Santa Fe Ring? Since Angel was sent by Washington, D.C., was Republican President Rutherford B. Hayes involved in Santa Fe Ring cover-up?

In my *Billy and Paulita*, I extrapolated those answers, which are blocked to historians by silence of corrupt secrecy of all responsible participants.

The August date marks one month after the lost Lincoln County War. The scene begins with Billy and fellow Regulator Tom O'Folliard during the flight from Lincoln County of other Regulators like Frank and George Coe. Then the scene shifts to Washington, D.C. and Frank Warner Angel's moral test.

* * * * * * *

AUGUST 17, 1878   7:52 AM   SATURDAY

Back in the Capitan Mountain cave, Billy gazed outward at a peculiar vision. During the night, countless newly-hatched spiderlings, each casting a silken tether, windblown, had criss-crossed the pines with a swaying, iridescent, filamentous maze.

Tom O'Folliard said to him, "Yginio's mom is good folks: stickin' tha' ax stuck in the stump so's we know i's safe hereabouts.

"An' tha' lady in Sumner shur was nice to give you a haircut at two AM." Billy smiled, saying her name was Celsa. She'd told him Pat Garrett had proposed to her sister, Juanita.

O'Folliard laughed. "I's funny how people there calls you two Li'l Casino an' Big Casino 'cause o' the poker playin'. You keep loanin' him. Does he pay back?"

"Not so far. But he keeps other people in - plays so badly that he puts money in their pockets."

"I don' unerstand why they'se sayin' you killt some clerk in the Injun resarvation las' Monday. We was jus' gettin' back them hosses they stole from us in Lincoln. A' leas' lookin' for 'em; an' takin' wha' we ended up with."

"I sure wish I'd found Sugar. But we got two of Brewer's that Jessie stole from the Feliz Ranch. Dick Brewer was a murdered Regulator. Had a farm near the Coes."

O'Folliard asked if it was true that the Coes were leaving that day, and did not notice the wince of abandonment. "Yes. To the San Juan Valley in the Farmington area. Northwest corner of this Territory. Going back to farming.

"But about that man who was killed - Morris Bernstein - he worked for that crooked Indian Agent, Frederick Godfroy. Seems he was shooting at some of the San Patricio men who rode in with us. I was blamed 'cause my name's known from the War."

O'Folliard asked if Yginio was going to live. "Yes. But they couldn't get those two bullets out of his back."

"Billy, them's real fine gloves you got in yer trunk. An' I never seen no sweater like that."

"They're from Tunstall." He blushed. "Mean a good deal to me."

"You figer Sumner's safe?"

"Sure. And from there we can go to Tascosa, Texas, to sell stock. Like Charlie told Catron in his letter, we Regulators will collect payment from him and other Ring men. It's part of the War.

"And I'll take you to a lookout to watch Chisum's big Texas drive. I once did cowboy work for him in Arizona. But I had to leave. A year ago today. Guess a lot's happened since then."

At that moment, in Washington D.C., one thousand five hundred twenty-one miles northeast of the Capitan Mountains, Frank Warner Angel paused at the threshold of the Cabinet room where five men waited, and tightened his grip on the handle of his carrying case with New Mexico Territory reports, before entering with habitual brash confidence.

Memorizing details to tell his wife, he got an unexpected memory of Ella, the exquisite woman in Moore's Hotsprings Hotel. In his wallet was her carte de visite photograph, naked except for a diaphanous shift.

The president sat at the head of a long table, a small flower-filled vase before him, and said to the secretary, "Mister Rogers, you can go now. We won't need a record of this meeting."

Affably, Rutherford B. Hayes continued, as Angel took a seat, "Your journey was a long separation from your wife and daughter;" surprising him by this kind awareness.

"And we are impressed, young man," said a lanky speaker, with startlingly wild, red hair and beard, sitting at the far end of the table. Before him and the others were piled Angel's forwarded copies.

Angel answered that he was actually thirty-three. Hayes chuckled. "To us, I'm afraid, that *is* young. I'll make the introductions. To your left is William Evarts, Secretary of State. Across from me is Carl Schurz, Secretary of the Interior and our resident fiery liberal. Carl works harder than any of us. With his one secretary and one clerk in the Patent Office Building he manages the Office of Indian Affairs, General Land Office, Pension Funds, Patent Bureau, Census Bureau, and Bureau of Education.

"Across from you is Attorney General Charles Devens of the Department of Justice. And to my left is John Sherman, Secretary of the Treasury and our champion of the greenback." Hayes chuckled again. "It seems that counterfeiting is the only thing you didn't find." Angel laughed.

Hayes continued, "You shed light on a part of the country as remote to us, in many ways, as Darkest Africa. We were pleased that you provided us with your tentative reports ..."

"Tentative?"

"So we can discuss your findings confidentially."

Hayes turned to John Sherman. "Our Angel is like one of your Secret Service operatives." Angel expressed curiosity about the unfamiliar entity. "That question will take us to the heart of your findings.

"But first, I want to make some relevant points. Our great War wasn't just about slavery, but about the role of federal government. In the South, people were willing to die for states' rights.

"Now that the central government won, it's my duty not only to protect citizens of all races, but to protect states' autonomy. Hence my slogan: 'put aside the bayonet.'

"For example, once I realized the newly-elected Republican governor of South Carolina, D.H. Chamberlain, needed federal troops to stay in power, I asked him to defer to his defeated Democratic opponent, Wade Hampton - who's now governor. I felt home rule would help the healing. The colored people didn't need Chamberlain. They've got the Fifteenth Amendment now."

Angel said, "But I've been reading about the Ku Klux Klan and ..."

"I'm not denying problems; but my conscience is clear. Our country needs help healing from the Civil War. Since the panic of seventy-three, what the American people want is economic stability. Everyone knows I'm not running for a second term. My legacy will be prosperity and a strong Republican party.

"And part of recovery is restoring confidence in the federal government after the Grant administration scandals. As you know, when Samuel Tilden lost, he said I'd won by fraud. And he had the credibility of having exposed New York's "Boss" Tweed Ring. And Tilden's still persisting. This May, he tried again to question my legitimacy.

"I'm convinced that those Grant scandals added to my close vote. Actually, their sad litany is crucial for our meeting today. In sixty-nine, Jay Gould and Jim Fisk - in collusion with Grant's brother-in-law - cornered the gold market to inflate prices.

" In seventy-two, there was the Crédit Mobilier scandal in which Union Pacific Railroad Corporation owners were also stock owners in its construction company, named Crédit Mobilier. Their profits were rumored to be in the millions from falsified building costs. And they'd been subsidized unwittingly by the federal government under the original Congressional Act for construction; but kept that money coming through bribes of corporation stock to congressmen.

"It's been called the biggest financial scandal in our history, but, to be fair, there weren't convictions. And, as loyal partyman, James Abram Garfield - in the House of Representatives since sixty-three and one of the Crédit Mobilier stockholders - told me: the scandal was exaggerated.

"Meanwhile, Ulysses S. Grant's Secretary of War was being bribed by merchants at army forts; and post office contracts were going to men who paid the right government official. Even Grant's private secretary was in the Saint Louis Whiskey Ring Scandal in which tax collectors were bribed with millions.

"So I'm determined to cleanse our party of that unsavory reputation.

"But to return to the Secret Service. It's a federal organization formed in sixty-two."

John Sherman added: "From the beginning, it's operated under the Department of the Treasury. In Lincoln's day, over half the paper money, and a good deal of coinage, was counterfeit. The Secret Service is a secret federal police force with power to go anywhere in the country to fight counterfeiting."

Hayes said, "And I joked that you were like an 'operative,' Attorney Angel, because its agents - called that - are as good at finding wrongdoers as yourself."

"Wrongdoers, indeed!" Angel said. "When you speak of scandal ..."

Hayes interrupted. "And, as to our Indian policy, we clearly can't tolerate agency funding scandals while we're trying to eliminate renegades like Victorio. Though it's a digression, I'll tell you that I'm considering a law to get rid of Reservations. I want to put Indians on farms with a twenty-five year title. That way, we can give that valuable land to our settlers. And now, let's turn to your findings."

Construing Hayes's tone as noble, Angel formulated his presentation accordingly. "Mister President, you've proved your lofty ideals by the very issues you've empowered me to investigate. As a staunch Republican, that emboldens me to speak without restraint. So I'll begin with my conclusion. I say this, not in vanity, but in moral indignation: I've discovered in New Mexico Territory, in the investigation of the murder of John Henry Tunstall, the largest scandal ever to come to light in our land, a scandal of proportions that would dwarf all the others. This scandal has occurred," he smiled, "possibly on soil never trod your Secret Service operatives. Had it not been for this single act of murder, what I found would have remained concealed by sheer distance alone.

"For in that Territory - so gigantic that Lincoln County, in which the crime occurred, could fit Massachusetts, Connecticut, Vermont, Rhode Island, and Delaware - there exists a land grab scheme in which one man has amassed six million acres. His name - as stated in my reports - is Thomas Benton Catron, New Mexico Territory's U.S. Attorney. What I've stumbled upon is well known to the local citizenry, but unknown to our populace at large. Its name is the Santa Fe Ring; and it runs the Territory as its fiefdom with Catron as king.

"Its consequence is unprecedented disenfranchisement, not only of the land owning, pre-Territorial, Mexican population, but of the Whites who've settled there. To the visitor - as I was - what is noteworthy about New Mexico Territory is not their strange mud-brick buildings, but the economic pall which hangs over it, because all money is sucked into that Ring.

"And the Santa Fe Ring operates like other Rings: by financial rewards and favor to politicians, judges, and law enforcement officers. But more perniciously, it operates by fear: intimidation, false arrests, removal of legally elected officials, illegal search and entry, and use of the military to enforce its power. And, Gentlemen, it operates by murder of its opponents.

"In fact, last month, as I was preparing my reports, the Ring staged a retaliative massacre of Mexican people - men, women, and children - in a town called San Patricio, near the town of Lincoln.

"Soon after, an attorney named McSween, who had been openly opposed to them, was murdered by the Ring, his besieged house burned down around him, his wife, her sister and her five little children, and men trying to defend them. All this was done, I have been told, while Colonel Dudley, commander of the local fort, participated as a Ring partisan, in violation of the Posse Comitatus Act. And the perpetrators of all those crimes were also the murderers of John Henry Tunstall."

Angel's handsome features contracted in a scowl. "Thus, these moral monstrosities completed the elimination of the only resistance to arise against their might." Angel smiled cynically.

"Though you could say there's one survivor: an eighteen year old, the youngest of my deponents - Tunstall's employee and witness to his murder. A William Bonney. In fact, I heard he was one of the few defenders to escape from that burning building."

Hayes spoke sympathetically. "I realize it's hard to know so much and not feel so much."

Angel felt an embarrassing urge to cry, so great was his yearning for goodness after wallowing in New Mexico Territory's evil. Angel said, "Gentlemen, I'm moved to share my deepest concern. We recently passed our Centennial: our celebration of the greatest democracy in history. In a mere four generations have the seeds of its destruction been planted? Thomas Benton Catron has rediscovered tyranny."

Hayes sighed deeply and said, "Attorney Angel, you've given us far more than we could have imagined. Am I to understand that all your reports were directed *solely* to Attorney General Devens and Secretary of the Interior Schurz?"

"Yes, Mister President," said Angel, noting nothing ominous about the question. "For the Department of Justice, I provided an overview of Lincoln County issues titled '*In the Matter of the   Lincoln County Troubles.*'

"A second report covers the murder: '*In the Matter of the Cause and Circumstances of the Death of John H. Tunstall, a British Subject.*' That one I divided into three questions: one, the cause of death; two, the circumstances of it, and, three, whether it was brought about by the lawless and corrupt action of U. S. officials. There's a separate report just on U.S. Attorney Catron." Angel turned to Schurz. "And for the Department of the Interior, I addressed the charges against Governor Axtell ..."

The president interjected smiling, "And don't leave out your almost four hundred page transcript of your depositions with Exhibits which you gave us all - just on the Tunstall matter. And your Uña de Gato land fraud investigation, your report on Surveyor General Henry M. Atkinson, and your Mescalero Indian Agency fraud investigations."

Hayes addressed the others. "Gentleman, we certainly have enough information to decide on a course of action. I call special attention to the section entitled '*Third,*' in Attorney Angel's second report to Devens, because it's about Tunstall's death."

They leafed through their copies and read: "*Third: Was the death of John H. Tunstall brought about by the lawless and corrupt action of United States Officials? After diligent inquiry and examination of a great number of witnesses, I report that his death was the result both indirectly and directly of the lawless and corrupt conduct of United States officials in the Territory of New Mexico.*

"*As to indirect causes, it is my opinion that John H. Tunstall, through his large and new mercantile endeavor and his recently acquired land holdings, which would have controlled most of the cattle range between the Mescalero Indian Reservation and the Pecos River through water rights to the Feliz and Peñasco Rivers, presented a financial threat to the existing political-judicial-economic alliance known as the Santa Fe Ring, whose leadership constituted the highest level of New Mexico officials: U.S. Attorney Thomas Benton Catron and Governor Samuel Beach Axtell.*

"*As to direct causes, it is my conclusion that the murder itself was a premeditated act done in compliance with directives, incentives, and promise of immunity from said Santa Fe Ring and its leaders. The act was committed under a guise of a local posse action to give it a screen of legality. Its organizer was a James J. Dolan whose business holdings were in competition with Tunstall's. And its promulgator was Lincoln County Sheriff William Brady, who employed known murderers, rustlers, and escaped convicts to do the deed.*"

When the cabinetmen finished reading, the president was rotating his little vase, peacefully studying its blossoms. Carl Schurz said to Angel, "If only you were not still in diapers during our revolution in Germany. Things would have turned out better." All laughed.

Hayes, smiling benevolently, said, "As you know, on June thirteenth, in response to your information, Department of the Interior Inspector, E.C. Watkins, was sent to the Mescalero Reservation. His report was forwarded on June twenty-seventh to Ezra A. Hayt, Commissioner of Indian Affairs.

"Watkins found that Agent Frederick Godfroy had, in Godfroy's own words, 'loaned' government supplies to that same James Dolan, his partner John Riley, a Doctor Joseph Blazer, and a known rustler, a John Kinney. In addition, Agent Godfroy was billing the government for rations for fifteen hundred Apaches, but could demonstrate only a few hundred. Obviously, Godfroy's removal is imminent.

" In the matter of the Uña de Gato Land Grant, we also agreed with your findings of fraud. Appropriate action will be taken."

"Thank you all," said Angel, welling triumph barely concealed.

Hayes continued, "But to return to your other reports - which you wisely introduced as having extreme implications - the matter is more complex. My inaugural slogan, which has apparently captured people's imagination, 'he that serves his party best serves his county best,' is crucially applicable. You are young, Attorney Angel, your intelligence and competence notwithstanding."

Hayes sighed and turned to the little vase of flowers, slowly dying in dismemberment, as they futilely soaked up water. "Part of being young is the believing that truth is enough. To a degree, we here have already discussed the issues you raised. And - if they could be proven - what you've discovered would, in fact, be a scandal to rock the county. That's why I reviewed past party troubles.

"Do you realize," Hayes's voice was assuming harsh firmness, "that if this scandal were exposed, it would not just dwarf - as you say - those scandals of the Grant administration, it would destroy this one?"

Angel felt his fingertips become cold. "Tilden would initiate my impeachment. And there is more. What you've discovered would give the next election to the Democratic party; and would also cause a major international incident with our important ally, England.

"This Tunstall report was initiated at the request of Ambassador Edward Thornton, beholden to Victoria, who, after the death of her spouse, Albert, is fetishistic about mourning. I wouldn't like consider our political and economic ramifications." Secretary of State William Evarts nodded grimly.

"What our country needs now is the continued guidance of the Republican Party. And, Tom Catron, this *possible* leader of this *possible* Santa Fe Ring, is a Republican. I may add that he is a man who was a Democrat, but once in New Mexico Territory, espoused our party as the one to receive his great power and influence - of which you may have discovered one unfortunate aspect.

"And that Territory's becoming a state is delayed only by resistance of many of us here in Washington to accepting so many Mexicans - people of mixed race - into our country. But the time will come. And a man like Catron will insure the direction of its vote. And, as you know, Catron gave you a deposition; but, to date, did not supply the additional information requested. So we can honestly say we've got no proof."

Angel struggled to resist the progression. The president was saying, "And a position of Assistant District Attorney for the Eastern District of New York State will become available by November - in less than three months. We here believe that your promotion would enhance your state."

With subdued voice, Angel said, "Thank you, Mister President."

"And we've prepared a revision for your Tunstall report to submit to you for your consideration. We hope you'll find in your heart that to serve the American people is to protect the Republican Party."

Hayes removed a sheet from his own stack and read it aloud: "*Third: After diligent inquiry and examination of a great number of witnesses, I report that the death of John H. Tunstall was not brought about through the lawless and corrupt conduct of United States officials in the Territory of New Mexico."*

Angel's face colored, then paled. "But what about the reports I submitted on Axtell and Catron? They contradict that."

"That's an excellent question," said Hayes. "It can be addressed. Samuel Beach Axtell's a Democrat, appointed as governor of Utah Territory by President Grant. There he became so embroiled in the Mormon conflict that - when New Mexico Territory's governor, Marsh Giddings, died in office - it was thought best to transfer him there. In Axtell's case, we can act.

"And, as to contradictions, putting together a puzzle is a delightful parlor game. My wife and I often leave one out on a small table. But before the pieces are assembled, the picture doesn't emerge.

"As you said, your reports went *solely* to the Departments of Justice and the Interior. Those on Axtell, Catron, and Atkinson will be stored in the Interior's offices. Those on Tunstall will go to the Department of Justice and to Ambassador Thornton.

"Pieces will *never again* be joined. So, one can say, 'No contradictions exist.'

"We'd like those *final* reports presented by say, October - just before that position of Associate District Attorney would begin.

"But we want to know *today* if our dedication to what's right for this country meets with your approval."

Secretary of the Treasury John Sherman said, "I want to repeat, Attorney Angel, that today's discussion is secret. It's a matter of national security, far beyond ..."

"I understand," said Angel and thought, "If I told this story, who'd believe it? They'd deny this meeting. There's no record of it. My career would be ruined."

He said quietly, "It appears that there's only one choice. I'll use this ... additional information." He signed the false document as a demonstration of intent.

"Well now," said Hayes, again affable, "I imagine after our labors, you, like the rest of us, are hungry." He chuckled. "Be forewarned that with the temperance views of myself and my wife, Lucy, we've got a liquor-free household. 'Lemonade Lucy,' I've been told she's called. And we're simple people. You're invited to our luncheon. It consists every day of bread, butter, and cold meats." He laughed. "I've already had my vice of the day."

"And that is?" asked Angel, tension dissipating with his decision.

"My one cup of coffee at breakfast," answered the president.

GOVERNOR LEW WALLACE

Billy Bonney's tragic fate manifested itself repeatedly as near-victories lost through immoral betrayals.

Most demonstrative is Billy's relationship with Lew Wallace, a handsome, rich, by then famous elitist who replaced Samuel Beach Axtell as Territorial governor after Investigator Frank Warner Angel's exposé resulted in his removal.

Lew Wallace also received the bulk of Billy's writings: Billy's negotiations for annulling his Lincoln County War indictments, then Billy's pleas for clemency when jailed. Though Wallace never helped Billy, it is noteworthy that he kept the boy's communications for the rest of his life.

Lew Wallace, almost 52 when he met Billy Bonney in March of 1879, had led a life of good fortune and achievements after his patrician birth in Indiana, where his father became governor and his step-mother was a noted suffragist. Educated in the law, he married the wealthy and literary Susan Elston, from the family that invented the Gatling gun.

In the Civil War, Wallace attained highest rank of Union Major General; and later, as a nationally-known attorney, was prosecutor at the Abraham Lincoln murder trial. He also achieved best-selling authorship of an historical novel on Cortez: *The Fair God*. In New Mexico Territory, he completed his next novel, *Ben-Hur: The Tale of the Christ,* which immediately became another best-seller. An accomplished artist, Wallace also patented mechanical inventions.

Lew Wallace's gubernatorial appointment by President Rutherford B. Hayes to the backwater of New Mexico was not the ambassadorship to exotic Turkey which he had desired. His stay in the Territory - from October of 1878 to May of 1881 - was cut short by finally gaining that ambassadorship from President James Abram Garfield. Wallace departed his brief governorship after his ill-considered interventions left Lincoln County with a "peace" of helpless impotence against the Santa Fe Ring, which he had inadvertently strengthened by his prosecution and vilification of its opponents, including Billy.

Wallace enjoyed his ambassadorship in Constantinople; then retired to Crawfordsville, Indiana as a local celebrity. From there, he traveled the country giving self-aggrandizing lectures on his colorful experiences. There is even a possibility that, before his death in 1905, Lew Wallace contemplated an Old West novel featuring Billy the Kid and utilizing, at last, his correspondence with the boy, which he had saved in perfect condition for that quarter century.

FICTIONALIZING LEW WALLACE'S BACKGROUND

The *Billy and Paulita* excerpt below introduces personality flaws that would cause Lew Wallace to betray his apparent bargain with Billy Bonney to annul his Lincoln County War murder indictments in exchange for eye-witness murder testimony. Those flaws would later yield Wallace's humiliation in the Dudley Court of Inquiry and revive his Civil War humiliation from the battle of Shiloh. So hubris and hypocrisy would be his breaking points in his moral test of pardoning Billy in the face of opposing Santa Fe Ring pressure. Abandonment of Billy would prove easier for Wallace.

The scene starts after the lost War with Billy's continued guerrilla rustling, while other Regulators flee the area. That overlaps the Washington, D.C. Cabinet meeting discussion about Lew Wallace as the Territory's replacement governor.

* * * * * * *

AUGUST 31, 1878   1:10 PM   SATURDAY

As Tom O'Folliard with Billy watched Chisum's giant cattle drive below, a plodding passive departure eastward, like innocence lost, Billy spoke excitedly about rustling plans. But they were glarrrious raiding of Cú Chulainn transposed to the Lincoln County War where, in archetypal recesses, waited the giant red bull fit for a queen. That same red bull, millennia before, had been captured in ochre and charcoal on cave walls in god glory awe; was later challenged by bull dancers in ancient Crete; was sacrificed in temples of Greece and Rome; and now, Billy's day, was murdered, pouring blood for spectators in Spain and Mexico, so his elemental powers could assuage humanity's impotence.

Billy said, "I've found stock outlets who aren't Ring men. Between Sumner and White Oaks - a town north of Lincoln - there's 'Whiskey Jim' Greathouse. He's got a way station and ranch.

"The Ring's biggest competition is Pat Coghlan. In the Tularosa area.

"And I'm still trying to meet a Dan Dedrick at his ranch called Bosque Grande. He somehow works with Coghlan. Also, Charlie and Doc will ride with us. They're moving to Sumner to fight the War too."

The outcome of that freedom struggle depended on a meeting then taking place one thousand four hundred thirty-five miles to the northeast of Chisum's herds, in Washington, D.C. in the White House Cabinet room. There President Rutherford B. Hayes addressed Secretary of the Interior Carl Schurz, Secretary of the Treasury John Sherman, Attorney General Charles Devens, and George McCrary, the clean-shaven, gray haired Secretary of War.

Hayes said, "U.S. Attorney Catron is a lucky man. The brazen irregularities in Governor Axtell's Lincoln

County Proclamations justify his removal. It remains only to chose his successor. For that, we'll meet here at three."

Only Carl Schurz stayed. Confidingly he said, "Rutherford, my friend, you - as well as Catron - are lucky. Providence protects you: in your election and in this Axtell. I would not like to contemplate the outcome if our Angel knew about the letters and petitions we have each gotten over the past two years from Cimarron, in Colfax County, where that Santa Fe Ring is the pet obsession of the citizenry - including that fanatical newspaper woman, Mary McPherson. The one Tom Catron wrote to us to disregard as 'a crazy person.'

"And, fortunately, our young blood-hound also did not sniff out that, in seventy, our own William Evarts was lucratively employed as an attorney by his *good friends*, Catron and Elkins, to add prestige - of his having been Attorney General the year before - to his legal opinion for them that the Maxwell Land Grant's title was sound for its sale - to get around Elkins's brother's questionable survey." Schurz added, "As President Johnson's Secretary of the Navy, Gideon Wells, said, 'Evarts is a man who accommodates himself to any set of principles.' "

"What of that?" Hayes declared irascibly, revealing the ruthless arrogance of his immense inherited wealth, and seen only by his intimates.

With irony and acceptance of futility, which he rationalized as mankind's foibles, Schurz sighed. "Merely that from our Olympian heights we are privileged to observe the irony of history unfolding."

From his papers, Schurz withdrew a document. "This one is from April of seventy-seven, only a year and three months before their war in Lincoln County. From Mary McPherson. Last night I added some check marks."

Hayes read: "*To the President: The undersigned in behalf of the people of the Territory of New Mexico herewith present the following Charge: that U.S. Attorney Thomas B. Catron, Judge Warren Bristol, Chief Justice Henry Waldo, and Governor Samuel B. Axtell have conspired together in a group* known as the Santa Fe Ring for the purpose of corrupting justice so as to deprive citizens of personal liberty and the right of fair trial, and to compass the revenues of the Territory and the property of its citizens including large land grants for purposes of private gain. We citizens therefore respectfully request their removal from office."

Schurz continued, "McPherson's son-in-law, Raymond Morley, a railroad engineer, joined with Cimarron attorney, Frank Springer, to buy the *Cimarron News and Press*. Morley's wife is McPherson's daughter. So every move the Ring made, they printed it in that paper. A local young gunfighter named Clay Allison even championed their cause. He reminded me of that young William Bonney, who so moved our Angel.

"You may recall that one of the first things *you* did as president was authorizing Fort Union troops to enforce warrants issued by Territorial Chief Justice Henry Waldo to seize or kill Morley and Springer if they resisted arrest - shades of Commander Dudley in Lincoln!

"Of course, Catron and Axtell were unhappy when that plot failed, but eventually they succeeded - by murder." Schurz pointed to another McPherson paragraph. "*An outrage was the assassination of a Methodist minister named Franklin J. Tolby, who was fighting the stranglehold of the Santa Fe Ring on our Territory. They murdered him after warning him to leave the County which he refused to do.*'

"Doesn't that remind you of the murdered Tunstall and McSween a year later? The Morleys and McPherson even printed, in their newspaper, that Clay Allison refused seven hundred dollars from Catron to do that deed.

"And look at this from McPherson last May. A list of charges identical to the ones Angel found against Axtell."

Hayes said, "And we're removing him. What else do you want?" Indignation remained. But Hayes had learned to tolerate exercises in idealism from this gadfly without sting.

"Only to contemplate, Rutherford. In Colfax County was no real uprising; though they called it the Colfax County War. How did these people in Lincoln County achieve all this one year later? I decided we missed something. I read McSween's pedantic deposition to Angel. I was not ready to fight.

"I believe there still remains alive the *real* leader of their Lincoln County People's Revolution. And you know, as well as I do, that was what it was."

Their eyes met, both aware that in place was the next potential enforcer: the Secret Service, poised, if needed, for political murder if the unrest continued. Hayes had already informed its Chief about the Lincoln County situation. Thus, Angel, naively by his reports, had established that Washington was merely one more link in the Santa Fe Ring; and had left its participants there on alert.

With his Cabinetmen reassembled, Hayes began by asking what they knew about Lew Wallace, his prospective pick for governor.

Secretary of War George McCrary said, "Ulysses S. Grant detested him for Shiloh. And in July of sixty-four, Wallace initiated the battle at Monocacy Junction without orders. Later, he claimed he saved President Lincoln from kidnapping. He once said to me, 'Washington lay exposed in its nakedness.' "

Carl Schurz joked: "The poet who was a general. Or the general who was a poet."

"Gentlemen," chuckled the president, "let's go over the specifics and make our decision. Troops won't kidnap me, but my wife will - for dinner." They laughed.

Schurz said, "I have taken a special interest in Wallace. Do not forget that I rescued my old professor from Spandau prison. I have a weakness for intellectuals." He adjusted his pince-nez and straightened his notes. "My assignment was to interview him. This is what I learned.

"Louis Wallace - who renamed himself 'Lew' because he thought it sounded better - was born in Brookville, Indiana, on April tenth of eighteen-seventeen. His father was the Governor of Indiana in thirty-seven. Lew became an attorney. For a wife he picked a very rich girl. In the War - probably because of his father - Governor Morton of Indiana made him Indiana's Adjutant General with the responsibility to raise troops. Then Lew was made Colonel of the Eleventh Regiment of Indiana Volunteers.

"It was for this regiment that this poetic romantic - so dashing that the paintings of him imply broken hearts - designed the Zouave costume. With the red pantaloons, tight green jackets, and little caps, to me the pictures look like organ grinder monkeys."

Hayes smiled. "It wasn't as bad as that, Carl. But they did stand out in parades."

"That I can imagine. And we will see how eccentric Lew is. We come to the battle of Shiloh in Tennessee. Do not forget - because we have seen such horrors later - Shiloh in sixty-two was the biggest battle ever fought on American soil. Twenty-three thousand seven hundred forty-six casualties; more than the total casualties of your Revolutionary War, War of Eighteen Twelve, and the Mexican War combined.

"Originally it was called the battle of Pittsburgh Landing. Wallace was positioned at Crump's Landing six miles north of Pittsburgh Landing, near the north to south Tennessee River.

"In my mind, the key to Shiloh is not often mentioned, which is that, through his own spies, Wallace learned that the Confederate army under General Albert Sidney Johnston was approaching. Did he inform General Grant? No. Why? He has said he assumed Grant would know something that big. Well, he didn't. And, the month before, Wallace had again been promoted, this time to Major General: the highest rank a man could reach at the time.

"Back to Shiloh. Two main routes went to Pittsburgh Landing: one direct - the River Road - one indirect, the Shunpike Road. With the terrain, the River Road went a bit east before going south. The Shunpike went quite west before looping back.

"Then came April fourth. Wallace's scout, Bell, reported to him that the rebel army was heading from Corinth to Pittsburgh Landing. So Wallace wrote a note - probably poetic - and gave it to his orderly Simpson to inform Grant. But - as revealed in the intense controversy that followed - Wallace told Simpson if he couldn't deliver it directly to Grant, he should *mail it*. Gentlemen, Simpson mailed it!

"Ulysses Grant said he never got the letter, which can be believed since - as you say in this country - 'all hell broke loose' two days later on April sixth, when everyone was asleep, except for the Confederate army. Wallace was awakened by his sentinel, who told him he heard guns from the south. So Wallace did the natural thing: went for breakfast on a steamboat on the Tennessee River.

"At eight-thirty, Grant's boat, the Tigress, passed his. Grant asked Wallace if he had heard gunfire. Wallace answered *only* that he had. So Grant told him to hold in readiness.

"At eleven-thirty, Grant sent Captain Baxter, his Chief Quartermaster, to tell Wallace to come to Pittsburgh Landing for a battle. Poor Baxter wrote those orders from Grant on a paper picked up in the Tigress's ladies' room. History has not told us what he was doing there. The note - whose penmanship Wallace criticized - Wallace later said he had lost. More unfortunate was what came next.

"Wallace had those two roads to get to the battle. Guess what he did?" The men were smiling. Schurz was their eccentric. "He had lunch. After that, he took the longer Shunpike, having decided that, by then, Grant must have the enemy retreating westward - which was where that road would first put him. In reality, a Confederate artillery of sixty-two cannon were firing on desperate Union men trapped at Pittsburgh Landing.

"Soon, Wallace was met by a messenger from Grant saying, 'Hurry up,' and, strangely - to Wallace - departing eastward.

"Nevertheless, Wallace blithely proceeded west until met by another Grant messenger. When that one also left in the 'wrong direction,' it occurred to Wallace that *he* had made a mistake. So what did he do? Stopped to wait for his stragglers.

"Then came two more couriers who reported that they were losing at Pittsburgh Landing, and pleaded with him to release troops. He refused. He felt it would make a bad impression if they did not arrive as a unit. But he did proceed southeast.

"That left Wallace with Snake Creek to cross. It was a bog. So he and his men descended waist deep. He later revealed that he decided not to worry about the uniforms. That is fortunate or this might still be a slave owning country - though poor Abe Lincoln might still be alive.

"At that point, Wallace was only a half mile from the battle. Since he was not Alexander the Great, famous for his lightning marches, he chose to bed down in the bog. He leaned on a tree. Sleep was further interrupted by mournful cries from the adjacent battlefield.

"Wallace did arrive the next morning. General Buell had already crossed the Tennessee River with eighteen thousand more troops. As you know, that day, Grant won.

"Then Grant removed Wallace from any future command of troops. Probably he hoped to humiliate him into leaving the army; but it only stimulated a flurry of writing, in which Wallace denied wrongdoing, but concluded that the war was young and they were all still learning

"But Lew was bored. So, in August of sixty-two, when his friend Governor Morton summoned him to assist in organizing the defense of Cincinnati, Ohio, he went - obviously alone. By coincidence, heading in that same direction were Confederate troops under General Kirby Smith. When Wallace found out, he took over Cincinnati without asking anyone, declared martial law, and composed a literary piece of sorts: a proclamation demanding that all inhabitants defend their city.

"Unable to get rid of him, the army next tried sending him to miserable Camp Chase, which held five thousand, renegade Union soldiers. His assignment was to prepare these derelicts to fight Indians in Minnesota. To everyone's surprise but his own, he did shape up and send off this criminal crew. I do not know, however, if they merely deserted again.

"Then came Lincoln's reelection. Wallace was sent to Baltimore, Maryland, to protect poling places. He got carried away, as usual, and was about to hang four men - declaring, without proof, that they were Confederate spies - when Lincoln leashed him.

"Then April fourteenth of sixty-five passed at Ford's Theater. Because he was a lawyer and loyal, Wallace was appointed by President Andrew Johnson as judge in the assassins' military trial.

"It has been the conclusion of our less hysterical times that Wallace bullied and hampered their lawyers. And making the eight defendants wear bizarre pointed caps covering their heads, does smack of his costuming dramas. As you all know, the hanging of the defendants, David Herald, George Atzarodt, and Lewis Payne, has left people uneasy because their fellow gallows victim, Mary Surratt - John Wilkes Booth's landlady - was considered innocent. The so-called accomplices, Doctor Samuel Mudd, who set Booth's broken leg; Edward Spangler; Samuel Arnold; and Michael O'Laughlin were also sentenced - again at Wallace's adamancy - to life in prison on the Dry Tortugas in Florida. President Johnson pardoned them later; though, by then, O'Laughlin had died of yellow fever.

"But this courtroom experience prepared Lew Wallace for his next assignment: heading the Andersonville War

Crimes trial against Confederate prison keeper, Captain Henry Wirz, in August of sixty-five. Wirz too was hanged, though without public regret.

"And Wallace continued to wax poetic. On July fourth of sixty-six he presented his old friend Governor Morton with the battle flags of the Indiana regiments and said ..." Schurz took up a paper: " '*In the armies of Persia was a chosen band called the Immortals bearing spears pointed with pomegranates of silver and gold. We, too, have our Immortals! And instead of a king to serve they have for leader that man of God and the people, Lincoln the Martyr.*' This writing makes me miss Abe even more. Gentleman, how do you point a spear with a pomegranate?" Several laughed.

"Then comes Mexico. Wallace had earlier convinced Lincoln and Grant that the Texan Confederates planned to join French Imperialists under Napoleon the Third's puppet king, Archduke Maximillian of Austria. So in late sixty-five, Lew did an arms running scheme for anti-imperialist Mexicans. They graciously took the arms and ungraciously never paid him.

"It is true that Lew Wallace has never shown venality. He has barely shown practicality.

"In sixty-six, he made an even stranger Mexican plan: offering their then president, Benito Juárez, to import American colonists to defend their border from Indians in exchange for free land. Can you imagine Juárez wanting to give up more land to Americans? But Wallace happily declared that the experience helped him finish his novel on Mexico, *The Fair God* - which has gotten so much literary acclaim.

"In seventy, Wallace ran for the House of Representatives from Indiana. The Democrats made much of Shiloh and the hanging of Missus Surratt. He lost, but blamed election fraud.

"Since seventy-four, he has been in private law practice in Crawfordsville, Indiana, and is working on a book on Jewish history called *Ben-Hur*. As you all know, he campaigned loyally in Florida for Rutherford's presidential bid."

Suave William Evarts said, "He almost got his reward this year. He was offered the ambassadorship of Bolivia, but refused. Probably the low salary."

Schurz laughed. "Not the five thousand dollars. He didn't like the landscape."

"So he might accept the Governorship of New Mexico Territory, which pays only two thousand six hundred dollars a year?" asked John Sherman.

"Apparently, yes. He thinks New Mexico Territory will look like Jerusalem and assist in completing his new book."

"Thank you, Carl," said Hayes, smiling. "Informative and amusing. Is Lew Wallace right as its next governor?"

"I will be a more serious," said Schurz, adjusting his pince-nez and reverting to token idealist. "This Lew Wallace, as I said, reminds me of my old professor. Then I risked my life to rescue him. Now I would let him stay. Intellectuals ruined our revolution. They were all mind and no heart. They cared only to act clever - not to act. I left the country in disgust.

"And, with Lew Wallace, possessing a mind able to be a lawyer, a general, and a writer, only gave him vanity to override orders with incorrect decisions, and to become despotic with horrible consequences like Missus Surratt. Does this bother him? Not at all. Because he feels nothing. We would send into this faraway battleground the opposite of our Angel. Please excuse my pun."

"Carl," smiled Hayes, "I'll continue that pun. We don't want an avenging Angel sent. This war needs to stay in darkness. I'm confident that Lew Wallace won't embarrass the Republican Party."

"And how many more will die?" asked Carl Schurz, exaggerating melancholy resignation.

"As many as have died likewise through history," said Hayes. "And now it's time for dinner."

FICTIONALIZING LEW WALLACE'S
MYTHOLOGIZING OF BILLY THE KID

To round-off the personality traits of Lew Wallace which impacted Billy Bonney's life, the newspaper articles he wrote about "Billy the Kid" in the beginning of the new century are fictionalized in *Billy and Paulita.*

By the time he wrote them, Lew Wallace had retired; and, though basking in his life of almost unremitting good fortune, he apparently still felt festering two unextractable thorns: his blame for the extreme casualties in the Civil War battle of Shiloh and his misleading pardon promise to Billy.

To deal with that pardon, in 1900 and in 1902, he presented long interview-style articles. The first, "Old Incident Recalled," was in the Crawfordsville *Weekly News-Review.* The second was in the *New York Sunday World Magazine* as "General Lew Wallace Writes a Romance of 'Billy the Kid,' Most Famous Bandit of the Plains: Thrilling Story of the Midnight Meeting Between Gen. Wallace, Then Governor of New Mexico, and the Notorious Outlaw, in a Lonesome Hut in Santa Fe."

Both articles - the latter reprinted in entirety later in this book - reveal Lew Wallace's attempts to rationalize his betrayal of Billy. For *Billy and Paulita*, both articles are fused and made twenty years earlier to overlap Billy's post-jailbreak tracking - emphasizing that Billy's capture, hanging sentence, and escape by murdering his deputy guards all occurred arguably as the betrayal of what Billy believed was a gubernatorial pardon bargain, with his own part fulfilled.

* * * * * * *

JUNE 3, 1881   11:17 AM   FRIDAY

Petrified, Manuel Brazil asked goat-faced Juan Rioval if he was positive. "Yes, patrón," the boy lied. "I have spoken with Beely Keed. He threatens revenge. You must leave.

"But I can be your eyes and ears. For this I think a hundred dollars is fair."

When Brazil refused, Rioval put on his sombrero and said, "I wish you luck that Shereef Garrett finds him before he finds you." Brazil offered fifty dollars and a horse for carrying messages. He had family in Anton Chico. He could go there.

Rioval said, "There, I say, you would be safe."

One thousand twenty-eight miles northeast of the Brazil ranch, in his Crawfordsville, Indiana, home, Lew Wallace, on his favorite easy chair, with his oversized writing board inventively balanced on its arms, said to his wife, "Susan, we're almost at the Holy Land.

"Back just yesterday and off to Constantinople by the end of the month. You must be curious as to these jottings I began in the cinder-infested bowels of our Indiana, Bloomington, and Western passenger car." She smiled lovingly and said of course.

"The angel of inspiration alighted on the first leg of our journey on the Atchison, Topeka, and Santa Fe line. It occurred to me that a legend is but truth writ bold. You may recall that I had mentioned a Billy the Kid, whose escape, just before hanging, is now fodder for newspaper reporters from coast to coast.

"I decided, who better to create the legend of Billy the Kid than the man at its center: myself? And rather than just use the tale as a chapter for my autobiography, I may someday turn it into a book. Tell me what you think.

He read aloud: "*Upon coming to the untamed wilds of New Mexico as Governor, with the mission of preserving peace, life, and property, I soon learned about Billy the Kid, the most notorious outlaw of the West and the quarry of every sheriff from the Rio Grande to Death Valley. I determined to rid the Territory of this scourge and end his spree of rustling and killing as many men as his twenty-one years of life. I knew I had to risk my own and arrange a face-to-face meeting.*

"*With much difficulty I had him contacted and set the rendezvous in a lonely hut on the outskirts of Santa Fe. He arrived holding Winchester rifle and six-shooter, and though a* stripling, had the cold piercing eyes of the hardened murderer. Using the pretense that I was working to solve the murder of an attorney to which he was a witness, I offered him a pardon in his pocket if he would testify then leave the Territory. I arranged his arrest to keep secret our plan. He even demanded that he be kept in irons so as not to lose his reputation as a desperado. But he soon tired of the confinement and, without testifying, slipped off the manacles in front of his terrified guards and left.

"After a series of at least thirty-nine more murders he was brought again to jail by the brave sheriff, Pat Garrett, surrendering at the point of fifty guns and having shot down three of his pursuers. From jail he sent me a note saying I had promised him a pardon and he had letters to prove it to everyone. But I thwarted his purpose by myself explaining to the newspapers the circumstances of his not keeping his side of the bargain.

"Of course he was sentenced to be hanged. To the judge he said, 'That frightens me not a bit. Billy the Kid was not born to be hung.' Nine men were placed to guard him in jail. The day before the hanging he dashed out the brains of the guard with him and seized his revolver and killed the others who ran to their comrade's assistance.

"Once more he was lose, and the one man on whom he swore a vendetta was myself and made the boast, 'I will ride to the Plaza in Santa Fe and put a bullet through Governor Wallace, who is responsible for my fix.' "

"Oh, Lew," exclaimed his wife, "I never imagined your danger. I would call it The Legend of Lew Wallace."

Abruptly, Wallace returned his notes to their folder. Her repeating "legend" had forced associations to "fable" and "falsehood," undoing the purpose of his fiction. He visualized the actual William Bonney, now relentlessly hunted, felt the unpleasant pang of his own perfidy, and decided that in future versions he would leave out the part about the pardon, because it obscured the drama.

He said, "Before we leave for Turkey, I shall contact the Crawfordsville Saturday Evening Journal and give them an interview about this fascinating exploit of mine."

COMMANDER N.A.M. DUDLEY

A source of Billy Bonney's words, as important as his Frank Warner Angel deposition, is his testimony in the Court of Inquiry for possible Court Martial of Fort Stanton's Commander Nathan Augustus Monroe Dudley. It had over a hundred transcribed testimonies by Lincoln County War participants. Billy's was given on May 28th and 29th of 1879.

By then, N.A.M. Dudley, an alcoholic, lackluster, career soldier, serving without distinction in the Civil War, had two Court Martials for offences including drunkenness on duty.

Dudley was 53 when promoted to Lieutenant Colonel and transferred, on April 5, 1878, from command at Fort Union, in the northern part of the Territory, to command of Fort Stanton.

The Lincoln County War began just 3½ months later; and Dudley's Ring-partisan intervention on July 19, 1878, caused defeat of Alexander McSween's side. His action was in violation of the Posse Comitatus Act, passed the month before, preventing military intervention in civilian strife.

Dudley's Court of Inquiry ran from May to July of 1879; and was based on plaintiff Susan McSween's accusation that he was responsible for her husband's murder and the arson of her house. The implication of conviction was treason.

Attorney Ira Leonard acted as co-counsel to Dudley's Court of Inquiry prosecutor, Captain Henry Humphreys, Fifteenth Infantry from Fort Bliss. Leonard wrote to Governor Lew Wallace, on May 23rd, that Dudley that was *"the most unmitigated old scoundrel that ever had existence."*

By the next month, on June 13th, seeing the writing on the wall, Attorney Leonard wrote to Wallace: *"If I ever saw three men* [the Court's three presiding military judges] *who have strained every effort to protect & shield an old scoundrel, this Court have done it."*

In that Court of Inquiry, Susan McSween, as the plaintiff and murdered Attorney Alexander McSween's widow, though not mentioning Billy, portrayed as terrible the six day siege of her house in the Lincoln County War, which trapped her, her husband; the freedom fighters; the law intern, Harvey Morris; and her sister Elizabeth, with her five little children.

It is known that Billy bolstered McSween during his mental decompensation in that siege. One can, thus, hypothesize Billy's inspiration in the death-defying escape on its last day.

And Billy was arguably the Court of Inquiry's most damning witness the next year, unshakable in his report of seeing three white soldiers shooting at his escaping group. That must have won him enmity of Dudley; Dudley's attorney, Henry Waldo; and their friends: Thomas Benton Catron and Judge Warren Bristol (ultimately Billy's hanging judge).

More subtle in its damage to Billy, was that Lew Wallace's necessary intervention in Lincoln County's unrest following the murder of Attorney Huston Chapman, had forced him to testify in early May against Colonel Dudley. Haughty Wallace's days of disrespectful trouncing by Dudley's attorney, Henry Waldo, apparently led to Wallace's future avoidance of Lincoln County and of Billy; until Wallace was rid of his governorship by early departure from the Territory on May 30, 1881.

Thus, one can hypothesize Wallace's entanglement of Billy Bonney with his own, noxious Dudley Court of Inquiry humiliation - all dredging up Civil War accusations of his failure in the two day battle of Shiloh. And for a selfish man like Wallace, that all spelled the end of hope for Billy's salvation by pardon. The result of Lew Wallace's withdrawal of protection ultimately unleashed the Ring against Billy.

Following fate's vagaries, one can, thus, start with Commander Dudley as intervening in the Lincoln County War, that leading to his Court of Inquiry which made Lew Wallace abandon Billy and made Billy a Ring target, which ended with the Ring's final solution of Billy's killing by Pat Garrett after the Secret Service had first achieved Billy's capture.

FICTIONALIZING COMMANDER DUDLEY

But history lacks Commander Dudley's motivation. For *Billy and Paulita*, I made venality his moral breaking point to explain his risking Court Martial. The scene starts with the Grand Jury's exoneration of Attorney McSween, which would later necessitate his Ring murder in the Lincoln County War.

* * * * * * *

APRIL 22, 1878   4:21 PM   MONDAY

In his parlor, Alexander McSween was feverish with excitement. With him were Regulators and jurymen. To hear his verdict, townspeople crowded at his open door.

Of those jurymen absent, three had worked for James Dolan; one was jury foreman, Dr. Joseph Blazer; and another was Desederio Zamora, a poor man, who had suspiciously put up the five thousand dollar bond for Jessie Evans's Tunstall murder indictment. To his audience, McSween exclaimed, "I've been declared innocent!" Wild cheering erupted.

Outside, Gottfried Gauss startled Sam Corbett by saying, "Yustiss. Now ve finish revenge."

McSween continued, "I will read my jurymen's words, that will echo through our history: '*The murder of John Tunstall for brutality and malice is without a parallel. By this inhuman act our county lost one of our best and most useful men.*'

"And they also held Governor Axtell responsible," McSween said. "They concluded: '*Especially do we condemn his Proclamation relating to John B. Wilson.*'

"Also, John Partridge Tunstall, Tunstall's father, is offering a reward for five thousand dollars for apprehension of his son's murderers.

"So the unjust saw the writing on the wall. Judge Bristol even approved our good friend, John Copeland, as sheriff. Copeland's leaving full-time management of his ranch, near Fort Stanton.

"With the Grand Jury generated warrants, he and his just-appointed deputy, Josiah Scurlock, will apprehend real criminals.

"And, in two days, we're having a mass meeting. I propose making a petition to tell Tunstall's murderers to get out of our town." Again there was cheering.

"I'll end with more good news. President Hayes is sending a Special Investigator here to get to the bottom of Tunstall's murder!" Animated talk began. "Wait. There's more.

"We've also gotten a new commander at Fort Stanton: Colonel Nathan Augustus Monroe Dudley. He's higher ranking than Purington, and was transferred from Fort Union on the fifth - obviously to assist us. Better yet, past commander, George Purington - who understands our situation - is staying on. We've been tested. But the world is God's crucible, refining us into pure gold."

During applause, Frank MacNab said to the Regulators, "I'm letting the Seven Rivers' rustlers know we're closing them out." He left, followed by Frank Coe.

Fred Waite looked at Billy's dark expression. "Ol' Chickasaw saying: 'Your own foolish general is more dangerous than your enemies combined.' " Billy was not listening. Dolan's promised river of blood now provoked certainty that McSween's victory would yield retaliation.

Right then, James Dolan was nine miles to Lincoln's northwest, in Fort Stanton, in the new commander's office. The tall soldier listened suspiciously to him, splendid white mustache waxed to pointy tips.

Dolan said, "And we citizens appreciated your providing a military escort for Judge Bristol and District Attorney Rynerson. Otherwise outlaws from Sheriff John Copeland's ranch, right near this fort, could have ambushed them.

"I assume Governor Axtell conversed with you in regimental headquarters in Santa Fe about our crisis?"

"Mister Dolan, I see no role in it for the military."

"Nor do I. We have excellent civilian resources." As if to rise, Dolan lifted his silver-headed cane, needed for his healing leg, but lingered. "Oh, I was to extend regards from U.S. Attorney Catron. He has *significant* interests in Lincoln County. So he and his Washington associate, Steve Elkins, wanted me to assure you that facts, which could undermine your credibility here, would not surface.

"By facts, I mean your Court Martial in November of seventy-one at Camp McDowell for numerous offenses including drunkenness on duty, for which you were suspended. And last year, your Court Martial for drunkenness and behavior unbecoming an officer, for which you were temporarily removed from your command at Fort Union.

"I know Tom Catron defended you - though it was unusual for a non-military lawyer to do so - and that he did it to protect someone of your stature, being second only to General Hatch in the Territory, from unjust accusations.

"So I'll speak freely as Tom's good friend. We know that attaining higher positions - and thus remuneration - in our peacetime army is difficult, given the reduction of the officer corps. Grateful citizens realize that it is prudent to assist those committed to their protection."

Dolan slipped an envelope from his frockcoat. "This is a token of our appreciation: eight hundred dollars." Dudley hesitated, then took it. "Might you be interested in hearing about our additional provisions to protect law and order?"

Dudley stiffened. "Understand me, Sir, I am not interested in something that smacks of irregularity."

"Forgive me. I am not implying a bribe. We citizens realize that any efforts could burden your already extensive duties. We feel the *least* we can do is make available to you that sum on a monthly basis - to double your current salary. And because of the hostile partisan situation, we would place it in a factitious account set up in the First National Bank of Santa Fe. Third party drafts could then be written against it by a co-signatory."

Dudley said, "The situation is more complex, Sir, than you may realize. *You* can make recommendations. *I* will decide whether they are appropriate for military action."

"I would not have expected otherwise. I take it that we have an agreement?" Dudley nodded with enough restraint to show reluctance. Dolan said, "By the way, another of Tom's friends is *George Purington.*" The hoped-for smile of dawning recognition was noted. "And some of the junior officers are friends as well: First Lieutenant Cyrus Delaney and Second Lieutenants Millard Filmore Goodwin, George Smith, and James French. And Post Surgeon Daniel Appel can be relied on too."

Dolan stood and said, "I hope I have been a service to you, to Lincoln town, and Lincoln County." The old soldier took the extended small white hand, as Dolan savored this crucial surrender.

To the alcoholic sworn to sobriety to protect his career, Dolan added, "And at a future occasion - since I come often to use the post telegraph - we can share that gift of excellent whiskey sent to you by our local innkeeper, Sam Wortley, in celebration of maintaining peace." Dolan had taken that precaution. Utter debasement might be necessary for his plans.

FICTIONALIZING DUDLEY'S MARCH ON LINCOLN

On July 19, 1878, Commander Nathan Augustus Monroe Dudley made his fateful and illegal march on Lincoln, ending its six day war and bringing about the murders of Attorney Alexander McSween and other freedom fighters, and the arson of his house. Since the Santa Fe Ring, which Dudley was assisting, prevailed, the historical truths of the machinations leading to his military intervention in violation of the Posse Comitatus Act are hidden.

So for *Billy and Paulita*, I reconstructed a scenario which began with the besieged McSween house, in which optimism reigned realistically. Its inmates, including Billy, were certain that they were prevailing; their strategic positioning of men throughout the town on July 14th had blocked Sheriff George Peppin's forces, which were beholden to local Ring boss, James Dolan. The Santa Fe Ring was about to lose.

Only the inconceivable intervention of troops could have turned the McSween's certain victory into certain defeat.

* * * * * * *

JULY 18, 1878   8:32 AM   THURSDAY

The people in the besieged McSween house had settled into optimistic waiting. At Elizabeth Shield's suggestion, everyone was having breakfast at the fully-expanded dining table. She had regenerated herself by deciding that, though it seemed frightening, they would never murder a family in their home. She was again successfully nursing baby Annie.

McSween had shaved, and was in a fresh suit. His wife, bangs curled in stubborn refusal to compromise her standards, was beside him, watching the sweaty men eating with incorrect forks and spoons from the confusing array.

"They shot Ben Ellis yestaday," French volunteered. "I headed ou' late las' night. I says to myself, 'I don' give a damn ...' "

"Please, Frenchie," said Susan McSween. "Not with the children."

"Sorry, Ma'am. I says, 'T' hell with i'. I ain' no bird in no cage. I seen Ben. Through the neck. Ellis, he's mighty riled up."

To their east, Dr. Taylor Ealy, medical kit in hand, accompanied by his wife, Ruth, supporting their baby daughter with one arm and holding little Pearl's hand, proceeded to the injured Ellis boy; watched by men in the foothills, wondering if they should shoot them.

In the House corral, James Dolan, with his silver-headed cane, was being assisted into his buggy by stocky John Kinney, who then took the reins for the trip to Fort Stanton. Dolan said, "I sent Jessie ahead with a message for Dudley that John Chisum was sending cowboys. And a cannon." Dolan smiled facetiously. "Anything is *possible*. And for our meeting with Dudley, all I need is for you to represent the law." Kinney laughed heartily. Dolan said, "The idiot must be awakened to his responsibilities."

At 4:18 PM, a mighty thunderclap drowned out Nathan Augustus Monroe Dudley's words. George Purington; Daniel Appel; and Second Lieutenants Millard Filmore Goodwin, George Smith, and James French shifted on uncomfortable chairs, all aware they were listening to a charade. "And, in conclusion," Dudley said, "we have all signed an agreement that the purpose of our Lincoln maneuver - in compliance with the Posse Comitatus Act - is the non-partisan protection of women and children; since civilian law enforcement under Sheriff Peppin is overwhelmed, even with the addition of John Kinney's Rio Grande Posse. And, on good information, reinforcements are on their way to the criminals from cattleman, John Chisum."

As Dudley completed Dolan's earlier instructions, he contemplated their threat sheathed in reassurance. Dolan had said, "We are *well* aware that you might be hesitating to protect us because you might risk conviction for treason and life in military prison if the resources of the army are used against American citizens.

"Unfortunately, refusing to send soldiers now *would not protect you.* Treason could be claimed by a vindictive person for your June twenty-eighth intervention in San Patricio with Sheriff Peppin."

Dudley's face had reddened as he capitulated to the inevitable. Intoxicated, relapsed into alcoholism to cope with the Ring's stranglehold, he had blustered with self-justification, "You underestimate me, Sir. I didn't rise to this rank by being a dullard. *My* actions have protected *our* mutual interests. I *strategically* awaited sufficient evidence of need for military intervention. Neither of us wants fodder for accusations since we *both* realize that the outcome 'might' be McSween's death."

Dolan had then expressed such effusive admiration that Dudley had felt true soldierly zeal.

Now a downpour pounded. To be heard, Dudley spoke more loudly. Passing their closed door, a middle-aged laundress heard, "Gentlemen, tomorrow we will break camp by four thirty AM and be ready to march by five. We should be in Lincoln by ten. I will be leading a column of two detachments - of forty infantry and twenty cavalry - commanded by Lieutenants French and Smith respectively. We will bring a mountain howitzer and Gatling gun."

Though the laundress's ability to speak English was limited, her comprehension was good. She ventured closer. Dudley said, "Purington, I want that blacksmith, Nelson, to work - if it takes all night - to get the howitzer ready. And I want the Gatling gun with five thousand rounds. And three days rations."

The godmother of the murdered infant of San Patricio ran toward the building where Juan Patrón was staying for protection. By the time she arrived, drops had ceased and the hot ground steamed.

At 9:48 PM, with rebozo over her head, the laundress trudged along the road from Fort Stanton. Passing the sinister House, she crossed herself. At the big home with a picket fence, described by Patrón, light slits made long bars on the black ground.

When its door opened, she stepped back, repelled by rank odor. "Señor McSween?" she queried, and was stiffly acknowledged. "I no speak good Engleesh. I from San Patricio. Mañana men comes. Howzer y Gading they bring." McSween said no one inside was named Howzer or Gading. "Please to understand. Cuidado. Make to be careful. All gente, all peoples, loves McSween."

"I understand. You come from San Patricio to wish us well."

When Billy walked in, McSween said, "Something remarkable just happened. A Mexican woman from San Patricio was just here."

Billy ran to the door. She was gone. Billy said he wished he had called him. "There was no need. She was an angel of mercy sent by God to confirm our path."

FICTIONALIZING DUDLEY'S COURT OF INQUIRY

The closing statement for the Court of Inquiry by Commander Dudley's attorney, Henry Waldo (Thomas Benton Catron's close friend), had to debunk Billy's fatally condemning testimony - for which Billy had risked his life by presenting. Based on the actual transcript, I created that scene for *Billy and Paulita* to demonstrate the lying and powerful push-back of the unbeatable Santa Fe Ring.

* * * * * * *

JULY 5, 1879   10:03 AM   SATURDAY

Henry Waldo stood for his closing argument, his demeanor mingling gravitas and indignation to Presiding Judge Colonel Galusha Pennypacker, and the two additional judges, Captain Henry Brinkerhoff and Major Nathan Osborne. Waldo spoke.

"Gentlemen, from the time this Court began, the Prosecution has acted with undue hostility: as if *this* was a Court Martial. That stance - combined with the fact that Ira Leonard worked so closely with Governor Wallace - left me, at least, suspicious about a hostile conspiracy. I wondered, who is this Leonard giving services without financial remuneration? If only Dickens had conceived such a hero." He rolled his eyes heavenward.

"As to the charges: all are patently absurd against a man of Colonel Dudley's unblemished reputation. Ridiculously, he is accused of aiding in killing one Alexander McSween and causing his house to be set on fire. But who were the witnesses? John Wilson, an ignorant old man who says he was menaced by the commander for not issuing warrants against outlaws besieging the town."

Waldo strode, slapping fine leather soles in angry staccato. "Another was Sue McSween. She contributed nothing. As to Colonel Dudley's conduct, all she told us was that she couldn't repeat his language when she accosted him in his camp." He smirked. "Our affidavits as to her character prove that it was *she* who *did* unmentionables.

"And as to the testimony of the hired man, George Washington, all we can say is that dull Negro never conceived those lies. They evince wicked help - for example, by a white attorney from Las Vegas.

"My good and patient soldiers, how your months have been wasted! There was a William Bonney alias Henry Antrim alias Kid, a murderer by profession, and accessory to the attempted murder of Special Courier Private Berry Robinson. His testimony was brief, yet he signalized his opening sentences with a lie. He swears that troops fell in with both the sheriff and his posse. Yet Sheriff Peppin; his deputies, Jack Long and Billy Matthews; his possemen, Robert Olinger, John Kinney, and Andrew Boyle; and the honorable soldiers themselves - Lieutenants Goodwin, Smith, and French; and the current commander, Purington - all attest that it did not occur. This boy also swore that three soldiers fired at him when he was escaping from the McSween building. It is sufficient to say that if he lies once, he would do so again.

"But let's examine that matter more closely. In the deceptive glare of the fire, it is doubtful that anyone could identify a man's clothes. This difficulty would be enhanced in the Kid's case, because he was looking from the center of the light out at the darkness - which is important. Toward the McSween building, objects were plainly discernable; so the opposite follows when conditions are reversed.

"Besides, it is certain that soldiers were not present, since the sergeant doing roll call testified that at a quarter past eight all the men were there. Yet the escape was then.

"In addition, Andrew Boyle informed us that some of his Seven River's possemen were dressed in soldier jackets and pants. To be generous, I can say that as the Kid fled he may have seen *them* and *thought* they were soldiers."

Performing, Waldo was enjoying himself. Tom Catron would be amused when he told him. Dressed *like* soldiers! That had been Dolan's idea, given to Boyle for testimony.

"And those guns - the Gatling and howitzer - that supposedly intimidated citizens. About them, from whom did we hear? Missus Montaño. Her lie was just her jealous Spanish pride because the soldiers had camped closer to the house of pretty Missus Baca." There was chortling from Osborn and Brinkerhoff.

On and on Waldo spoke, mucoid tobacco spittle accumulating in his glass. "Suppose that Colonel Dudley addressed Sheriff Peppin exactly as the *Negro* soldier, Private James Bush, stated. It would simply show the Colonel in sympathy with his attempt to carry out law. Implying otherwise shows only malicious intent by a *Negro* Private against an officer."

Two hours passed. Still Waldo continued. "When we look at the honest, brave, and resolute white faces of the sheriff and his posse, and think of the miserable horde of Mexicans and cut-throats who opposed to them, and when we reflect upon the skill shown by the sheriff's posse in isolating the criminals to the house of McSween, we know that no power under heaven could have prevented them from accomplishing their goal. Troops made no difference. Then where is the blame? There is none.

"And as looting of the Tunstall Store - an officer of the U.S. Army accused of that!

"Now I must come to the regrettable testimony of Governor Wallace. I would suggest that he was trying to blame someone for the failure of his Amnesty Proclamation, since what the McSween villains needed was gallows, not a pardon."

Henry Waldo mopped his face as if ending a long, but well fought, battle. "Gentlemen, the foul conspiracy to disgrace and ruin Colonel Dudley, concocted by Lew Wallace, Ira Leonard, and Sue McSween, has ended in failure. Colonel Dudley comes forth unscathed. All that remains is to thank the Court for its patient attention."

After their midday meal, Captain Henry Humphreys gave his closing presentation to the three judges yawning with postprandial lassitude. "Good Sirs, we have listened to the seemingly endless words of the Defense, and recalled wise words about one guilty: 'He protesteth too much.' " The tall slim Captain, with ill-fitting jacket making him appear unable to fill its space, spoke with deep sincerity. "So we'll just state the truth." Neither he nor Leonard had realized that their last hope was forcing that truth on their recalcitrant listeners.

"We contend that we've already proved each of our charges. And, we contend that witnesses brought by Colonel Dudley for refutation were merely partisans of the Murphy-Dolan faction - including James Dolan himself. And one needs no more proof of the dire consequences of Colonel Dudley's partisan intervention than the fact that Dolan party efforts had been unproductive from the fourteenth of July to the nineteenth when Colonel Dudley arrived and turned the tides.

"And we have shown the absurdity of Colonel Dudley's claim that his only purpose was to protect women and children. In the burning house were Missus McSween, her sister, and five children. Thus we have shown that Colonel Dudley's criminal acts make him unfit for service in the noble army of the United States and subject to Court Martial. Thank you for your time."

Presiding Judge Colonel Galusha Pennypacker announced adjournment for discussion with his fellow judges. At four thirty, Pennypacker read the judges' decision: "*The following is the Opinion of the Court: In view of the evidence adduced, Colonel N.A.M. Dudley is not guilty of any violation of law or of orders. And his act of proceeding to the town of Lincoln was prompted by the most humane and worthy motives and by good military judgment under exceptional circumstances. Proceedings before a Court Martial are therefore unnecessary.*"

Words of Friends and Foes

WORDS OF BILLY BONNEY'S CONTEMPORARIES

Recorded words benefit from their historical context; and Billy Bonney's tumultuous times yielded a plethora of letters, depositions, investigative reports, and court testimonies related to Lincoln County's "troubles," its war, and the aftermath.

A half-century later, came participants' memoirs, written by Billy's acquaintances who finally felt safe enough from Santa Fe Ring retaliation to capitalize on his reputation to enhance their own; though early movies and historians had already transmogrified him from revolutionary to outlaw.

So, for better and for worse, adding context to Billy Bonney's own productions are writings by his friends and foes.

WORDS OF FRIENDS

One could say that besides his real friends, like a Silver City teacher or his fellow Regulators, Billy Bonney also acquired more "friends" after his reflected glory got them late-in-life publishers for their otherwise unmarketable autobiographies.

Other people, once actually cherished by Billy, like John Tunstall, did not mention him in their writings. Nevertheless, their words assist in understanding his own.

Billy Bonney's tremendous fame began when he was still alive and popular with his fellow freedom fighters and anti-Ring partisans. All indication is that he was aware of his notoriety, even relishing it and reading his own press.

Equally noteworthy, are absent contemporary voices, whose silence about Billy measures the danger of being associated with the Lincoln County War's losing side or with that troublemaking vocal boy.

Indeed, Regulators who stuck with Billy - Charlie Bowdre and Tom O'Folliard - are, not coincidentally, buried beside him; their killings separated from his by only seven months.

So only silence about Billy came from Regulator Fred Tecumseh Waite: Billy's half-Chickasaw friend and partner in ownership of the John Tunstall-granted Peñasco River ranch; who escaped his own Lincoln County War murder indictments by escaping New Mexico Territory to live a politically active life in Oklahoma Indian Territory.

Silence only came from Regulator Josiah "Doc" Scurlock, who likewise fled Territorial legal clutches and a hangman's noose to become a teacher in Texas.

Less intellectually sophisticated than Waite and Scurlock, but equally silent, were Regulators John Middleton and Henry Brown (the latter's own subsequent history in Kansas oddly combining law enforcement and outlawry).

Silence about Billy also came from the otherwise assertive widow of Alexander McSween, Susan; besieged during the Lincoln County War in her house with Billy for a week. Willing to fight her own military and civil cases against Commander N.A.M. Dudley, she never acknowledged Billy's brave Court of Inquiry testimony for her case, or came as a witness on his behalf in his Mesilla hanging trial.

And what about the silence of Justice of the Peace John "Squire" Wilson, sole witness to the Billy-Wallace clemency meeting in his house; and also a witness and participant from the time of Alexander McSween's unjust legal harassment, to John Tunstall's murder, to the Lincoln County War?

And what about the silence of Attorney Ira Leonard, who had sought Billy's pardon from 1879 to 1881; and who first represented him - successfully - in the Mesilla hanging trial; but suddenly abandoned him to hostile legal counsel by the court-appointed lawyer, Albert Jennings Fountain?

Apparent self-protection from Ring thuggery by many of his erstwhile friends was Billy Bonney's and history's loss.

MARY RICHARDS

Mary Richards, 28, born in Southampton, England, was the last of Billy Bonney's three, Silver City, public school teachers. She started her job at fall semester on September 14, 1874, two days before Billy's mother's death, when he was almost 15 and left homeless. My guess is that she tutored him after that, while he worked for his room at a local hotel, then had a butcher's job while living in a boarding house; until his jailing for theft and escape to Arizona Territory in September of 1875.

Her observations imply closeness. She related a touching anecdote of Billy discovering they were both ambidextrous, and wondering if they were related. She also described Billy's "artistic nature," and his being "no more of a problem in school than any other boy growing up in a mining camp."

Credited to Mary Richards, by virtue of her generous educating, may be the fine quality of Billy's writings in Spencerian penmanship. And even Billy's later great affection for his first ranch boss, Londoner, John Tunstall, may have been enhanced by warm association with her British accent.

JOHN HENRY TUNSTALL

Though he never mentioned Billy Bonney in his profuse letter writing, gentle John Henry Tunstall, the wealthy British store-keeper and rancher, as Billy's first New Mexico boss after Billy's 1877 return to the Territory - fresh from the killing of Frank "Windy" Cahill - transformed him from outlaw to rebel with a cause, by inspiration and by 1878 martyrdom.

Given the dramatic impact on Billy of that older man (almost 25), it is noteworthy to realize that their whole relationship lasted only 4½ months.

Though short, Billy's connection with John Tunstall was described by George Coe in his 1934 autobiography titled *Frontier Fighter: The Autobiography of George Coe Who Fought and Rode With Billy the Kid*. A homestead farmer who lived near Lincoln, George Coe knew Tunstall; and, after Tunstall's murder, became a Regulator. George Coe also intuitively captured Billy's yearning for a father figure, and wrote:

Tunstall seemed really devoted to the Kid. One day I was in Lincoln and I asked him about Billy.

"George, that's the finest lad I ever met," he said. "He's a revelation to me every day and would do anything to please me. I'm going to make a man out of that boy yet. He has it in him."

Billy himself indicated his pride in his Tunstall association by confirming, in his June 8, 1878 deposition to Attorney Frank Warner Angel, ownership of land on the Peñasco River which Tunstall had granted to him and fellow employee, Fred Waite.

And Tunstall's letter writing to his loving family in London recorded events which later gave context to his own Santa Fe Ring ambush death; as well as foreshadowing his inoculation of idealism and fighting for justice that would, three years later, bring Billy to his own willing martyrdom, also by assassination and also for Santa Fe Ring ends.

ALEXANDER McSWEEN

Billy Bonney's de facto boss after John Henry Tunstall's murder was 35 year old Lincoln attorney, Alexander McSween, who, like Tunstall, never wrote about Billy.

Bi-cultural Billy, however, may have assisted McSween's Santa Fe Ring opposition by bridging that cause to the local Hispanic residents of San Patricio and Picacho, who ultimately became the majority of Lincoln County War freedom fighters.

And the vicious Santa Fe Ring attacks on McSween - from a fraudulent embezzlement case against him to his wartime murder - probably further politicized Billy.

In the Lincoln County War's besieged McSween house, Billy had even became McSween's confident, as evidenced by Billy's Dudley Court of Inquiry testimony that McSween showed him a letter he wrote to Commander Dudley demanding explanation for the military's threat to him and his property. And, as McSween deteriorated mentally under strain of the Lincoln County War siege, Billy may have bucked him up.

But by 1881, McSween's widow, Susan, claimed to merely recall Billy as "lively" during the siege; and offered him no assistance in his hanging trial.

JOHN "SQUIRE" WILSON

Lincoln County Justice of the Peace John "Squire" Wilson theoretically could have gotten Billy his pardon and saved his life. Wilson knew everything - from John Tunstall's murder evidence to Lincoln County War events - even being wounded himself by a stray bullet in Sheriff William Brady's ambush.

Though no writings by John Wilson exist about Billy, his acts imply that he once had documents confirming Billy's deputizing, since, after Tunstall's murder, he appointed Billy Deputy Constable under Town Constable Atanacio Martinez, along with Tunstall employee, Fred Waite, to serve murder warrants on the killers. Lost also are Wilson's arrest warrants themselves - which would have been for Tunstall's Ring murderer possemen like James Dolan, William "Buck" Morton, Frank Baker, and Andrew "Buckshot" Roberts; and possibly even Sheriff William Brady himself.

Importantly, all these official acts of Wilson, acting as Justice of the Peace, establish Billy and the McSween side as law enforcement appointees, and vindicate them throughout the Lincoln County War period.

Wilson's failure to achieve justice points to the pervasive corrupt power of the Santa Fe Ring. Service of the Tunstall murder warrants failed because of obstruction by Ring-partisan Lincoln County Sheriff William Brady, himself leader of the Tunstall murder posse. That was why Wilson deputized Tunstall's foreman, Dick Brewer, to form his own posse - including Billy - to achieve those arrests.

"Squire" Wilson's anti-Ring partisanship generated backlash by corrupt Governor Samuel Beach Axtell, who, by proclamation, illegally removed his Justice of the Peace powers in March of 1878 - purposefully leaving Sheriff Brady the only agent of law enforcement in Lincoln County.

Stubborn Wilson merely ignored Axtell's proclamation, performing as Justice of the Peace, and even bravely remaining in town throughout July's 1878 Lincoln County War.

During that war, as Justice of the Peace, Wilson was forced, by physical threat, by invading Commander N.A.M. Dudley, to issue false warrants against Alexander McSween and others, including Billy, for an alleged attack on his courier, Private

Berry Robinson. The purpose was a Ring attempt to give a color of rightness to Dudley's military intervention in violation of the Posse Comitatus Act.

The next year, in March of 1879, Justice of the Peace Wilson hosted the pardon negotiation meeting of Billy and Governor Lew Wallace in his Lincoln house. Thus, Wilson was sole witness to any agreement. And the newly discovered letter by Billy enables hypothesizing about Wilson's even greater role in those Wallace-Billy arrangements.

Later in 1879, Wilson testified against Commander Dudley in the Fort Stanton Court of Inquiry, and attested to his being coerced to issue the anti-McSween warrants during the War.

But in late March and early April of 1881, Wilson offered no assistance to Billy as a witness for his defense in his Mesilla hanging trial.

Interestingly, Wilson was likely in Lincoln later that month, on April 28th, when the boy made his great escape from the courthouse-jail; though he remained forever silent as to his opinions or possible insider knowledge about that drama.

JUAN PATRÓN

A Lincoln local and respected Hispanic community leader, Juan Patrón was a political risk to the Murphy-Dolan faction; but escaped death when purposefully shot, in 1875, by Dolan's partner, John Riley. Patrón was left with a crippling limp.

Patrón had been one of John Tunstall's first Lincoln friends; and, later, as an Alexander McSween partisan, Patrón realistically believed himself at risk of murder by Ring-partisan, Fort Stanton Commander N.A.M. Dudley.

Friend also to Alexander McSween's widow's attorney, Huston Chapman, Juan Patrón again was almost shot inside his own Lincoln house by James Dolan's associate, Billy Campbell, on the same February 18, 1879 night on which Chapman himself was murdered soon thereafter by Dolan and Campbell on Lincoln's single street.

Being also the town jailor, Juan Patrón appears to have offered his house, rather than the wretched pit jail or the dangerous Fort Stanton brig, for Billy's feigned arrest and incarceration in his Governor Wallace clemency deal.

Additionally, the newly authenticated Billy Bonney letter indicates that Juan Patrón may have assisted the pardon plan itself. If so, it was a touching attempt to protect the boy whom Patrón regarded as a Lincoln County War freedom fighter and Hispanic advocate.

But Juan Patrón never wrote about Billy; nor did he long outlive him. As a flagrant Ring opponent, he was murdered in suspicious circumstances by April of 1884.

HISPANIC FREEDOM FIGHTERS

To this day, among many in New Mexico's Hispanic population, Billy Bonney is regarded as a freedom fighter; the San Patricio massacre, the Lincoln County War killings of Picacho and San Patricio men, and the earlier Ring grabs of family grants all remembered bitterly by descendants.

Specific martyrs came from the McSween house siege and arson; with San Patricio's killed and unsung fighters, Francisco Zamora and Vincente Romero. And Yginio Salazar, Billy's good friend, almost died during the burning building escape; and lived his long life with pain and two war bullets in his back.

In 1931, Paco Anaya, a Fort Sumner friend of Billy's, wrote a manuscript which posthumously became a book titled. *I Buried Billy*, as a respectful farewell. Anaya would have known the Maxwell family's Hispanic sheep herders, who respected Billy's Robin Hood stance and hid him near the town from May to July of 1881.

GOTTFRIED GAUSS

German-born Gottfried Gauss, 56 at the time of Billy Bonney's great escape from the Lincoln courthouse-jail, played a part in Billy's Lincoln County history from his October of 1877 arrival as a John Tunstall ranch hand - and Gauss was Tunstall's cook - to Billy's 1881 jailbreak, when Gauss was the Lincoln courthouse-jail's caretaker.

Importantly, Gottfried Gauss's direct experience of traumas and injustices of the period before Tunstall's murder and through the Lincoln County War and defeat, left him attached to Billy and with a bitter anti-Ring stance.

In fact, before Billy's arrival, Gottfried Gauss had been employed at an early incarnation of the House (ultimately Billy's courthouse-jail), when it was L.G. Murphy & Company. Gauss later claimed he was cheated out of wages and profits from its brewery, which he ran. This personal taste of Ring injustice added to Gauss's future anti-Ring sentiments.

Those traumas make Gauss the possible provider of Billy's jailbreak revolver, in the hypothetical scenario of the gun's outhouse placement. And Gauss's later eye-witness statements about Billy's jailbreak - including the boy's killings of Deputies James Bell and Robert Olinger - are obviously circumspect. And Gauss took his secrets to the grave.

But Gauss is part of Billy Bonney's written record.

Billy himself, in his Frank Warner Angel deposition of June 8, 1878, mentions Gottfried Gauss's presence at Tunstall's Feliz River ranch before the ambush-murder, and during earlier intimidation by Sheriff Brady's possemen of the ranch hands there. Billy's transcriptionist wrote:

The persons at the ranch were R. M. Brewer, John Middleton, G. Gauss, M. Martz, R.A. Widenmann, Henry Brown, F.T. Waite, W<u>m</u> McClosky and this deponent.

The night before John Tunstall's fatal return ride with his men and horses to Lincoln from that ranch, the plan was for Gottfried Gauss to remain there alone. Thus, Gauss endured traumas of the arriving, baying, Brady, mob posse; and then news of Tunstall's killing. Billy's transcriptionist wrote:

Deponent further says that on the night of the 17th of February A.D. 1878 J.H. Tunstall arrived at the ranch and informed all persons there that reliable information had reached him that J.B. Matthews was gathering a large party of outlaws and desperados as a posse and the said posse was coming to the ranch, the Mexicans in the party to gather up the cattle and the balance of the party to kill the persons at the ranch. It was thereupon decided that all persons at the ranch excepting G. Gauss, were to leave ...

So Gottfried Gauss was first to encounter Tunstall's murder posse. Gauss was present again in 1881 - with those bitter memories - as caretaker, when Billy made his jailbreak.

Ten years later, Gauss was quoted in the *Lincoln County Leader* of March 1, 1890. He implied an enabling role of non-intervening Lincolnites and his own sympathy for Billy. Possibly it was he who directed Deputy Robert Olinger to the courthouse's east side, where armed Billy waited ready with Olinger's shotgun at its second story window. Gauss stated:

> I was crossing the yard behind the courthouse, when I heard a shot fired then a tussle upstairs in the courthouse, somebody hurrying downstairs, and deputy sheriff Bell emerging from the door running toward me. He ran right into my arms, expired the same moment, and I laid him down, dead. That I was in a hurry to secure assistance, or perhaps to save myself, everybody will believe.
>
> When I arrived at the garden gate leading to the street, in front of the courthouse, I saw the other deputy sheriff Olinger, coming out of the hotel opposite, with the four or five other county prisoners, where they had taken their dinner. I called to him to come quick. He did so, leaving his prisoners in front of the hotel. When he had come up close to me, and while I was standing not a yard apart, I told him that I was just after laying Bell dead on the ground in the yard behind. Before he could reply, he was struck by a well-directed shot fired from a window above us, and fell dead at my feet. I ran for my life to reach my room and safety, when Billy the Kid called to me: "Don't run, I wouldn't hurt you – I am alone, and master not only of the courthouse, but also of the town, for I will allow nobody to come near us." "You go," he said, "and saddle one of Judge (Ira) Leonard's horses, and I will clear out as soon as I have the shackles loosened from my legs." With a little prospecting pick I had thrown to him through the window he was working for at least an hour, and could not accomplish more than to free one leg. He came to the conclusion to wait a better chance, tie one shackle to his waistbelt, and start out. Meanwhile I had saddled a small skittish pony belonging to Billy Burt (the county clerk), as there was no other horse available, and had also, by Billy's command, tied a pair of red blankets behind the saddle ...
>
> When Billy went down the stairs at last, on passing the body of Bell he said, "I'm sorry I had to kill him but I couldn't help it."

On passing the body of Olinger he gave him a tip with his boot, saying, "You are not going to round me up again." And so Billy the Kid started out that evening, after he had shaken hands with everybody around and after having a little difficulty in mounting on account of the shackle on his leg, he went on his way rejoicing.

IRA LEONARD

Billy's best friend in a high place, Ira Leonard, became widow Susan McSween's lawyer against Commander N.A.M. Dudley after the Ring's murder of Attorney Huston Chapman, who had been Leonard's office mate in Las Vegas, New Mexico.

Born in New York state, Leonard was 46 when he met Billy in Lincoln in 1879, when the boy was risking his life to testify in the April Grand Jury against Chapman's killers.

It seems likely that Leonard knew from the start about Billy's belief in a gubernatorial clemency deal, because, assuming the promise to be real, he kept Lew Wallace informed about Billy's courtroom testimony: the crux of its bargain.

In a letter to Wallace dated April 20, 1879, Leonard wrote about Billy's courtroom pressure from the district attorney:

> *I will tell you Gov. that the prosecuting officer of this Dist.* [Ring partisan William Rynerson] *is no friend to the enforcement of the law. He is bent on going for the Kid & ... is proposed to destroy his testimony & influence. He is bent on pushing him to the wall. He is a Dolan man and is defending him by his conduct all he can.*

In addition, the Grand Jury's presiding judge was Ringman Warren Bristol, whose judgeship Leonard hoped to gain through intervention by Governor Wallace; though Leonard eventually received a different judgeship from him.

Surely sealing Ira Leonard's personal anti-Ring sentiments and his certainty of Ring danger, was an assassination attempt on himself on April 25, 1879 in Lincoln. It mimicked the nighttime shooting of his friend, Huston Chapman, two months before; and arguably was also done by James Dolan.

On May 20th, Ira Leonard wrote to Governor Lew Wallace about the lead-up to his own near-murder:

He [District Attorney William Rynerson] *aroused among the friends of the outlaws here a feeling of antagonism against me that resulted in their posting on a tree to which I had my horse hitched addressed to me informing me that if I did not leave the country "they would take my scalp and send me to hell."*

Ira Leonard was also in Lincoln, from May to July of 1879, as co-counsel to the military prosecutor in the Dudley Court of Inquiry; where Billy testified for them in May.

To Governor Lew Wallace, on May 23rd, Leonard wrote that Dudley was *"the most unmitigated old scoundrel that ever had existence;"* adding, on June 13th, *"If I ever saw three men* [the Court's presiding judges] *who have strained every effort to protect & shield an old scoundrel, this Court have done it."*

Apparently moved by Billy's efforts, and on good terms with Wallace, Leonard continued attempts to get Billy his pardon. Most dramatic was his October of 1880 intervention with Secret Service Operative Azariah Wild, in which he almost succeeded in arranging a different pardon in exchange for Billy's testimony against counterfeiters pursued by Wild.

And after Billy's Stinking Springs capture and three months of Santa Fe incarceration, in March of 1881, Leonard protectively accompanied him on the long train ride south to Mesilla for the murder trials under Judge Warren Bristol.

On March 30, 1881, Leonard represented Billy before Bristol for the first indictment - the murder of Andrew "Buckshot" Roberts - and got that case dismissed on a technicality; before abruptly abandoning further representation, possibly after a Ring threat. Leonard left Billy's defense for the William Brady and George Hindman indictments to court appointed, inimical attorneys: Albert Jennings Fountain and John D. Bail.

Subsequently, Ira Leonard helped remarried Susan McSween Barber in settling the estates of John Tunstall and her first husband, Alexander McSween.

Unfortunately, there are no later writings by Ira Leonard about Billy; a possible measure of his fear about advertising his past alliance with the boy - well founded after living through his own 1879 assassination attempt and whatever threat made him flee Mesilla in the middle of his successful defense in Billy's first murder trial.

FRANK AND GEORGE COE

Frank and George Coe, cousins and homesteading farmers, aged 26 and 21 respectively when Billy met them when he himself was still 17, became his fellow Regulators. They knew and admired Billy from his arrival in Lincoln County in September of 1877, and throughout the Lincoln County War period. After that, the Coe cousins fled for safety to the northwest portion of the Territory, near Farmington; not returning to Lincoln County until 1884.

Frank and George Coe were indicted in the Lincoln County Grand Jury of 1878, along with Billy and other Regulators, for the April 4, 1878 killing of Andrew "Buckshot" Roberts at Blazer's Mill, private property within the Mescalero Apache Indian Reservation.

FRANK COE

As an old-timer, Frank Coe wrote about Billy Bonney in an unpublished letter to a William Steele Dean, dated August 3, 1926. In it, he emphasized Billy's multiculturalism, and above-average height (5'6" was average), belying later denigrating mythology by enemies of Billy's "shortness."

Coe stated:

[He was] 5ft 8in, weight 138 lb stood straight as an Indian, fine looking a lad as I ever met. He was a lady's man, the Mex girls were all crazy about him. He spoke their language well. He was a fine dancer, could go all their gaits and was one of them. He was a wonder, you would have been proud to know him.

Frank Coe, also gave the following quote about Billy to the *El Paso Times* of September 16, 1923:

He was brave and reliable, one of the best soldiers we had. He never pushed his advice or opinions, but he had a wonderful presence of mind; the tighter the place the more he showed his cool nerve and quick brain.

Frank Coe also stated about Billy Bonney:

He never seemed to care for money, except to buy cartridges with; then he would much prefer to gamble for them straight. Cartridges were scarce, and he always used about 10 times as many as any one else.

GEORGE COE

George Coe, with his cousin Frank, was a Lincoln County homestead farmer, and also a friend of fellow farmer and eventual Regulator, Josiah "Doc" Scurlock. Before the war period, George and "Doc" Scurlock were already anti-Ring, having been harassed and arrested by brutal Sheriff William Brady on false accusation of harboring a murderer.

In 1934, old-timer George published *Frontier Fighter: The Autobiography of George Coe Who Fought and Rode With Billy the Kid.* In it, Coe called Billy a "dramatic individual" to whom John Tunstall had "kindly feeling." Coe emphasized Billy's charisma, intelligence, singing, and dancing. He wrote:

Billy came down to the Dick Brewer Ranch on the Ruidoso. He was the center of interest everywhere he went, and though heavily armed, he seemed as gentlemanly as a college-bred youth. He quickly became acquainted with everybody, and because of his humorous and pleasing personality grew to be a community favorite. In fact, Billy was so popular there wasn't enough of him to go around. He had a beautiful voice and sang like a bird. One of our special amusements was to get together every few nights and have singing. The thrill of those happy evenings still lingers – a pleasant memory – and tonight I would give a lot to live through one again. Frank Coe and I played the fiddles, and all of us danced, and here Billy, too, was in demand.

About Lincoln County War fighting, George Coe quotes Billy's militant fervor, seen also in Billy's later writings:

As for going out and giving up to that outfit, we'll die first.

That statement matches Billy's equally bellicose and brave words in his letter, the next year, to Governor Lew Wallace:

I am not afraid to die like a man fighting but I would not like to be killed like a dog unarmed.

HENRY HOYT

Henry Hoyt was a 24 year old medical doctor, working as a mail rider, when he met Billy Bonney in Tascosa, Texas, three months after the lost Lincoln County War.

Billy and fellow Regulators, Charlie Bowdre and Tom O'Folliard, were conducting petty rustling against Ringmen targets. It was guerilla-style warfare of retribution, about which they had threateningly forewarned in their "Regulator" letter of July 13, 1878 to Thomas Benton Catron's brother-in-law, Edgar Walz, his Lincoln County ranch manager.

One outlet for their horses was Tascosa; where Billy, having become attached to intellectual and charming Hoyt - as he had already with John Tunstall and would with Lew Wallace - gifted him with a fine sorrel horse. Apparently, to avoid suspicion - and with the possibility that the horse, Dandy Dick, had belonged to murdered Sheriff William Brady and may have been stolen from Ring sympathizers, Charles Fritz, or Edgar Walz - Billy created an elaborate bill of sale for Hoyt.

Dated October 24, 1878, written in Spencerian penmanship, it uses correct legalese and is furthermore signed by two witnesses. Its beautiful signature is Billy's most artistic and famous - and most forged.

Noteworthy is that teenaged Billy, still 18, impressed Dr. Hoyt to the extent that he saved the small document. And for years after Billy's death, Hoyt believed that he owned the only sample of "Billy the Kid's" handwriting. Hoyt eventually got an autobiographical book out of that contact: his 1929 *A Frontier Doctor.*

Henry Hoyt, like the Coe cousins, Frank and George, admired Billy's intelligence and bi-culturalism. In his book, he wrote the following about Billy:

After learning his history directly from himself and recognizing his many superior natural qualifications, I often urged him, while he was free and the going was good, to leave the country, settle in Mexico or South America, and begin all over again. He spoke Spanish like a native and although only a beardless boy was nevertheless a natural leader of men. With his poise, iron nerve, and all-around efficiency properly applied, he could have made a success anywhere.

HOYT CONTACTS THE WALLACE FAMILY

In the 1920's infancy of Billy the Kid historical research, Henry Hoyt learned that the Lew Wallace family had its own William Bonney letters; and, on April 27, 1929, by letter, he contacted Lew Wallace's grandson, Lew Wallace Jr.

Hoyt enclosed a photocopy of Billy's tintype and his own Bill of Sale, with the following note on its back, written in 1927, two years before that accompanying letter:

Copy of a bill of sale written by Wm H. Bonney - alias "Billy the Kid" Oct 24th 1878 - at Tascosa, Panhandle of Texas, U.S.A., and given to me for my protection in case my ownership of this horse, which Billy had presented to me - was ever questioned. It is witnessed by Howard & McMasters, owners of the leading store in Tascosa where it was written. It is without doubt the only specimen of the handwriting of this famous young outlaw now in existence. He was 19 years old when he wrote this - was killed by the famous gun man, Sheriff Pat Garrett 3 years later, and died with a record of having killed 22 men, one for every year of his life. He was a remarkable character, a natural leader of men, and was largely forced into the life of an outlaw by his circumstances over which he had no control.

Henry F. Hoyt
Long Beach California. 1927

Henry Hoyt's 1929 letter itself, to Lew Wallace Jr., was typed, and is as follows:

Dear Mr. Wallace: -

This time it is me who is apologizing for the long delay in answering your favor of June 20th 1928. You have doubtless forgotten, but I wrote for some information regarding the old mining proposition in New Mexico in which both your illustrious grandfather and myself were interested. I desired the information - dates, etc, in connection with a manuscript I was preparing for publication of my memoirs from 30-50 years ago.

Incidentally, I am one of the few men living who was well acquainted with that famous outlaw "Billy the Kid" and for many years supposed I had the only specimen of his handwriting in existence, a Bill of Sale for a horse he presented me with, and wrote out himself, to protect me should my ownership ever be questioned, a very important matter in that part of the world in that period. This paper I have preserved all these years.

Shortly before I wrote you last year I learned of the letter your grandfather wrote Billy the Kid and the latter's reply, then in the possession of Mr. Maurice G. Fulton, of Roswell, N.M., so opened up a correspondence with him that resulted in his exchanging copies of both letters with me for a copy of my Bill of Sale.

As I happened to know about this correspondence, both from the Kid and General Wallace, and mention it in my manuscript, I naturally would like to include these letters among the illustrations in my book - that is to be published this fall by the Houghton Mifflin Company of Boston - and am asking your kind permission to do so.

I am enclosing a photo-copy of my souvenir of the Kid - Wm H. Bonney - with my permission to use the same for publication at your pleasure. You will find a written and signed by me, statement on the back explaining it. As I do not know if you have a copy of the only picture of Billy the Kid in existence or not, I am also sending a copy of it, with my permission to use it in any way you wish. By looking closely you will see a chain crossing his chest. This is a long braided hair chain attached to a ladies gold watch that I presented to Billy for his sweetheart at Ft Sumner, who is still living.

I presume this had something to do with his later giving me Dandy Dick the best horse he had. You will notice in my note on the back of the bill of sale that it was written **before** I learned of the letters between he and General Wallace.

If my manuscript is published verbatim and you should ever read the book you will find some interesting incidents of my acquaintance with your grandfather and the young outlaw.

Trusting you will grant me permission to publish those historic and intensely interesting letters, I remain,

Sincerely yours,
Henry F. Hoyt

JOHN P. MEADOWS

A cattle rancher living in New Mexico from early 1880, John P. Meadows, when an old-timer, capitalized on his yarns about having known and liked Billy Bonney by giving interviews to historians; and by performing in a historical pageant called "Days of Billy the Kid in Story, Song and Dance" on February 26, 1931 in Roswell, New Mexico.

Subsequently, Meadows transcribed his "Days of Billy the Kid" act; and it appeared in serialized newspaper accounts in the *Roswell Daily Record* on March 2nd , 3rd, and 4th of 1931. Existing also is a seventy-eight page, typed manuscript with John Meadows's additional information on Billy, also dated 1931. And from August 8, 1935 to June 25, 1936, the *Alamogordo News* printed almost forty reminiscence articles by Meadows.

John Meadows professed prolific recall of Billy Bonney's "quotations" fifty years after their alleged utterances. Also, his grasp of the contemporary history was paltry, as evidenced by the compendium of his recollections in a 2004 book edited by a John P. Wilson and titled *Pat Garrett and Billy the Kid as I Knew Them: Reminiscences of John P. Meadows.*

Nevertheless, as Billy's obvious fan and sympathizer, John Meadows - delicately skirting Billy's 20th century outlaw reputation - added color bordering on the credible.

Meadows wrote in *Reminiscences*:

> I will indicate that the man who is generally chronicled as having turned outlaw really had some excellent traits along with some of his bad ones. I don't know how many [men] he had killed - in fact, I don't know that he had killed any - and I didn't care ... I liked him right off the reel, and I do to this day, though it has been fifty years since Pat Garrett captured him by killing [him].

John Meadows also provided insight into how that unusual boy was able to grab the attention and respect of many older men, themselves living on the verge of violence. Meadows wrote memorably:

> When he was rough, he was as rough as men ever get to be, yet he had a good streak in him.

Most dramatic, however, was John Meadows's claim that after Billy's great escape on April 28, 1881, he headed south to Meadows's new ranch on the Peñasco River, arriving there in the beginning of May. That implies Billy's sensible plan of continuing southward over the border to Chihuahua in Old Mexico, where his bi-lingual skills and Hispanic affinities would have made a natural fit.

Meadows wrote:

> I never saw the Kid again until after he had been sentenced to be hanged and came to my place on the Peñasco one night when he was on the dodge.

Meadows, claiming it as part of that visit by Billy, quoted his jailbreak statement, made from the courthouse balcony, to the watching Lincoln townspeople, concerning his killing of Deputy James Bell. Its repetition to Meadows may imply that his killing of Bell bothered Billy enough to share those uncomfortable feelings with a friend:

> I did not want to kill Bell, but I had to do so to save my own life. It was a case of have to, not of wanting to.

As to Billy's insouciant defiance after his escape, John Meadows's gives a quote implying that Billy's decision of where to go next may have been made while he lingered ambivalently at his Peñasco ranch. Immediately upon leaving, Billy apparently proceeded northeast to Fort Sumner, to Paulita Maxwell, and to near-certain death at Sheriff Pat Garrett's hand. Meadows wrote that Billy said:

> I am not going to leave the country, and I am not going to reform, neither am I going to be taken alive again.

JOHN MEADOWS ON LOST BILLY WRITINGS

Interestingly and importantly, John Meadows's book, *Pat Garrett and Billy the Kid as I Knew Them*, also refers to some writings by Billy Bonney which have remained undiscovered. And Meadows certainly had no doubt about the boy's literacy.

Quite reminiscent of the Hoyt Bill of Sale is Meadows's reference to another bill of sale from 1880. Meadows states:

The Kid said, "I've sold my forty-two head of cattle to Pankey, and I'll send him the bill of sale by you." Then he made a bill of sale out, and George Fulgum and I witnessed it.

More dramatic, is John Meadows's reference to Billy's possessing a letter from Governor Lew Wallace about the pardon promise. Though Meadows's rendition of the bargain is incorrect - based on "standing trial" instead of "testifying in a trial" - the fact of a letter's existence repeats Billy's own claim to Wallace by letter from the Santa Fe jail. Meadows wrote:

He had a letter which he showed me from the governor, Lew. Wallace, which said that if he came in and stood his trial and was convicted, the governor would pardon him.

Billy's March 2, 1881 jail letter to Governor Wallace stated:

I have some letters which date back two years and there are Parties who are very anxious to get them but I will not dispose of them until I see you. that is if you come immediately.

E.C. "TEDDY BLUE" ABBOTT

E.C. "Teddy Blue" Abbott, a roving cowboy about Billy Bonney's age, had merely heard of Billy in 1878; and published, as an old-timer, in 1955, *We Pointed Them North: Recollections of a Cowpuncher.* Like George Coe, Abbott recorded Billy's atypical multiculturalism, writing:

The Lincoln County troubles was still going on, and you had to be either for Billy the Kid or against him. It wasn't my fight ... it was the Mexicans that made a hero of him.

"Teddy Blue" Abbott, thus, was possibly one of the first strangers to capture the star quality of that teenager who came to represent the freedom fight of the Territory's oppressed people.

WORDS OF FOES

For someone with a short life, Billy Bonney accumulated a long list of powerful foes - Lincoln County sheriffs and deputies, two governors, district attorneys and a district judge, a fort's commander, the Secret Service, and Santa Fe Ringmen. Even Secretary of the Interior Carl Schurz heard about "the Kid" via a pejorative letter from Governor Lew Wallace. Their hostile lies colored Billy Bonney's history to the present.

LEW WALLACE

Arguably, the most important person in Billy Bonney's life was Lew Wallace. Billy refused, despite all contrary evidence, to abandon hope that Wallace would save him.

Billy's obsession - rooted in dynamics of illegitimate birth to an abandoning father, followed by a rejecting step-father - left him in a never-ending search for a paternal substitute. Of his options, honorable John Tunstall and Alexander McSween had been murdered; selfish John Chisum had become traitorous during the Lincoln County War; Fred Waite had abandoned the Territory; and Ira Leonard had proved too timid.

Only Lew Wallace, the best "father" of them all, elicited Billy's courtship, first as a granter of legal clemency; then as an imagined compatriot in a fight for justice; and finally as the last opportunity for a life-saving pardon.

Of course, Lew Wallace was a tragic choice; though coincidentally himself engrossed with Billy; but as literary fodder. Wallace's hypocrisy is clear in his June 8, 1902 *New World Magazine* story, "Romance of Billy the Kid," which, using his twenty year old Billy letters, reverses the pardon bargain to make himself a hero, with outlaw Billy as its betrayer. That farcical article may have been Wallace's nidus for an intended Old West historical novel - yet another thrust at his best-seller formula like his *Fair God* and *Ben-Hur*.

Instead, Wallace died by 1905; and preservation of Billy's letters, generated in the boy's futile attachment to him, became Lew Wallace's contribution to Billy's real judgment day.

But Lew Wallace's June 8, 1902 *New World Magazine* outlaw myth article stated:

General Lew Wallace Writes a Romance of 'Billy the Kid' Most Famous Bandit of the Plains

Thrilling Story of the Midnight Meeting Between Gen. Wallace, Then Governor of New Mexico, and the Notorious Outlaw, in a Lonesome Hut at Santa Fe.

Gen. LEW WALLACE, author of "Ben Hur," is completing his autobiography, which will be issued in a few weeks.

The most thrilling chapter in this remarkable personal narrative tells of the midnight meeting in a lonely hut between Gen. Wallace, at the time Governor of the Territory of New Mexico, and "Billy the Kid," the most notorious outlaw the far West has ever produced.

From advance sheets of Gen. Wallace's book the following account of this strange rendezvous has been copied and compiled for the Sunday World Magazine. The story has never been printed in any newspaper or magazine before.

The episode occurred in 1879. The outlaw was at the zenith of his wild career. Gen. Wallace conceived the idea that he might gain certain important information by a face-to-face talk with the outlaw. With much difficulty the meeting was finally arranged. It was not without a strong element of danger to both participants, but they trusted each other and the trust was not betrayed.

The Midnight Rendezvous.

On the night of the meeting two men sat, shortly before midnight, silent and expectant, in the hut which had been chosen for the rendezvous, which was on the outskirts of Santa F, N.M.

Their gaze was fastened on the door, and, as the minutes slipped away the tension grew more severe, the silence more oppressive.

One man was the owner of the rude home that stood desolate in the shifting sands of the great mesa.

The other was Gen. Lew Wallace, Governor of New Mexico.

The hands of the clock pointed to 12.

The hush deepened. Suddenly it was broken by the sound of a resolute knock on the door of the cabin.

"Come in," said the Governor of New Mexico.

The door flew open and, standing with his form outlined by the moonlight behind him, was "Billy the Kid." In his left hand he carried a Winchester rifle. In his right was a revolver. The weapons, quick as a flash, covered the two occupants in the room.

"I was to meet the Governor here at midnight. It is midnight: Is the Governor here?"

The light of the candles flickered against a boyish face, yet the man who stood in the doorway was the most notorious desperado in all the West. He had killed scores of men: he was the quarry of every sheriff from the Rio Grande to the bordering foothills that shut in Death Valley.

The Boy Outlaw.

In facial features "Billy the Kid" was a mere stripling. His narrow shoulders were rounded, his posture slightly stooping, his voice low and effeminate. But his eyes were cold and piercing, steady, alert, gray like steel.

Gen. Wallace rose to his feet and held out his hand, inviting the visitor forward for a conference.

"Your note gave the promise of absolute protection," said the outlaw, warily.

"I have been true to my promise," replied the Governor. "This man," pointing to the owner of the cabin, "and myself are the only persons present."

The rifle was slowly lowered, the revolver returned to its leather holster. "Billy" advanced and the two seated themselves at opposite sides of the narrow table.

Gen. Wallace was able to effect an important arrangement with the outlaw, of which he gives the details. In fact, a very friendly understanding was established between the two.

Explaining the purpose of the interview and its result with "Billy," Gen. Wallace says:

"Shortly before I had become Governor of New Mexico, Chapman, a young attorney in Lincoln, had been murdered.

[AUTHOR'S NOTE: This lie about Chapman's murder date is to remove Wallace's responsibility. The real date was February 18, 1879, 4½ months into Wallace's term; during which he had ignored Lincoln County's crisis - until Chapman's murder forced his coming there.]

Half a dozen men were arrested, accused of the crime. Among them was Jesse James.

[AUTHOR'S NOTE: Preposterously adding Jesse James demonstrates Wallace's literary mode of dime novel fantasy; but also highlights the extent of his lying.]

While it was more than probable that one or more of the men charged with the murder were guilty, it was impossible to prove the allegation, for the witnesses, filled with terror, fled the country. When I reached New Mexico it was declared on every hand that "Billy the Kid" had been a witness to the murder. Could he be made to testify?

"That was a question on the tip of every tongue.

"I had been sent to the Southwest to pacify the territory; here was an opportunity I could not afford to pass by. Therefore I arranged the meeting by note deposited with one of the outlaw's friends, and at midnight was ready to receive the desperado should he appear. He was there on time – punctual to the second.

"When 'Billy the Kid' stepped to the chair opposite mine, I lost no time in announcing me proposition.

Agrees to the Plan.

" 'Testify,' I said, 'before the Grand Jury and the trial court and convict the murderer of Chapman and I will let you go scot-free with a pardon in your pocket for all your misdeeds.' [Author's boldface]

[AUTHOR'S NOTE: Here is confirmation of Wallace's pardon promise to Billy.]

" 'Billy' heard me in silence; he thought several minutes without reply.

" 'Governor,' said he, "if I were to do what you ask they would kill me."

" 'We can prevent that," said I.

[AUTHOR'S NOTE: Wallace inverts the deal's creation by omitting Billy's letter proposing it, and making himself the initiator; thus hiding Billy's bravery and emphasizing only Billy's concern about being killed. In addition, the bogus arrest was Billy's idea; but Wallace here both claims and embellishes that plan.]

"Then I unfolded my plan. 'Billy' was to be seized while he was asleep. To all appearances, his capture was to be genuine. To this he agreed, picking the men who were to effect his capture. He was afraid of hostile bullets and would run no risk. Another stipulation was to the effect that during his confinement he should be kept in irons. 'Billy the Kid' was afraid also of the loss of his reputation as a desperate man."

137

[AUTHOR'S NOTE: Wallace makes only a snide dig about "reputation; though Billy was risking his life.]

The plan agreed upon in the cabin on the lonely mesa at midnight was carried out to the letter. "Billy the Kid" was seized the following morning and confined in the Lincoln County jail. It was here that Gen. Wallace, in spite of the fears of the guards, permitted the outlaw to give an exhibition of his skill with the revolver and the rifle. "Billy," standing or riding, using either the one weapon or the other, sent every bullet true to its mark.

"Billy," said the General, "there's some trick to that shooting. How do you do it?"

"Well, General," replied the desperado, "there is a trick to it. When I was a boy I noticed that a man in pointing to anything he wished observed, used his index finger. With long use, unconsciously, the man had learned to point it with unerring aim. When I lift my revolver, I say to myself, 'Point with your finger.' I stretch the finger along the barrel and, unconsciously, it makes the aim certain. There is no failure; I pull the trigger and the bullet goes true to its mark."

[AUTHOR'S NOTE: This shooting exhibition may have occurred, but the aiming part may be apocryphal, since it is incorrect.]

"Billy," though at his own request kept in irons, did not remain long confined. One morning the guards led him to breakfast. Returning, the desperado drawled in the feminine voice that was a part and parcel of his character:

"Boys, I'm tired. Tell the Governor I'm tired."

The manacles slipped like magic from his wrists. The guards stood stupefied, and "Billy the Kid," laughing mockingly, walked leisurely from the jail yard, through the gate and across the street. Easily, gracefully, he threw himself into the saddle on the back of a horse standing near at hand and, putting spurs to the animal, dashed away. "Billy" was gone. He had not escaped in the night; he had walked away in the broad light of day, with his guards, heavily armed, standing about him.

[AUTHOR'S NOTE: Of all Wallace's lies, this scenario is the cruelest. In fact, Billy had remained incarcerated from April to June of 1879, testifying in the April Lincoln Grand Jury as per his pardon bargain; and getting the indictments. In May, he further risked his life testifying in the Dudley Court of Inquiry. Only in June, when

Wallace's pardon had not come and Ringman District Attorney William Rynerson got Billy's venue for his murder indictments changed to Doña Ana County for a hanging trial, did Billy exit their mutually-planned sham arrest. And Wallace ends with the low blow of giving him an effeminate voice, claimed by no contemporary.]

"Boys," I'm tired," he said, and looked them straight in the eyes.

They were not in collusion with the desperado; Gen. Wallace satisfied himself of the fact.

But how account for "Billy's" escape?

Hypnotism, some say – hypnotism or that strange something that lurked in the depths of the steel-gray eyes.

[AUTHOR'S NOTE: This concoction of the guards' coercion, is Wallace's cover-up of Billy's popularity. His jailor was part of the sham arrest of the pardon deal; and townspeople saw him as hero, not desperado.]

The desperado's freedom, however, was not long-lived. He was arrested soon afterward for a series of murders, and was brought again to the Lincoln County Jail. Patrick Garrett was Sheriff. He was probably the one man in New Mexico who did not fear "Billy the Kid." He was his match in every respect – as calm, as desperate, as certain.

[AUTHOR'S NOTE: The timing is a lie. Billy left jail in June of 1879. The Stinking Springs capture was on December 22, of 1880. And Wallace's demonizing of Billy continues by adding a fictional "series of murders."]

Perhaps "Billy" knew this. At any rate he must have considered himself in desperate straits. He sent for Gen. Wallace. The General refused to respond. Then the outlaw sent him a note. The note said:

"Come to the jail. I have some papers you would not want to see displayed."

"I knew what he meant," said Gen. Wallace, reminiscently. "He referred to the note he received from me in response to which he appeared in the hut on the mesa. He was threatening to publish it if I refused to see him. I thwarted his purpose by giving a copy of the latter and a narrative of the circumstances connected with it to the paper published in the town. It was duly printed and upon its appearance a copy was sent to "Billy" in his cell. He had nothing further to say."

Not Daunted by His Sentence.

In the end the desperado was convicted and sentenced to be hanged. When the sentence was read he stood before the trial judge and said:

"Judge, that doesn't frighten me a bit. 'Billy the Kid' was not born to be hung."

He was a thorough fatalist. He believed he bore a charmed life. He believed he would not die until his "time came," and then death was inevitable.

From the court-room "Billy" was led back to the jail. Nine men were put on guard, and he was never allowed a moment from the sight of one of them.

On the day before that set for his execution one man sat in front of Billy while he ate his dinner. During the meal the guard forgot himself and suddenly stooped. "Billy's" quick eye took in the situation in a glance.

With a leap he sprang upon the bending man and dashed his brains out with his handcuffs. He seized the dead guard's revolver and, his steel-gray eyes gleaming, he walked forward deliberately and routed all the other guards, who ran to the assistance of their comrade.

Once more "Billy the Kid" escaped in the full light of day through the doors of the jail. He forced a blacksmith to break the manacle chains, seized a good horse that stood nearby and rode away.

He called back as he spurred the animal into a gallop:

"Tell the judge that I said "Billy the Kid' was not born to be hung."

But "Billy" had forgotten one thing; he had not reckoned on the character of the man who was Sheriff of the county. He had forgotten Patrick Garrett. Garrett shut his teeth hard, like a man who is determined to accomplish his purpose, no matter the obstacles presenting themselves. He set out to take "Billy the Kid," dead or alive.

[AUTHOR'S NOTE: Twice Wallace published a personal offer of $500 for Billy's capture to achieve his hanging.]

Garrett received information that "Billy" had gone back to an old fort in the mountains to see his sweetheart. Garrett followed. He lay in wait in the dooryard of the home of "Billy's" love, and finally his vigil was rewarded when he saw the door open one night and a man step out into the white light of the moon.

His hat was off, he was in his stocking feet and he wore only shirt and trousers. He passed out into the night.

Garrett crept to the door and passed in.

He covered the girl's father with his gun.

"Not a word," he said, and slid behind the headboard of the bed.

The Death of "Billy the Kid."

The door opened again and "Billy the Kid" entered. He seemed to scent danger as a camel scents rain; instinct taught him that something was wrong. He cried to the cowering old man in Spanish:

"Who's here?" he asked. "Who's here?"

Garrett raised his revolver; two shots rang out on the quiet air and the room filled with smoke. A form tottered, then crashed to the floor. In the nerveless hand was a smoking revolver; for the first and last time the notorious New Mexican outlaw had missed his aim. Garrett escaped unwounded. But there were two bullet wounds in the body of "Billy the Kid" and both pierced the heart. Garrett's aim was unerring.

To-day there is a little lowly heap of earth located in Las Cruces, N.M. To the curious stranger some idle native may, now and again, point out this little grave and explain, with a certain pride, that Las Cruces possesses the final resting place of the worst bad man that ever infested the Southwestern border. An ancient Mexican, who sometimes shows this grave to visitors, once made the cautious remark regarding its occupant that, had he lived, he would probably have turned out to be a bad man.

"And how old was 'Billy' when he died?" asked one curious stranger.

"Twenty-one, senor," replied the ancient. "He died, almost one might say, before he fully began to live."

"You say he was bad?" remarked another stranger.

"He is said to have killed many men."

"How many? How many, amigo, had this man killed at the time he himself died?"

"He had killed," replied the ancient Mexican, **"twenty-one men, one for each year of his age, may the saints defend us,"** said **the Mexican.** [Author's boldface]

[AUTHOR'S NOTE: Wallace may have been the inventor of this mythology of Billy's twenty-one victims. He had also added Billy's shooting at Garrett, in his fantasized death scene.]

"He was a good man, and very kind to poor people. Yet, had he lived, he might, according to the opinion of some, have turned into a bad man."

Gen. Wallace also tells in his autobiography how and why "Billy the Kid" started on his career of crime:

A Waif of New York City.

"The man whose deeds of blood had drawn upon him the eyes of an entire nation, was born a New York waif. Before he was more than ten years of age he was brought to Indiana, and in Terre Haute and Indianapolis, where he was reared, he was known as William Bonne. In 1876, when he was about seventeen years old, he suddenly left his home, crossed the Mississippi and went to the country of the men of his kind – the frontier of the far West.

"Billy began his career with an oath to kill John Chisum, his first employer when the lad reached the plains. Chisum and the "Kid' had been unable to agree on terms of settlement for a season's work. The result was the lad's fearful vendetta, sworn not only against Chisum, but against all of Chisum's other employees as well.

" 'For each herdsman employed by you whom I kill," Billy sent him word, 'I will deduct $5 from our unsquared account. If I kill you,' he added grimly, 'my bill will be receipted in full.'

"Then his bloody career began. It was not long until William Bonne, the waif, reared in the peaceful surroundings of Indiana, became the most feared man in the Southwest. At the same time, he was the most revered, the most adored and the most respected man in the Territory.

"It was the kind of good reward that sometimes comes to bad men."

[AUTHOR'S NOTE: This ambiguous end pays strange homage to Billy Bonney, with its non-sequitor of "bad men" being "revered" and "adored." It is as if the real Billy, his real fulfillment of the pardon deal, and the injustice of his hanging trial and murder breaks through the clouds of Lew Wallace's obfuscations for a last brief moment. Wallace may have inadvertently revealed grudging admiration and residual envy that contributed to betraying Billy. But did Wallace feel guilt? Given his selfish hypocrisy, the best bet is that his novelist persona was using those truths only for literary contrast, and glossing over conscience by anticipating a future best seller on the Old West. And this article summarizes well the malicious myth of Billy the Kid he helped to create.]

NATHAN AUGUSTUS MONROE DUDLEY

The 1879 Court of Inquiry transcript for Fort Stanton's commander, Nathan Augustus Monroe Dudley, exemplifies the Santa Fe Ring's power to cover up its partisans' crimes.

Governor Lew Wallace had earlier removed Dudley from command by calling him a local "irritant": his interpretation of Susan McSween's attorney, Huston Chapman's, accusations about murder and arson during the Lincoln County War. Chapman had added that Lincoln's citizens remained in fear of Dudley's murderous potential.

So the Ring murdered Huston Chapman.

But that did not solve the Ring's problem, since Chapman's law associate, Ira Leonard, took his place. Two months later, the Ring tried to assassinate Leonard, but failed.

So Ring strategizing took a "legal" route. Ignoring Dudley's past two past Court Martials, they had him request his own Court of Inquiry for potential Court Martial - assured that he would win. His attorney would be Thomas Benton Catron's friend and the Territory's best trial lawyer, Henry Waldo; and the Chief Judge of three would be Dudley's best friend from Fort Union: Colonel Galusha Pennypacker, 16th Infantry. Ring partisans also gave affidavits maligning Susan McSween's morality and veracity, to sabotage her credibility as a witness.

Into that Court's lions' den had naively entered both Billy Bonney and Governor Lew Wallace to testify against Dudley; hopeless acts that would ultimately poison their relationship and Billy's pardon possibility.

Dudley himself testified from June 28th to 30th of 1879 as that forty-nine day trial's last witness. On July 5, 1879, its three judges - ignoring all evidence - cleared him of any wrongdoing.

Dudley, arrogantly lying, had endured, as his greatest risk, Billy's testimony of seeing his white soldiers firing a volley at him and others fleeing the burning McSween house. "Volley" meant "in unison" and "under orders." And "white," in that context, likely meant officers. Dudley's proceeding to Court Martial should have occurred - and even to hanging for treasonous murder of American citizens.

Dudley's examination was done by Attorney Henry Waldo for defense ("*by Col. Dudley*" in the transcript); and by military prosecutor Captain Henry Humphreys, Fifteenth Infantry out of Fort Bliss ("*Recorder*" in the transcript). Humphreys was assisted by Attorney Ira Leonard, who was present in court.

Attorney Waldo alleged that Dudley's march on Lincoln did not violate the Posse Comitatus Act because he had come as a "humanitarian" to protect women and children.

Of course, that ignored the fact that the McSween side had been winning and that his military presence insured their defeat; as well as the burning of the besieged McSween house with its trapped women and children: Susan McSween, her sister, and her sister's five little children. It also ignored Dudley's refusal of Susan McSween's request for protection. Concealed was Dudley's role as a Ring-partisan.

Dudley's own mendacious words demonstrate the arrogance of power and sense of immunity to the law created by Santa Fe Ring protection.

Attorney Henry Waldo began the questioning as follows:

Q. by Col. Dudley. Do you admit to having gone to Lincoln on the 19th day of July last, if so, state what induced you to go there at that time?

Answer. I did go to Lincoln on the 19th day of July last. I was induced to go to Lincoln being thoroughly convinced that it was my solemn duty to do so. I had been in command of the post. My object in going to Lincoln was to give protection to women and children and parties, and parties who were not engaged in the disturbances then existing in Lincoln.

Q. by Col. Dudley. State whether or not in going there it was done in pursuance of any promise by you, or of any agreement or understanding, direct or indirect, between you and Sheriff Peppin, or anyone on his behalf?

Answer. There was no agreement, no.

After the long Henry Waldo examination, the prosecution had a short incompetent cross-examination, which made no use of the dramatic testimony of witnesses like Billy Bonney; and which was blocked anyway by Attorney Waldo's constant objections, which were sustained by the three corrupt judges; as follows:

Q. by Recorder. What induced you to think it was your solemn duty to go to Lincoln on the 19th day of July last, upon what authority did you base that action, and was your sole and only object that of a humanitarian?

Answer. My knowledge of the affairs in Lincoln, my sense of duty as an Officer of the Army. It was decidedly as I understood the word.

Q. by Recorder. If you went there in the capacity of a humanitarian, why did you not carry out that purpose and prevent the bloodshed and destruction of property that was going on there instead of promoting the disturbance by allowing a warrant to be issued against McSween and others?

Objected to by Lieut. Col. Dudley, by his counsel ...

Objection sustained.

N.A.M. Dudley's exoneration by this Court of Inquiry re-established Santa Fe Ring control in Lincoln County by demonstrating the futility of opposition. The resulting "peace," of which Lew Wallace foolishly boasted to President Hayes and Secretary of the Interior Carl Schurz as his doing, was actually the people's helpless disillusionment about justice.

In addition, that corrupt outcome sealed Billy's fate, since prideful Lew Wallace responded to both the verdict and his lambasting by Attorney Henry Waldo with such repugnance that he abandoned Lincoln County for the two year remainder of his administration - and that included Billy's pardon.

And Billy, as arguably the most damning witness, won only more enmity of the Ring - sealing his own future killing.

AZARIAH WILD

By 1880, it must have been clear to Santa Fe Ringmen that Billy Bonney had to die. Refusing to leave the Territory after the lost Lincoln County War like most of the Regulators, he had become a self-appointed gadfly, and possible future leader of another uprising of oppressed citizens. And Billy's reputation for fierceness, coupled with public anger at the Lincoln County War's horrors and its antecedent San Patricio massacre, boded his side's future victory.

To eliminate Billy, an organization with the license for clandestine murder was enlisted: the Washington, D.C. Secret Service, a branch of the Treasury Department with broad powers, but with special focus on counterfeiting. The fact that the Chief of the Secret Service, James Brooks himself, was contacted after merchant, James Dolan, received merely a counterfeit $100 bill, indicates high level Ring machinations; likely by Thomas Benton Catron's past legal partner and Washington counterpart for the Santa Fe Ring: Territorial Representative Stephen Benton Elkins. Actually passing the fake bill had been drifter, Billy Wilson, employed by the actual counterfeiter: Dan Dedrick.

The Special Operative, one of only forty in the country, chosen for what would arguably become one of the Secret Service's first political murders, was Azariah Faxon Wild. Then 45, he was stationed in New Orleans, and was sent to New Mexico Territory in September of 1880.

Billy Bonney, innocent of counterfeiting or of its Santa Fe Ring-fabricated "outlaw rustling gang," would be framed as the "gang's" leader; until gullible, lazy, and duped Azariah Wild, relying only on Ring-partisan sources - primarily James Dolan and Thomas Benton Catron's brother-in-law Edgar Walz - would organize and finance the boy's pursuit as "leader" of what Wild eventually fantasized as the country's largest counterfeiting and rustling gang.

As required by Secret Service guidelines, Azariah Wild wrote daily reports of his activities on preprinted forms, like the following, from any base of operations. Before his coming to New Mexico Territory, it was New Orleans:

146

𝔘.𝔖. 𝔗𝔯𝔢𝔞𝔰𝔲𝔯𝔶 𝔇𝔢𝔭𝔞𝔯𝔱𝔪𝔢𝔫𝔱
SECRET-SERVICE DIVISION

New Orleans   District

James J. Brooks,
Chief U.S. Secret Service

Sir: I have the honor to submit the following, my report as _Chief_ Operative of this District for _Monday_ the _29ᵗʰ_ day of _December, 18_79, written at _New Orleans, Louisiana_, and completed at _9_ o'clock _A_ M on the _30ᵗʰ_ day of _December, 18_79

By October 6, 1880, at the start of Billy Bonney's framing by Ring informers, Azariah Wild made his first garbled reference to him (misspelling "Antrim" as "Antrom"), as follows:

> _There is an outlaw in the mountains here who came here from Arizona after committing a murder there named William Antrom alias Wᵐ Bonney alias Billy Kid with whom these cattle thieves meet, and by many it is believed that they the cattle thieves and shovers of the queer [sic - counterfeiters] receive the counterfeit money. I have found no evidence thus far to support their suspicions._

Ironically, that same month of October 1880 - one month before Ring-selected Pat Garrett was elected Lincoln County Sheriff - Operative Azariah Wild almost implemented a pardon for Billy, superseding the need for Governor Lew Wallace's original option.

Generating that new chance was Billy's loyal attorney (and by then also judge) Ira Leonard, as seen in Wild's October 8ᵗʰ report. In that report, is the noteworthy and intriguing statement: _"Antrom has recently written a letter to Judge Leonard."_ That letter would have been Billy's offer of another exchange of testimony for a pardon - this time against the actual counterfeiter - assumedly, Dan Dedrick. Sadly, it is another of Billy's writings that is lost - or possibly expurgated later, in Washington, D.C., by the efficient Santa Fe Ring.

Azariah Wild wrote in his report to Chief James Brooks:

I left Fort Stanton at 7 o'clock A.M. on the stage and reached Lincoln the County seat at 8:30 A.M. ... The object of my visit to Lincoln was to see Judge Ira Leonard ... In my report of October 5th ... I spoke of an outlaw whose name was Antrom alias Billy Bonney. During the Lincoln Co. War he killed men on the Indian Reservation for which he has been indicted in the territorial and the United States Court. Gov. Wallace has issued a proclamation granting immunity to those not indicted but as Antrom has been indicted the proclamation did not cover his (Antrom's) case and he (Antrom) has been in the mountains as an outlaw ever since a space of about two years time.

Governor Wallace has since written Antrom's attorney on the subject saying he should be let go but has failed to put it on shape that satisfied Judge Leonard (Antrom's attorney).

It is believed and in fact is almost known that he (Antrom) is one of the leading members of this gang.

Antrom has recently written a letter to Judge Leonard which has been shown to me in confidence that leads me to believe that we can use Antrom in these cases provided Gov. Wallace will make good his written promises and the U.S. Attorney will allow the case pending in the U.S. Court to slumber and give him (Antrom) one more chance to reform. [Author's boldface]

I have promised nothing and will not except to receive and propositions he Leonard and his client see fit to make and submit them to U.S. Attorney Barnes.

Judge Leonard has written Antrom to meet him (Leonard) at once for consultation.

The chances are that the conversation will take place within the next week when I will report fully to you and submit whatever propositions they see fit to make to US. Attorney Barnes for such action as he deems proper to take.

Unfortunately for Billy, James Dolan probably learned from Wild about that new pardon opportunity, and convinced him to arrest Billy at the planned meeting with Attorney Leonard for coordination of Billy's testimony in exchange for a pardon.

But Billy was finally cautious. He robbed the mail stagecoach on October 16th, read Wild's report about that trap, and avoided the meeting; but lost his pardon chance. Arrest, Billy knew, would have led only to a speedy hanging trial.

By October 29, 1880, Azariah Wild, totally misled by Ringmen, wrote this report to Chief James Brooks:

> *I am now perfectly confident that there is a counterfeiting gang here who are making counterfeit $100- and $50- notes as I am of anything that I do not know absolutely certain, and that I have not seen with my own eyes ...*
>
> *The force of desperados now at Fort Sumner the headquarters of the gang numbers twenty six. They openly say they number sixty two in Lincoln Co. and defy the authorities ..*
>
> *I especially call your attention to the location: All the outlaws or nearly all have been driven out of Texas and Arizona, and concentrated at Fort Sumner. They have two ranches. One seventy-five miles (the Pat Coghlan Ranch) the other twelve miles from Fort Sumner (the Dan Dedrick Ranch). They have a band of their men out stealing horses, cattle, robbing mails, and people whilst the balance of their force remain on the ranch guarding the stock they have stolen ...*
>
> *This is a case that requires time to work but I candidly believe I can work it successfully by taking time. If I had a good man with me it would be of great service.*

By November 11th, convinced that the gang was led by "the Kid," and with Pat Garrett already a Deputy Sheriff and appointed by Wild as a Deputy U.S. Marshal, Wild wrote about their planned "raid on Fort Sumner" by his "force" of Texans, against "the worst (organized) gang of men that this country has." That posse included Wild's ignorant addition of murderer/rustler/San Patricio massacre leader/ Lincoln County War Ring-side fighter, John Kinney. Wild stupidly wrote:

> *John Kinney has qualified as Deputy U.S. Marshal so I have a man to represent the U.S. Marshal while the other parties will act as a Posse Comitatus.*

By November 22nd, the posse was after the "Kid outfit":

> *The Sheriff* [sic - Deputy Sheriff Will Hudgens] *at White Oaks with his Posse went out 13 miles from town and attempted to arrest Billy Kid, William Wilson and others on Monday the 22nd instant and had to return to town empty handed. Kid force out numbered that of the Sheriff.* [Author's note: It is Wild's fantasy as to "*out numbered.*"]

By December 23, 1880, Tom O'Folliard had been fatally shot by Pat Garrett (on the 19th), as Azariah Wild reported. By then, Wild was so hysterically paranoid while grandiosely fantasizing about capturing the gigantic "Kid gang," that he included "*Jessie* [sic] *James*" in it! Wild wrote:

> *I am also in receipt of reliable character that Deputy Marshal P.F. Garrett has killed one of the Kid & Wilson gang, and badly wounded another in attempting to arrest them. He is still in pursuit of the balance of the outlaws. Jessie James is surely here under the name of Campbell.*

On December 26, 1880, Special Operative Azariah Wild left New Mexico Territory and returned to his New Orleans headquarters. He was apparently unaware of Pat Garrett's capture of Billy at Stinking Springs on December 22, 1880.

But on January 1, 1881, Wild described his certainty that the desired capture or killing of Billy Bonney would occur as planned. He stated in his report to Chief James Brooks:

> *I have this day received information of an almost positive nature, that Deputy U.S. Marshal P.F. Garrett has the Kid and Wilson gang of outlaws at his mercy and that he will either kill or arrest them.*

WARREN BRISTOL

Warren Bristol was the Ring-partisan judge of the Third Judicial District of New Mexico Territory. He was 55 when he first met Billy Bonney when indicting him in the 1878 Lincoln County Grand Jury for the murders of Sheriff William Brady, Deputy Sheriff George Hindman, and Andrew "Buckshot" Roberts. Ultimately, corrupt Warren Bristol was Billy's hanging judge in his March to April 1881 trials in Mesilla.

Warren Bristol had also been the crucial implementer of the Santa Fe Ring's strategy to destroy its economic competitor, John Henry Tunstall, through a fraudulent embezzlement case against his friend, Attorney Alexander McSween. Bristol's judgments against McSween included attachment of Tunstall's property by alleging him as McSween's "partner." Bristol was, thus, the enabler of Tunstall's murder and key contributor to injustices culminating in the Lincoln County War.

And Judge Bristol's interventions punctuate legal outrages throughout the Lincoln County War period.

In the Grand Jury of 1878, Lincoln Ring boss, James Dolan, along with other Sheriff Brady possemen, was indicted for the Tunstall murder. Bristol would later make sure that all the Ringmen's cases, up to 200, were dismissed on technicalities.

That obstruction of justice would lead to Billy's true statement in 1881, after his hanging sentence from Bristol, that it was unfair that he alone, of all Lincoln County War participants, should have received the full penalty of the law.

Again, prior to the Grand Jury of 1879, after Governor Lew Wallace had implemented the arrest and incarceration in Fort Stanton of James Dolan, Billy Campbell, and Jessie Evans as murderers of Attorney Huston Chapman, as well as of Seven Rivers men for crimes including rustling, it was Judge Bristol who approved their Ring-biased attorneys' request for their habeas corpus freeing (though Campbell and Evans had already escaped the lax imprisonment earlier).

Judge Bristol's maliciousness is seen in his management of Billy's 1881 trial. A translator was denied for the Hispanic jurymen. And his instructions, seen below, left no option but conviction for murder in the first degree - its only penalty then being hanging. Bristol did his job well to insure Billy's death.

JUDGE BRISTOL'S JURY INSTRUCTIONS

Territory of New Mexico
District Court 3d Judicial
District Doña Ana County
April Term A.D. 1881

In the Third Judicial
District Court April Term / 1879

Territory of New Mexico	)
vs	)
	) *Murder*
William Bonney alias Kid	) *1st Degree*
Alias William Antrim	)

Gentlemen of the Jury:
The defendant in this case William Bonney alias Kid alias William Antrim is charged in and by the indictment against him which has been laid before you with having committed in connection with certain other persons the crime of murder in the County of Lincoln in the 3d Judicial District of the Territory of New Mexico in the month of April of the year 1878 by then and there unlawfully killing one William Brady by inflicting upon his body certain fatal gunshot wounds from a premeditated design to effect his death.

The case is here for trial by a change of venue from the said County of Lincoln.

The facts alleged in the indictment if true constitute Murder in the 1st and highest degree and whether these allegations are true or not true are for you to determine from the evidence which you have heard and which is now submitted to you for your careful consideration.

In the matter of determining what your verdict shall be it will be improper for you to consider anything except the evidence before you.

You as Jurors are the exclusive judges of the weight of the evidence. You are the exclusive judges of the credibility of the witnesses. It is for you to determine whether the testimony of any witnesses whom you have heard is to be believed or not. You are also the exclusive judges whether the evidence is sufficiently clear and strong to satisfy your minds that the defendant is guilty.

There is no evidence tending to show that the killing of Brady was either justifiable or excusable by law. As a matter of law therefore such killing was unlawful and whoever committed the deed or was present and advised or aided or abetted and consented to such killing committed the crime of murder in some one of the degrees of murder.

There is no evidence before you showing that the killing of Brady is murder in any degree than the first.

Your verdict therefore should be either that the defendant id guilty of the murder in the 1st degree or that he is not guilty at all under this indictment.

Murder in the 1st degree consists in the killing of one human being by another without authority of law and from a premeditated design to affect the death of the person killed.

Every killing of one human being by another that is not justifiable or excusable should be necessarily a killing without authority of law.

As I have already instructed you to consider murder in the 1st degree it is necessary that the killing should have been perpetrated from a premeditated design to effect the death of the person killed.

As to this premeditated design I charge you that to render design to kill premeditated it is not necessary that such design to kill should exist in the mind for any considerable length of time before the killing.

If the design to kill is completely formed in the mind but for a moment before inflicting the fatal wounds it would be premeditated and in law the effect would be the same as though the design to kill had existed for a long time.

In this case in order to justify you in finding this defendant guilty of murder in the 1st degree under the peculiar circumstances as presented by the indictment and the evidence you should be satisfied and believe from the evidence to the exclusion of every Reasonable doubt of the truth of several propositions.

1ˢᵗ That the defendant either inflicted one or more of the fatal wounds causing Brady's death or that he was present at the time and place of the killing and encouraged – incited – aided in – abetted – advised or commanded such killing.

2d That such killing was without justification or excuse.

3d That such killing of Brady was caused by inflicting upon his body a fatal gunshot wound.

And 4ᵗʰ that such fatal wound was either inflicted by the defendant upon a premeditated design to effect Brady's death or that he was present at the time and place of the killing of Brady and from a premeditated design to effect his death he then and there encouraged – incited – aided in – abetted – advised or commanded such killing.

If he was so present – encouraging – inciting – aiding in – abetting – advising – or commanding the killing of Brady he is as much guilty as though he fired the fatal shot.

I have charged you that to justify you in finding the defendant guilty of murder in the 1ˢᵗ degree you should be satisfied from the evidence to the exclusion of every reasonable doubt that the defendant is actually guilty.

As to what would be or would not be reasonable doubt of guilt I charge you that belief in the guilt of the defendant to the exclusion of every reasonable doubt does not require you to so believe absolutely and to mathematical certainty – That is to justify a verdict of guilty it is not necessary for you to be as certain that the defendant is guilty as you are that two and two are four or that two and three are five.

Merely a vague conjecture or bare possibility that the defendant my be innocent is not sufficient to raise reasonable doubt of his guilt.

If all the evidence before you which you believe to be true convinces and directs your understanding and satisfies your reason and judgment while acting upon it conscientiously under your oath as jurors and if this evidence leaves in your minds an abiding conviction to a moral certainty that the defendant is guilty of the crime charged against him: then this would be proof of guilt to the exclusion of every reasonable doubt and would justify you in finding the defendant guilty.

You will apply the evidence to this case according to the instructions I have given you and determine whether the defendant is guilty of murder in the 1st degree or not guilty.

Murder in the 1st degree is the greatest crime known to our laws. The legislature of this Territory has enacted a law prescribing that the punishment for murder in the 1st degree shall be death.

This then is the law: No other punishment than death can be imposed – for murder in the 1st degree.

If you believe and are satisfied therefore from the evidence before you to the exclusion of every reasonable doubt that the defendant is guilty of murder in the 1st degree then it will be your duty to find a verdict that the defendant is guilty of murder in that degree naming murder in the 1st degree in your verdict and also saying in your verdict that the defendant shall suffer the punishment of death.

If from the evidence you do not believe to the exclusion of every reasonable doubt that the defendant is guilty of murder in the 1st degree or if you entertain a reasonable doubt as to the guilt of the defendant, then in that case your verdict should be not guilty.

_532_

Territory
   Vs.   ) Murder
William Bonney
Alias "Kid" alias
William Antrim

Charge to Trial Jury

Filed in my office this 9th day of April A.D. 1881.
George R. Bowman
Clerk

ALBERT JENNINGS FOUNTAIN

By April 8, 1881, Billy Bonney needed an ally. His loyal attorney, Ira Leonard, had abruptly abandoned his defense after attaining the unexpected victory of quashing the first of Billy's three indictments: for the murder of Andrew "Buckshot" Roberts. The next case was Billy's indictment for the murder of Sheriff William Brady. And after that, if he was not already sentenced to hang, would be the trial for the murder of Deputy Sheriff George Hindman.

For Billy, Judge Warren Bristol appointed local law-and-order newspaper owner, Apache vigilante, and politically active 42 year old attorney, Albert Jennings Fountain. Fountain's co-counsel was John D. Bail. Both saw Billy as an outlaw.

Fountain gave a lackadaisical defense, as can be seen from his closing argument in which he made no attempt to counter any of Judge Bristol's prejudicial instructions to the jurymen.

So Billy was declared guilty on the trial's second day: April 9th. On April 13th, Bristol set his hanging for May 13th.

A measure of Billy's desperation for legal representation to appeal this sentence, was his attempt to get money to retain Fountain privately. That led to his writing his last known letter - to Attorney Edgar Caypless, who was already carrying out his replevin suit against Pat Garrett's posseman, Frank Stewart, for stealing Billy's bay racing mare at Stinking Springs. Billy's hope was that he could then sell her to cover Fountain's legal fees. The money never came through in time.

ATTORNEY ALBERT JENNINGS FOUNTAIN'S JURY INSTRUCTIONS

Territory of New Mexico
vs   ) Murder
William Bonney alias Kid alias William Antrim
In the District Court of Doña Ana
County March 1881 term.

Instructions asked for by Defendants counsel. The Court is asked to instruct the Jury as follows: to wit:

1st Instructions asked –

Under the evidence the Jury must either find the defendant guilty of Murder in the 1st degree, or acquit him.

2nd Instruction asked –

The jury will not be justified in finding the defendant guilty of Murder in the 1st degree unless they are satisfied, from the evidence, to the exclusion of all reasonable doubt, that the defendant actually fired the shot that caused the death of the deceased Brady, and that such shot was fired by the defendant with the premeditated design to effect the death of the deceased, or that the defendant was present and actually assisted in firing the fatal shot or shots that caused the death of the deceased, and that he was present in a position to render such assistance and actually rendered assistance from a premeditated design to effect the death of the deceased.

Instruction asked –

If the Jury are satisfied from the evidence to the exclusion of all reasonable doubt that the defendant was present at the time of the firing of the shot or shots that caused the death of the deceased Brady, yet, before they will be justified in finding the defendant guilty, they must be further satisfied from the evidence and the evidence alone, to the exclusion of all reasonable doubt, that the defendant either fired the shots that killed the deceased, or some one of them, or that he assisted in firing said shot or shots, and that he assisted in firing said shot or shots, or assisted in firing the same, or assisted the parties who fired the same either by his advice, encouragement or procurement or command, from a premeditated design to effect the death of Brady. If the Jury entertains any reasonable doubt upon any of these points they must find a verdict of acquittal.

A.J. Fountain
J.D. Bail

PATRICK "PAT" FLOYD GARRETT

Billy Bonney's mortal enemy was Lincoln County Sheriff and U.S. Deputy Marshal Patrick "Pat" Floyd Garrett.

Garrett, with his posse, had attempted Billy's group's ambush murder in Fort Sumner on December 19, 1881 (killing Tom O'Folliard), and again on December 22nd at Stinking Springs (killing Charlie Bowdre). Capturing Billy there, Garrett ensured his eventual hanging trial in Mesilla. Finally, Garrett was Billy's lone assailant in the fatal, Fort Sumner ambush of July 14, 1881. Garrett was then 31.

Pat Garrett, however, was no Ringman. And with pride in his wealthy plantation origins, he undertook his missions with a lawman's dispassion, rather than with an avenger's vindictiveness or a Ringman's greed.

Elected Lincoln County Sheriff on November 2, 1880, with Santa Fe Ring blessings and Secret Service backing, Pat Garrett, having acquired this best job of his life, was assigned to terminate Billy Bonney by legal hanging or legal bullet.

It is unclear whether Pat Garrett knew or cared about the political issues of the Lincoln County War and its aftermath, which had branded Billy an outlaw, killer, and counterfeiter; or if he personally believed those accusations. Knowing Billy from early 1878 as an acquaintance after he left the Texas buffalo range to settle in Fort Sumner, Garrett was possibly aware of their exaggeration.

But Garrett certainly did hope to capitalize on his fame after his nationally publicized killing of "outlaw Billy the Kid." The vehicle was a book, written by his journalist border, Ashmun "Ash" Upson, in dime-novel style. Its title was *The Authentic Life of Billy the Kid: The Noted Desperado of the Southwest, Whose Deeds of Daring and Blood Made His Name a Terror in New Mexico, Arizona, and Northern Mexico.*

Though it failed financially for Garrett, its claims set the ball rolling for Billy-as-desperado mythology that still taints real history. In *The Authentic Life's* lurid hyperbole and fabrications, Billy kills willy-nilly - Anglos, Native Americans, and Mexicans - in unknowable and huge quantities.

As "Ash" Upson's creation raved:

The Kid had a lurking devil in him. It was a good-humored jovial imp, or a cruel and bloodthirsty fiend, as circumstances prompted. Circumstances favored the worser angel, and the Kid fell.

But Pat Garrett decently mitigated Ash Upson's maligning. In probably his own words, his book stated:

It will never be known whether the Kid recognized me or not. If he did, it was the first time during all his life of peril that he ever lost his presence of mind, or failed to shoot first and hesitate afterwards. He knew that a meeting with me meant surrender or fight. He told several persons about Sumner that he bore no animosity against me and had no desire to do me injury. He had also said that he knew, should we meet, he would have to choose between the several alternatives of surrendering, or killing me, or getting killed himself.

Only Garrett's honesty and vague quilt about Billy's recognizing him and choosing "getting killed himself," gave a clue that graciously left open the door for revisionist history.

JIM EAST

A Texan posseman of Pat Garrett's at Billy's Stinking Springs capture, Jim East, almost 28, also witnessed Billy's Maxwell family farewell at Fort Sumner and on the way to jail. East, thus, became a "reporter" to later historians about Billy's suspiciously affectionate parting with Paulita Maxwell. East's information was later confirmed by an unpublished letter to him from the early historian, Walter Noble Burns.

On June 3, 1926, Walter Noble Burns typed to Jim East:

I also know that the Kid and Paulita were sweethearts - at least I heard that story on most good authority many times. But I was unable to write it frankly because my publishers were afraid any such statement might lay them open to a libel suit.

JOHN WILLIAM POE

Among the last people to see Billy Bonney alive were those waiting to kill him in ambush along with Sheriff Pat Garrett: his deputies John William Poe, almost 30, and 25 year old Thomas "Kip" McKinney. Neither deputy knew Billy or Lincoln County War history.

Unlike Garrett, John William Poe sought no literary gain from Billy's murder. But he wrote its long description, titled "The Killing of Billy the Kid," as a letter, dated July 10, 1917, to the famous cattleman, Charles Goodnight. In 1933, it was printed as a book of that title, with introduction by historian Maurice Garland Fulton.

Charles Goodnight was a founder of the Texas Panhandle Cattleman's Association, which had employed John William Poe, in 1880, as a cattle detective stationed in White Oaks, New Mexico Territory.

Earlier, in Texas, Poe had been a Deputy U.S. Marshal. By 1880, like other Texans - and like Secret Service Operative Azariah Wild - he became convinced that rampant cattle rustling was by Billy the Kid and his "gang." He was unaware of the Lincoln County War freedom fight; instead believing Santa Fe Ring propaganda that Billy's loyalists were merely outlaws and Hispanic "natives" (the latter identification reflecting period racism). Poe met Billy only minutes before the July 14, 1881 shooting; and, not recognizing him, supposed he was Peter Maxwell's worker or a family friend.

In his "The Killing of Billy the Kid," John William Poe stated his cattle detective mission for the Texas Panhandle Cattleman's Association as:

... putting an end to the wholesale raiding and stealing of cattle, which had been and was then carried on by Billy the Kid and his gang of desperados ...

Poe knew only fanciful exploits of Billy's "gang":

... they were operating from the Panhandle of Texas through a great part of New Mexico and Arizona.

As prelude to Billy Bonney's killing, Poe claimed to have determined Fort Sumner as his hide-out; though Poe may have concocted this story to protect Billy's actual traitor or traitors. Poe's claim, however, was that he had an "informer" at the White Oaks livery of the Dedrick brothers, to whom Billy sold rustled stock. That "informer" stated, according to Poe, that:

> ... while in his sleeping quarters at night, he had overheard a conversation between the two men [Mose and Sam Dedrick], which convinced him that the Kid was yet in the country, making his headquarters in Fort Sumner ...

Poe also credited himself with convincing Pat Garrett, "who seemed to have but little confidence in our being able to accomplish the object of our trip," to "go to Fort Sumner with the determination of unearthing the Kid if he were there."

In Fort Sumner, as a stranger, Poe did reconnaissance, becoming convinced that "nervousness" of the people meant Billy's presence; and attributed "nervousness" to "terror" of "the Kid."

Shortly before midnight on July 14, 1881, stationed on the mansion's porch - with Deputy "Kip" McKinney nearby - and with Pat Garrett inside Peter Maxwell's room, Poe claimed to first encounter Billy. He wrote:

> ... I was entirely off my guard, the thought coming into my mind that the man approaching was either Maxwell or some guest of his who might have been staying there. He came on until he was almost within arm's-length of where I sat, before he saw me ...
>
> Upon his seeing me, he covered me with his six-shooter as quick as lightning, sprang onto the porch, calling out in Spanish, "Quien es?" (Who is it?) - at the same time backing away from me toward the door through which Garrett only a few seconds before had passed ...

After Billy's shooting, Poe first doubted that the victim was Billy; quoting himself: "Pat, the Kid would not come to this place; you have shot the wrong man."

But Poe immediately accepted the truth of Billy Bonney's killing after the corpse was identified by Pat Garrett, Peter Maxwell, and the townspeople, who took it for a pre-burial vigil. The next morning, identification of the body as Billy's was again made by the six man Coroner's Jury.

But well-meaning though ignorant John William Poe made his conclusion that continued the pernicious mythology of outlawry and murder that would contaminate the history and repute of "Billy the Kid" for the next 130 years. Poe wrote:

> Garrett's first shot had penetrated his breast just above the heart, thus ending the career of a desperado who, while only about twenty-three years of age at the time of his death, had killed a greater number of men than any of the many desperados and "killers" I have known or heard of during the forty-five years I have been in the Southwest.

THOMAS "KIP" MCKINNEY

Pat Garrett's other deputy for ambushing Billy Bonney, Thomas "Kip" McKinney, as an old-timer, attempted to mount the bandwagon of self-serving publicity about Billy the Kid by building on Stinking Springs posseman Jim East's claims of a romance existing between Billy and Paulita Maxwell.

So "Kip" McKinney lasciviously fabricated that Billy's murder site was actually Paulita Maxwell's bedroom in the family mansion, rather than her brother's; even adding a sadistic fantasy of her being bound as a decoy. McKinney appears to have added racist spice of making Billy a "half-breed Indian."

McKinney's nasty tale was published, along with that period's historical misinformation and universal vilification of Billy, in a 1912 book by Frederick William Grey titled *Seeking Fortune in America*.

Frederick William Grey wrote:

> Billy the Kid, of whom I made mention before, was a noted desperado, but of quite a different stamp. He never fought fair like Thompson, and never gave the other man

a ghost of a show if he could help it. He was a half-breed Indian, or at least had Indian blood in him. When he was finally killed, it was proved that he had killed more than one man for every year he had lived ... Finally, as I said before, Sheriff Pat Garrett (a product of Uvalde) and Kip Kinney went after him. They found out a Mexican girl whom the Kid used to visit, and lay in wait for him there after tying and gagging her. Garrett stayed in the house behind a sofa and Kip was to stay outside to see that the Kid did not get to his horse again after the shooting commenced. The Kid rode up when night fell and walked into the house; but, like all hunted animals, his suspicions were easily aroused, for he had hardly entered the dark room when he drew his pistol and asked who was there. As he called out, Garrett rose from behind the sofa, and, sighting the Kid against the light of the doorway, fired twice, killing him instantly. This was not showing much sporting spirit in Garrett, but the man was a murderer of the worst type, killing men just for the sport of it.

SETTING A BAD STAGE

Given the words of Billy Bonney's foes, the last thing the public audience for Billy the Kid would have believed in this early 20th century period of historical ignorance and mythologized desperado horrors, was that Billy Bonney was highly literate.

Nineteenth Century Handwriting

Universal Literacy

Billy Bonney benefited from mid-nineteenth century, public schools' achievement of pervasive literacy along with standardized cursive penmanship. Handwriting quality came to reflect a writer's social standing and the Victorian ideal of "character formation" through practice and self-control.

Pens, Ink, and Paper

PENS AND ACCOUTREMENTS

The 18th century writing implement was a trimmed quill feather. By the early 19th century, that pointed design was translated into metal with a steel tip, or "nib." Soon, that semi-cylindrical nib was improved for control of the ink's flow and deposit by addition of side slits and a hole above the central slit, and by increasing flexibility to the writer's pressure.

America's first steel pen company was founded in 1858 by a Richard Esterbrook, Jr., in Camden, New Jersey - a year before Billy Bonney's birth. Soon, production outpaced British-made nibs; and Esterbrook's became the world's largest pen business.

Elongated penholders for nibs were usually wood or bone; with gold and ivory as luxuries presumably never used by Billy Bonney in his school days; while being hunted as an outlaw; or as a prisoner awaiting first trial, then hanging.

The penholder's base enhanced grip with circumferential bands called "ferrules," or with cork sheaths.

Using that type of pen required skill. The curved nib, with its hole above its split, held minimal ink, requiring frequent dipping. Risk was always splattering and puddling.

Penwipers were also needed to prevent nib corrosion by the acidic ink. One can doubt homeless Billy Bonney's use of that nicety, since he wrote in urgency of the moment. And the other accoutrements - like blotters, pen rests, ink-stands, pen trays, and inkwells - would have depended on his hosts.

IRON-GALL INK AND ITS PREDECESSORS

For centuries, writing was done by ink. Ancient inks were smudgy wood-soot, mixed with glue or gum. A break-through by the Greeks was an acidic mixture of iron and tannin which ate into a parchment skin; and later was used on paper.

By Billy Bonney's day, such ink came from gallotannic acid, a product of the female gall wasp, which laid eggs on oak trees. The trees' defensive encapsulation of developing larvae, along with release of gallic and tannic acids, made swollen "oak galls" or "gallnuts." From them were extracted those acids.

But gallic and tannic acids, though "biting into paper" to prevent smudging, were colorless. Added to achieve purple-blackness was iron salt (sulfate of iron) and dyes like indigo. The resulting fluid was known as "iron-gall ink."

Over time, however, that iron-based ink oxidized by rusting to brown. And its acid could eat through paper. So luck of good preservation kept for posterity Billy's written words.

PAPER

Paper achieved writing's portability and mass production, replacing earliest stone and dried clay with Egyptian plant fiber papyrus, Hellenistic and Medieval parchment (velum) from animal hides, and Central America beaten bark.

By Billy Bonney's period, paper technology was advanced - America being its leader in production by mills; though its availability in remote New Mexico Territory was often limited.

Paper was made from pulped cellulose plant fibers from rags - of flax, cotton, or linen - or from ground wood; or from a mixture of both. For manufacturing, those water-logged fibers, binding to each other, were spread, bleached, and dried as a sheet; then cut to size.

Pulp, by its variations, aids experts in paper identification - of importance to studying Billy Bonney's writings. Not only does pulp give consistency and thickness to a sheet of paper, but with differing finishing processes, its fibers leave tactile or visually recognizable surfaces, or "grain." Grades of roughness also affect writing - or ink splattering! (Pulp texture can be seen on page 314 in Figure 27's paper magnification.)

Furthermore, pulp mixtures varied with each hand-mixed batch. So, though commercially manufactured by machines with continuous rollers by the late 19th century, individual paper batches had unique fiber patterns, localized pulp densities, and shared production defects.

An example of defects are "paper-maker's tears": pale dots of water or worker's perspiration dripped on newly-made sheets, leaving thinned tiny circles. Or clumped pulp made thickened dark knots, visible when a sheet is held to light.

Paper sheets also were manufactured in different thicknesses by varying fibers, fillers, or sizing; the completed stationery being thereby classified by "weight."

In addition, late 19th century stationery itself displayed social connotations. Embellishments - like stamped embossures on a page's upper left corner - were added as advertising logos by some paper mills. Stationers, the retailers, also added embossures with table-top lever-operated embossing machines, which compressed the paper between two dies for a customized raised design - like little versions of today's notary seals.

Mills packed stationery as 480 sheet reams, which were divided for stationers into smaller packets called "quires."

Pertinent to Billy Bonney's letters, is that quires, at times, were "folios": a single long sheet folded in half (like a modern greeting card). A folio could yield a four-sided letter, or could be torn in half for two single pages with a ragged left edge.

As to envelopes, more common was folding a letter and attaching its free edge with a wax seal. No envelopes survive to indicate whether Billy Bonney used them; but his first known letter is folded horizontally into thirds - but unsealed.

PENMANSHIP PEDAGOGUE:
PLATT ROGERS SPENCER

Home schooling for Billy Bonney by his mother is possible; but the likely source of his standardized penmanship was in New Mexico Territory's Silver City where, from the ages of 13½ to 14½, he attended public school under three teachers: Dr. Webster, Miss Pratt, and Mary Richards.

It is also possible that the last teacher, Mary Richards, who admittedly liked Billy, tutored him off-hours in 1875 during his last, orphaned year in Silver City. That year followed the death of his mother in September of 1874. After that, Billy supported himself with butcher shop work and petty theft; until he was finally jailed for a burglary in September of 1875 and escaped to Arizona Territory at almost 16.

PLATT ROGERS SPENCER

Fittingly, Billy Bonney, who became part of the unique mythology of the American Frontier, wrote in a uniquely American hand. It was named "Spencerian" after its originator, Platt Rogers Spencer, a calligrapher who lived from 1800 to 1864 and mass-produced his cursive writing style and techniques with instructional texts and copybooks. Spencerian style predominated into the 20th century.

Platt Rogers Spencer - a clerk as a boy, and later an abolitionist and head of the business empire of his writing manuals and writing schools - claimed inspiration for his graceful alphabet from natural forms, and coupled his standardized teaching method with his ideals of emancipation and education.

Following Spencer's death, his sons continued his writing business as "the Spencerian Authors," prolonging what was called "the golden age of penmanship" into Billy's day.

The Spencerian system was replaced in the 1920's by the similar copybook methodology and style of the Palmer Method.

FICTIONALIZING BILLY'S WRITING CLASS

In *Billy and Paulita*, I fictionalized Mary Richards's Silver City class of September 1874, with Billy introducing Platt Rogers Spencer and his writing system. That system would inspire real Billy Bonney's script for the rest of his life, and was distinctively modified by him based on its principles.

"Who remembers the name of the penmanship we shall learn today?"

Chauncey tried to read from an older student's copybook: "Speceriam."

"Very good. It's 'Spencerian,' the name of its inventor. Could someone tell me what they learned about him in quiet reading period yesterday?" There was no response. "You, there, Henry Antrim." Dreamily, he had been staring at her. "Please stand." He was mute. About to rescue him, she thought, "Their primitive educations may have left them irreparably slow."

Billy began. "Platt Rogers Spencer was born in New York State, like me; but not in New York City, like me. He was born in eighteen hundred, exactly. He always wanted to write good, even when he was little. Then he moved to Ohio. I was about his age when we moved to Kansas. In Ohio, he liked the looks of round pebbles on the shore of Lake Erie. So he drew lines around them. I guess he used sticks. When he was twelve, he wanted a piece of paper. So I'd imagine he was real poor. But he finally got one. He figured out that the best way to write's to make lines like Nature makes. Like water moving 'round rocks. And like vines. I guess by then he was older. Then he decided that writing's a rhythm. H e must have liked to dance. He said you had to use your whole arm and finger muscles. And, to practice, he gave everyone as many copy books as they wanted." There was silence of astonishment.

"My goodness," said Mary Richards, "no school boy in England could have recited better."

SPENCERIAN PENMANSHIP

All Billy Bonney's known writings are in Spencerian style. Akin in its philosophy to Victorian corseting of women as restricting wayward flesh, and compatible with contemporary ideals of "moral character" and "willpower," Spencerian training sought rigid control of muscle and bone throughout the body to create its idealized and uniform cursive script.

WRITING BY ROTE

The concept of standardized teaching of a writing style goes back to the Renaissance, where manuals or "copybooks" presented alphabets for emulation. American schools of the 1600's used wood-mounted printed alphabets, covered by protective clear horn - thus called "horn books."

Those teaching aids were replaced later in that century by cardboard "battledores" with idealized alphabet and numerals. They evolved into later "primers" and "spellers."

The progression toward standardized writing in American society was motivated by increasing emphasis on literacy for clear communication in burgeoning businesses and culture. Establishing uniformity in a time when most documents were handwritten, were "writing systems" stressing use of standardized script, assisted by specified body position and arm and hand use.

THE SPENCERIAN METHOD

Platt Rogers Spencer's first publication, in 1848, was *Spencerian or Semi-Angular Penmanship*. Other publications by him followed from 1855 to 1863, just before his death.

In 1874, his sons, the "Spencerian Authors," published their illustrated teaching manual as *Theory of the Spencerian System of Practical Penmanship for Schools and Private Learners Developed by Questions and Answers with Practical Illustrations: Designed to Be Used by Pupils in Connection With the Use of Spencerian Copybooks.*

Billy Bonney may have used earlier or later versions.

WRITERS' POSITIONS

The Spencerian System emphasized seating position, including straight posture and proscribed foot positioning. Seating was "Front" or "Right-Side;" all to create ideal placement for the pen-holding hand, with its forearm on the desk, to maximize precise movement for the cursive style.

FIGURE 1: Writing positions (From H.C. Spencer. *Theory of Spencerian Penmanship.* 1874. Courtesy of the Ames Historical Society.)

HOLDING THE PEN

Essential to achieving Spencerian alphabet formation was the pen-holding hand, which executed smooth and supported gliding throughout writing.

Necessary was the forearm's remaining on the desk. With raised wrist, the hand moved on nails of its arched ring and pinky fingers "touching the paper directly under the palm." The system's rigidity is seen in the manual's instructions:

Take the pen between the first and second fingers and the thumb, observing 1st, that it crosses the second finger on the corner of the nail; 2nd, that it crosses the fore finger forward of the knuckle; 3rd, that the end of the thumb touches the holder opposite the lower joint of the fore finger; 4th, that the top of the holder points towards the right shoulder; 5th, that the wrist is above the paper, and the hand resting lightly on the nails of the third and fourth fingers; 6th, that the point of the pen comes *squarely* to the paper.

EXPLANATION.

A.—*Muscular rest* of the forearm, near the elbow.
B—Rest of the hand, on the surface of the nails of the 3d and 4th fingers.
C—*Wrist*, three quarters to one inch from the table.
D—*End of the thumb*, opposite the first joint of the fore finger—drawn back so that one half the pen is in view.
E—Three quarters of an inch from the left corner of second finger nail to the point of the pen at L.
F—Pen crosses the forefinger just forward of the knuckle joint.
G—*Hand well inclined over to the left*, that its upper surface may face the ceil-

ing above, and the upper end of the pen pointsto the right shoulder.
H—The *right edge of the hand*—which should never touch the paper.
I—The *pen*, held with the neb *square* on the paper, so that pressure will produce the smallest possible mark—and grasped just tight enough to guide it, and no more.
K.—End of the second finger dropped gently under the pen, which crosses it obliquely at the root of the nail.

To produce whole arm movement, raise the forearm some two inches and a half at A (see left drawing, Card 1), and slide on to the movable rest at B.

FIGURE 2: Holding the pen (Platt Rogers Spencer. *Spencerian Penmanship.* 1857.)

WRITING DRILLS

Spencerian training manuals gave "opening exercises": "Position at Desk," "Adjusting Arms," "Opening Inkstand," and "Taking Pens." "Closing procedures" were: "Wipe Pens," "Close Inkstand," and collect pens and copybooks "in the reverse order of their distribution."

Standardization was also sought by teachers' commands, even timed by metronomes with precision of a military drill.

For its ideal of uniformity, the Spencerian Method dissected the alphabet into basic forms named "elements" or "principles." They were ovals, curves, and lines (called "straight line," "right curve," "left curve," "extended loop," "direct oval," "reversed oval," and "capital stem"), all having rightward slant of fifty-two degrees.

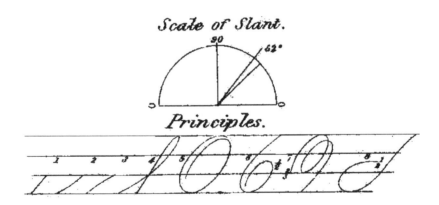

FIGURE 3: "Elements" for the Spencerian alphabet (From H.C. Spencer. *Spencerian Key to Practical Penmanship.* 1874. Courtesy of the Ames Historical Society.)

SPENCERIAN WRITING

Once exact seating and pen-grip were achieved, muscles of the body were coordinated into a choreography achieved by repeated drills of the "elements" of ovals, curves, and lines; and by combining them into an alphabet by "proper movements" of arm, hand, and fingers.

The goal was controlled but fluid movement from the shoulder, with the forearm sliding freely on the desk; while the writing hand, balanced on its supporting nails of last two fingers, also slid. So the "whole-arm" worked for each letter, maximizing standardized grace.

The resulting writing maintained the rightward slant of fifty-two degrees, established by the "elements" of ovals and slanted lines.

Spencerian upper case letters are less familiar to modern eyes than its lower case letters, which look much like today's. Those capital letters are ornate, with loopings and flourishes, and terminating decorative curlings and wisps.

Spencer's emphasis on "elements" is most reflected in Billy Bonney's distinctive signatures, which used the "capital stem," a right-slanted subtle curve ending with a small left-sided loop for his B and H in "William H. Bonney."

For publication, Platt Roger Spencer concluded his mission by a ditty: "Our intention has been to present to the public a system 'Plain to the eye, and gracefully combined, / To train the muscle and inform the mind.' "

That all this obsessive rigmarole was actually necessary to achieve the "correct" appearance of Spencerian penmanship, is evidenced by the altered look of Billy Bonney's writing from the Santa Fe jail - where he obviously lacked facilities for correct position.

And those less perfect results bothered him enough to offer their explanation. From the Mesilla jail, he apologized to one of his attorneys, Edgar Caypless, in his letter of April 15, 1881, stating: *"excuse bad writing. I have my handcuffs on."*

SPENCERIAN WRITING EXERCISES

Practice and rote were essential to Platt Rogers Spencer's system. Exercises were done on chalkboard or paper to practice underlying principles of the alphabet's design elements.

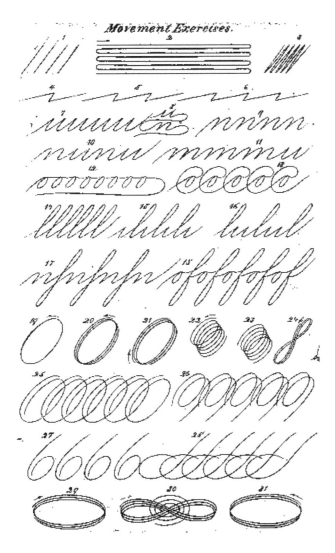

FIGURE 4: Spencerian writing exercises (From H.C. Spencer. *Spencerian Key to Practical Penmanship.* 1874. Courtesy of the Ames Historical Society.)

Spencerian Capital Letters

Spencerian capitals varied by degrees of flourishing. Billy Bonney apparently learned, or preferred, the simplest forms, which are presented below as the first letters in this chart demonstrating the style's variations.

A		N	
B		O	
C		P	
D		Q	
E		R	
F		S	
G		T	
H		U	
I		V	
J		W	
K		X	
L		Y	
M		Z	

Spencerian Lower Case Letters

The Spencerian lower case alphabet resembles modern cursive writing, though with a strict rightward slant.

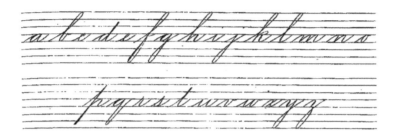

FIGURE 5: Lower case alphabet (From H.C. Spencer. *Spencerian Key to Practical Penmanship*. 1874. Courtesy of the Ames Historical Society.)

Spencerian Flourishes and Shading

Spencerian penmanship had calligraphic options for flourishing and shading letters by altering pen nib pressure.

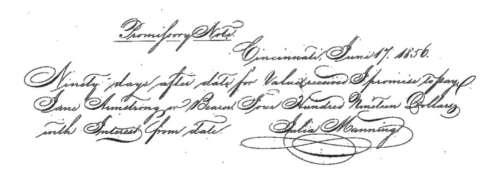

FIGURE 6: Example of Spencerian flourishes and shadings (From H.C. Spencer. *Theory of Spencerian Penmanship*. 1874. Courtesy of the Ames Historical Society.)

Spencerian Writing Sample

Ideal Spencerian style, with florid flourishes and shadings, is seen below in a letter contemporaneous with Billy Bonney's own writings; and is from General Edward Hatch, the highest ranking military officer in New Mexico Territory.

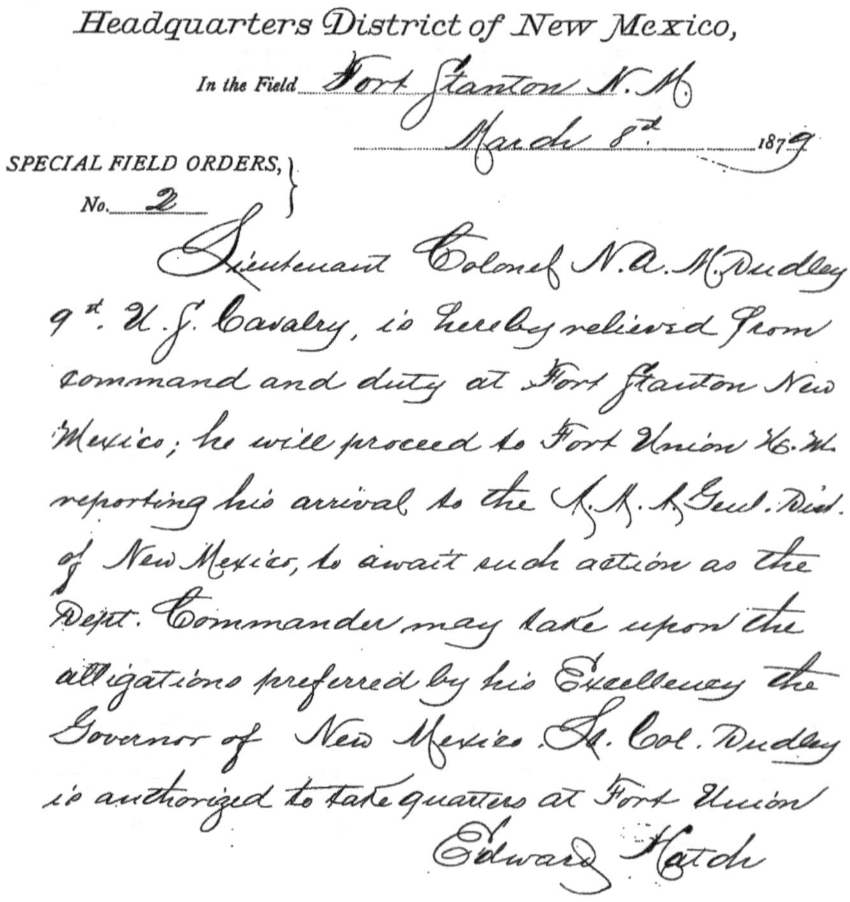

Headquarters District of New Mexico,

In the Field Fort Stanton N.M.

March 8th. 1879

SPECIAL FIELD ORDERS,
No. 2

Lieutenant Colonel N.A.M. Dudley 9th. U.S. Cavalry, is hereby relieved from command and duty at Fort Stanton New Mexico; he will proceed to Fort Union N.M. reporting his arrival to the A.A.A. Genl. Dist. of New Mexico, to await such action as the Dept. Commander may take upon the allegations preferred by his Excellency the Governor of New Mexico. Lt. Col. Dudley is authorized to take quarters at Fort Union

Edward Hatch

FIGURE 7: Example of Spencerian penmanship. (From the Indiana Historical Society, Lew Wallace Collection.)

Billy Bonney's Writing Style

BILLY BONNEY'S SPENCERIAN STYLE

Billy Bonney masculinized Spencerian penmanship with jaunty artistry. His writings, though maintaining the requisite rightward slant and alphabet style, banished frilly and effeminate flourishes; with his words ending in abrupt short strokes. For *Billy and Paulita*, I fictionalized him, at 15½, explaining to another character who admires his handwriting: "It's Spencerian. But I changed it. It was curly - like vines. I like big trees with wind blowing through branches better."

And Billy used the Spencerian "elements" to design his varied signatures as freely as he varied aliases. With a continuous line, he united letters unexpectedly and creatively: the most beautiful example being his fused H and B for the "W HBonney" in his Hoyt Bill of Sale.

Less successful, possibly because of paper roughness, was his attempt at Spencerian "shading" by nib pressure, tried only on that Hoyt Bill of Sale. It made blots, which one can guess were annoying, since he was attempting to create an official-looking document with appropriate legalese and witnessing.

Already mentioned, is Billy's pride in his writings' appearance, as demonstrated by his April 15, 1881 Mesilla jail letter to Attorney Edgar Caypless, where he apologized for handcuffs causing "*bad writing.*" And his earlier, Santa Fe jail letters to Governor Lew Wallace have cramped words and less slant, indicating lack of a writing good surface or handcuffs. The appearance of those four Santa Fe jail letters, differing from his prior ones of March 1879, has caused questioning of the later letters' authorship. But that doubt is belied by Billy's distinctively modified Spencerian style and his grammatical idiosyncrasies remaining constant throughout his productions.

BILLY BONNEY'S SPENCERIAN ALPHABET

CAPITAL LETTERS

SPENCERIAN	BILLY	WRITING SOURCE
A	*A*	APPENDIX 7: December 12, 1880, Letter to Governor Wallace (Analla) *Analla*
B	*B*	APPENDIX 7: December 12, 1880, Letter to Governor Wallace (Bonney) *Bonney*
C	*C*	APPENDIX 5: March 20,, 1879, Letter to Governor Wallace (Commanding) *Comanding*
D	*D*	APPENDIX 3: March 13, 1879, Letter to Governor Wallace (Dear) *Dear*
E	*E*	APPENDIX 3: March 13,1879, Letter to Governor Wallace (Excellency) *Excellency*
F	*F*	APPENDIX 2: October 24, 1878, Hoyt Bill Of Sale (F. Hoyt) *F. Hoyt*
G	*G*	APPENDIX 3: March 13, 1879, Letter to Governor Wallace (General) *General*
H	*H*	APPENDIX 1: June 8, 1878, Deposition to Frank Warner Angel (H. Bonney) *H. Bonney*
I	*I*	APPENDIX 3: March 13, 1879, Letter to Governor Wallace (I remain) *I remain*
J	*J*	APPENDIX 3: March 13, 1879, Letter to Governor Wallace (J.J. Dolan) *J. J. Dolan*
K	*K*	APPENDIX 3: March 13, 1879, Letter to Governor Wallace (Kid Antrim) *Kid Antrim*

SPENCERIAN	BILLY	WRITING SOURCE
L	*L*	APPENDIX 5: March 20, 1879, Letter to Governor Wallace (Lincoln) *Lincoln*
M	*M*	APPENDIX 5: March 20, 1879, Letter to Governor Wallace (Mountains) *Mountains*
N	*N*	APPENDIX 11: March 27, 1881, Letter to Governor Wallace (New) *New*
O	*O*	APPENDIX 7: December 12, 1880, Letter to Governor Wallace (Officer) *Officer*
P	*P*	APPENDIX 4: March 20, 1879, 1880, Letter to "Squire" Wilson (P.S.) *P. S.*
Q	————	NONE (Q)
R	*R*	APPENDIX 7: December 12, 1880, Letter to Governor Wallace (Respect) *Respect*
S	*S*	APPENDIX 4: March 20, 1879, 1880, Letter to "Squire" Wilson (Soldiers) *Soldiers*
T	*T*	APPENDIX 4: March 20, 1879, Letter to "Squire" Wilson (Thursday) *Thursday*
U	————	NONE (U)
V	*V*	APPENDIX 7: December 12, 1880, Letter to Governor Wallace (Vegas) *Vegas*
W	*W*	APPENDIX 4: March 20, 1879, Letter to Governor Wallace (Watch) *Watch*
X	————	NONE (X)
Y	*Y*	APPENDIX 7: December 12, 1880, Letter to Governor Wallace (Yerbys) *Yerbys*
Z	*Z*	APPENDIX 7: December 12, 1880, Letter to Governor Wallace (Zuber) *Zuber*

LOWER CASE LETTERS

SPENCERIAN	BILLY	WRITING SOURCE
a	*a*	APPENDIX 2: October 24, 1878, Hoyt Bill of Sale (and) *and*
b	*b*	APPENDIX 3: March 13, 1879, Letter to Governor Wallace (body) *body*
c	*c*	APPENDIX 3: March 13, 1879, Letter to Governor Wallace (called) *called*
d	*d*	APPENDIX 5: March 20, 1879, Letter to Governor Wallace (dog) *dog*
e	*e*	APPENDIX 4: March 20, 1879, Letter to Governor Wallace (escaped) *escaped,*
f	*f*	APPENDIX 5: March 20, 1879, Letter to Governor Wallace (for) *for*
g	*g*	APPENDIX 5: March 13, 1879, Letter to Governor Wallace (give) *give*
h	*h*	APPENDIX 2: October 24, 1878, Hoyt Bill of Sale (hand) *hand*
i	*i*	APPENDIX 3: March 13, 1879, Letter to Governor Wallace (indeed) *indeed*
j	*j*	APPENDIX 9 : March 2, 1881, Letter to Governor Wallace (jail) *jail*
k	*k*	APPENDIX 5: March 20, 1879, Letter to Governor Wallace (killed) *killed*
l	*l*	APPENDIX 3: March 13, 1879, Letter to Governor Wallace (late) *late*
m	*m*	APPENDIX 4: March 20, 1879, Letter to "Squire" Wilson (may) *may*

SPENCERIAN	BILLY	WRITING SOURCE
n	*u*	APPENDIX 4: March 20, 1879, Letter to "Squire" Wilson (note) *note*
o	*o*	APPENDIX 3: March 20, 1879, Letter to Governor Wallace (of) *our*
p	*p*	APPENDIX 2: October 24, 1878, Hoyt Bill of Sale (presents) *presents*
q		NONE (q)
r	*r* *v*	APPENDIX 5: March 20, 1879, Letter to Governor Wallace (road) *road* or APPENDIX 7: December 12, 1880, Letter to Governor Wallace (Portales) *Portales*
s	*s*	APPENDIX 4: March 20, 1879, Letter to "Squire" Wallace (same) *same*
t	*t*	APPENDIX 7: December 12, 1880, Letter to Governor Wallace (they) *they*
u	*u*	APPENDIX 3: March 13, 1879, Letter to Governor Wallace (understand) *understand*
v	*v*	APPENDIX 10: March 4, 1880, Letter to Governor Wallace (very) *very*
w	*w*	APPENDIX 4: March 20, 1879, Letter to "Squire" Wilson (who) *who*
x	*x*	APPENDIX 3: March 13, 1879, Letter to Governor Wallace (explain) *explain*
y	*y*	APPENDIX 5: March 20, 1879, Letter to Governor Wallace (yesterday) *yesterday*
z	*z*	APPENDIX 3: March 13, 1879, Letter to Governor Wallace (citizens) *citizens*

BILLY BONNEY'S SPENCERIAN PENMANSHIP MODIFICATIONS

Billy Bonney expressed his rebellious and artistic sides by consistent personalizing of his Spencerian handwriting, while staying true to its basic alphabet and fifty-two degree slant.

BILLY'S FLOURISHES

Billy rejected Spencerian flourishes terminating words, giving his writing a modern clipped look, as exemplified in his March 20, 1879 letter to Governor Wallace [APPENDIX 5].

BILLY'S SHADING

Spencerian writing had the fancy option of shading letters by increasing pressure on the nib. Billy's attempt appears only in his October 24, 1878 Hoyt Bill of Sale [APPENDIX 2], and unsuccessfully blots.

BILLY'S LETTER SLANT

Though maintaining the correct Spencerian alphabet slant in his early writings from 1878 and 1879, by 1880, when on the run from the law, and in 1881, when in the Santa Fe jail, Billy Bonney wrote more upright. Apparently distressed by losing proper form, he explained the problem in a Mesilla jail letter to one of his attorneys, Edgar Caypless, as being from wearing handcuffs. But this appearance change from early to late letters has caused erroneous claims that his later letters were by another author - though only the slant differs.

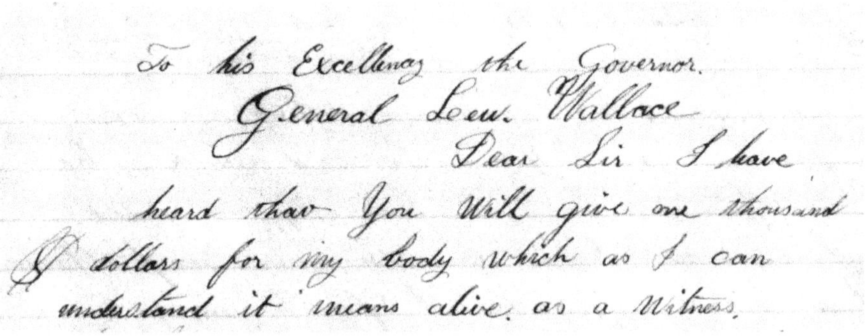

To his Excellency the Governor.
General Lew. Wallace
Dear Sir I have
heard that You Will give one thousand
$ dollars for my body which as I can
understand it means alive. as a Witness.

FIGURE 8: Billy Bonney's March 13, 1879 letter to Governor Lew Wallace [APPENDIX 3]

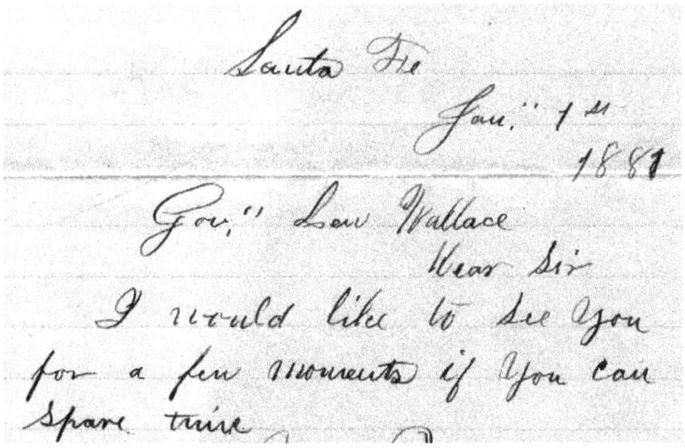

Santa Fe
Jan. 1st
1881
Gov. Lew Wallace
Dear Sir
I would like to See You
for a few moments if You can
Spare time

FIGURE 9: Billy Bonney's January 1, 1881 letter to Governor Lew Wallace [APPENDIX 8]

BILLY'S CHANGED LOWER CASE LETTER R

The only alphabet change from Billy Bonney's early to late letters is his lower case "r." Possibly he was influenced by Governor Lew Wallace's letter to him dated March 20, 1879. Wallace, a non-Spencerian penman, used an alternative "r."

Billy's "r" switch is seen by comparing the greeting "Sir" in his March 13, 1879 and December 12, 1880 letters sent to Lew Wallace. By the latter, Billy used Wallace's "r," as seen in Wallace's own letter to Billy dated Match 20, 1879.

LEW WALLACE'S CASE LETTER R

Governor Lew Wallace used a non-Spencerian lower case "r," as seen in his March 20, 1879 letter to Billy Bonney. Billy used that version of "r" henceforth.

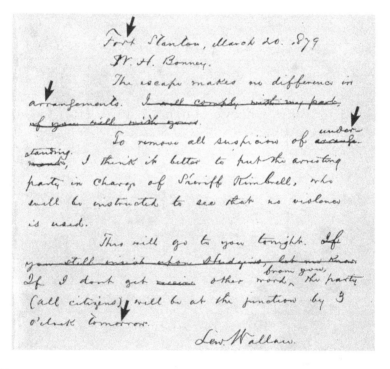

FIGURE 10: Governor Lew Wallace's March 20, 1879 letter (Indiana Historical Society, Lew Wallace Collection.)

BILLY'S EARLY LOWER CASE LETTER R

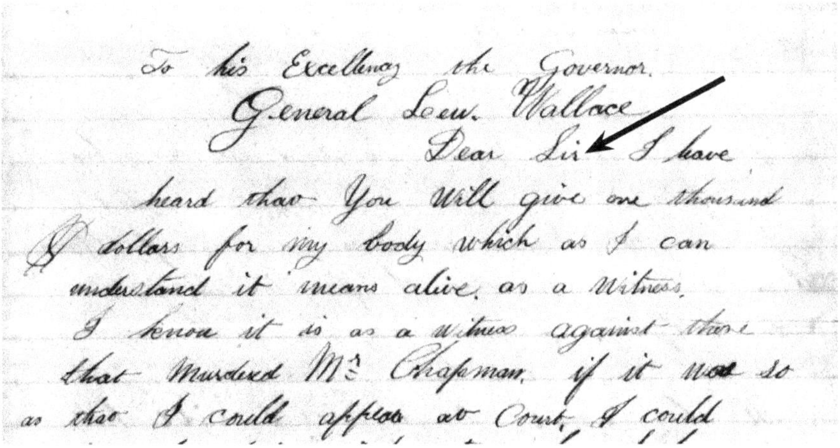
To his Excellency the Governor.
General Lew. Wallace
Dear Sir I have
heard that You will give one thousand
$ dollars for my body which as I can
understand it means alive. as a Witness.
I know it is as a witness against those
that Murdered Mr. Chapman. if it was so
as that I could appear at Court, I could

FIGURE 11: Billy Bonney's March 13, 1879. Letter to Governor Lew Wallace [APPENDIX 3]

BILLY'S LATER LOWER CASE LETTER R

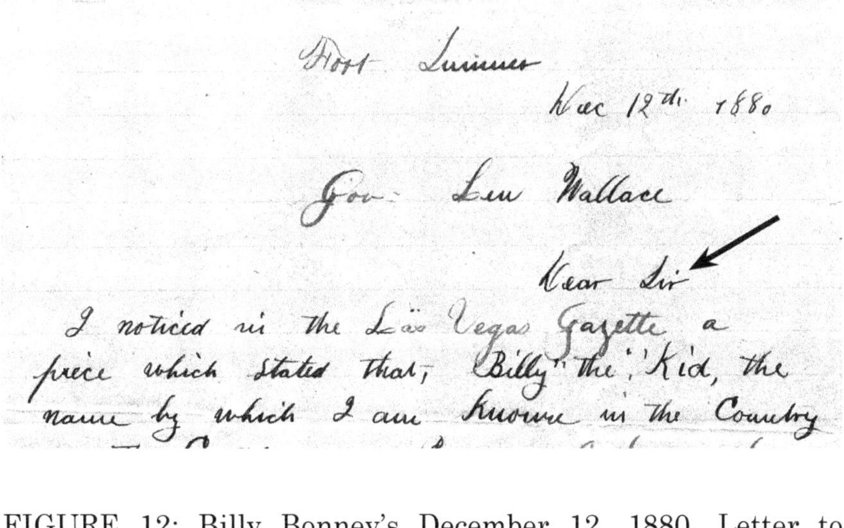
Fort Sumner
Dec 12th 1880
Gov. Lew Wallace
Dear Sir
I noticed in the Las Vegas Gazette a
piece which stated that, "Billy" the "Kid, the
name by which I am known in the Country

FIGURE 12: Billy Bonney's December 12, 1880. Letter to Governor Lew Wallace [APPENDIX 7]

BILLY BONNEY'S SIGNATURES

Billy Bonney's embellishments of the Spencerian alphabet occur most clearly in his signatures, which he used for subtle communication of his emotions and his missive's motives. They evidence practice, experimentation, and artistic goals. As can be seen in their listing on page 192, all differ somewhat.

UNITING LETTERS IN SIGNATURES

Billy's most famous signature - and the one most forged - is from his October 24, 1878 Hoyt Bill of Sale [APPENDIX 2]. It has clever joining of the initial "H" with the "B" of Bonney.

That joining trick was expanded for his March 20, 1879 letter to "Squire" Wilson [APPENDIX 4] by uniting all the capitals - though sacrificing the ideal Spencerian slant.

More awkward were Billy's signatures on his later jail letters because of his handcuffs or writing options. Examples are seen in his letters to Governor Lew Wallace of January 1, 1881 [APPENDIX 8] and March 27, 1881 [APPENDIX 11].

January 1, 1881:

March 27, 1881:

FLOURISHES IN SIGNATURES

Small flourishes exist only in Billy Bonney's signatures: for "Bonney's" terminating "y," and lead-ins to "W" for "William."

THE "Y": The "y," as in Billy's March 20, 1879 letter to "Squire" Wilson [APPENDIX 4], has a leftward puffy loop for partial underlining of his signature. That modest flourish repeats in all of Billy's signatures.

THE "W": Variable, though more showy, are Billy's starts of "W's," as seen in the grouping of all his known signatures from June 8, 1878 to March 27, 1881.

ALL KNOWN
BILLY BONNEY SIGNATURES

October 4, 1878. Signature at end of a court reporter's transcribed deposition to Investigator for the Departments of Justice and the Interior, Frank Warner Angel, about the murder of John Henry Tunstall [APPENDIX 1]

William H Bonney

October 28, 1878. Bill of Sale for a horse to Dr. Henry Hoyt [APPENDIX 2]

W H Bonney

March 13(?), 1879. Letter to Governor Lew Wallace to request a pardon [APPENDIX 3]

W. H. Bonney

March 20, 1879. Letter to Lincoln County Justice of the Peace John "Squire" Wilson about the planned pardon meeting with Governor Lew Wallace [APPENDIX 4]

W H Bonney

March 20, 1879. Letter to Governor Lew Wallace to arrange the feigned arrest for the pardon bargain [APPENDIX 5]

W H Bonney

March 24(?), 1879. The newly authenticated "Billie" letter fragment, probably to Governor Lew Wallace, giving information about Territorial outlawry with Lincoln County War references [APPENDIX 6]

Billie

December 12, 1880. Letter to Governor Lew Wallace denying personal outlawry and the murder of Jim Carlyle [APPENDIX 7]

William Bonney

January 1, 1881. First Santa Fe jail letter to Governor Lew Wallace requesting a meeting about the pardon [APPENDIX 8]

W.H.Bonney

March 2, 1881. Second Santa Fe jail letter to Governor Lew Wallace requesting a meeting about the pardon [APPENDIX 9]

Wm H Bonney

March 4, 1881. Third Santa Fe jail letter to Governor Lew Wallace requesting a meeting about the pardon [APPENDIX 10]

Wm H. Bonney

March 27, 1881. Fourth Santa Fe jail letter to Governor Lew Wallace requesting a meeting about the pardon [APPENDIX 11]

WBonney

BILLY BONNEY'S GRAMMATICAL IDIOSYNCRASIES

Though reasonably sophisticated in penmanship, Billy Bonney betrayed his limited formal education by a few, consistent, grammatical errors and misspellings. They assist in confirming a written document as his own.

INITIAL ABSENCE OF LETTER DATING

Billy appeared to be a rapid learner, realizing letter dating after his first dateless one to Governor Lew Wallace, written probably on March 13, 1879 [APPENDIX 3].

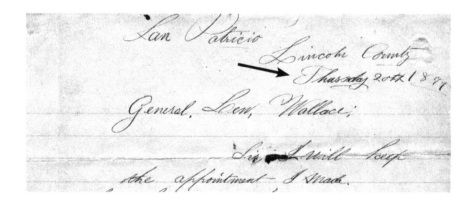

Seven days later, in Billy's March 20th letter to Governor Wallace [APPENDIX 5], he used a date - as he did henceforth.

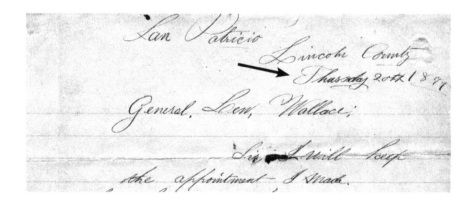

NO CAPITALIZATION AT SENTENCES' START

A consistent error is Billy Bonney's unawareness of capitalizing the first word of a sentence, as indicated in his March 13(?), 1879 letter to Governor Wallace [APPENDIX 3].

CAPITALIZATION FOR WORD EMPHASIS

Billy Bonney capitalized words for emphasis. Examples abound. Some are indicated below.

1) October 24, 1878 Hoyt Bill of Sale [APPENDIX 2]

2) March 13(?), 1879 letter to Governor Wallace [APPENDIX 3]

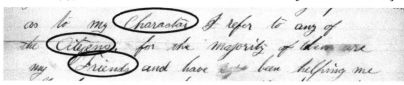

3) March 20, 1879 letter to "Squire" Wilson [APPENDIX 4]

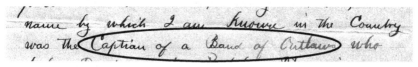

4) March 20, 1879 letter to Governor Wallace [APPENDIX 5]

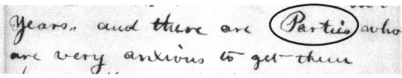

5) December 12, 1880 letter to Wallace [APPENDIX 7]

6) March 2, 1880 letter to Wallace [APPENDIX 9]

CONSISTENT SPELLING ERRORS

SOUNDING OUT FOR SPELLING

Though an excellent speller - with "indictments" correct in his first letter to Governor Lew Wallace, Billy misspelled when "sounding out" a word like *"Camul"* for "Campbell" in his December 12, 1880 letter [APPENDIX 3] - possibly hearing Texan accent for (Billy) Campbell. He also has *"Enimies"* for "Enemies" in his March 20, 1879 letter [APPENDIX 5]; and *"murderded"* in his March 13 (?), 1879 letter to Wallace.

CONSISTENCY OF ERRORS

Billy's misspellings remain consistent from early to late writings, assisting in confirmation of his authorship. *"Annser"* for "answer" is three times in his March 13, 1879 letter to Wallace [APPENDIX 3]; and is also in his jail letters to him of March 4, 1881 [APPENDIX 10] and March 27, 1881 [APPENDIX 11]. Billy also misspells *"untill,"* in his Wallace letters of March 20, 1879 and March 2, 1881.

1) March 13, 1879 letter to Wallace with *"annser"*

2) March 27, 1881 letter to Wallace with *"annser"*

CONSISTENT PUNCTUATION ERRORS

OMISSION OF PERIODS

Besides not capitalizing a sentence's first word, Billy Bonney often omitted periods. An example is shown in his March 20, 1879 letter to Lew Wallace [APPENDIX 5]; with no period between *"can depend on"* and *"I am not afraid ..."*

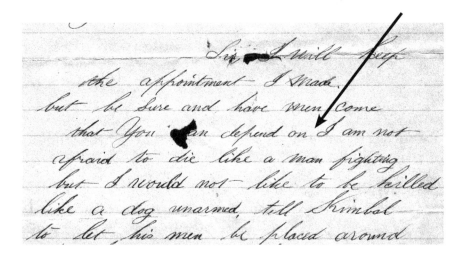

OMISSION OF QUESTION MARKS

Billy Bonney did not use question marks; as shown in his letter of March 27, 1881 to Lew Wallace [APPENDIX 11].

Anonymous Regulator Manifesto Letter

Regulator Manifesto Letter

The Regulator Manifesto letter may be Billy Bonney's first written production; but only its unattributed copy exists. Dated July 13, 1878 - ten days after Americans celebrated their Revolutionary liberation's fourth of July anniversary, and one day before sixty "McSween's," under leadership of Attorney Alexander McSween, rode into Lincoln to start the Lincoln County War freedom fight - it is signed only "*Regulator*."

It is the Regulators' clearest statement of their idealistic determination to fight Santa Fe Ring oppression; and it foreshadows Billy Bonney's post-war retaliatory stock rustling.

This Regulator Manifesto letter's recipient was Thomas Benton Catron's brother-in-law, Edgar Walz. Walz was, at the time, managing Catron's 40,000 acre cattle ranch in Lincoln County, and functioning as Catron's Santa Fe Ring presence there; along with local boss, James Dolan.

Edgar Walz, in turn, apparently found the Manifesto either sufficiently alarming or incriminating to give it to Fort Stanton's Post Adjutant - not coincidently a Ring loyalist: Second Lieutenant 9th Cavalry Millard Fillmore Goodwin.

Goodwin, in turn, took legal precautions to make its "*true copy*." First he obtained its certification in writing by recent Ring-biased Justice of the Peace David M. Easton. Concealed is that Easton was no longer a Justice of the Peace; having resigned after the Regulators killed Andrew "Buckshot" Roberts near his office at Blazer's Mill on April 4, 1878. The Dolan-Peppin side, however, continued to use Easton's voided warrants against McSweens during the Lincoln County War, while keeping secret his resignation. That sham of his still being an active official may have been used here also.

David Easton wrote on the copy's second page:

I certify that the above is a true copy of a letter received by Edgar A. Walz on July 14" 1878.

(sgd) D.W. Easton

Below Easton's certification, the apparent copyist, Thomas Blair, Captain 15th Infantry, signed and wrote: *"A true copy."*

Bottom-most was the signature of Post Adjutant Goodwin, who repeated the statement: *"a true copy."*

It is noteworthy that Edgar Walz would, by late 1878, and through 1880, become one target of Billy Bonney's guerilla rustling. Walz was also an important informer against Billy to Secret Service Operative Azariah Wild from September of 1880 to Wild's departure that December.

Though only the copy exists, the lost original was attributed to Charles Bowdre - with minimal evidence - by an early historian of the period, Maurice Garland Fulton. Fulton claimed Edgar Walz had identified handwriting as Bowdre's.

The copy is in the Washington, D.C., National Archives Records of the Adjutant General's Office.

MYSTERY AUTHORSHIP

My opinion is that Billy Bonney is the more likely author - by writing it himself or by dictation to Charlie Bowdre.

It matches Billy's zealot reputation through skirmishes before and after John Tunstall's murder; through the life insurance embezzlement case's harassment of Alexander McSween; and through Regulator killings of Frank Baker, William "Buck Morton, Sheriff William Brady, and Deputy George Hindman. Fueling it is also rage at the San Patricio massacre, only 10 days before; and fervor for the Lincoln County War Battle about to start the next day.

It also matches Billy's known literary skill and melodrama. For example, on March 20, 1879, he wrote to Governor Lew Wallace: *"I am not afraid to die like a man fighting but I would not like to be killed like a dog unarmed."*

THE REGULATOR MANIFESTO

In Camp, July 13, 1878.

Mr. Walz. Sir: - We are all aware that your brother-in-law, T.B. Catron sustains the Murphy-Kinney party, and take this method of informing you that if any property belonging to the residents of this county is stolen or destroyed, Mr. Catron's property will be dealt with as nearly as can be in the way in which the party he sustains deals with the property stolen or destroyed by them.

We returned Mr. Thornton the horses we took for the purpose of keeping the Murphy crowd from pursuing us with the promise that these horses should not again be used for that purpose. Now we know that the Tunstall estate cattle are pledged to Kinney and party. If they are taken, a similar number will be taken from your brother [sic - in-law]. It is our object and efforts to protect property, but the man who plans destruction shall have destruction measured on him. Steal from the poorest or richest American or Mexican, and the full measure of the injury you do, shall be visited upon the property of Mr. Catron. This murderous band is harbored by you as your guest, and with the consent of Catron occupies your property.

Regulator

FICTIONALIZING THE REGULATOR MANIFESTO

For *Billy and Paulita,* the creation of the Regulator Manifesto letter was fictionalized as Billy Bonney's dictation to Charles Bowdre.

In that pre-war period, the Regulators were taking refuge in the Hispanic towns of San Patricio and Picacho, close to Lincoln.

The excerpt states:

JULY 13, 1878   9:16 AM   SATURDAY

In the Picacho house of Martin Chávez, Billy, O'Folliard, and Bowdre were at a table. Men there and in San Patricio, infuriated by the massacre, were preparing for the ride into Lincoln the following day. Other Regulators guarded the adobe in which McSween still slept. Bowdre, with poised pen, said to Billy, "Yaw good with words. Ah wan' tah write Edgar Walz an' Catron 'bout how we Regalators protect people an' propahty from their Ring. An' that we'll take revenge."

Billy dictated, "Mister Walz Sir. We all know that your brother-in-law Mister Catron sustains the Dolan party. Steal or destroy property of the poorest or richest American or Mexican and the full measure of the injury you do shall be visited upon his property. REGULATORS."

Deposition to Attorney Angel

Hope Comes to Lincoln County

The Santa Fe Ring's biggest mistake was not the murder of John Henry Tunstall, but murdering a British citizen. The latter triggered England's envoy, Sir Edward Thornton, to demand an investigation by President Rutherford B. Hayes, with allegations by Tunstall's family and Attorney Alexander McSween of involvement of United States officials.

So, in May of 1878, 2 1/2 months after the crime, Attorney Frank Warner Angel was sent to New Mexico Territory as an Investigator for the Departments of Justice and the Interior.

If the Hayes administration's motive was cover-up - as is likely - they picked the wrong man. Attorney Angel was intelligent, diligent, and honest; and not only deciphered the role of the Santa Fe Ring in his stay of many months, but also sympathized with the McSween side. And he energetically amassed evidence. His final Tunstall murder report had thirty-nine depositions besides Billy Bonney's. Just before Billy, Angel listened to depositions by Tunstall-side sympathizers: Alexander McSween and Gottfried Gauss.

Deposition of Billy Bonney

Billy Bonney's deposition of June 8, 1878 represents his first recorded words and his first known writing: a signature. It also establishes a pattern for his three remaining years of life: testifying bravely, in letters and courts, for truth.

The deposition itself presents the sophisticated vocabulary, excellent recall, and clarity of description that characterize all Billy Bonney's future words.

BILLY'S MINDSET

When Billy Bonney, then 18, gave his transcribed deposition to handsome and articulate Attorney Frank Warner Angel on June 8, 1878, he likely believed that Washington simply sought the truth to enable arrest of John Tunstall's killers. After all, Investigator Angel had come on the behest of President Rutherford B. Hayes himself. There could be no reach of Santa Fe Ring influence to that level - or so the Lincoln citizens who were Billy's friends would have believed.

And Billy's new boss, Attorney Alexander McSween, was so optimistic about justice being done that he had spent days preparing almost a hundred pages of exhibits for his own long deposition, given just two days before Billy's.

By contributing his deposition, Billy also proved his mettle. Unbeknownst to Angel, he was risking his life. After Tunstall's February 18, 1878 Ring murder, Billy had lived through horrifying injustices. From February 20th to 22nd, he and Fred Waite (and briefly Town Constable Atanacio Martinez) had been incarcerated in Lincoln's dank pit jail by Ring-controlled Sheriff William Brady to block their serving Tunstall murder warrants. Then, with Regulators' determination to right the wrongs, Billy had been involved in the March and April killings of Tunstall murderers - Frank Baker, William "Buck" Morton, Sheriff William Brady, Deputy George Hindman, and Andrew "Buckshot" Roberts. In that April's Grand Jury, however, he and others had been indicted for the last three deaths.

So Billy's coming to Lincoln for that deposition, risked arrest (with certain hanging) or being shot by Ringman Lincoln County Sheriff George Peppin (present at Brady's ambush).

By that June 8, 1878, Billy was also traumatized and angry. He had lost kind John Tunstall - and his first stability since his mother's death - and had been wrenched from being a ranch owner to being a hunted indicted murderer.

On that June 8th, political tensions were also a tinder keg. The next month the Lincoln County War Battle would erupt. Alexander McSween was hiding for his life; and Sheriff Peppin was raiding Regulator stronghold, San Patricio, preliminary to leading the massacre there one month later: on July 3rd.

WITNESS TO THE DEPOSITION

Billy Bonney's deposition was under oath, and officially witnessed by the man whose role would continue in anti-Ring opposition and in Billy's life: Justice of the Peace John "Squire" Wilson. By that June 8, 1878 day, Wilson had already played a part in Tunstall's autopsy and Coroner's Jury report; had written the arrest warrants for Tunstall's killers; had deputized Billy and Fred Waite under Town Constable Atanacio Martinez to serve the murderers' warrants; and had deputized Tunstall's foreman, Dick Brewer, to form a posse to capture those killers. But Wilson had been thwarted. Ringman Governor Samuel Beach Axtell himself blocked the law by his illegal proclamation voiding Wilson's powers and outlawing Tunstall's deputized men; forcing them to become vigilantes as the Regulators.

So, justly angry, and comprehending Billy's risk-taking, "Squire" Wilson now heard and notarized the boy's deposition. By the next year, Wilson would covertly assist Billy when new hope arrived in Lincoln: replacement governor, Lew Wallace.

DEPOSITION OF JUNE 8, 1878

The Lincoln transcriptionist for Attorney Frank Warner Angel recorded Billy's words in slanted spidery script on legal-length paper, with six pages numbered 314 to 319. Then Billy signed; and Justice of the Peace Wilson witnessed. It stated:

Territory of New Mexico)
County of Lincoln)

William H. Bonney being duly sworn, deposand says, that he is a resident of said county, that on the 11th day of February A.D. 1878 he in company with Robt. A. Widenmann and Fred T. Waite went to the ranch of J.H. Tunstall on the Rio Feliz, that he and said Fred T. Waite at the time intended to go to the Rio Peñasco to take up a ranch for the purpose of farming. That the cattle on the ranch of said J.H. Tunstall were throughout the County of Lincoln, known to be the property of said Tunstall; that on the 13th of February A.D. 1878 one J.B. Matthews claiming to be Deputy Sheriff came to the ranch of said J.H. Tunstall in company with Jesse Evans, Frank Baker, Tom Hill and   Rivers, known outlaws who had been confined to the Lincoln County jail and had succeeded in making their escape, John Hurley, George Hinman,   Roberts and an Indian aka Poncearo the latter said to be the murderer of Benaito Cruz, for the arrest of the murderers of whom (Benaito Cruz) the Governor of this Territory offers a reward of $500. - Before the arrival of said J.B. Matthews, deputy Sheriff, and his posse, having been informed that said deputy sheriff and posse were going to round up all the cattle and drive them off and kill the persons at the ranch, the persons at the ranch cut portholes into the walls of the house and filled sacks with earth, so that they, the persons at the ranch, should they be attacked or their murder attempted, could defend themselves, this course being thought necessary as the sheriffs posse was composed of murderers, outlaws and desperate characters none of whom has any interest at stake in the County, nor being residents of said County. That said Matthews when within about 50 yards of the house was called to stop and advance alone and state his business, that said Matthews after arriving at the ranch said that he had come to attach the cattle and property of A.A. McSween, that said Matthews was informed that A.A. McSween had no cattle or property there, but that if he had he, said Matthews could take it. That said Matthews said that he thought some of the cattle belonging to R.M. Brewer, whose cattle were also at the ranch of J.H. Tunstall, belonged to A.A. McSween, that said Matthews was told by said Brewer that he Matthews, could round up the cattle and that he, Brewer, would help him. That said Matthews said that he would go back to Lincoln to get new instructions and if he came back to the ranch he would come back with one man. That said Matthews and his posse were then invited by R.M. Brewer to come to the house to get something to eat. -

Deponent further states that Robert A. Widenmann told R.M. Brewer and the others at the ranch, that he was going to arrest Frank Baker, Jesse Evans and Tom Hill said Widenmann having warrants for them. That said Widenmann was told by Brewer and the others at the ranch that the arrest could not be made because if it was made they, all the persons at the ranch would be killed and murdered by J.J. Dolan & Co. and their party. That Jesse Evans advanced upon said Widenmann, said Evans swinging ~~it~~ his gun and catching it cocked and pointed directly at said Widenmann. That said Jesse Evans asked said Widenmann whether he, Widenmann, was hunting for him, Evans, to which Widenmann answered that if he was looking for him, he, Evans, would find it out. Evans also asked Widenmann whether he had a warrant for him; Widenmann answered that it was his (Widenmann's) business. Evans told Widenmann, that if he ever came to arrest him (Evans) he, Evans would pick Widenmann as the first man to shoot at, to which Widenmann answered that that was all right, that two could play at that game. That during the talking Frank Baker stood near said Widenmann, swinging his pistol on his finger, catching it full cocked pointed at said Widenmann. - The persons at the ranch were R.M. Brewer, John Middleton, G. Gauss, M. Martz, R.A. Widenmann, Henry Brown, F.T. Waite, W<u>m</u> McClosky and this deponent. J.B. Matthews after eating started for Lincoln with John Hurley and Ponceano the rest of the party or posse saying they were going to the Rio Peñasco. Deponent started to Lincoln with Robt. A. Widenmann and F.T. Waite and arrived at Lincoln the same evening and again left Lincoln on the next day, February the 14<u>th</u> in company with the above named persons, having heard that said Matthews was going back to the ranch of said J.H. Tunstall with a large party of men to take the cattle and deponent and Widenmann and Waite arrived at said ranch the same day. - Deponent states that on the road to Lincoln he heard said Matthews ask said Widenmann whether any resistance would be offered if he Matthews returned to take the cattle, to which said Widenmann answered that no resistance would be offered if the cattle were left at the ranch but if an attempt was made to drive the cattle to the Indian Agency and kill them for beef as he, said Matthews had been heard to say would be done, he, said Widenmann, would do all in his power to prevent this.

Deponent further says that on the night of the 17<u>th</u> of February A.D. 1878 J.H. Tunstall arrived at the ranch and informed all the persons there that reliable information had reached him that J.B. Matthews was gathering a large party of outlaws and desperados as a posse and that said posse was coming to the ranch, the Mexicans in the party to gather up the cattle and the balance of the party to kill the persons at the ranch. It was thereupon decided that all persons at the ranch excepting G. Gauss, were to leave and W<u>m</u> McClosky was that night sent to the Rio Peñasco to inform the posse who were camped there, that they could come over and round up the cattle, count them and leave a man there to take care of them and that Mr. Tunstall would also leave a man there to help round up and count the cattle and help to take care of them, and said McClosky was also ordered to go to Martin Martz, who had left Tunstall's ranch when deponent, Widenmann and Waite returned to the town of Lincoln on the 13<u>th</u> of February, and ask him said Martz to come to the ranch of said Tunstall and aid the sheriffs posse in rounding up and counting the cattle and to stay at the ranch and take care of the cattle.

Deponent left the ranch of said Tunstall in company with J.H. Tunstall, R.A. Widenmann, R.M. Brewer, John Middleton and F.T. Waite, said Tunstall, Widenmann, Brewer, Middleton and deponent driving the loose horses, Waite driving the wagon. Said Waite took the road for Lincoln with the wagon, the rest of the party taking the trail with the horses. Deponent says that all the horses which he and party were driving, excepting 3 had been released by sheriff Brady at Lincoln, that one of these 3 horses belonged to R.M. Brewer, and another was traded by Brewer to Tunstall for one of the released horses.

Deponent further says, that when he and the party had traveled to within about 3 miles from the Rio Ruidoso he and John Middleton were in drag in the rear of the balance of the party and just upon reaching the brow of a hill they saw a large party of men coming towards them from the rear at full speed and that he and Middleton at once rode forward to inform the balance of the party of the fact. Deponent had not more than barely reached Brewer and Widenmann who were some 200 or 300 yards to the left of the trail when the attacking party cleared the brow of the hill and commenced firing at him, Widenmann and Brewer. Deponent Widenmann and Brewer rode over a hill towards another which was covered with large *rocks and trees in order to defend themselves and make a stand. But the attacking party, undoubtedly seeing Tunstall, left off pursuing deponent and the two with him and turned back to the caño in which the trail was. Shortly afterwards we heard two or three separate and distinct shots and the remark was then made by Middleton that they, the attacking party must have killed Tunstall. Middleton had in the meantime joined deponent and Widenmann and Brewer. Deponent then made the rest of his way to Lincoln in company with Robt. A. Widenmann, Brewer, Waite and Middleton stopping on the Rio Ruidoso in order to get men to look for the body of J.H. Tunstall.*

Deponent further says that neither he nor any of the party fired off either rifle or pistol and that neither he nor the parties with him fired a shot.

William H. Bonney

Sworn and subscribed before me this eighth day of June A.D. 1878.

John B. Wilson
Justice of the Peace

ANALYSIS OF THE DEPOSITION

Behind the meticulous factual renditions in Billy Bonney's deposition, is his concealment of all feelings. In his later productions, after his fame - first local then national - he allowed himself flippancy. But never would pain and anger, which must have been intense that June 8th day, be revealed.

Emotions finally exploded wordlessly in Billy's frenzied killing of Deputy Robert Olinger in his April 28, 1881 jailbreak. Olinger, on Tunstall's murder posse, in the Lincoln County War, at the Mesilla hanging trial, and as his sadistic guard at Lincoln's courthouse-jail, epitomized all the injustices.

And this deposition, though Billy was unaware, was his first step to becoming all by himself: "standing pat against the world" on Lincoln's courthouse-jail balcony during his great escape, and addressing his audience of townspeople.

Billy stated for Attorney Angel:

Territory of New Mexico)
County of Lincoln   )

> *William H. Bonney was duly sworn, deposand says, that he is a resident of said county, that on the 11ᵗʰ day of February A.D. 1878 he in company with Robt. A. Widenmann and Fred T. Waite went to the ranch of J.H. Tunstall on the Rio Feliz, that he and said Fred T. Waite at the time intended to go to the Rio Peñasco to take up a ranch for the purpose of farming.*

[AUTHOR'S NOTE: Billy, though initiating his description of Tunstall's harassment by the Ring side, slips in, poignantly and proudly, that he intended ranching on the Peñasco River along with another Tunstall employee, Fred Waite. That ranch would have been given to them under the Homestead Act by Tunstall. As a British citizen, Tunstall could not use that method of getting land. But he apparently intended to provide ranches to his employees, forming a confederation of ownership along the river. That control of water supply would yield a monopoly for his cattle ranching stretching northward to his Feliz River Ranch, and eastward to the Pecos River, uniting him with John Chisum's giant herd. That plan was a key step in ending the Ring's economic stranglehold. And, when Billy spoke these words, he had to know that Tunstall's dream, as well as his own, was lost.]

> *That the cattle on the ranch of said J.H. Tunstall were throughout the County of Lincoln, known to be the property of said Tunstall;*

[AUTHOR'S NOTE: Billy is aware of the Ring's trumped up embezzlement charge against Alexander McSween; and its attempt to seize Tunstall's property as being owned in partnership with McSween. So Billy is emphasizing Tunstall's sole ownership of the cattle. He is also beginning the explanation of the property attachment attempts by Ring-partisans which would lead to Tunstall's murder by Sheriff Brady's posse.]

> *that on the 13ᵗʰ of February A.D. 1878 one J.B. Matthews claiming to be Deputy Sheriff came to the ranch of said J.H. Tunstall in company with Jesse Evans, Frank Baker, Tom Hill and   Rivers, known outlaws who had been confined to the*

*Lincoln County jail and had succeeded in making their escape,
John Hurley, George Hinman,   Roberts and an Indian aka
Poncearo the latter said to be the murderer of Benaito Cruz,
for the arrest of murderers of whom (Benaito Cruz) the
Governor of this Territory offers a reward of $500. -*

[AUTHOR'S NOTE: Billy is here condemning mingling of so-called law enforcers in Lincoln County ("*J.B. Matthews claiming to be a Deputy Sheriff*") with outlaws who were the Ring's thug enforcers, and who had ridden with Sheriff Brady's posse to murder Tunstall. Billy is, however, also being ironic as to Jessie Evans and his boys (Baker, Hill and Rivers) and their pit jail escape. That episode went back to their September 18, 1877 theft of Tunstall's finest horses. But it is possible that Billy was with them, since that was the one month he rode with their gang. Interestingly, Gottfried Gauss, who became an indirect witness to Tunstall's murder - and who may have assisted Billy in his 1881 jailbreak - was present at that horse theft. More important, Billy may have been the one to break out Jessie and his boys from the pit jail on October 28, 1877. Even though Billy had started working for Tunstall, he may have retained some initial loyalty to Jessie. That irony, of knowing more than his words say, is seen in the newly authenticated letter of Billy's in which he calls Frank Baker "*deceased,*" when Billy was among Regulators who "made him deceased" by fatal shooting!]

[AUTHOR'S NOTE: As an aside, Billy here presents a reward of "$500" as impressive. That lets one to wonder what he thought of the astronomical sum of $1000 that Governor Wallace would place on his own head the following year.]

Before the arrival of said J.B. Matthews, deputy Sheriff, and his posse, having been informed that said deputy sheriff and posse were going to round up all the cattle and drive them off and kill the persons at the ranch, the persons at the ranch cut portholes into the walls of the house and filled sacks with earth, so that they, the persons at the ranch, should they be attacked or murder attempted, could defend themselves, this course being thought necessary as the sheriffs posse was composed of murderers, outlaws, and desperate characters none of whom has any interest at stake in the County, nor being residents of said County.

[AUTHOR'S NOTE: Billy cleverly is making clear the dangerous demeanor of local "law enforcement," building up to establishing that public officials were involved in murdering Tunstall.]

That said Matthews when within about 50 yards of the house was called to stop and advance alone and state his business, that said Matthews after arriving at the ranch said that he had come to attach the cattle and property of A.A. McSween, that said Matthews was informed that A.A. McSween had no cattle or property there, but that if he had he, said Matthews could take it.

[AUTHOR'S NOTE: Billy demonstrates clear understanding of the attachment's fake claim that McSween's property included Tunstall's by virtue of a "partnership." Billy denies that, but emphasizes Tunstall's inspirational stance of declaring that "the life of one man was worth more than all he owned" and no resistance would be offered to unjust seizure of his cattle. Billy is also describing the Ring's attempts to elicit a violent response from Tunstall's employees to justify killing him in "self-defense."]

That said Matthews said that he thought some of the cattle belonging to R.M. Brewer whose cattle were also at the ranch of J.H. Tunstall, belonged to A.A. McSween, that said Matthews was told by said Brewer that he Matthews could round up the cattle and that he, Brewer, would help him.

[AUTHOR'S NOTE: Billy gives another example of Matthews's provocation of taking cattle under false pretenses; but Matthews is again foiled in attaining a fight.]

That said Matthews said that he would go back to Lincoln to get new instructions and if he came back to the ranch he would come back with one man. That said Matthews and his posse were then invited by R.M. Brewer to come to the house to get something to eat. -

[AUTHOR'S NOTE: Matthews apparently needed to get new strategy from James Dolan, having received only foreman Dick Brewers non-confrontational hospitality.]

Deponent further states that Robert A. Widenmann told R.M. Brewer and the others at the ranch, that he was going

to arrest Frank Baker, Jesse Evans and Tom Hill said
Widenmann having warrants for them. That said Widenmann
was told by Brewer and the others at the ranch that the arrest
could not be made because if it was made they, all the persons
at the ranch would be killed and murdered by J.J. Dolan& Co.
and their party. That Jesse Evans advanced upon said
Widenmann, said Evans swinging it his gun and catching it
cocked and pointed directly at said Widenmann. That said
Jesse Evans asked said Widenmann whether he Widenmann,
was hunting for him, Evans, to which Widenmann answered
that if he was looking for him, he, Evans, would find it out.
Evans also asked Widenmann whether he had a warrant for
him; Widenmann answered that it was his (Widenmann's)
business. Evans told Widenmann, that if he ever came to arrest
him (Evans) he, Evans would pick Widenmann as the first man
to shoot at, to which Widenmann answered that that was
all right, that two could play at that game. That during the
talking Frank Baker stood near said Widenmann, swinging
his pistol on his finger, catching it full cocked pointed at said
Widenmann. -

[AUTHOR'S NOTE: Billy is establishing the dangerously
threatening behavior of Jessie and his boys. Probably Billy gave
evidence against them in Tunstall's Coroner's Jury inquest,
contributing to their warrants and 1878 Grand Jury indictments.]

The persons at the ranch were R.M. Brewer, John
Middleton, G. Gauss, M. Martz, R.A. Widenmann, Henry
Brown, F.T. Waite, Wᵐ McClosky and this deponent. J.B.
Matthews after eating started for Lincoln with John Hurley and
Ponceano the rest of the party or posse saying they were going to
the Rio Peñasco. Deponent started to Lincoln with Robt. A.
Widenmann and F.T. Waite and arrived at Lincoln the same
evening and again left Lincoln on the next day, February the
14ᵗʰ in company with the above named persons, having heard
that said Matthews was going back to the ranch of said J.H.
Tunstall with a large party of men to take the cattle and
deponent and Widenmann and Waite arrived at said ranch the
same day. -Deponent states that on the road to Lincoln he heard
said Matthews ask said Widenmann whether any resistance
would be offered if he Matthews returned to take the cattle, to

which said Widenmann answered that no resistance would be offered if the cattle were left at the ranch but if an attempt was made to drive the cattle to the Indian Agency and kill them for beef as he, said Matthews had been heard to say would be done, he, said Widenmann, would do all in his power to prevent this.

[AUTHOR'S NOTE: Billy is making clear that he, Widenmann, and Waite were functioning, of necessity, as Tunstall's bodyguards.]

Deponent further says that on the night of the 17ᵗʰ of February A.D. 1878 J.H. Tunstall arrived at the ranch and informed all the persons there that reliable information had reached him that J.B. Matthews was gathering a large party of outlaws and desperados as a posse and the said posse was coming to the ranch, the Mexicans in the party to gather up the cattle and the balance of the party to kill the persons at the ranch.

[AUTHOR'S NOTE: On this day before the murder, Billy is establishing Tunstall's knowledge of mortal risk of the murderous posse. Noteworthy, is that Billy can be observed concealing all his feelings about the upcoming most traumatic event of his life.]

It was thereupon decided that all persons at the ranch excepting G. Gauss, were to leave and Wᵐ McClosky was that night sent to the Rio Peñasco to inform the posse who were camped there, that they could come over and round up the cattle, count them and leave a man there to take care of them and that Mr. Tunstall would also leave a man there to help round up and count the cattle and help to take care of them, and said McClosky was also ordered to go to Martin Martz, who had left Tunstall's ranch when deponent, Widenmann and Waite returned to the town of Lincoln on the 13ᵗʰ of February, and ask him said Martz to come to the ranch of said Tunstall and aid the sheriffs posse in rounding up and counting the cattle and to stay at the ranch and take care of the cattle.

[AUTHOR'S NOTE: This example of Tunstall's pacifism in the face of such injustice and provocation must have profoundly affected Billy as being a new way of seeing the world. It gives insight as to how Tunstall changed Billy's life from that of a violent delinquent to becoming a rebel with a cause.]

*Deponent left the ranch of said Tunstall in company with
J.H. Tunstall, R.A. Widenmann, R.M. Brewer, John Middleton,
F.T. Waite, said Tunstall, Widenmann, Brewer, Middleton and
deponent driving the loose horses, Waite driving the wagon.
Said Waite took the road for Lincoln with the wagon, the rest of
the party taking the trail with the horses. Deponent says that all
the horses which he and party were driving, excepting 3 had
been released by sheriff Brady at Lincoln that one of these
3 horses belonged to R.M. Brewer, and the other was traded by
Brewer to Tunstall for one of the released horses. -*

[AUTHOR'S NOTE: Again Billy is meticulously establishing that
Tunstall was free of legal blame; and that his murder was without
justification. Billy accounts for all the horses, making clear that
they were immune to the attachment or accusation of its violation.]

*Deponent further says, that when he and the party had
traveled to within about 3 miles from the Rio Ruidoso he and
John Middleton were in drag in the rear of the balance of the
party and just upon reaching the brow of a hill they saw a large
party of men coming towards them from the rear at full speed
and that he and Middleton at once rode forward to inform the
balance of the party of the fact. Deponent had not more than
barely reached Brewer and Widenmann who were some 200 or
300 yards to the left of the trail when the attacking party
cleared the brow of the hill and commenced firing at him,
Widenmann and Brewer.*

[AUTHOR'S NOTE: Though he does not say it, Billy was at the
most dangerous position, possibly by choice: "drag" - the rear -
was where an attack would have occurred; and did.]

*Deponent, Widenmann and Brewer rode over a hill towards
another which was covered with large rocks and trees in order
to defend themselves and make a stand.*

[AUTHOR'S NOTE: That location for "a stand," which is the first
large hill to the right of the northward directed trail which expands
to a clearing, can still be seen about 600 yards from Tunstall's
murder site, which was to the left of the trail.]

*But the attacking party, undoubtedly seeing Tunstall, left off
pursuing deponent and the two with him and turned back to the
caño in which the trail was.*

[AUTHOR'S NOTE: Here again can be seen Billy's emotional
restraint. Did he feel guilt? It does appear that only after the fleeing
men stopped, did they realize that Tunstall was not with them.]

*Shortly afterwards we heard two or three separate and distinct
shots*

[AUTHOR'S NOTE: Exemplified here is the meticulous detail
characterizing Billy's thinking. In the Dudley Court of Inquiry the
next year, his rendition of troops shooting at them would be as
precise. Here he is knowingly describing Tunstall's fatal shots: one
through his shoulder, another a coupe de grâs to his head, and a
possible echo sounding a third - as Billy and the others may have
testified the next day at Tunstall's six man Coroner's Jury inquest.]

*and the remark was then made by Middleton that they, the
attacking party must have killed Tunstall. Middleton had in
the meantime joined deponent and Widenmann and Brewer.
Deponent then made the rest of his way to Lincoln in company
with Robt. A. Widenmann, Brewer, Waite and Middleton
stopping on the Rio Ruidoso in order to get men to look for the
body of J.H. Tunstall. -*

[AUTHOR'S NOTE: Again, Billy's emotional restraint is evident.]

*Deponent further says that neither he nor any of the party
fired off either rifle or pistol and that neither he nor the parties
with him fired a shot.*

[AUTHOR'S NOTE: Lack of provocation is Billy's message. But did
survivor's guilt remain with him always?]

William H. Bonney

[AUTHOR'S NOTE: This is Billy Bonney's first known signature,
and is laboriously out of practice. Conceivably, he last wrote
Spencerian script when 15 ½, in Silver City. And he chose "*William
H. Bonney*" from his possibilities of William Henry McCarty, Henry
Antrim, or Billy Bonney.]

FIRST BETRAYAL OF BILLY

There was no way that the hopeful Lincoln citizens, including Billy, could know that Frank Warner Angel's investigation was a sham - possibly Angel himself was unaware until forced to make this conclusion covering up the Ring:

> *After diligent inquiry and examination of a great number of witnesses, I report that the death of John H. Tunstall was not brought about through the lawless and corrupt conduct of United States officials in the Territory of New Mexico."*

And the Washington, D.C. officials, nevertheless, took no chances. Angel's reports were concealed, and only published seventy-five years after Billy's killing when found in the National Archives by the great historian of the Lincoln County War period, Frederick Nolan. He cited them, in 1956, in his *New Mexico Historical Review* article: "Sidelight on the Tunstall Murder."

And Billy's fate, though he could not know, was already sealed that June 8, 1878 by what would become his continuing stance as the Ring's gadfly. The indictments he already had, along with other Regulators, for murders of Andrew "Buckshot" Roberts, Sheriff William Brady, and Deputy George Hindman, would bring him, in three years, to Mesilla, before Ring-partisan, hanging judge, Warren Bristol. Billy's sentence there would justify his homicide, 3 months and 5 days later, by Sheriff Pat Garrett, in the name of the law. And Billy would be the only person to be punished for Lincoln County War crimes.

But entering the fight for justice that June 8th, may have stimulated Billy to bone up on his Spencerian writing skills. All his future signatures would be improved over the clumsy one he provided for his Angel deposition. In fact, the next one, on a bill of sale almost five months later, would be his most beautiful and creative, and end up being his most forged.

Bill of Sale to
Henry Hoyt

THE REBEL RUSTLER

Eight months after his life fell apart with John Tunstall's murder, about five after his deposition to Investigator Frank Warner Angel yielded no justice, and almost three after Lincoln County War defeat, Billy Bonney, almost 19, wrote a bill of sale for a horse on October 28, 1878 [APPENDIX 2].

BILLY'S MINDSET

With unhealable traumatic wounds of multiple and horrible losses and futile rage at iniquity, by October 28, 1878, Billy Bonney was starting anew by reverting to his Arizona rustling ways and stealing horses. He had to earn money. Traitorous cattle king John Chisum had reneged on paying the Regulators. But Billy also had a political agenda. It was guerilla rustling.

Riding with past Regulator friends, Charlie Bowdre and Tom O'Folliard - and initially with "Doc" Scurlock and John Middleton, who soon left the Territory - Billy was adhering to the "Regulator Manifesto" of July 13, 1878 by wreaking retribution on Ring head, Thomas Benton Catron, through his brother-in-law, Edgar Walz, then managing Catron's 40,000 acre ranch in Lincoln County's Carrizozo.

Another rustling target was the ranch of Charles Fritz, whose deceased brother, Emil Fritz, had been the excuse for Ring harassment of Attorney Alexander McSween by the life insurance policy embezzlement case which culminated in the murders of Tunstall and McSween. Emil Fritz had also been a founder of Lincoln's House, Ring headquarters for local bosses: Lawrence Murphy, John Riley, and James Dolan.

TEXAS STOCK OUTLET AND BILLY'S REPUTATION

The stock outlet for Billy's fledgling rustling business of late 1878 was Tascosa, Texas. That was where he met the man for whom the bill of sale was written: Dr. Henry Hoyt.

That document yields a riddle: Why did Hoyt keep it? The horse was merely a gift from a scruffy teenager. If it was originally stolen, that was common. And Hoyt often got horses. Though a medical doctor, he was then working as a mail rider.

The answer may be the first clue to the historical importance of that bill of sale: it implies that, by late 1878, Billy Bonney had a "reputation" extending to Texas.

Why would Billy get one? My guess is that the Santa Fe Ring was taking notice. Unlike their other opponents, Billy had stayed; and he eluded capture. As a Regulator, he had helped kill their partisans: Sheriff William Brady topping that list. And Billy was testifying against them, not only by his Angel deposition, but likely in Tunstall's Coroner's Jury, helping to get indictments in the 1878 Grand Jury. And he was a freedom fighting hero to oppressed Anglo and Hispanic citizens.

What was the reputation? The Ring had only one for opponents: "outlaw."

A Charlie Siringo may have spread that outlaw reputation in Tascosa. Henry Hoyt knew Siringo as LX Ranch foreman. Siringo knew Ma'am Jones's family at Seven Rivers - from which had ridden the Seven Rivers boys against Tunstall and McSween. By 1920, Charlie Siringo capitalized on his minimal connection to Billy by writing *The History of Billy the Kid*.

In 1878, when Henry Hoyt met Billy selling horses in Tascosa, there was mutual admiration. In 1927, when Billy was the famous "Billy the Kid," Hoyt wrote on a copy of his Bill of Sale about him: *"He was a remarkable character."*

That was a key: By late 1878, Billy stood out: charismatic, brilliant, audacious, and a rising outlaw star. Of course, the Bill of Sale was a wonderful souvenir for the young doctor!

By 1929, Hoyt's prescience paid off: based on owning that Bill of Sale, he justified writing to famous Lew Wallace's grandson and publishing a book, *A Frontier Doctor* - commercially viable mostly for his anecdotes about Billy as Billy the Kid, and about how he got that Bill of Sale.

THE HOYT BILL OF SALE

Reflecting the "Regulator Manifesto," the Hoyt Bill of Sale seems to be Billy Bonney's insider joke. And it reveals much about him: from handwriting, content, and signature.

The horse in question is called a "sorrel," which is a flashy chestnut red with white mane and tail. Hoyt states in his book that its name was "Dandy Dick." That name says it all.

Dandy Dick was murdered Sheriff William Brady's horse, possibly once a gift from James Dolan (as had been Brady's 1,000 acre Walnut Grove Ranch outside Lincoln). After Brady's killing, the horse was at Ringman ranches of Edgar Walz or Charles Fritz. Stolen Dandy Dick was, for Billy, "spoils of war."

A bill of sale, thus, was needed to protect Hoyt. But it deviously gives away the audacious theft while taunting the master's killing by providing precise brands. One can almost see Billy sneering. In this document, Billy began cocky irony that would persist in his writings as anger's substitute.

Surprisingly, Billy used correct legalese. Besides giving date, location, and buyer, he words a contract. One can only guess how he learned. But Exhibits provided by Alexander McSween to Frank Warner Angel for his own deposition have: *Know all persons by these presents.* Possibly Billy, privately reading over his own deposition at the Lincoln courthouse prior to signing it, found and read McSween's.

Also correct is Billy's addition of signed witnessing at the end by George Howard and James McMasters, owners of the store and saloon where the document was apparently written.

As to its penmanship, it is Billy's most flamboyant, and his only writing attempting Spencerian shading, though his nib caught and splattered ink at *"Branded"* and *"B"* of the brand.

In addition, after his Angel deposition's clumsy signature, Billy must have practiced. The Bill of Sale has a clever and beautiful innovation. He is now *"W HBonney;"* the "W" starting with a tiny flourish and ending with a sweep integrating it with the "H." Best of all, with very complex penwork and artistry, the "H" fuses with the "B" of "Bonney." It would become Billy's most forged signature.

Billy wrote:

Tascoso Texas
*Thursday Oct 24*th
1878

Know all persons by these presents that I do
hereby Sell and deliver to Henry F. Hoyt one Sorrel
Horse Branded BB on left hip and other indistinct
Branded on Shoulders for the sum of Seventyfive
$ dollars in hand received
W HBonney

ANALYSIS OF BILL OF SALE

Billy uses business-like wording and excellent vocabulary.

Know all persons by these presents

[AUTHOR'S NOTE: This is the correct legalese for a contract.]

that I do hereby Sell and deliver

[AUTHOR'S NOTE: Precisely, both "*sell and deliver*" are included; but as is his style, Billy capitalized the crucial word: "*Sell.*"]

to Henry F. Hoyt

[AUTHOR'S NOTE: Precise Billy has even questioned Hoyt about his middle initial.]

one Sorrel Horse Branded BB on left hip and other indistinct Branded on Shoulder

[AUTHOR'S NOTE: Since brands are recorded, this slyly identifies the horse as dead Sheriff Brady's. And "*other indistinct*" brand is teasing, since rustlers blurred past brands, then added their own. So Billy is saying that prior to Brady, Dolan had stolen the horse!]

for the sum of Seventyfive $ dollars in hand received.

[AUTHOR'S NOTE: Again playful, this is an astronomical sum.]

W HBonney

WHERE TO NEXT?

However hard his life had been to that day of October 28, 1878, Billy showed his plucky resilience by that Bill of Sale. He is exuberantly writing and exercising magnanimity's power: a boy gifting a doctor with a fine horse. One can guess that the sale of Billy's other stolen horses had gone well. (Tascosa was having a horse shortage in this period.) And grateful Hoyt even gave Billy a gold watch with a hair chain as friendly recompense.

In the next two years, Billy would rely more on New Mexico Territory repositories for his stolen horses and cattle; though their numbers were petty compared to major Territorial rustlers like John Kinney out of Mesilla.

Billy's main receivers appear to have been the Pecos River area Bosque Grande Ranch of counterfeiter, Dan Dedrick; Dedrick's two brothers' White Oaks livery; and the Tularosa ranch of Pat Coghlan. Amusingly, when Billy would later report on rustling and outlawry to new governor, Lew Wallace, he would omit all their names - giving other criminals instead!

In this same period of the Hoyt Bill of Sale, Billy was also supporting himself with gambling; the popular game, in his day, being draw poker. He rode a circuit from Fort Sumner and Portales (where he hoped to make a way station with fellow Regulator Charlie Bowdre) to Anton Chico and Las Vegas.

One can assume that Billy's card game was not fair-and-square. His tintype hints at methodology, since on his left pinky he displays a "gambler's ring." Though passed off as jewelry in his day, it was a "shiner;" polished mirror-like on top, but rolled to the palm when playing, to read cards dealt over it. With Billy's intelligence, he would be able to recall each player's hand. And, by 1876, indexes - the number and suite on card corners - had been introduced, making that reading easier.

That this outlaw life-style was not what Billy wanted long-term, is evidenced by his letters - only 4½ months away - to Governor Lew Wallace, in which he proposes to risk all so that he can re-enter society free of the legal obstacle of his Lincoln County War murder indictments.

Governor Wallace's Amnesty Proclamation

WRITING A TALE OF THE CHRIST

When new Territorial Governor, Lew Wallace, 51, arrived in New Mexico on October 1, 1878 he was famous and unhappy. The fame came from his high-profile Civil War career as a Major General, his role as prosecuting attorney in the Abraham Lincoln murder trial, and his status as a best-selling author of an historical novel named *The Fair God.*

He was unhappy because his ambition had been for an ambassadorship to exotic Turkey, to add first-hand color for his book in progress: *Ben-Hur-A Tale of the Christ.* He was also unhappy because his patrician wife, Susan, hated dusty adobe-built Santa Fe, calling it one "ugly brickyard."

Lew Wallace was also a man under pressure, having been appointed by President Rutherford B. Hayes to end the Lincoln County "troubles." And he would learn that the controlling political cabal of the Santa Fe Ring had its own agenda for him. Not irrelevantly, his neighbor in a law office at the east side of the plaza was Attorney Thomas Benton Catron himself.

Lew Wallace also had one primary interest: himself. So, through the remainder of 1878, he ignored Lincoln County, and set about repairing the long-neglected, huge, 17th century Palace of the Governors, in which were his office and family apartments. And he busily penned his tale of the Christ.

Pathetically, the Lincoln County citizens must have seen Lew Wallace as the coming of their own savior; especially with his following on the heals of fired Ring-partisan Governor Samuel Beach Axtell. They even had a sympathetic, honest, Lincoln County Sheriff, George Kimbrell. And "Squire" Wilson had stayed on as Justice of the Peace. Active too, as jailor and community leader, was Juan Patrón. And Tom Catron had resigned as U.S. Attorney ten days after Wallace arrived.

UPDATE TO WASHINGTON

Lew Wallace, with his blessed life - except for criticisms about Shiloh, which he disputed - was an optimist with abundant self-confidence. He had made clear to President Rutherford B. Hayes and to his Washington, D.C. liaison and confidant, Secretary of the Interior Carl Schurz, that he could end the Lincoln County strife within six months of his arrival.

Wallace also appears to have anticipated a solution free of his own wasting time delving into specifics. All indication is that he ignored the notebook given him by Investigator Frank Warner Angel listing Santa Fe Ringmen. In addition - though that may have been a Washington manipulation - there is no indication that he ever read Frank Warner Angel's reports.

WRITING TO CARL SCHURZ

Looking back at his whole career, one can call Lew Wallace heavy-handed and authoritarian. In New Mexico Territory, his plan for "peace" was declaration of martial law, rounding up of troublemakers by troops, and hanging many - as he had attempted in Cincinnati during the Civil War. Prosecuting Abraham Lincoln's accused murderers, he achieved hanging even of John Wilkes Booth's innocent landlady, Mrs. Surratt.

So Wallace proposed martial law to Carl Schurz as follows:

Santa Fe, New Mexico.   *October 5, 1878.*

Hon. C. Schurz, Secretary Interior Department. Washington, D.C.

As to the basis of the request which I have to prefer relative to affairs in the county of Lincoln in this Territory, I beg attention to the following reports.

(No. 1 - Dudley's to Hatch, September 29, 1878. No. 2 - Sherman's, Oct. 4, 1878. No. 3 - Bristol's, Oct. 4, 1878.)

* * *

These papers are all official, and disclose plainly the condition of the county. With no organized militia in the Territory or arms belonging to it; with the court closed, the sheriff shut up in the fort, the Marshal unable to make arrests, the good people unable to protect themselves, the regulars fixed to their posts by orders necessitated by Act of Congress, June 18, 1878, I am powerless to maintain the peace or remedy the unhappy state of affairs in the section referred to. In my judgment nothing remains for me to do except call upon the President to exercise his constitutional authority, and declare the existence of insurrection in the county of Lincoln, place the county without loss of time under martial law, suspend the writ of habeas corpus therein, and appoint a military commission to come and hold sessions there for the trial and punishment of offenders. In no other way can citizens be made safe in person and property. The Legislature of the Territory is not assembled, nor can it be in time to accomplish any quick result; no doubt it would unite with me in this request. I am loath to put such a mortification upon such a high spirited people; at the same time I do not hesitate to charge the necessity for it to the aforesaid Law, by which the regulars in the Territory are forbidden as posse comitatii.

The proclamation of the President should be limited to a time when the militia of the Territory can be organized and armed. By mail today I send requisition for the quota of arms due.

I suggest obtaining the active co-operation of the Texas rangers on their side of the line. Doubtless the Texas State authorities will be glad to join the movement. Their combination with the regulars on this side will bring permanence of peace, by stamping out the robber element and breaking up their corrals and depots of plunder. The great need is a few rugged examples.

I send this by telegraph, because to wait on the mails will but further time for outrage and murder.

Lew. Wallace,
Governor of New Mexico.

THE RING MAKES ITS MOVE

The Ring sized up Lew Wallace well. As he planned Palace repairs, they misled him about "real" sources of the "troubles": outlaws, who happened to be their Lincoln County War opponents - including Billy Bonney.

FIRST MENTION OF THE KID TO WALLACE

The *"Marshal"* in Wallace's October 5th letter Carl Schurz was U.S. Marshal John Sherman in Santa Fe. The day before, Sherman had written to Wallace, becoming the first public official to identify Billy Bonney; meaning that by his fourth day in office, Wallace knew of *"W*m *H. Antrim alias Kid alias Bonny,"* a most-wanted outlaw. U.S. Marshal Sherman wrote:

Office of the United States Marshall,
TERRITORY OF NEW MEXICO.

Santa Fe, Oct 4th *1878*

Hon Lew Wallace
    Gov New Mexico
Sir:
        I have the honor to acknowledge the receipt of your favor of the 3rd inst requesting a statement of the facts relative to certain information received by you, that of terrorism now existing in Lincoln County N.M. had prevented me from executing certain warrants, regularly issued upon indictments, found in the proper Court, against residents of that County & placed in my hands as United States Marshal for official action.
        *In reply I beg to state that I have such warrants for Charles Bowdry, J.G. Scurlock, **W**m **Antrim alias Kid alias Bonny.** Steven Stevens,   Scroggins, George Coe, John Middleton, Henry Brown and   Waite, residents of Lincoln Co, charged with the murder of William Roberts, which I am powerless to execute owing to the disturbed condition of affairs in that County -*

resulting from the acts of a desperate class of men that now control it, in such force as wholly to paralyze the efforts of its law abiding citizens.

In that County two contending factions seem to have attracted to their respective standards a lawless body of armed men who by pursuing a merciless system of retaliation and by committing murder in its most revolting form in cold blood and with reckless disregard of human life that would disgrace savages, have either driven out of that County or frightened into abject submission, the remaining inhabitants, who having had neither sympathy with nor interest in, the causes that led to the present deplorable condition there, - have in striving to avoid acting with either faction, been alternatively the victims of both.

One of my deputy marshals William Brady, who was also Sheriff of Lincoln Co was deliberately assassinated at mid-day while passing along the public stretch within fifty yards of the Courthouse of that County and tho' since then I have personally visited the scene of these outrages and have endeavored by every means in my power both in person and by deputy, to execute the process of the Court, I regret to say that I find myself unable to make arrests there with the civil power under my control. It is impossible for me to be personally present in that County at all times, and since the death of Brady I have not been able to find a reliable deputy who, with the feeble force I can place at his disposal as a posse, will risk his life, to make such arrests in the face of the resistance offered by the well armed and organized desperados who now infest that County.

The Militia of New Mexico, being wholly without organization, no immediate assistance from that source can be expected and in my judgment there is now no means of enforcing the law in that County without aid from US troops.

I have the honor to be
Your very obedient Serv
John Sherman Jr.
U.S. Marshal

WALLACE'S SIMPLE SOLUTION

Besides martial law and hanging, Lew Wallace liked the grand gesture of Amnesty Proclamations. And in New Mexico Territory, in which everyone appeared to be accusing someone of crimes - in which he took no interest - the solution appeared to be to pardon everyone. Presumably, courts would happily not be clogged with litigation, and the accused would be relieved to get on with their mundane lives. Because complaints had also been against the military - for marching on Lincoln - Wallace threw troops in also.

On November 13, 1878, forty-four days after arriving, Governor Wallace printed his "Proclamation," in Spanish and English, and in newspapers. Its result would be unexpected and irritating to him.

But in four months, his "Proclamation" would initiate his unusual relationship with an unusual teenager: Billy Bonney, not included in its offers of amnesty because of having been already indicted for three Lincoln County War period murders; and being eager to avoid the next step in the legal progression of "undergoing pains and penalties consequent upon sentence."

Lew Wallace, thinking to end Lincoln County problems, instead opened a Pandora's box of other problems on that November 13, 1878, when he printed for all to read:

PROCLAMATION BY THE GOVERNOR

For the information of the people of the United States, and of the citizens of New Mexico in especial, the undersigned announces that the disorders lately prevalent in Lincoln County in said Territory, have been happily brought to an end. Persons having business and property interests therein, and who are themselves peaceably disposed, may go to and from that County without hindrance or molestation. Individuals resident there, but who have been driven away, or who, from choice, sought safety elsewhere, are invited to return, under assurance that ample measures have been taken, and are now and will be continued in force, to make them secure in person and property. And that the people of Lincoln County may be helped more speedily to the management of their civil affairs, as contemplated by law, and to induce them to lay aside forever the divisions and feuds which, by national notoriety, have been so prejudicial to their locality and the whole Territory, the undersigned, by virtue of authority in him vested, further proclaims a general pardon for misdemeanors and offenses committed in the said County of Lincoln against the laws of said Territory in connection with the aforesaid disorders, between the first day of February 1878, and the date of this proclamation.

And it is expressly understood that the foregoing pardon is upon the conditions and limitations following;

It shall not apply except to officers of the United States Army stationed in the said County during the said disorders, and to persons, who, at the time of the commission of the offense or misdemeanor of which they may be accused, were, with good intent, resident citizens of the said Territory, and who shall have hereafter kept the peace, and conducted themselves in all respects as becomes good citizens.

Neither shall it be pleaded by any person in bar of conviction under indictment now found and returned for any such crimes or misdemeanors, nor operate the release of any party undergoing pains and penalties consequent upon sentence heretofore had for any crime or misdemeanor.

In witness whereof I hereunto set my hand and caused the seal of the Territory of New Mexico to be affixed.

SEAL

Done in the city of Santa Fé, this 13th day of November, A.D. 1878.

Lewis Wallace,

By the Governor,
W.G. Ritch,
Secretary

Billy's First Letter
to Lew Wallace

THE "ANNULY" BARGAIN

In March of 1879, Billy Bonney began to write letters to Governor Lew Wallace which he hoped would change his life. They did, but not as he intended. He had been stimulated by Wallace's "Proclamation" about amnesty, by certainty that Wallace understood Lincoln County War issues, and by the astronomical reward of $1000 Wallace had put on his head.

BILLY'S MINDSET

Gambler Billy had an ace up his sleeve: knowing the governor was under pressure after the murder of Attorney Huston Chapman the prior month, on February 18th; and Billy was not only its eye-witness, but the killers were his old Ring nemeses: James Dolan and Jessie Evans (along with Jessie's new gang member, Billy Campbell).

Also, the Chapman murder was infuriatingly on the first anniversary of Tunstall's killing by the same men; and five months after Alexander McSween's murder, also by them.

Chapman himself was a Regulator hero, retained by widow, Susan McSween, to prosecute Colonel Dudley for the Lincoln County War's murder and arson. And Billy - initiated by his Angel deposition - may have already offered Chapman his eye-witness testimony to Dudley's shooting soldiers for any future civil or military action of his against that commander.

Also, that night of February 18, 1879 signaled Billy's childhood's end. Starting with his peace meeting with Dolan and the others, it ended with Chapman's killing and mutilation by fire (so reminiscent of McSween's). Thus, that murder - and contemplated testifying against those murderers - would end forever any possibility of peace between Billy and the Ring.

So, by March of 1879, Billy, hardened by grim tests and regaled as the people's hero, emerged with cocky conviction of being any man's equal. And with the moral core retained from Tunstall, he also wanted to reclaim life as a law-abiding citizen; as he had just attempted in that Dolan peace meeting.

FIRST LETTER TO LEW WALLACE: MARCH 13(?), 1879

There was reason for Billy Bonney to trust Lew Wallace. Wallace represented the McSweens' single Lincoln County War victory: removal of Ringman governor, Samuel Beach Axtell. Anyone would reasonably assume that Wallace understood the political issues that had made him a mid-term replacement.

In the month after Huston Chapman's killing, on about March 13th, Billy wrote a letter to that new governor proposing his testifying against the man's murderers in exchange for the annulling of his Lincoln County War murder indictments.

Billy's ironic wit would audaciously translate Wallace's reward for him of $1000 (presumably dead or alive as an outlaw-murderer) to its being merely a feeler for him as an informer in exchange for clemency! Essentially Billy wanted to include himself in Wallace's Amnesty Proclamation.

Used was also his sly manipulativeness, which had enabled Billy's homeless survival since 14½. He played to Wallace's guilt, knowing, like others in Lincoln, about Attorney Chapman's complaint letters to him about neglecting the beleaguered citizens. Now Billy could save the day.

One can assume Billy's great care in creating his letter; all his abilities and charms came into play. Everything depended on that two-sided sheet, where his brilliance shone with even "indictments" spelled correctly.

Inculcated with Spencerian philosophy linking presentation to character - though on the run from bounty hunters after that $1000 reward, and from soldiers sent out by Wallace - Billy strove for an ideal letter, obtaining fine stationery embossed with the national capital building.

How did he get the necessary paper, pen, ink, and desk? Later, in discussion of Billy's newly discovered letter - fourth in his March 1879 set to Lew Wallace - I will hypothesize as to where he was when writing and who were the people assisting him in his courageous plan for personal freedom and convicting Ringmen.

Billy wrote, with characteristic lack of capitalizing at start of sentences and capitalizing for emphasis, as follows:

> *To his Excellency the Governor*
> *General Lew Wallace*
> *Dear Sir I have heard*
> *that You will give one thousand $ dollars for*
> *my body which as I can understand it means alive as a*
> *witness. I know it is as a witness against those that*
> *murderd Mr Chapman. if it was so as that I could appear*
> *at court, I could give the desired information. but I have*
> *indictments against me for things that happened in the*
> *late Lincoln County War and am afraid to give up because*
> *my Enimies would Kill me the day Mr Chapman was*
> *murderded I was in Lincoln, at the request of good*
> *citizens to meet Mr J.J. Dolan to meet as Friends, so as to*
> *be able to lay aside our arms and go to Work. I was*
> *present when Mr Chapman was murderded and know*
> *who did it and if it was not for those indictments I would*
> *have made it clear before now if it is in your power to*
> *Anully those indictments I hope you will do so so as to give*
> *me a chance to explain. please send me an annser telling*
> *me what you can do You can send annser by bearer*
>
> *I have no wish to fight any more indeed I have*
> *not raised an arm since your proclamation. As to my*
> *Character I refer to any of the Citizens. for the majority of*
> *them are my Friends and have been helping me all they*
> *could. I am called Kid Antrim but Antrim is my*
> *stepfathers name.*
>
> *Waiting an annser I remain*
> *Your Obedient Servant*
> *W.H. Bonney*

ANALYSIS OF THE LETTER

That March 13(?), 1879 letter, the first and most famous of Billy Bonney's, is dated hypothetically, because the actual date is missing - as if he was unaware that dating was standard. He never made that mistake again.

The letter has tremendous value for analyzing Billy - and ultimately Lew Wallace - based not only on its actual words, but its context, innuendos, intents, and results. One can assume that even its creation was transformative for Billy.

First, Billy wrote as an unabashed equal to the highest official in the Territory - one appointed by the president.

Next was the governor's heady reward, probably the highest Billy ever knew. At $1000, it would be $10,000 in our day; giving this 19 year old a first measure of his rebel fame and his enemies' fear (since he saw himself as a Regulator soldier, or *"fighter"* as he put it). Someone had felt he was worth that sum. He may have wondered if his informer to Wallace was Ring boss, James Dolan, afraid of his fomenting another uprising. Or was Wallace's informer the Ring's spy, Saturnino Baca, past tenant of the McSweens, who, present in the Lincoln County War with his family, was used as excuse to bring in Dudley's soldiers; thus, playing a crucial role in the McSweens' defeat?

And Lew Wallace had come to Lincoln; and though available to Dolan and Baca lies, was seen as more amenable to McSween side's provable truths. To Billy, writing his letter to Governor Wallace meant victory could be attained at last.

So he played all his cards.

The letter displayed his best Spencerian penmanship, but was self-effacingly signed *"W.H. Bonney"* - contrasting the Hoyt Bill of Sale's flamboyant *"W HBonney"* - and humbled further by complimentary closing of *"Your Obedient Servant."* But important words are capitalized assertively and aggressively.

Charm contrasts brash confidence. To the governor himself, Billy impudently reinterprets the reward, saying: *"You will give one thousand $ dollars for my body which as I can understand it means alive as a Witness;"* thus, converting the huge sum to representation of his own great value - alive!

Cleverly and seductively Billy uses correct legalese by requesting the governor to "annul" (spelled "*annuly*") his indictments; rather than to "pardon" - technically used for those already convicted. He also puts his crimes in the correct context for the actual Amnesty Proclamation: as being committed during Lincoln County War fighting (not randomly). And he happens to omit that all were for murder!

ANALYSIS OF THE LETTER OF MARCH 13(?), 1879

To his Excellency the Governor
General Lew Wallace
Dear Sir I have heard
that You will give one thousand $ dollars for my body

[AUTHOR'S NOTE: Billy begins with treating the astounding reward like an advertisement; but displays fearlessness, since he recognizes "*for my body*" - as in "dead or alive" - but makes an ironic play on the word "body" to begin his audacious negotiation.]

which as I can understand it means alive as a witness.

[AUTHOR'S NOTE: Here is Billy's first switcheroo; taking control irrespective of Wallace's status as the Territory's highest official.]

I know it is as a witness against those that murderd Mr Chapman.

[AUTHOR'S NOTE: Here is Billy's second switcheroo: taking his own "*understanding*" of "*witness*" to be fact. His expertise in a gambler's Three Card Monte pays off!]

if it was so as that I could appear at court, I could give the desired information.

[AUTHOR'S NOTE: Billy presents the bait for the pardon deal.]

but I have indictments against me for things that happened in the late Lincoln County War and am afraid to give up because my Enimies would Kill me

[AUTHOR'S NOTE: Appealing to sympathy: he has enemies who would kill him. He needs the powerful man's protection.]

The day Mr Chapman was murderded I was in Lincoln, at the request of good citizens

[AUTHOR'S NOTE: Here is a character recommendation and also an advertisement of his power: citizens "*requested*" him to come.]

to meet Mr J.J. Dolan

[AUTHOR'S NOTE: Billy is covering his bases in case Wallace is aware of James Dolan's role as the Ring boss.]

to meet as Friends, so as to be able to lay aside our arms and go to Work.

[AUTHOR'S NOTE: This refers to the Lincoln County War as: "*lay aside arms.*" So the "*good citizens*" felt *his, Billy's*, declaring peace was important. And Billy makes clear his motive of going back to "*work*": as demanded in the Amnesty Proclamation.]

I was present when Mr Chapman was murderded and know who did it and if it was not for those indictments I would have made it clear before now

[AUTHOR'S NOTE: This is the hook for the pardon deal.]

if it is in your power to Anully those indictments I hope you will do so so a to give me a chance to explain.

[AUTHOR'S NOTE: The actual annulling deal is Capitalized (though misspelled): and is the correct legal word for canceling indictments - pardon is after sentencing.]

please send me an annser telling me what you can do You can send annser by bearer

[AUTHOR'S NOTE: This is assertive facilitating, demonstrating confidence in his loyal bearers, who would not betray his location.]

I have no wish to fight any more

[AUTHOR'S NOTE: Do not miss that again, by *"fight,"* Billy is referring to the Lincoln County War and its aftermath. He does not see himself as an outlaw, but as a soldier.]

indeed I have not raised an arm since your proclamation. as to my Character I refer to any of the Citizens,

[AUTHOR'S NOTE: Here again are character references.]

for the majority of them are my Friends and have been helping me all they could.

[AUTHOR'S NOTE: This implies that he is the people's champion. By March 4, 1881, that becomes a threat of jail rescue: *"I guess they mean to Send me up without giving me any Show but they will have a nice time doing it. I am not entirely without friends."*]

I am called Kid Antrim but Antrim is my stepfathers name.

[AUTHOR'S NOTE: Billy was known by various aliases at this time, but he is making this odd clarification for Wallace: attributing *"Antrim"* to his rejecting step-father, who had abandoned him to homelessness after his mother's death. Since that is irrelevant to his clemency plea, it appears an unconscious desire to define himself as not an Antrim, but as an orphan. It appears to be a reaching out to Wallace as another, idealized father-figure. And it marks the start of Billy's tragic obsession with the man.]

Waiting for an annser I remain
Your Obedient Servant,

[AUTHOR'S NOTE: Cautious humility is expressed by *"Obedient servant."*]

W.H. Bonney

[AUTHOR'S NOTE: Under five months after Billy's flamboyant Hoyt Bill of Sale signature, this signature is cautiously humble and conservative.]

A FANTASIZED ALLIANCE

This first letter of Billy Bonney to Governor Lew Wallace was a big gamble. Billy certainly knew that the reward's actual focus was "body." He was worth "$1000" to the Ring dead. There was no surety that Wallace would not set a trap for his hanging arrest. Billy had to know that danger. The letter measured his desire for a law-abiding life.

That Billy took this course, has moving implications. By March of 1879, most Regulators had fled; either to distant areas of the Territory like the Coe Cousins: or to the states, like Fred Waite, Jim French, John Middleton, Henry Brown, and Josiah Scurlock. When Billy ultimately did face these murder indictments, the defendant list was long. Only he was there to prosecute. Thus, stubbornly and righteously in this letter, Billy, homeless so long, is asking the governor to permit him to stay without fear in the place he finally considered home.

And for a boy drifting since early adolescence, Lincoln County's Anglo and Hispanic communities of which he was now a part, as well as his involvement with the Maxwell family and Paulita, must have seemed worth the gamble.

Also reflected in that letter is Billy Bonney's newly recognized personal power. How titillating it must have been to him. Secret was his proposal to the man who could defeat the Santa Fe Ring. Secret was his offer of testimony that could bring Ring-boss, James Dolan, and Billy Campbell to hanging; and Jessie Evans to prison as their murder accessory. Secret was that he may already have made an offer to Attorney Huston Chapman to testify against Commander Dudley. And Billy must have believed that Wallace knew another secret: that his deposition to Investigator Frank Warner Angel already incriminated basically the same men as Tunstall's murderers.

But touchingly, Billy is reaching out to Lew Wallace for more than clemency. On his own, having lost John Tunstall and Alexander McSween, he is seeking a new ally - a father figure - with power to guarantee winning the fight started by those good men. To him, that was worth risking death.

Billy-Wallace Meeting

ARRANGING A MEETING

Billy Bonney - and most Lincolnites - assumed Lew Wallace understood and opposed the Santa Fe Ring's corruption, which had yielded his mid-term governorship. That error would kill Billy in two years. But Billy's sought gubernatorial meeting must have been awaited by his allies with hope.

Inconceivable was that this famous man was just a narcissistic romanticizer - like authoring his historical fictions - just creating drama for his amusement and aggrandizement.

Billy was staking his life on a man mindlessly subduing the Territory merely to apply for Turkey's ambassadorship and to depart; which he did by mid-May of 1881, short of his full term.

Wallace would leave no true solution, but take literary inspiration about the wild West, with Billy the Kid as its paragon of bloodthirsty outlawry. Thus, their communications would be saved by Wallace like a taxidermied specimen of the boy himself. Indeed, the Billy-Wallace letters exist for history only because of Lew Wallace's avaricious callous plan.

The destructiveness of Lew Wallace's irresponsible and fey personality cannot be underestimated. In the Civil War's 1862 battle of Shiloh, as a Major General having enough Union troops to ensure victory, he ignored couriers with General Ulysses S. Grant's orders, and missed the first day of battle. That yielded 23,746 casualties; more than in the Revolutionary War, War of Eighteen Twelve, and the Mexican War combined. Though Wallace finally arrived for the next day's victory, he was refused all future troop command by General Grant.

Post-war, as the Lincoln murder trial prosecutor, he forced on the doomed defendants peaked witch-like masks. Billy was about to enter Wallace's fantasy world - and become its demon.

WALLACE'S TRICKY LETTER OF
MARCH 15, 1879

Lew Wallace's March 15, 1879 written response to Billy Bonney's bargain letter of March 13(?), 1879, shows that he was imagining a meeting with a bandit king of the wild and wooly West; as well as having no interest in the causes of ongoing "troubles" or of Attorney Huston Chapman's murder.

Instead, since his Amnesty Proclamation to eliminate most prosecutions had not ended violence, Wallace merely created his own explanation: outlaws were stirring disrest by rustling. And, coming personally to Lincoln, he planned to quiet restive citizens by capturing and hanging those outlaws with soldier posses, and by returning rustled cows after interviewing the locals for brands. (That exercise must have bored him, since he saved no notes. And in his Dudley Court of Inquiry, under cross-examination, Wallace recalled no names or specifics of those interviews.)

Then, in the midst of that tedious, uninspiring, plebian squabbling, apparently from out of the blue, dropped the amazing letter of a W. H. Bonney, offering to solve Wallace's most nagging problem by testifying against Huston Chapman's killers, already arrested and being held at Fort Stanton.

So Wallace must have checked around little Lincoln town about this W. H. Bonney. Assumedly, the traumatized citizens - living through three murdered mutilated bodies and a war with brutal military intervention in just one year - were reticent. Less reticent would have been Ring-partisans like Saturnino Baca and Edgar Walz. Billy Bonney, "the Kid" was their outlaw, an important source of their problems.

So wily attorney, Lew Wallace, who had managed to hang John Wilkes Booth's innocent landlady, Mrs. Surratt, was ready to set a trap for this despicable but foolish boy. It would be the start of his pardon trick: to extract useful testimony from Billy with the lure of clemency; then hang him.

Almost immediately, Governor Lew Wallace responded to Billy's letter. Wallace wrote:

Lincoln, March 15, 1879.

W.H. Bonney.
> *Come to the house of Old Squire Wilson (not the lawyer) at nine (9) o'clock next Monday night alone. I don't mean his office, but his residence. Follow along the floor of the mountain south of the town, come in at that side, and knock on the east door. I have the authority to exempt you from prosecution, if you will testify to what you say you know.*
>
> *The object of the meeting at Squire Wilson's is to arrange the matter in a way to make your life safe. To do that the utmost secrecy is to be used. So come alone. Don't tell anybody – not a living soul – where you are coming or the object. If you could trust Jesse Evans, you can trust me.*
> *Lew Wallace*

ANALYSIS OF WALLACE'S LETTER OF MARCH 15, 1879

The Lew Wallace letter's arrogant preposterousness is evident. A new-comer to Lincoln, Wallace gives Billy directions around town. More seriously, it reflects his unawareness that the boy had been employed there by John Tunstall and had fought there in its major war, just eight months earlier.

As naïve, is Wallace's linking Billy to Jessie Evans, the murderous Ring rustler and enforcer with whom Billy rode only in September of 1877. More worrisome, is Wallace's obvious lack of input from Justice of the Peace "Squire" Wilson, who knew everything: Billy's 1878 law enforcement roles and freedom fighting. Wilson knew that Billy was no outlaw.

A forewarning is Wallace's sentence: *"I have the authority to exempt you from prosecution, if you will testify to what you say you know."* It is just a lawyer's trick of misleading wording. Having the "authority," does not mean it will be used. Craftily, by *"to exempt,"* Wallace avoids Billy's use of annul (*"annuly"*) or clemency or pardon. Later, Billy's Attorney Ira Leonard would state to Secret Service Operative Azariah Wild that no proper form of a pardon had been put in writing by the governor.

Wallace had set a trap. Billy fell into it two days later.

Meeting of March 17, 1879

Billy's fateful meeting with Governor Lew Wallace was on March 17, 1879, at 9 PM, at "Squire" Wilson's little adobe on Lincoln's single street. Whether it was "secret" is questionable, given perspective from the newly authenticated Billy letter.

Nevertheless, with Wilson as witness, Billy thought he got a verbal agreement of exchanging his testimony for negating his indictments, since he proceeded with that perilous plan.

That Wallace intended betrayal is indicated 23 years later in his interview for *New York World Magazine* of June 8, 1902, titled, with himself as hero: "General Lew Wallace Writes a Romance of 'Billy the Kid' Most Famous Bandit of the Plains." In it, he lies that Billy never testified; but admits his ruse:

"Testify," I said, "before the Grand Jury and the trial court and convict the murderer of Chapman and I will let you go scot-free with a pardon in your pocket for all your misdeeds."

Changed Circumstances

Governor Wallace, right after that March 17th meeting with Billy Bonney, received a lesson in Ring power. Rounding up "outlaws" for punishing would be difficult, if not impossible. Eventually, Billy alone would get that "punishing."

Wallace's initial interviews with Lincolnites apparently made "bad guys" of James Dolan, Billy Campbell, Jessie Evans, and Seven Rivers boys as being Tunstall's killers, Ring wartime fighters, McSween's murderers, and Chapmen's assassins. So Wallace incarcerated over twenty of them in Fort Stanton, unaware that Commander N.A.M. Dudley was their partisan; as were other officers, including past commander, George Purington. The fact that his prisoners were left to roam the Fort like guests did not alert Wallace either.

By March 19th, two days after Wallace's meeting with Billy, Jessie Evans and Billy Campbell "escaped," heading to Texas. Losing suspects to indict led to more letters among Billy, Wallace, and Wilson on March 20th. But Billy trusted Wallace.

Billy's Letter Flurry to Wallace and Wilson

HECTIC FATEFUL DAY OF MARCH 20, 1879

On March 19th, two days after the Billy-Wallace pardon meeting at "Squire" Wilson's house, all learned about the Fort Stanton escape of Huston Chapman's murderers: Jessie Evans and Billy Campbell. It was Wallace's first sign that ending the "troubles" was not as simple as he had envisioned.

And Billy, unsure whether the pardon deal was ruined now that only suspect James Dolan remained in custody, the next day exchanged a flurry of letters with Wallace; with Justice of the Peace "Squire" Wilson as their go-between.

Once reassured by a letter from Wallace, with delivery by an additional unknown messenger, Billy next wanted precise arrangements as to his sham arrest and safety provisions.

Important to observe is Billy's trust of Wilson; another sad overestimation. Doubtless Wilson sympathized with McSweens and Billy, but Wilson would remain forever silent as to Billy's pardon or his later defense in the Mesilla hanging trial.

Noteworthy also is the propinquity of that March 20th's letter-writers. Wallace was at José Montaño's house in Lincoln, close to Wilson's. The unnamed "bearer" would have a short ride to San Patricio: the location Billy put on his letters.

But one should question Billy's "address." With a $1000 bounty on his head, Billy would not be expected to advertise his location. Analysis of his newly discovered letter implies that "San Patricio" was, as he would say, "a blind."

And the first recipient of Billy's letter flurry, might have also been his accomplice in the pardon planning: none other than closed-mouthed cautious "Squire Wilson" himself.

BILLY'S LETTER TO "SQUIRE" WILSON

With his network of friends, Billy would quickly have learned about the Evans-Campbell escape, and extrapolated its risk to his clemency deal. So, on March 20th, he wrote to Justice of the Peace John "Squire" Wilson to check on the feigned arrest plan with Governor Lew Wallace.

The letter must have been delivered early, because time remained that day for communications between Lincoln and San Patricio; that is, if Billy was not hiding right in Lincoln!

But once Wilson got the letter, he could just walk to José Montaño's to pick up Wallace's written response. Billy wrote:

San Patricio

Thursday 20th

1879

Friend Wilson.

Please tell You know who that I do not know what to do, now as those Prisoners have escaped. So send word by bearer. a note through You it may be he has made different arrangements if not and he still wants it the same to Send :William Hudgins: as Deputy, to the Junction tomorrow at three Oclock with some men you know to be all right. Send a note telling me what to do

WHBonney

P.S. do not send Soldiers

WALLACE'S LETTER TO WILSON

Fort Stanton. March 20, 1879

Squire Wilson

I enclose a note for Bonney. Read it, and forward at once. I presume the messenger is waiting.

If you know why Kimbrell should not go rather than Hudgens, hold on till I get over this evening.

Yours, Lew Wallace.

WALLACE'S ENCLOSED RESPONSE TO BILLY

The *"note for Bonney"* enclosed with Wallace's letter to Wilson is in the Lew Wallace Collection as a draft. It implies that Wallace was unaware of the dark implications of the Evans-Campbell escape to his plans, as well as its adding greater risk to Billy if imprisoned. In addition, with lawyer's slyness, Wallace had ominously crossed out *"I will comply with my part if you will with yours;"* as if taking no chances by putting any form of "promise" in writing. Wallace wrote:

> The escape makes no difference in arrangements. ~~I will comply with my part if you will with yours~~.
> To remove all suspicions of ~~arrangement~~ understanding, I think it better to put the arresting party in charge of Sheriff Kimball, who will be instructed to see that no violence is used.
> This will go to you tonight. ~~If you still insist upon Hudgens, let me know.~~ If I don't ~~get~~ receive other word from you the party (all citizens) will be at the junction by three o'clock ~~tomorrow~~.

BILLY'S SECOND LETTER TO WALLACE

Billy's second letter that day of March 20th must have gone out soon after he received Lew Wallace's written response to his own "Friend Wilson" letter. The dangerous plans depended on trusting Wallace. Arrest, which Billy devised himself, was what he had avoided for the past year, since John Tunstall's murder, its retaliations, and the Lincoln County War itself had made him a prime candidate for Ring-style elimination .

Billy's letter reflects that awareness, as well as his literary skill - epitomized in its quotation: *"I am not afraid to die like a man fighting but I would not like to be killed like a dog unarmed."* But even in this extremis, Billy was trying to forge with Wallace a mutual fight for justice; including giving the past General advice on how to capture escapees!

Billy's overwrought excitement at this new relationship with a new father-figure was evident even to him, since he apologizes at the letter's end for *"having so much to say."*

San Patricio

Lincoln County
Thursday 20th 1879
General. Lew. Wallace:

*Sir. I will keep the appointment
I made. but be Sure and have men come that You
can depend on I am not afraid to die like a man fighting but
I would not like to be killed like a dog unarmed. tell Kimbal
[sic - Sheriff Kimbrell] to let his men be placed around the
house and for him to come in alone: and he can arrest us. all
I am afraid of is that in the Fort we might be poisoned or
killed through a window at night. but You can arrange that all
right. tell the Commanding Officer to watch)Let Goodwin(
he would not hesitate to do anything there Will be danger on
the road of Somebody Waylaying us to kill us on the road to
the Fort. You will never catch those fellows on the road
Watch Fritzes. Captain Bacas. ranch and the Brewery they Will
either go to Seven Rivers or to Jicarillo Mountains they
will stay around close untill the scouting parties come in.
give a spy a pair of glasses and let him get on the mountain
back of Fritzes and watch and if they are there there will
be provisions carried to them. it is not my place to advise
you, but I am anxious to have them caught, and perhaps
know how men hide from Soldiers, better than you. please
excuse me for having so much to say*
and I still remain Yours Truly

W H. Bonney
P.S.
*I have changed my mind Send Kimbal to Gutieres just below
San Patricio one mile, because Sanger and Ballard are or were
great friends of Camels [sic - Billy Campbell's] Ballard told me
today yesterday to leave for you were doing everything to catch
me. it was a blind to get me to leave tell Kimbal not to come
before 3 oclock for I may not be there before*

ANALYSIS OF BILLY'S LETTER TO WALLACE OF MARCH 20, 1879

Besides bravado, Billy's letter of March 20, 1879 displays his search for a father. It was lifelong; but Lew Wallace was his last attempt. Billy's first letter to him almost waved adoption papers by disavowing any current familial connection: *"I am called Kid Antrim but Antrim is my stepfathers name."*

Illegitimate, Billy may never have known his father McCarty. His stepfather, from his mother's 1873, Santa Fe marriage, was William Henry Harrison Antrim; with whom she, Billy, and his brother first lived in Indiana. Antrim moved them to Silver City for mining, and cast the boys to the streets after their mother's death in 1874. Nevertheless, from 1875, in Arizona, where Antrim settled, Billy tried to contact him. But upon Billy's 1877 return to New Mexico, he abandoned "Antrim" for "Bonney" - possibly his mother's maiden name.

The next transference was to kind John Tunstall, whose death made Billy a rebel courting Alexander McSween - even volunteering as a protector for him in the Lincoln County War.

But cattle king, John Chisum, betrayer of Tunstall, McSween and the Regulators, got the same hatred as Antrim. After capture, to a reporter, Billy blamed Chisum for his woes.

Most fatherly was Attorney Ira Leonard, who, as Susan McSween's attorney after Huston Chapman's murder, met Billy when he was in Lincoln's sham arrest and testifying for Wallace. Leonard would later advocate for his pardon and defend Billy at his hanging trial. But he would abandon him at that trial - perhaps after a death threat - leaving Billy with Attorney Albert Jennings Fountain, satisfied to see him hang.

Buffalo hunter, Patrick Floyd Garrett, Billy's decade-older acquaintance from Fort Sumner, seemed a father-figure candidate; though his becoming a capturing lawman who killed Tom O'Folliard and Charlie Bowdre should have seared Billy's filial longings. Yet, at the moment of ambush in the Maxwell mansion, Billy may have recognized Garrett's unusual height in the darkness, and became inhibited from shooting for a fatal moment. Garrett himself, in his post-killing book, contemplated that possibility with fleeting guilt.

ANALYSIS OF THE LETTER OF MARCH 20, 1879

Of all Billy Bonney's potential father substitutes, Lew Wallace seemed his preference. For him, Billy tried hardest to be appealing - as if the pursued pardon, over time, became equivalent to being loved at last. For Wallace came Billy's weighty and revealing decision presented in his March 20, 1879 letter to the man. It can be interpreted as filial courtship.

San Patricio

Lincoln County
Thursday 20th 1879
General Lew Wallace:

Sir. I will keep the appointment I made. but be Sure and have men come that You can depend on

[AUTHOR'S NOTE: Stoically, Billy is attempting to structure protection, knowing his extreme risk in an arrest. His customary use of capitalizations for emphasis includes "*Sure*" for certainty and "*You*" for Wallace taking personal responsibility.]

I am not afraid to die like a man fighting but I would not like to be killed like a dog unarmed.

[AUTHOR'S NOTE: Besides its beautiful wording - alternating "*to die*" with "*to be killed*" - this makes clear Billy's proud self image as a soldier, a "*man fighting*."]

tell Kimbal [sic -Sheriff Kimbrell] *to let his men be placed around the house and for him to come in alone: and he can arrest us.*

[AUTHOR'S NOTE: Billy trusted Sheriff Kimbrell, a McSween-side sympathizer. The "*us*" refers to Billy's Regulator friend, Tom O'Folliard, who was to accompany him in the arrest.]

all I am afraid of is that in the Fort we might be poisoned or killed through a window at night.

[AUTHOR'S NOTE: After the Lincoln County War, Billy and the Lincolnites had no trust of Commander Dudley or his officers. Many believed that the killing of Attorney Huston Chapman was at his behest - since Chapman was about to have Dudley prosecuted for murder and arson in the Lincoln County War. Billy is also prescient about Ring-style assassination. By April 25, 1879, in Lincoln, a bullet through a window would almost kill Attorney Ira Leonard, Chapman's replacement.]

but You can arrange that all right.

[AUTHOR'S NOTE: Not only is this a compliment, it measures Billy's pride at having the powerful man on his side and as a "partner" in their plan to get justice for Chapman's killing.]

tell the Commanding Officer to watch)Let Goodwin(he would not hesitate to do anything

[AUTHOR'S NOTE: Second Lieutenant Millard Fillmore Goodwin could have been one of the three white soldiers firing on Billy and others during the escape from the burning McSween house. But Billy must have been unsure; though he was aware that Goodwin was a Ring partisan. In his testimony in the Dudley Court of Inquiry, Billy does not identify the shooting soldiers by name.]

there Will be danger on the road of Somebody Waylaying us to kill us on the road to the Fort.

[AUTHOR'S NOTE: This is the measure of courage, since, at this point, Billy assumed he would be incarcerated in the Fort, nine miles from Lincoln. To be recognized also, is Billy's awareness that the long road was excellent for ambush. Nevertheless, two months later, he would offer to testify at the Dudley Court of Inquiry and be transported, without protection, for two days in a row along that same road.]

You will never catch those fellows on the road Watch Fritzes. Captain Bacas. ranch and the Brewery they Will either go to Seven Rivers or to Jicarillo Mountains they will stay around close until the scouting parties come in.

[AUTHOR'S NOTE: Here is filial Billy, the governor's partner in justice, sharing his knowledge to assist in re-arresting Jessie Evans and Billy Campbell.]

give a spy a pair of glasses and let him get on the mountain back of Fritzes and watch and if they are there there will be provisions carried to them.

[AUTHOR'S NOTE: Here is excited Billy giving the great general advice on spying. *"Fritzes"* is the ranch of Charles Fritz, a Ring sympathizer, and brother of deceased House founder, Emil Fritz. Also, the ambush murder of the Regulator leader, Frank MacNab, (who had replaced murdered leader Dick Brewer) was done the year before, on April 29, 1878, by Seven Rivers boys hiding at this same Fritz ranch. It was a likely lay-over for Evans and Campbell.]

it is not my place to advise you,

[AUTHOR'S NOTE: The wry humor should not be missed. Most of the letter was indeed cocky, and audaciously advised Wallace without the slightest awe at his lofty position. Billy certainly sees himself as the equal of any man - and here even as a superior in terms of survival wiles and interpretation of local politics.]

but I am anxious to have them caught, and

[AUTHOR'S NOTE: Billy has his own agenda, and not just for the amnesty deal. He is seeking the prosecution of Ring murderers who killed many people dear to him.]

perhaps know how men hide from Soldiers, better than you.

[AUTHOR'S NOTE: Billy allows himself a full flash of his playful humor. He even capitalizes *"Soldiers,"* since it was Fort Stanton troops that Wallace sent out trying to catch him - without avail!]

please excuse me for having so much to Say

[AUTHOR'S NOTE: Billy must have been as excited as when John Tunstall gave him and Fred Waite a Peñasco River Ranch.]

and I still remain Yours Truly,

[AUTHOR'S NOTE: In Billy's mind, their relationship has progressed from *"Your obedient servant"* of his first pre-meeting letter to *"Yours Truly."*]

W H. Bonney

P.S.
I have changed my mind

> [AUTHOR'S NOTE: Not only is this assertive, but it implies that Billy's mind was going a hundred miles an hour!]

Send Kimbal to Gutieres just below San Patricio one mile, because Sanger and Ballard are or were great friends of Camels [sic - Billy Campbell's] *Ballard told me ~~today~~ yesterday to leave for you were doing everything to catch me. it was a blind to get me to leave.*

> [AUTHOR'S NOTE: This clearly is not a secret arrangement as Wallace had believed. People on both sides of the Ring are following it. Billy may also be mentioning "*a blind*" to demonstrate that he is putting faith in Wallace's being trustworthy.]

tell Kimbal not to come before 3 oclock for I may not be there before

> [AUTHOR'S NOTE: Note the emphasis on time: "*not to come before 3 oclock.*" This adds credence to Billy's not being in San Patricio, as he headed this letter, and needed time to get there.]

BILLY'S SHAM ARREST

The planned feigned arrest occurred the day after Billy's letter, on March 21, 1879, just four days after Billy had first met Lew Wallace in person.

Billy knew that the Ringmen wanted him dead; and arrest with hanging was the best way of accomplishing that. He was cutting things close; but Sheriff George Kimbrell, who had replaced Ring-partisan Sheriff George Peppin, who had quit, was a guarantee of protection during the arrest itself.

And jail arrangements changed for the better - with Billy kept neither in Fort Stanton (in which he would never have survived) or in Lincoln's noxious, underground, pit jail. He was kept in the Lincoln house of McSween sympathizer, his friend, and the county jailor, Juan Patrón. And Billy could testify for indictments even if suspects Evans and Campbell were gone. The most villainous defendant remained: James Dolan.

Wallace
Interviews Billy

INFORMING ON OUTLAWS

One can guess that in March of 1879 peripatetic Lew Wallace, stuck in primitive Lincoln, was bored. Possible amusement was clever desperado Billy Bonney, "jailed" just east of his Montaño house lodging. Dreary interviewing of dreary townspeople, whose refusal to let sleeping dogs lie, was delaying his Palace of the Governors renovation, his writing of *Ben-Hur*, and his amusing his equally bored wife and son.

Billy was likely bored also, with the Grand Jury almost a month away; though his sham incarceration in friendly hospitality of Juan Patrón's home must have been pleasant; as must have been knowledge of Lew Wallace as a neighbor.

That short walk on Lincoln's red dirt road may have inspired Wallace to interview Billy with takes-one-to-know-one logic. And Wallace's other interviews apparently yielded no understanding of the war issues that had led to Huston Chapman's murder - which had necessitated his coming.

Noteworthy is that, of his interviews, Lew Wallace saved only his Billy Bonney interview notes from March 23, 1879, titling them with frontier romanticism: *"Statements by Kid."*

Those jottings demonstrate Billy's knowledge of Territorial outlawry and rustling; as well as his attempt to ingratiate himself with Wallace and to be his ally on the side of the law. One wonders, however, what Billy made of the governor's questions, irrelevant to the ongoing Lincoln County crisis.

But Billy was cunning. He omitted reporting his own rustling associates, Charlie Bowdre and Tom O'Folliard, and their outlets: Pecos River area Dan Dedrick; Dedrick's brothers in White Oaks, Mose and Sam; and Tularosa-based Pat Coghlan - himself second only in magnitude to Ring-rustlers!

WALLACE'S INTERVIEW OF BILLY

Lew Wallace's notes on his Billy Bonney interview about local outlawry, which he titled *"Statements by Kid, made Sunday night March 23, 1879,"* were not part of the pardon deal initiated by Billy's first letter just ten days earlier. Boding ill, Wallace even omitted Billy's real name for that heading.

Wallace's notes, lacking political context, are meaningless lisitings of people and places. Missing is the Santa Fe Ring's rustling from John Chisum's giant herd of 80,000 cattle to meet beef contracts for Fort Stanton and the Mescalero Indian Reservation. Missing is murdered Tunstall's and murdered McSween's opposition. Missing is the Lincoln County War, and Commander Dudley's intervention which brought in Attorney Chapman to prosecute. Missing as outlaws are the Ringman public officials, law enforcement officers, and military brass. So the notes reveal Wallace's ignorance of political motives for Chapman's murder, as well as his inability to connect that murder to the war, seven months earlier, in that very town - where McSween house ruins were not far from the place on the street where Chapman's burning corpse sprawled on the red street the month before; that place, almost in front of the Montaño house, being where Wallace probably trod daily.

The newly authenticated letter by Billy Bonney, discussed next, appears to be the boy's follow-up attempt at clarifications. For example, Billy refers to the "Buckshot" Roberts Regulator killing (one of his pardon deal indictments) at the Mescalero Indian Reservation Agency when describing their search for Tunstall's stolen stock and its rustlers. Billy writes: *"those were the men we were in search of when we went to the Agency."*

But Wallace's *"Statements by Kid"* reflects just apathetic reduction of mutual accusations of Ring and anti-Ring factions in Lincoln County to "outlawry."

Billy's words for *"Statements by Kid,"* however, are his redeeming anti-outlawry contributions and his attempts to connect that information to the Tunstall and McSween murders and the war. His words belie Lew Wallace's 1881, as well as his late-in-life, fabrications for not granting Billy a pardon, as being based on Billy's alleged incorrigible refusal to reform from "outlawry."

LEW WALLACE INTERVIEW NOTES: MARCH 23, 1879

On legal-length paper, Lew Wallace wrote his Billy Bonney interview notes in his small, neat, non-Spencerian script. Wallace appeared to have some pre-existing knowledge - like about Shedd's Ranch, a rustled stock holding-place - which he used as headings; and assumedly for lines of questioning. And Billy's fund of knowledge was breath-taking.

Wallace wrote:

William Bonney ("Kid")
relative to arrangement
with him.

Notes:

3-23-1879

Statements by Kid, made Sunday night March 23, 1879

1. There is a cattle trail beginning about 5 miles above Yellow Lake in a cañon, running a little west of north to Cisneza del Matcho (Mule Spring) and continuing around the point of the Capitan Mountains down toward Carrizozo in the direction of the Rio Grande. Frank Wheeler, Jake Owens and Dutch Chris are supposed to have used this trail taking a bunch of cattle over. Vansickle told K. so. They stopped and killed two beavers for Sam Corbett – hush money to Vansickle to whom they gave the beavers. Vansickle also said the Owens-Wheeler outfit mentioning "Chris" Ladbessor using this trail for about a year, but that lately their horses had given out, and of 140 head which they started to work they had only got through with 40. That now they were going to the Reservation to make a raid on the Indian horses to work on.

The Rustlers.

The "Rustlers," Kid says: were organized in Fort Stanton. Before they organized as "Rustlers" they had been with Peppin's posse. They came from Texas. Owens was conspicuous amongst them. They were organized before the burning of McSween's house, and after that they went on their first trip down the county as far as the Coe's ranch and thence to the Feliz where they took the Tunstall cattle. From the Feliz they went to the Pecos, where some of them deserted, Owens amongst them. (Martin, known to Sam Corbett) was in charge of the Tunstall cattle, and was taken prisoner, and saw them kill one of their own party. On the same trip they burnt Lola Wise's house, and took some horses. Coe at the time was ranching at the house. On this trip they moved behind a body of soldiers, one company, and a company of Navajo Scouts. They moved in sight of the soldiers, taking horses, insulting women. Lorenzo Trujillo (Jus. Peder) Juan Trujillo, Jose M. Gutierres, Pancho Sanchez, Santos Tafoya, are witnesses against them. They stopped on Pecos at Seven Rivers. Collins, now at Silver City, was one of the outfit – nick-named the Prowler by the cowboys. At Seven Rivers. There joined them Gus Gildey (wanted at San Antonio for killing Mexicans) Gildey is carrying the mail now from Stockton to Seven Rivers – James Irvin and Reese Gobles, (rumored that their bodies were found in a drift down the Pecos) – Rustling Bob (found dead in the Pecos, killed by his own party) – John Selman (whereabouts unknown) came to Roswell while [Captain] Carroll was there –

The R's [Rustlers] stayed at Seven Rivers; which they left on their second trip via the Berenda for Fort Stanton. On their return back they killed Chavez boys and the crazy boy, Lorenzo – and the Sanchez boy, 14 years old. They also committed many robberies. They broke up after reaching the Pecos, promising to return when some more horses got fat.

Shedd's Ranch

The trail used going from Seven Rivers to Shedd's was round the S.W. part of the Guadalupe Mts. by a tank on the right hand of trail: from Shedd's the drives would be over to Las Cruces Jesse Evans, Frank Baker (killed) Jim McDaniels (at Cruces, ranging between Cruces and El Paso) Reed at Shedd's bought cattle from them – also sold cattle to E.C. Priest, butcher in Cruces. "Big Mose" (at Cruces last heard from) and ⸻, deserter from cavalry – (went to Arizona)

Mimbres

Used to be called Mormon City – situated 30 miles on the road to Cruces from Silver City south. A great many of what are known as "West Harden gang" are there. Among them Joe Olney, known in Mimbres as Joe Hill; he has a ranch in old Mexico somewheres near Coralitos. He makes trips up in this country: was at Penasco not long ago.

San Nicholas Spring

Is about 18 miles from Shedd's Ranch on the road to Tularosa, left hand road. There's a house at the spring and about 4 or 5 miles from it N.W. is another corral of brush and a spring, situated in a cañon. There Jim McDaniels used to keep stolen Indian horses. McD. one of the Rio Grande posse. Kid says the latter is still used.

The Jones Family

Came from Texas. Used to keep saloon at Fort Griffin. The family consists of the father, Jim Jones, John Jones, boy about 10 years old, a girl about 13, and the mother. Marion Turner lives with the family, and he killed a Mexican man at Blazers Mill "just to see him kick." He had no cattle when the War started. The Jones, John and Jim, killed a man named Riley, a partner of theirs, on the Penasco 3 or 4 years ago.

ANALYSIS OF THE WALLACE
INTERVIEW NOTES

Statements by Kid, made Sunday night March 23, 1879

There is a cattle trail beginning about 5 miles above Yellow Lake in a cañon, running a little west of north to Cisneza del Matcho (Mule Spring) and continuing around the point of the Capitan Mountains down toward Carrizozo in the direction of the Rio Grande. Frank Wheeler, John Owens and Dutch Chris are supposed to have used this trail taking a bunch of cattle over. Vansickle told K. so.

[AUTHOR'S NOTE: Of interest to understanding Billy as a person with widespread influence, is realizing the variety of people he knew intimately, along with his understanding of Territorial geography. None of his modern history books communicate that grasp; but it is a key to comprehending his threat to the Ring as a future leader of another uprising. And here he is just 19.]

They stopped and killed two beavers for Sam Corbett – hush money to Vansickle to whom they gave the beavers. Vansickle also said the Owens-Wheeler outfit mentioning "Chris" Ladbessor using this trail for about a year, but that lately their horses had given out, and of 140 head which they started to work they had only got through with 40. That now they were going to the Reservation to make a raid on the Indian horses to work on.

The Rustlers.

The "Rustlers," Kid says, are organized in Fort Stanton. Before they organized as "Rustlers" they had been with Peppin's posse. They came from Texas.

[AUTHOR'S NOTE: Billy is discussing the Seven Rivers boys; but Wallace appears to miss his linking them to a military outpost and a sheriff's posse. This is Lincoln County War information, which Billy may actually have been giving; but Wallace's ignorance of names - like "Peppin" the wartime sheriff- reduced it to vague irrelevancy.]

Owens was conspicuous amongst them. They were organized before the burning of McSween's house,

[AUTHOR'S NOTE: Billy is clearly using the Lincoln County War - "*the burning of McSween's house*" - as a time reference.]

and after that they went on their first trip down the county as far as the Coe's ranch and thence to the Felix where they took the Tunstall cattle.

[AUTHOR'S NOTE: Here Wallace garbles the period right after Tunstall's murder. His ignorance of event sequence prevents his making sense of Billy's information.]

From the Feliz they went to the Pecos, where some of them deserted, Owens amongst them. (Martin, known to Sam Corbett) was in charge of the Tunstall cattle, and was taken prisoner, and saw them kill one of their own party.

[AUTHOR'S NOTE: Tunstall had chosen "Dutch" Martin Martz as a neutral for supervision of his Feliz ranch cattle during Sheriff Brady's attachment, just before his murder. And Sam Corbett was hired by Tunstall as salesman at his Lincoln store. Billy may have been giving the roots of the Lincoln County War; though Wallace is on a meaningless tangent.]

On the same trip they burnt Lola Piso's house, and took some horses. Coe at the time was ranching at the house. On this trip they moved behind a body of soldiers, one company, and a company of Navajo Scouts. They moved in sight of the soldiers, taking horses, insulting women. Lorenzo Trujillo (Jus Perez) Juan Trujillo, Jose M. Gutierres, Pancho Sanchez, Santos Tafoya, are witnesses against them. They stopped on Pecos at Seven Rivers. Collins, now in Silver City, was one of the outfit – nick-named the Panther by the cowboys. At Seven Rivers there joined them Gus Gildey [sic-Gildea] (wanted at San Antonio for killing Mexicans) Gildey is carrying the mail now from Stockton to Seven Rivers – James Irvin and Reese Gobles, (rumored that their bodies never found in a drift down the Pecos) – Rustling Bob (found dead in the Pecos, killed by his own party) – John Selman (whereabouts unknown) came to Roswell while [Captain] Carroll was there –

[AUTHOR'S NOTE: Billy is giving outlawry information with incredible detail. In Arizona, Billy may have known Gus Gildea, once a John Chisum cowboy and back then working at Henry Clay Hooker's Sierra Bonita Ranch.]

The R's [Rustlers] stayed at Seven Rivers; which they left on their second trip via the Berenda for Fort Stanton. On their return back they killed Chavez boys and the crazy boy, Lorenzo – and the Sanchez boy, 14 years old. They also committed many robberies. They broke up after reaching the Pecos, promising to return when some more horses got fat.

Shedd's Ranch

The trail used going from Seven Rivers to Shedd's was round the S.W. part of the Guadalupe Mts. by a tank on the right hand of trail: from Shedd's the drives would be over to Las Cruces Jesse Evans, Frank Baker (killed)

[AUTHOR'S NOTE: Billy, who rode with Jessie Evans in September of 1877, may have learned this route then. But he is also referring to a pre-war event: the Regulator killing of Frank Baker - "*Frank Baker (killed)*" - in which Billy took part. Wallace seems unaware of this meaning or its Regulator implication.]

Jim McDaniels (at Cruces, ranging between Cruces and El Paso) Reed at Shedd's bought cattle from him – also called to E.C. Porest, business in Cruces. "Pug Mose" (at Cruces last heard from) and   , deserter from Carnby – (went to Arizona)

Mimbres

Used to be called Mormon City – situated 30 miles on the road to Cruces from Silver City south.

[AUTHOR'S NOTE: One can imagine Billy keeping a straight face as he casually mentioned Silver City - where he was last on September 23, 1875, escaping through its jail's chimney as an arrested burglar facing a ten year sentence.]

A great many of what are known as "Mot Hardin gang" ate there. Among them Joe Olney, known on the Mimbres as Joe Hill; he has a ranch in old Mexico somewheres near Coralitos. Shumarker lives up in this country: was at Penasco not long ago

San Nicholas Spring

Is about 18 miles from Shedd's Ranch on the road to Tularosa, left hand road. There's a house at the spring and about 4 or 5 miles from it N.W. is another corral of brush and a spring, situated in a cañon. There Jim McDaniels used to keep stolen Indian horses. McD. one of the Rio Grande posse. Kid says the latter is still used.

[AUTHOR'S NOTE: In this time-frame, Billy may have been using major cattle rustler, Pat Coghlan, in the Tularosa area, for his own rustled stock - and cannily omits his name. That fact may have assisted in Billy's intimate knowledge about that area!]

The Jones Family

Came from Texas. Used to keep saloon at Fort Griffin. The family consists of the father, Jim Jones, John Jones, boy about 10 years old, a girl about 13, and the mother.

[AUTHOR'S NOTE: This family of Ma'am and Heiskell Jones was the first to befriend Billy when he returned to the Territory from Arizona in 1877. That is why Billy knows their past history. John Jones was a particular friend, later killed by Robert Olinger.]

Marion Turner lives with the family, and he killed a Mexican man at Blazers Mill "just to see him kick." He had no cattle when the War started.

[AUTHOR'S NOTE: Again Billy is using the Lincoln County War as a reference. One wonders how much information Wallace was missing in the jottings that his notes represent. But in analyzing the newly authenticated Billy letter next, one gets a clearer idea of how Billy actually stated these wartime references.]

The Jones' John and Jim kills a man named Riley, a partner of theirs, on the Penasco 3 or 4 years ago.

[AUTHOR'S NOTE: Wallace appears here to have garbled information. John Jones killed a man in Texas, necessitating the family's relocation to New Mexico. The family had a store in Roswell, and no partner on the Peñasco River.]

FATHER-FIGURE IMPRINTING

History is made not only by events but by the psychology of its participants. Like a duckling that considers "mother" to be any moving constant in its first fourteen days of life, Billy Bonney, by March 23, 1879, seven days after their meeting, unconsciously imprinted on Lew Wallace as a father.

Though Wallace missed the import of the information he received from the boy - and one wonders how much he left out - "*Statements by Kid*" reflects the sheer effort Billy was exerting to be appreciated for his knowledge and helpfulness. If anything, Billy seemed like a law enforcer in the making.

But concurrently, Lew Wallace was writing his *Ben-Hur: A Tale of the Christ*. Could it be that a sadistic scene in that book was inspired by the pardon bargain he was dangling before Billy Bonney, and by his power over this brilliant and trapped teenager?

In *Ben-Hur*, Wallace has Judah Ben-Hur's galley ship slave master, Arrius, converse about a pardon for him. Arrius says to Ben-Hur: "Perhaps I do but play with thee."

The "Billie" Letter Fragment

A NEW BILLY THE KID LETTER

Authenticated by me here is a Billy Bonney letter, found when researching this and my other Billy the Kid books. I named it the "Billie" letter fragment.

Owned by Lew Wallace, it is among his papers, donated by his family, in 1940, to the Indiana Historical Society in Indiana as the Lew Wallace Collection. It remains archived there.

FIRST NOTE OF "BILLIE" LETTER FRAGMENT

I first saw the "Billie" letter fragment as its two page, typed copy, dated "**5/14/47**" at its bottom, and with a short annotated commentary by its unknown copyist on its first page's top.

I obtained that copy from the collection of Herman Weisner, a New Mexican historian and Old West document researcher, now deceased, whose papers are housed in Las Cruces at New Mexico State University's Branson Library in its Rio Grande Historical Society Collection. They lack an original version, implying that Weisner was not its original typist - though he is known to have visited the Indiana Historical Society.

The Indiana Historical Society kept the real fragment in their Lew Wallace Collection's archival box for 1880, because an unknown past archivist had bracketed in pencil, without basis, "[1880?]" at its top. They do not have the typed version.

Whoever made the copy, however, considered its being by Billy Bonney, but denied that. However, in the Robert Mullin papers in the Midland, Texas, Nita Stewart Haley Memorial Library, on his same, typed, non-original copy, early historian Robert Mullin had scrawled: "*Important, Billy's letter.*"

So disputed authorship left the fragment in limbo; and the copy's typed annotation at its top states:

(LETTERS OF LEW WALLACE)

(Page torn from notebook about 8 by 9, ruled, black ink, two sides. *Pencil notation in different handwriting at top of sheet. Handwriting resembles but is not identical with letters signed Bonney.)
(1880)*

Since the copyist denied its being a Billy the Kid letter, why did he or she make a copy? An answer is lost with the author.

But the copyist was wrong. And the opportunity to reveal another letter by Billy Bonney - one that could add perspective to his relationship with Governor Lew Wallace and to their earliest pardon negotiations - remained in obscurity for sixty-three more years.

Meanwhile, the Lew Wallace Collection's "Billie" letter fragment was moved in 1999, with the rest of the papers, from the State Library to the magnificent Indiana Historical Society building, where it was stored loose in that 1880 archival box: while Billy's known letters were kept in a vault.

THE FATEFUL FAX

When my Billy the Kid research began in 1999, I acquired copies of Herman Weisner's documents - among them the "Billie" letter fragment. (As an aside, his collection's index lists extensive Thomas Benton Catron papers; but almost all seem expurgated by theft!) As to that fragment, I trusted the annotated refutation; and disregarded that typed copy.

But eleven years later, beginning intense study of Billy Bonney's letters for this book, I became intrigued by the fragment's content, and requested a copy of the original from the Indiana Historical Society to check the handwriting myself. My first glance at their fax was a heart-pounding moment of finding a treasure. It was obviously by Billy Bonney.

It was a discovery waiting to happen. After all, Lew Wallace had saved it with his New Mexico Territory papers; probably originally right with his other Billy the Kid letters.

And, contrary to the copyist's opinion, its Spencerian penmanship matched Billy Bonney's handwriting in his March 1879 letters to Governor Lew Wallace and to Justice of the Peace John "Squire" Wilson.

But its Indiana Historical Society label of "1880" was misleading; since Billy's letters after 1879, when he was on the run or in jail, have a more upright script.

That Indiana Historical Society fax also exhibited Billy's idiosyncrasies: like no capitalization at sentences' beginnings and capitalization of words for emphasis.

And the ragged left margin, called mistakenly by the annotating copyist "`torn from notebook`," would ultimately assist in confirming the place and date of that letter's writing.

The content is spectacular, reflecting Billy's eye-witness knowledge about Lincoln County War incidents. Evident too is his ironic wit: like calling "*deceased*" John Tunstall's killer, Frank Baker - when Baker was, in fact, Billy's (along with other Regulators') homicide victim!

But what about the signature: just "*Billie*;" and not "Billy?"

WHAT ABOUT "BILLIE ?"

As to the fragment's "*Billie*" signature, Billy Bonney used many names: by birth, Henry McCarty; as stepson, Henry Antrim; and as self-invented Billy Bonney. And "*Billie*" may have been his usual spelling, since his other signatures use only "*W.H.*," "*W.*," "*W<u>m</u>*," or "*William*" along with "*Bonney.*"

That "*ie*" may hold other clues. Interestingly, it is still used by the historical, New Mexican, and part-Hispanic, Maxwell family to this day: an elderly, deceased, uncle being "Mannie" instead of "Manny." So Billy, who identified heavily with Hispanic culture, may have preferred and chosen an Hispanic-style diminutive spelling.

Billy's "*ie*" also appears in a diary entry by Sallie Chisum, John Chisum's pretty niece, who amusingly listed pages of "*Presents*" from her suitors. She called him "*Willie*," writing:

286

"Indian Tobacco sack presented to me on the 13 of Aug 1878 by William Bonney. two candi hearts given me by Willie Bonney on the 22 of August."

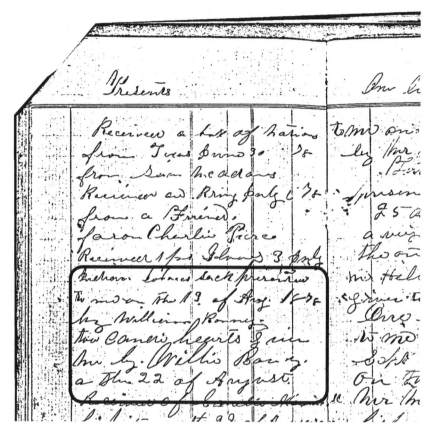

FIGURE 13: Sallie Chisum's Diary entry page 142 (From Historical Center for Southwest New Mexico, Roswell Archives: Sallie Chisum Diary 1878 to 1879.)

A NEEDLE IN A HAYSTACK

My trip to the Indiana Historical Society was obviously needed to examine the "Billie" letter fragment directly.

And I had the heroic plan of turning every page in the Lew Wallace Collection's thousands with the hope of finding the fragment's missing front page or pages - if accidentally mislocated. I would likewise search the Lew Wallace Collection at Indiana State University's Lilly Library in Bloomington.

September of 2010 was when I went. Though I did not find the missing front part, the fragment itself - along with related letters by others - permitted the "Billie" fragment's authentication; along with new insights to Billy Bonney's pardon negotiations, his perspective on the Lincoln County War, and possible secret allies assisting him.

THE "BILLIE" LETTER FRAGMENT

When I arrived in Indianapolis, the "Billie" letter fragment was loose in the Indiana Historical Society's Lew Wallace Collection's archival box for 1880; with its penciled-in date of "[1880?]," as seen by its typing copyist in 1947. [APPENDIX 6]

I am pleased to say that after my authentication, to the satisfaction of archivists at the Lew Wallace Collection, the "Billie" letter fragment is now housed in a special vault along with Billy Bonney's other letters.

GENERAL PHYSICAL DESCRIPTION

The "Billie" letter fragment is in excellent condition, measuring 8 inches wide x 9 ¾ inches long. Its single page has a ragged left side (which made the copyist assume it had been torn from a notebook). Its other three edges are sharply cut.

Its fancy, medium weight paper is off-white with faint blue, horizontal guidelines, which leave a top margin deeper on the back side than the front side: 1¾ inches and 3/4 inches respectively. At the bottom of both sides, the space under the last horizontal guideline to the page bottom is only ¼ inch, since the page bottom cuts off between lines. The handwriting, however, ignoring top margins, starts higher on both sides.

On the upper left corner of the front top margin is a moderately sharp, raised embossure of a "lady's head," measuring approximately 1/2 inch long and 3/8 inch wide. The back of that convex embossure appears on the rear of the page as its concave image on the upper right margin.

The writing is dark brown, typical of aged, oxidized, iron-gall ink. And the signature name is merely "Billie."

288

CONTENTS OF THE "BILLIE" LETTER FRAGMENT

This is the two-sided "Billie" letter fragment, with original blank spaces [APPENDIX 6]. Analysis is on pages 321 to 326.

on the Pecos. all that I can remember are the So Called <u>Dolan</u> Outfit but they are all up here now: and on the Rio G<u>rande</u> this man Cris Moten I believe his name is he drove a herd of)80(head one Year ago last December in Company with Frank Wheeler Frank <u>Baker</u> deceased Jesse Evans George Davis alias Tom Jones. Tom Hill, his name in Texas being Tom Chelson also deceased. they drove the cattle to the Indian Reservation and sold them to John Riley and JJ Dolan. and the cattle were turned in for Beef for the Indians the Beckwith family made their boasts that they came to Seven Rivers a little over four years ago with one Milch Cow borrowed from John Chisum they had when I was there Year ago one thousand six hundred head of cattle. the male members of the family are Henry beckwith and John Beckwith Robert <u>Beckwith</u> was killed the time McSweens house was burned. Charles Robert Olinger and Wallace Olinger are of the same gang. their cattle ranch is situated at Rock Corral twelve miles below Seven Rivers on the Pecos. Paxton and Pierce are Still below them forty miles from Seven Rivers there are four of them Paxton: Pierce: Jim Raymen, and Buck Powel. they had when I seen them last about one thousand head of cattle: at Rocky Arroya there is another Ranch belonging to Smith who Operated on the Penaco last year with the Jesse Evans gang those and the places I mentioned are all I know of this man Cris Moten at the time they stole those Cattle was in the employ of J.J. <u>Dolan</u> an C<u>o</u> I afterwards Seen Some of the cattle at the Rinconada Bonita on the reservation those were the men we were in search of when we went to the Agency. the Beckwith family were attending to their own Business when this War started but GW. Peppin told them that this was John Chisums War and so they took a hand thinking they would loose their Cattle in case that he Chisum won the fight. this is all the information I can give you on this point

Yours Respectfully Billie

AUTHENTICATION BY HANDWRITING

When compared to Billy Bonney's March 13(?), 1879 first letter to Governor Lew Wallace, the "Billie" letter shows the same Spencerian style, with rightward slant and with Billy's personalized alphabet and lack of flourishes.

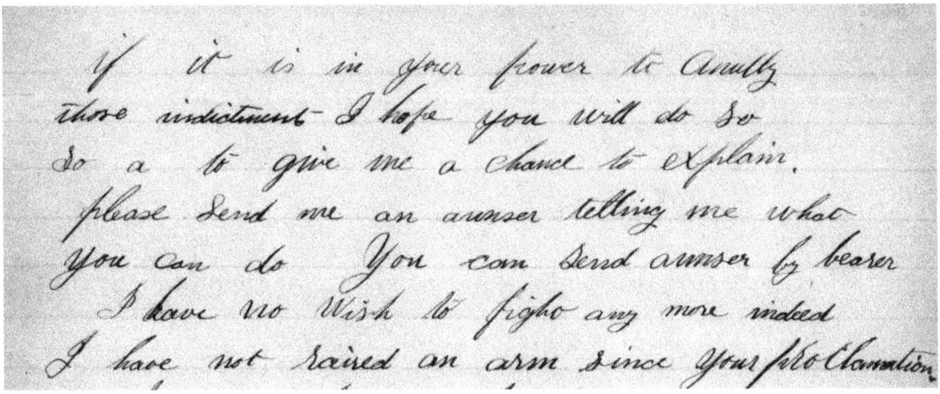

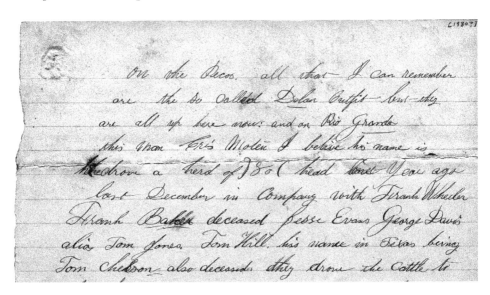

FIGURE 14: Letter to Governor Wallace from March 13, 1879 [APPENDIX 3]

FIGURE 15: "Billie" letter fragment [APPENDIX 6]

SPECIFIC WORD COMPARISONS

KNOWN BONNEY LETTER	"BILLIE" LETTER
March 13, 1879 letter to Wallace [APPENDIX 3] *(signature: J. J. Dolan)*	Line 11 *(signature: J J Dolan)*
December 12, 1880 letter to Wallace [APPENDIX 7] *(signature: J. S. Chisum)*	Line 14 *(signature: John Chisum)*
March 20, 1879 letter to Wallace [APPENDIX 5] *(Seven Rivers)*	Line 13 *(Seven Rivers)*
March 13, 1879 letter to Wallace [APPENDIX 3] *(Lew. Wallace)* March 20, 1879 letter to Wallace [APPENDIX 5] *(Lew. Wallace;)* December 12, 1880 letter to Wallace [APPENDIX 7] *(Lew Wallace)* January 1, 1881 letter to Wallace [APPENDIX 8] *(Lew Wallace)* March 4, 1881 letter to Wallace [APPENDIX 10] *(Lew Wallace)*	Line 19 *(Wallace)*

KNOWN BONNEY LETTER   "BILLIE" LETTER

COMPLIMENTARY CLOSINGS

March 13, 1879 letter to Wallace [APPENDIX 3] *Your Obedient Servant*	*Yours Respectfully*
March 20, 1879 letter to Wallace [APPENDIX 5] *Yours Truly*	
December 12, 1880 letter to Wallace [APPENDIX 7] *Yours Respec*	
January 1, 1881 letter to Wallace [APPENDIX 8] *Yours Respect*	
March 2, 1881 letter to Wallace [APPENDIX 9] *Yours Respect*	
March 4, 1881 letter to Wallace [APPENDIX 10] *Yours Respect*	

KNOWN BONNEY LETTER   "BILLIE" LETTER

THE NAME "BILLIE"

December 12, 1880 letter to Wallace Line 19 [APPENDIX 7] *Billie Wilsons horses*	SIGNATURE *Billie*

AUTHENTICATION BY STYLE IDIOSYNCRASIES

As already noted, Billy Bonney's style idiosyncrasies were: no capitalizations at sentence starts and capitalizing for emphasis. Both are indicated below in the "Billie" letter.

NO CAPITALIZATION AT SENTENCE START

CAPITALIZATION OF WORDS FOR `EMPHASIS

Authentication by Repetitive Grammatical Error

Though using excellent grammar and sophisticated vocabulary, Billy Bonney mistakenly used "seen" as the past tense of "see" - instead of "saw."

That error appears in his May 28, 1879 Dudley Court of Inquiry testimony as his *"Answer"* to prosecutor, Captain Henry Humphreys (*"Recorder"*), about his eye-witness account of people killed in the escape from the burning McSween house on July 19, 1878; as well as people Billy saw shooting at them.

*Answer. I **seen** five killed, I could not swear to who killed them, I **seen** some of them that fired.*

Q. by Recorder. Who did you see that fired?

Answer. Robt. Beckwith, John Hurley, John Jones, those three soldiers, I don't know their names.

That "seen-saw" error is repeated twice in the rear side of the "Billie" letter fragment: 1) *"when I seen them last"* and 2) *"I afterwards Seen Some of the cattle"* as indicated below:

Authentication by Stationery

Fortunate for authenticating the "Billie" letter fragment is its having been written on distinctive lined stationery with an unique embossed stamp of a "lady's head."

And Billy Bonney *himself* used that same "lady's head" stationery for two letters he signed on March 20, 1879. It was also used by others in Lincoln from March to June of 1879.

Since the other users were all Billy's anti-Ring allies, the stationery also assists in determining the fragment's date as well as in extrapolating its historical significance.

PAPER

Antique paper tells tales of its origins to an expert paper conservator like Susan Rogers at the Indiana Historical Society. For me, she examined the "Billie" letter fragment, comparing it to the other sheets having the "lady's head" seal.

Crucial for conclusions is that 19th century paper was hand-made; meaning that sheets from individual batches differ by recognizable variations acting like fingerprints.

Comparisons of a paper sheet include overall thickness; color; pulp patterns of fiber direction and clumping; surface texture; imperfections, like "paper maker's tears;" sheet format, as single page or as a folded folio; ruled horizontal lines and margins; and decorations like embossures.

Pulp fiber direction and clumping is not only visually recognizable with back-lighting, but determines "flexibility": the arc or drape a dangled sheet will assume parallel to the lay of its fibers. Surface texture or roughness is revealed by slanting or "raking" light. "Tearing" (splattered sweat droplets of papermakers), with backlighting, looks like tiny white dots.

Susan Rogers determined that all the "lady's head" stamped stationery examples were same-sized, cream colored, middle weight, of probable rag-wood pulp mixture, and with matching blue ruled lines and matching dropped top margins.

Most dramatic, was discovering that two of the "lady's head" stationery users' sheets - as will be seen - were from the same batch as came the "Billie" letter fragment itself!

FOLIO FORMAT

A clue on the single sheet "Billie" letter is its torn left margin, which led the copy's 1947 typist to theorize wrongly that the page was "`torn from a notebook`."

But that riddle was solved by the "lady's head" stamp, since it let me find, in the Lew Wallace Collection, other users. And those writing multi-paged letters retained the *folio format*: meaning paper folded like a big greeting card with four sides for writing! For a fifth page, they tore apart a folio, making the ragged left margin - just as on the "Billie" letter fragment.

Knowing that the fragment came from a folio opened a tantalizing possibility that missing from that letter was a whole folio: four more pages - all the more loss to history.

"LADY'S HEAD" EMBOSSED STAMP

Decorating some stationery from the 1850's through 1880's were embossed images on the upper left margin, stamped by machine for a raised cameo effect.

Folios were embossed when folded, leaving the stamped impression of the seal less sharp on the second page.

The blurred "lady's head" seal on the "Billie" letter fragment's single sheet implies that it was a second folio sheet.

The "Billie" letter's "lady's head" seal measures about 3/8 inch wide by 1/2 inch long on all examples of the "lady's head" stationery found in the Lew Wallace Collection. All examples of "lady's head" stationery were contemporaneous; and their writers were from the Lincoln area.

Decorative seals were added to stationery at two possible locations. Paper manufacturers, for advertisement, embossed stamps with their own name and logo. Retailers - known as stationers, often dry goods stores selling varied merchandise - could also order blank paper from manufacturers, packed by the ream at 480 or 500 pages of 24 to 25 folios, or by the "quire" as packets of 24 or 25 sheets. They could then add their own fancy stamp by using a custom-ordered die attached to a hand press: for example, like the distinctive "lady's head" embossure.

"BILLIE" LETTER "LADY'S HEAD" STAMP

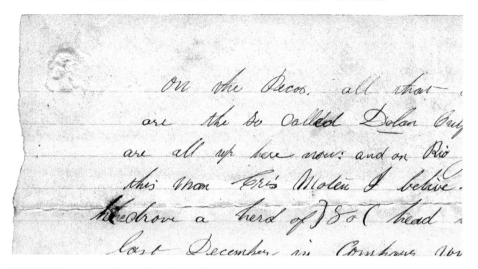

FIGURE 16: "Lady's head" stamp on the "Billie" letter fragment [APPENDIX 6]

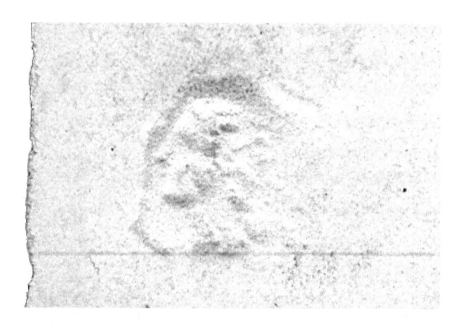

FIGURE 17: Enlarged "lady's head" stamp from the "Billie" letter fragment [APPENDIX 6]

BILLY'S OTHER "LADY'S HEAD" STATIONERY

Important for authenticating and dating the "Billie" letter fragment is my discovery that two of Billy Bonney's known signed letters, both dated March 20, 1879 - to Justice of the Peace John "Squire" Wilson and to Governor Lew Wallace - are on identical "lady's head" stationery.

"LADY'S HEAD" ON BILLY'S LETTER TO WILSON OF MARCH 20, 1879

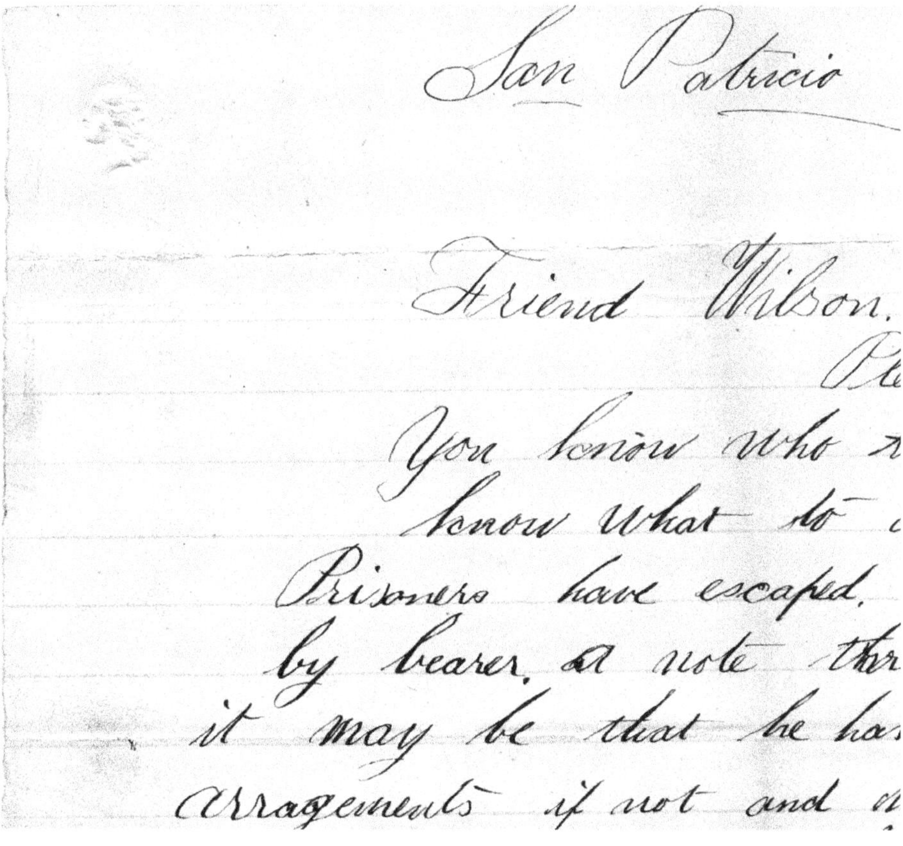
San Patricio

Friend Wilson.

You know who

know what to

Prisoners have escaped.

by bearer. a note

it may be that he

arragements if not and

FIGURE 18: "Lady's head" stationery for Billy's March 20, 1879 letter to "Squire" Wilson [APPENDIX 4]

"LADY'S HEAD" ON BILLY'S LETTER TO WALLACE OF MARCH 20, 1879

Billy Bonney used a single folio sheet, but started on its "back side," giving this letter its "lady's head" seal reversed.

FRONT SIDE WITH "LADY'S HEAD" REVERSED

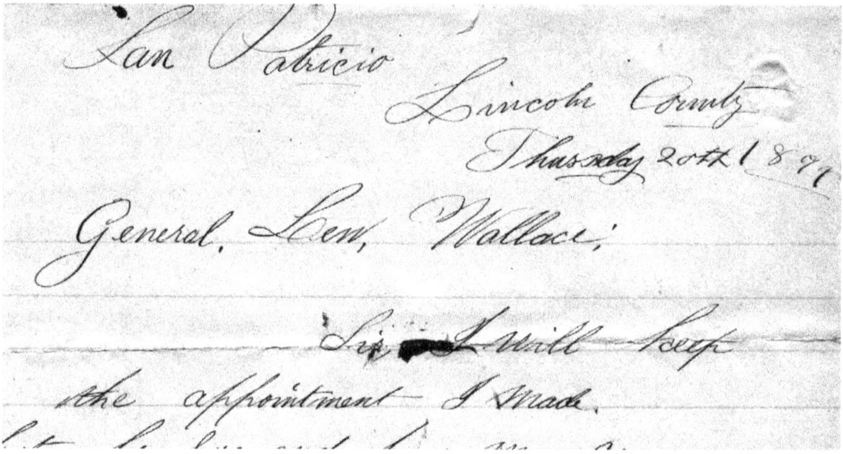
San Patricio
Lincoln County
Thursday 20th 1879
General. Lew. Wallace;
Sir I will keep
the appointment I made.

REAR SIDE WITH "LADY'S HEAD" CORRECT

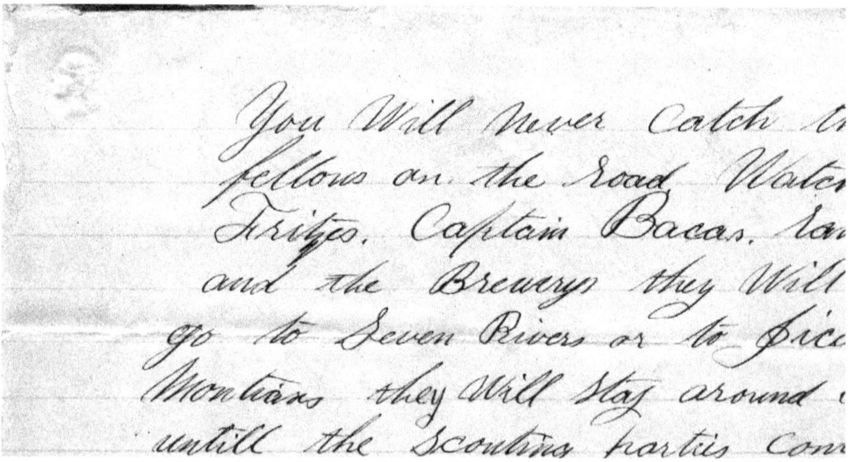
You Will never Catch th
fellows on the road Watc
Fritzes. Captain Bacas. ra
and the Brewerys they Will
go to Seven Rivers or to Jic
Montains they Will Stay around
untill the Scouting parties Com

FIGURE 19: "Lady's head" stationery for Billy's March 20, 1879 letter to Governor Wallace [APPENDIX 5]

OTHER USERS OF THE "LADY'S HEAD" STATIONERY

Besides Billy Bonney, others who used the "lady's head" stamp stationery in the Lincoln area, in the narrow time-frame of March to June of 1879, were: Juan Patrón, John "Squire" Wilson, George Taylor, and Deputy Sheriff Robert M. Gilbert.

JAILOR JUAN PATRÓN

Lincoln County War McSween partisan, friend of Billy Bonney, and his jailor for the pardon deal sham arrest, Juan Patrón used "lady's head" stationery for two letters, both dated March 29, 1879, both to Governor Lew Wallace, and both written when Billy was jailed in his house. Single pages, they are from a torn folio. And their paper batch is the same as that of the "Billie" letter fragment!

Juan Patrón's March 29th letters both report failure to apprehend the two escaped murderers of Attorney Huston Chapman - Jessie Evans and Billy Campbell - who fled Fort Stanton incarceration. The first letter has the best quality "lady's head" embossure in the existing stationery samples.

FIRST PATRÓN LETTER OF MARCH 29, 1879

Lincoln, N.M.
                               March 29, 1879
His Exc. Gov. Lew Wallace,
        Fort Stanton, N. Mex.
Sir:
        Lieutenant Martin Sanches arrived this afternoon, and could not find the parties he was after. The "parties" suspected were peaceful miners.
        Our horses are in very poor condition, hardly able to walk. We have no new information of the whereabouts of the outlaws.
                               Expecting your orders, I remain
                               Very respectfully,
                               Juan B. Patron

SECOND PATRÓN LETTER OF MARCH 29, 1879

Lincoln, N.M.

March 29, 1879

His Exc. Lew Wallace,
    Governor of New Mexico
Dear Sir: I am in receipt of yours of this date.
I will immediately send a party of men as you direct.
Sanches came in this afternoon and was unsuccessful in his expedition.
    We have no clue as to the whereabouts of Evans or Campbell.
Everything is quiet down here.
                        Truly Yours,
                        Juan B. Patron

FIRST "LADY'S HEAD" PATRÓN LETTER

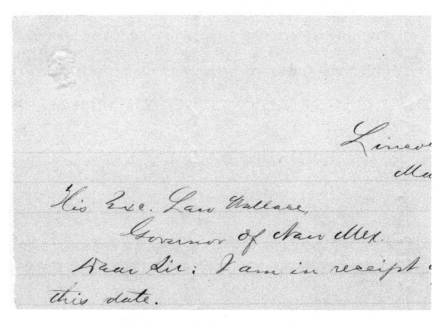

FIGURE 20: Juan Patrón's first March 29, 1879 letter to Governor Lew Wallace with the embossed "lady's head" (Indiana Historical Society. Lew Wallace Collection.)

SECOND "LADY'S HEAD" PATRÓN LETTER

The clarity of both "lady's head" seals on Juan Patrón's letters eventually led to recognizing the identity and symbolism of the "lady's head."

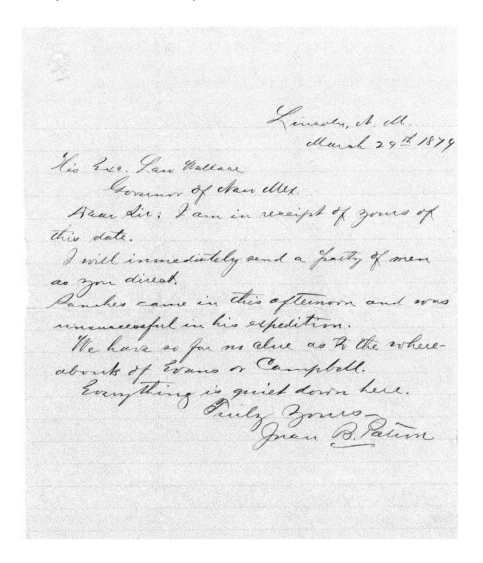

FIGURE 21: Juan Patrón's second March 29, 1879 letter to Governor Lew Wallace with the embossed "lady's head" (Indiana Historical Society. Lew Wallace Collection.)

JUSTICE OF THE PEACE "SQUIRE" WILSON

Also using the "Billie" letter fragment's "lady's head" stationery in the same time-frame as did jailor Juan Patrón, was another public official: Lincoln County Justice of the Peace John "Squire" Wilson. His Lincoln house was a short distance southwest on the mile-long single street from Patrón's, where Billy was staying in his pardon deal's sham incarceration.

Wilson's house was also where Governor Lew Wallace and Billy had their March 17, 1879 meeting to discuss annulling the boy's indictments in exchange for his eye-witness Grand Jury testimony on murderers of Attorney Huston Chapman.

Matching Wilson's wild jagged script and unimpressive literacy is an unsigned, undated, one page fragment having the "lady's head" seal. (One side was used upside-down). A note at a page bottom, in Lew Wallace's hand, states it was by "*Sqr. Wilson.*" Its penmanship and "lady's head" stationery is identical to Wilson's dated letter of April 8, 1879. The latter is signed with his initials: "*JBW,*" and is Wilson's last letter using that stationery. Afterwards he switched to different paper.

Wilson's initialed, April 8, 1879, "lady's head" stationery letter was written on a single page with ragged left margin. It was a warning to Governor Wallace, and stated:

Lincoln april 8th 79
Dear Governer Wallace
it is said that G Pepin told a mexican that the ~~of a~~ pimping Governer thought Himself safe at town. But the first thing He knew He would Be killed & then the other officers of such as sheriff & probate & Justices could easily Be Done away With So you can se what they are after Be very careful about yourself also said you Would not Be attacked on the Road when you had an escort But in town   confidential
*   Yours in truth*
*   J B W*

WILSON'S "LADY'S HEAD" STATIONERY LETTER OF APRIL 8, 1879

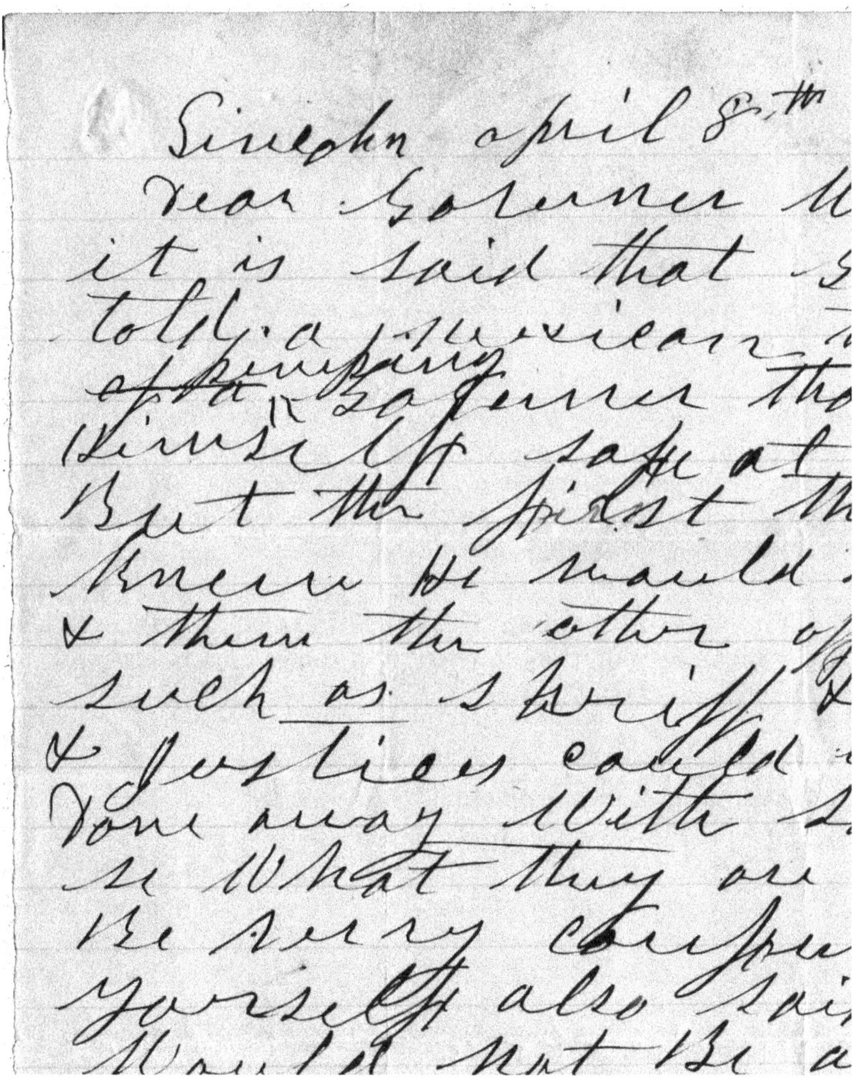

Sinchn april 8th
Dear Governor W
it is said that S
told a mexican t
of keeping
ofa so Gunner tha
Himself safe at
But the fidst th
Knew He would
& them the other of
such as sheriff &
& Jostices could
Done away With S
se What they are
Be very careful
yourself also sai
Would not Be a

FIGURE 22: "Squire" Wilson's "lady's head" stationery letter of April 8, 1879 (Indiana Historical Society, Lew Wallace Collection.)

WILSON'S UNDATED "LADY'S HEAD" LETTER

John "Squire" Wilson's undated, unsigned, one page fragment, like the "Billie" letter fragment, reports for Governor Lew Wallace cattle holdings and outlawry.

Either just a note - or missing its first and last pages - it has a ragged left side; and its possible start has the "lady's head" is on its bottom left. Wallace wrote on that side's bottom: *"Paper from Sqr.Wilson."* That side states:

Nash Has about 120 Head in with Paxton and Pearce dont know His Brand Buck Powel & Raynor also Has about 300 head in the Herd of Paxton & Pearce Brand Figure 9 probably on Left side & Hip that is all in the teritory Just over the line in texas Beckwith creling & olinger Have about 1400 Head all together Beckwiths Brand RB connected on Left Hip creling & olinger AHB connected on Left side the Jones Boys Have some cattle on the west side of the River about Popes crossing dont know many some Branded ⚏ Speaks & others Have some of tunstalls cattle

The other side of that "Squire" Wilson letter fragment has the "lady's head" on the top right; and the ragged margin to the left. That side states:

Chisums Herd about 1200 Head Range from 12 mile Bend to Good Bend distance about 50 miles Roil & others But Roil principal Business in charge of Herd ———
Vonsuikel Herd camp at Bosque Grandy about 350 Head Brand V on shoulder it on side Ꞥ N on Hip known as the copelarys cattle ——— Thomas Gardners Herd Seven Rivers about 140 Head ℐ Believe on side & Hip ——— Paxton & Pierces Herd about 900 Brand ⟋ℐℓ on side & Hip ———

Probable fighting men John Jones Jim Jones Bil Jones George Davis Mron turner Bob Speaks Gunter John Smith or Silton & tom cat or Silvan & that is all I know about Seven Rivers that are Desperate men

WILSON'S UNDATED LETTER'S
"LADY'S HEAD" STATIONERY

This undated and unsigned "Squire" Wilson letter matches his distinctive handwriting and has Lew Wallace's note on its bottom confirming that it was from *"Sqr. Wilson."*

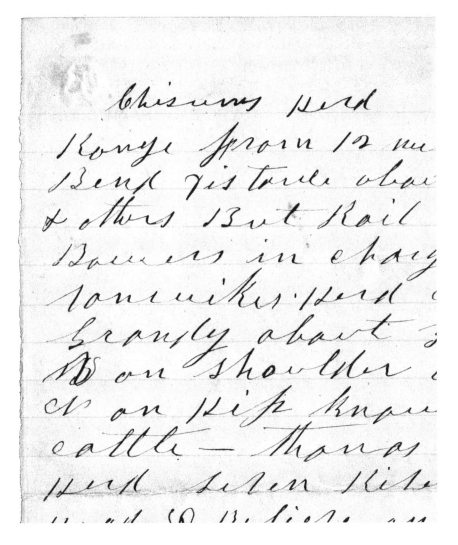

FIGURE 23: "Squire" Wilson's undated "lady's head" stationery letter's back side, probably March of 1879 (Indiana Historical Society, Lew Wallace Collection.)

LEGAL ASSISTANT GEORGE TAYLOR

Also writing on "lady's head" stationery to Governor Lew Wallace from Lincoln in the same time-frame as Juan Patrón and "Squire" Wilson was a George Taylor. He was the legal assistant to Attorney Ira Leonard, who was then in Lincoln to represent Susan McSween for her April 1879 Grand Jury case against Commander Dudley for murder and arson, as well as to prepare for his Dudley's Court of Inquiry role starting in May.

George Taylor's four page letter to Governor Wallace, dated April 25, 1879, is in folio form, with unseparated pages.

GEORGE TAYLOR'S "LADY'S HEAD" STATIONERY
ON APRIL 25, 1879

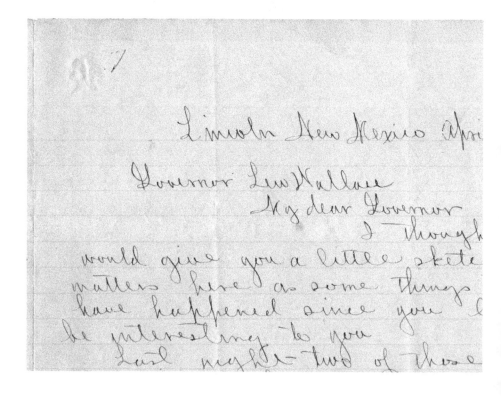

FIGURE 24: George Taylor's "lady's head" stationery letter of April 25, 1879 (Indiana Historical Society, Lew Wallace Collection.)

GEORGE TAYLOR'S "LADY'S HEAD" STATIONERY
LETTER OF APRIL 25, 1879

George Taylor's letter of April 25, 1879 matches the content of the other writers using the "lady's head" stationery, in that he was a reporting to Governor Lew Wallace about Lincoln County "troubles" from an anti-Ring side.

Lew Wallace put his own note on the letter's last page: *"May 21ˢᵗ, 79, From Geo. Taylor. Esq ___ giving act of the shooting into Judge Leonard's house."*

It should be noted that, in the letter below, the "Wilson" George Taylor refers to is local attorney, Sidney Wilson, not Justice of the Peace John "Squire" Wilson.

George Taylor wrote:

Lincoln New Mexico April 25ᵗʰ-79

> *Governor Lew Wallace*
> > *My dear Governor*
> > > *I thought I would give you a little* sketch of matters here as some things that have happened since you left may be interesting to you.
> > > *Last night two of those outlawed scoundrels who are so numerous around here made a dash through town horseback and fired into our building.*
> > > *Judge Leonard had changed the place of his bed and they seemed to be aware of the fact for the bullets were directed where he lay, fortunately the side of the house was struck and no damage done but had they not been going so rapidly when they fired they may have accomplished their purpose which was evidently to kill or injure the Judge so he cannot prosecute them.*
> > > *Col Rynerson the prosecuting attorney for the territory is either afraid or anxious to screen these villains you have arrested; he is entering into his work with no spirit and leaves all the work for the Judge only interfering to raise obstacles in the way of bringing the rascals to justice.*
> > > *I have no confidence in him he has been engaged in murderous scrapes himself and can't help but have a*

fellow feeling for men who are in the same trouble he has been in himself.

Wilson is in great trouble, the men who employed him are now trying to get back their horses and arms from him; he is denouncing them as a set of ___ cutthroats and murderers and swearing he will never defend another one of them, he told me he had heard them make desperate threats against parties who have been prominent in arresting them, and particularly against Judge Leonard against whom they are very hostile. singulously they have no feeling against Rynerson but all their animosity is directed against the Judge.

You should have laughed had you seen us rushing around for our weapons when we were fired into last night, it was a complete surprise to as we had not anticipated anything of the kind. I thought when you were here you took most too many precautions I see now I was mistaken there is no telling when the scoundrels will make a break on us, they are thirsting for revenge and plunder and the instant the military are withdrawn from here we will have the same bloody contests over again that have taken place here before.

We are now well armed and ready to give the outlaws a good reception when they come as they surely will if that military scoundrel Col Dudley is exonerated from his crimes and again placed in command: it is a mystery to me how that man can be permitted to disgrace the army as he does, using it to persecute and murder the honest people of this county and aid and protect the most desperate thieves and outlaws in the United States in their crimes.

The mining interests are looking better every day. I believe we will soon have some good developments made.

I will write you the news as they occur, I hope you will soon return as these outlaws stand in great dread of you and your presence here gives us all a greater sense of security than even the military as they could not prevent the outrage of last night.

Respectfully
George Taylor
Lincoln New Mexico

DEPUTY SHERIFF ROBERT M. GILBERT

Another "lady's head" stationery user was anti-Ring Lincoln County Deputy Sheriff Robert M. Gilbert. On June 1, 1879, he wrote to Governor Wallace about law enforcement problems.

On February 19, 1878, Gilbert had been one of six Coroner's jurymen for John Tunstall. Their judgment of murder yielded Justice of the Peace Wilson's warrants used by the Regulators.

That June 1, 1879, Robert Gilbert was a deputy under Sheriff George Kimbrell, the McSween-side partisan who made the sham arrest for Billy Bonney's Wallace pardon deal.

SEALS ON GILBERT'S JUNE 1, 1879 LETTER

The Robert M. Gilbert letter is the last known use of the "lady's head" stationery. Five pages long, its intact folio is folded backwards, reversing the seal to its upper right corner. Its fifth page, a half- folio, has the seal correctly on its front.

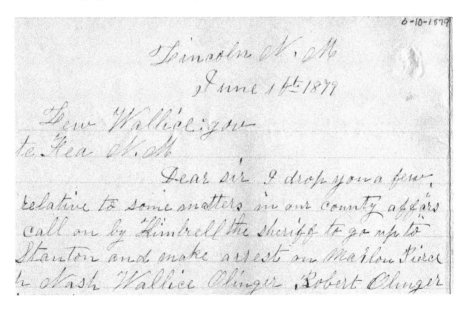

FIGURE 25: First page of Deputy Sheriff Robert M. Gilbert's "lady's head" stationery letter of June 1, 1879, with reversed seal on reverse-folded folio (Indiana Historical Society, Lew Wallace Collection.)

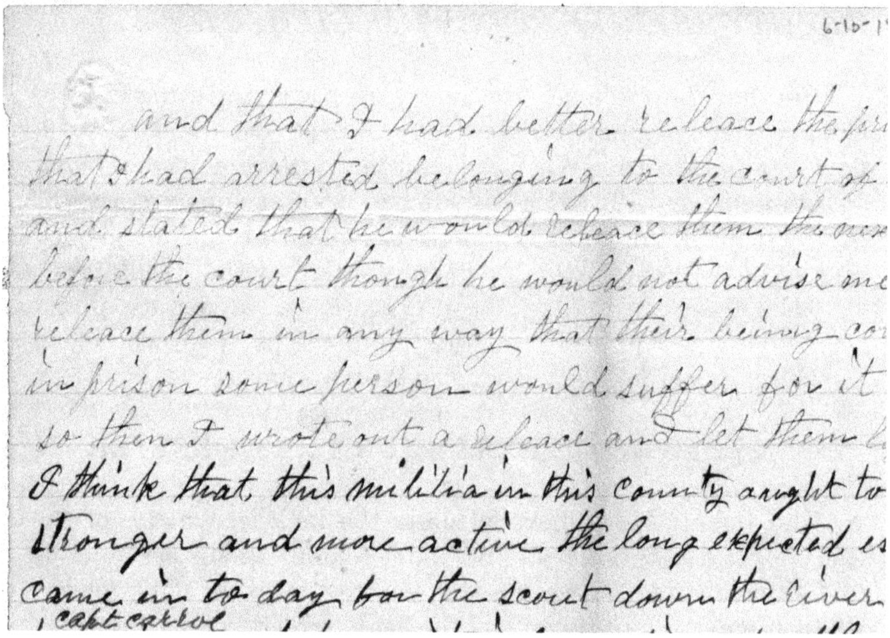

and that I had better release the pri[soners?]
that I had arrested belonging to the court of
and stated that he would release them the [men?]
before the court though he would not advise me
release them in any way that their being co[n-]
in prison some person would suffer for it
so then I wrote out a release and let them [go?]
I think that this militia in this county aught to
stronger and more active the long expected [men?]
came in to day for the scout down the river
cabt carrol

FIGURE 26: Fifth page - a half-folio - of Deputy Sheriff Robert
M. Gilbert's "lady's head" stationery letter of June 1, 1879,
with "lady's head" seal correctly positioned (Indiana Historical
Society, Lew Wallace Collection.)

ROBERT GILBERT LETTER OF JUNE 1, 1879

Deputy Sheriff Robert M. Gilbert's letter of June 1, 1879
to Governor Lew Wallace describes his being foiled in arresting
Lincoln County War lawbreakers by their Ring partisans.

Lincoln N.M
June 1st 1879

Hon Lew Wallice: gov
Sante Fea N.M

Dear sir I drop you a few lines
relative to some matters in our county affairs I was call on by
Kimbrell the sheriff to go up to Fort Stanton and make arrest on
Mailon Pierce Joseph Nash Wallice Olinger Robert Olinger

Marion Turner and Andrew Boyle and on arriving ~~all~~ at the
commanders quarters was informed by the commanders wife
that he was very sick suffering with ~~nuelg~~ neralga I said that
I wanted to see him that I was Deputy Sheriff Gilbert she then
said that she would see him and I remained on side of the house
for some time and then she came out and asked me what
I wanted I said to her I wanted a posse of 5 or 6 men to arrest
some men in the post for whome I had warrants for and
I wanted the men quick and if the commander pleased to attend
to my wants soon so in a few minutes the commander Capt
Purington came out and asked me who I had warrants for in
the Post I said the warrants were issued from the district court
he then asked me to let him see the warrants I says as you are
commander of the post I have no objection and handed the
warrants to him and he remarked that Judge Warren Bristol
promised that these warrants should not be sent here and asked
how I got them I said they were put in my hands by Sheriff
Kimbrell then he stated that I would have to wait untill the
court of inquiry broke up so that he could see Judge Waldo. so
in a course of time Waldo came and in a few minutes he said
make out the requisition and mention the names of all that you
want to arrest I said is that really necessary and he said yes
that he would not give a posse to arrest himself then I said
I would make it out and did giving the above names and gave it
to him and seeing Turners name said why did you not showe
me the warrant for Turner before I said I did not think of it or
did not think it any use he then asked me for the warrant and
I said to him that it was isued from Justice court he then
remarke that I could have men to arrest under Justices warrant
then I said give me the posse and I will leave Turner out he then
sent for the posse after nearly 2 hours delay and when the posse
came he instructed them not to assist in arresting Mr Turner
but assist in arresting the others so I went in search for the men
found Mr Pierce and arrested such and no persons els for a
while finally Turner came out cursing me and saying that I had
no posse to arrest him and d-d your old soul you cant arrest me
I then threw my gun on him and said I will show you and did
and conducted him and Pierce to the guard house and released
the possee the commander said to me that some person had
come up from Lincoln and had told the boys that there was

warrants out for them I supposed it was the account of not more than two being found and my previously wanting to be in a hurry to make the arrest and stating that the parties may leave which he said they would not! so I went back up to the Settlers store and found Andrew boil and started to make an arrest on him and he said that he protested the arrest as he had a summons from from the United States I said that did not make any difference do you resist the arrest and at the time Judge Waldo stepted up to me and said do you not know how to arrest a man and slaped me on the shoulder and said that is way) which I did the same to Boile and said go with me at which time boile rose and started along with me when Waldo remarked to me that he would have me punished for contempt of court I remarked that I cannot help it I had already made the arrest and walked on with the prisner down to the commanding quarters and delivered Mr Boil at this time waldo came and said that he was attorney gen of the Ter and why did I not ask him for advise I said that I did not even know that you were attorney gen of the Ter then some one present said why did you not see a lawyer concerning the arresting these men and I stated that I counseled with lawyers and Dondly remarked that Judge Leonard was no lawyer I mentioned no names of lawyers of any person Judge Waldo read some law stating very clearly that no arrest could be made on witnesses during their attendance on courts to and from and that I had better releace the prisners that I had arrested belonging to the court of inquiry and stated that he would releace them the next day before the court though he would not advise me to releace them in any way that their being confined in prison some person would suffer for it so then I wrote out a releace and let them loos I think that this militia in this county ought to be stronger and more active the long expected escort came in today for the scout down the river and has capt carrol orders not to assist in rounding up cattle nor holding them nor to make any arrest were there is no sheriff only to guard prisners very scrct orders Capt Carrol seems to in good spirits do all you can for this part of the county and as speedy as possible R.M. Gibert

Deputy Sheriff
Lincoln county. N M

WHO IS THE "LADY?"

The "lady's head" stamp embossure on the "Billie" fragment was an invaluable link for confirming it as Billy Bonney's and extrapolating historical implications of that letter.

But who was the "lady?" And did that stamp have any special meaning to its stationery's users?

Since the "lady's head" embossure was crimped onto folio-folded paper by a hand press, its crispness varied with pressure; and the second page's duplicate was always less sharp.

The most perfect "lady's head" image appears on Juan Patrón's first letter of March 29, 1879 to Governor Lew Wallace. One can make out not only her classical profile and wavy wind-blown hair; but also, behind her, is a rod topped by a drooping cap - a symbol lost to most modern viewers.

But in Billy's day, she would have been easily recognizable; and her cap is the give-away. The "lady's head" is "Lady Liberty," holding her freedom cap on a pole.

That "Lady Liberty" image goes back to the Roman Empire, where the conical Phrygian cap symbolized freedom from tyranny, because it was worn by liberated slaves.

That representation of freedom was adopted in 18th century, revolutionary France as the goddess of Liberty, and named Marianne. She was first painted by a Jean-Michel Moreau in 1775 in traditional Roman dress along with her Phrygian cap topping her war pike. By 1790, in France, the Phrygian cap became, simply, the "liberty cap."

The "Lady Liberty" symbol came to the United States by the late 18th century also, and was commonly used on coins and other public venues through the 19th century. Most frequently in profile, she was depicted wearing the liberty cap or holding it on a pole (representing her pike in revolutionary France).

And the "Lady Liberty" on the "Billie" letter's stationery is exactly that image.

My historical analysis to follow demonstrates that no better symbol could have been used by that stationery's writers in that brief period. One can even venture to say that running out of local supply became an accidental symbol for the running out of time for liberty in Lincoln County.

LADY LIBERTY STAMP ENLARGED FROM THE FIRST JUAN PATRÓN LETTER OF MARCH 29, 1879

That the "lady's head" embossure on the "Billie" letter fragment is "Lady Liberty," can be seen clearly from the enlarged stamp on Juan Patrón's first of two March 29, 1879 letters to Governor Lew Wallace. And the letter's paper came from the same batch as did the "Billie" letter fragment's.

FIGURE 27: Enlarged "Lady Liberty" stamp from Juan Patrón's first letter of March 29, 1879 to Governor Lew Wallace; also enlarging and demonstrating pulp patterns (Indiana Historical Society. Lew Wallace Collection.)

Non-"Lady's Head" Stationery Users

Other stationery, useful in analyzing the "Billie" letter fragment, appeared contemporaneously in the Lincoln area.

GOVERNOR LEW WALLACE

Lew Wallace inadvertently demonstrated limited paper supply in Lincoln by insensitively using dead John Tunstall's stationery, probably from his store across the street. Ironically, Wallace's subject on March 6, 1879 was Billy Bonney:

OFFICE OF
JOHN H. TUNSTALL,
Lincoln, Lincoln County, New Mexico.

Lincoln, N.M. .... *187.........*

Lincoln, N.M., March 6, 1879
Gen. Edward Hatch.
Con'g Dist. New Mexico
Sir.
I have just ascertained that "The Kid" is at a place called Las Tablas, a plazita up near Capitan's ranch. He has with him Thomas Folliard He was *and was going out of the Territory, but stopped there to rest his horses, saying he would stay a few days. He was at the house of one Higinio Salazar.*

You will oblige me by sending a detachment after the men; and if they are caught secure them on in Fort Stanton, for trial at *as accessories to the murder of Chapman.*

If the men are found to have left Las Pables I beg they may be pursues until caught. The details are com-
manded to you for
judgment.

      Very respectfully
      Your friend and servant,
      Lew. Wallace
      Gov. New Mexico

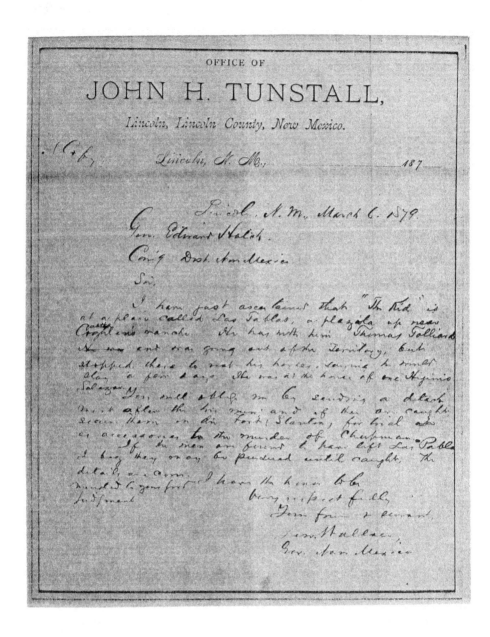

FIGURE 28: Lew Wallace letter about Billy Bonney on John Henry Tunstall letterhead, dated March 6, 1879 (Indiana Historical Society. Lew Wallace Collection.)

PROBATE JUDGE FLORENCIO GONZALES'S
LETTER OF OCTOBER 8, 1878

Lincoln County Probate Judge Florencio Gonzales had protected Alexander McSween from some of James Dolan's litigation; and lived in San Patricio: Regulator safe haven and massacre site on July 3, 1878, before the Lincoln County War.

On October 8, 1878, Florencio Gonzales wrote new governor, Lew Wallace, about lawlessness. His stationery had a national capitol building embossure. As such, it provides another clue to circumstances surrounding the "Billie" letter fragment, since that capital stationery was used by Billy himself for his first letter of March 13(?), 1879 to Wallace.

Also, Billy had headed his March 20, 1879, "Lady Liberty" stationery letter to Lew Wallace as being from "*San Patricio*."

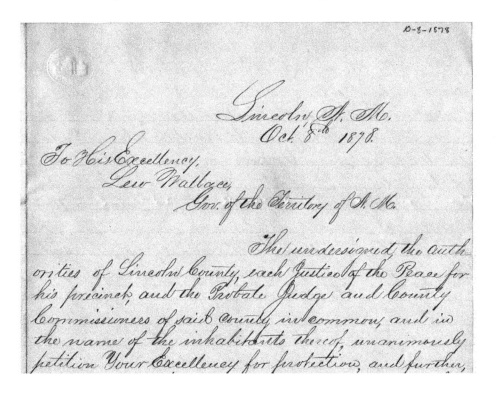

FIGURE 29: Lincoln County Probate Judge Florencio Gonzales capital building stationery stamped letter of October 8, 1878 (Indiana Historical Society, Lew Wallace Collection.)

JAILOR JUAN PATRÓN'S LETTER OF APRIL 12, 1879

The "Lady Liberty" stationery, available in early 1879 in the Lincoln area, seems to have petered out, with Deputy Robert M. Gilbert's June 1st letter being its last example. Jailor Juan Patrón's letter, by April 12th, had the national capitol building embossure. Justice of the Peace "Squire" Wilson's paper, by May 18th, was the long, lined, legal-style being used in town by Attorney Ira Leonard. And, as I determined, in the entire remaining Lew Wallace Collection, "Lady Liberty" stationery never appeared again.

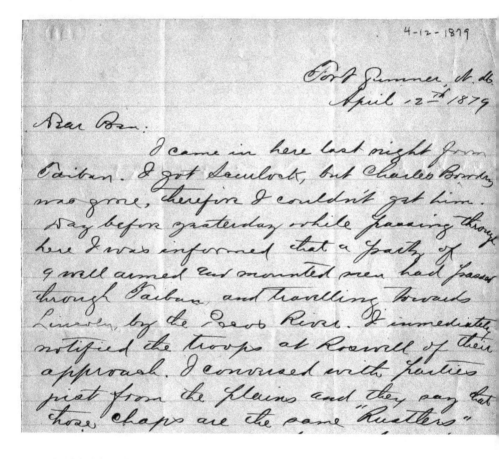

FIGURE 30: Juan Patrón national capitol building stamped stationery letter of April 12, 1879 (Indiana Historical Society, Lew Wallace Collection.)

"SQUIRE" WILSON LETTER OF MAY 18, 1879

On May 18, 1879, "Squire" Wilson used legal-length paper looking identical to that being used by Attorney Ira Leonard, in Lincoln and participating in the Dudley Court of Inquiry.

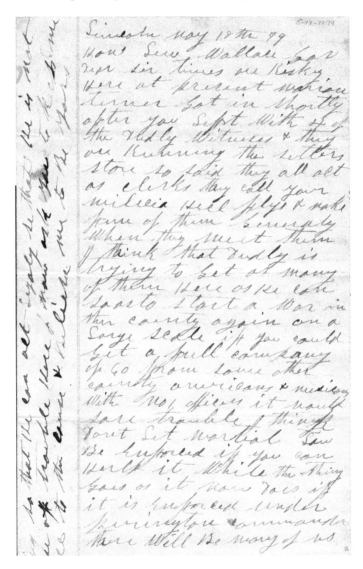

FIGURE 31: Wilson's legal-length stationery letter of May 18, 1879. (Indiana Historical Society, Lew Wallace Collection.)

AUTHENTICATION BY CONTENT

Authenticating Billy Bonney's authorship of the "Billie" letter fragment is assisted by its content: information that, arguably, only Billy would use or know.

As to its recipient, that content jibes with Lew Wallace's 1879 request to Lincolnites, after Huston Chapmen's murder, for feedback on outlawry. It matches reporting by the other anti-Ring users of the "Lady Liberty" stationery from that March to June. Also, Wallace retained it in his Territorial papers. So Lew Wallace is concluded to be its recipient.

The fragment also fits with Billy's ongoing pardon negotiations with Governor Wallace; most obviously in that Billy used that same "Lady Liberty" stationery for two of his own signed letters for those arrangements that March.

The "Billie" letter fragment's subjects appear to continue Billy's March 23, 1879 Lew Wallace interview, "*Statements by Kid*," already discussed. But unlike those cattle rustling and outlawry "*Statements by Kid*," where Wallace missed any broader context, the "Billie" letter fragment alludes to explanations of Lincoln County War period events as well as issues pertinent to Billy's wartime murder indictments, which were the essence of their pardon negotiations.

Thus, referenced are 1878 Regulator killings in March of Frank Baker, and in April of Andrew "Buckshot" Roberts at Blazer's Mill in the Mescalero Indian Agency; and house arson and killing of Alexander McSween - all connected to the current Lincoln County "troubles," and justifications of Billy's acts. The "Billie" letter fragment's using "*mentioned*," further implies it as elaborating on his Wallace interview.

As such, the fragment is unique among Billy Bonney's letters. It is less a pardon plea, and more a sharing of Billy's insights. One can imagine that its missing front might have Billy Bonney's own description of the Lincoln County War and Chapman's murder - about which he would testify in a month.

One can only wish that someday the rest of the fragment is found - possibly in the collection of an early historian who accidentally carried it off with other papers, never realizing that he or she now possessed arguably the most important document in the history of Billy the Kid.

"BILLIE" LETTER CONTENT COMMENTARY

on the Pecos.

[AUTHOR'S NOTE: Frustratingly, the fragment begins with a sentence ending. But *"on the Pecos"* were three major foci of participants in Lincoln County's "troubles" and outlawry. There was cattle king John Chisum, who proved traitor to his alliance with Tunstall and McSween; and even refused to pay the Regulators their promised wages. Worse, there were the Seven Rivers boys: the Jones and Beckwith families; the Olinger brothers, Wallace and Robert; and their Captain, Andrew Boyle. All had participated in murders of men on Billy's side: Frank MacNab before the Lincoln County War, and all the deaths in the War itself. They would have been in the group shooting at Billy during the burning building escape. And, in that period, James Dolan had a cow camp south of Seven Rivers on the Pecos; there worked the foreman, William "Buck" Morton, whom the Regulators would kill as a Tunstall murderer. And the Dolan cow camp received rustled stock for the Santa Fe Ring, stock rustled by Jessie Evans and his boys: other Tunstall murderers.]

all that I can remember are the So Called <u>Dolan</u> Outfit but they are all up here now:

[AUTHOR'S NOTE: This is an example of special information that Billy Bonney would know: the fact that by 1879 James Dolan and his henchmen no longer had the Pecos cow camp after he went bankrupt in 1878 from mercantile competition with John Tunstall. Intriguingly, Dolan's name is underlined for emphasis; and Dolan certainly was the Santa Fe Ring boss in Lincoln County. Dolan probably was key to bringing in Commander N.A.M. Dudley during the Lincoln County War when, staying in town, he realized that the McSween side about to win.]

and on the Rio <u>Grande</u> this man Cris Moten I believe his name is he drove a herd of)80(head one Year ago last December in Company with Frank Wheeler

[AUTHOR'S NOTE: The reference to *"Cris Moten"* (possibly *"Dutch Chris"*) and the *"Rio Grande"* appears as Billy's expanded description of a rustler gang in Wallace's *"Statements by Kid," made Sunday night March 23, 1879"* which said: *"in the direction of the Rio Grande. Frank Wheeler ... and Dutch Chris are supposed to have used this trail taking a bunch of cattle over."*]

Frank <u>Baker</u> deceased Jesse Evans George Davis alias Tom Jones. Tom Hill, his name in Texas being Tom Chelson also deceased.

[AUTHOR'S NOTE: Billy continues to list rustler gang members, and they are Jessie Evans's boys: Frank Baker, George Davis, and Tom Hill, crucial names missed by Wallace in his "*Statements by Kid.*" Billy would have known these men, first because he rode with Jessie and his boys in September of 1877; second because they were Ring rustlers and enforcers who were directly involved in murdering Tunstall; and Evans was in the Chapman killing.]

[AUTHOR'S NOTE: Billy snidely calls Frank Baker (underlined) "*deceased.*" Baker, as a Tunstall murderer, was a Regulator killing on March 9, 1878; and Billy was likely one of his killers!]

[AUTHOR'S NOTE: As intimate, is Billy's knowing the death of Evans's gang member, Tom Hill, as well as his alias and place of origin. Though Billy again only says "*deceased,*" it was an obscure killing; implying that Billy kept track of erstwhile associates. During an Evan's gang robbery, Hill was shot by a Cherokee partner of a German sheep herder named John Wagner near Shedd's Ranch: a Ring outlet for rustled stock, and a safe haven for Jessie and his boys. In that shooting, Jessie was hit in the right wrist.]

they drove the cattle to the Indian Reservation and sold them to John Riley and JJ Dolan. and the cattle were turned in for Beef for the Indians

[AUTHOR'S NOTE: This amazing statement demonstrates an insider's knowledge of the mercantile and criminal dynamics of the Santa Fe Ring which had led to Tunstall's murder and the Lincoln County War. It is also the central point which Wallace missed in all his interviewing: <u>the Territorial rustling was a Ring endeavor to meet beef contracts for the Mescalero Indian Reservation and for Fort Stanton.</u> It had been the plan of Tunstall and McSween to replace the Ringman with their own contracts to both entities. That was why Tunstall created a cattle ranch in the Feliz River, and a secondary one on the Peñasco River, with Billy and Fred Waite as Homestead Act owners. And that Ring competition was why Tunstall had to die. So, here Billy is giving Wallace the dynamics he needed to really end the Lincoln County "troubles" - dynamics which Wallace ignored.]

the Beckwith family made their boasts that they came to Seven Rivers a little over four years ago with one Milch Cow borrowed from John Chisum   they had when I was there Year ago one thousand six hundred head of cattle.

[AUTHOR'S NOTE: This is Billy's wry sense of humor, about the Beckwith family "borrowing" a cow from Chisum; but in four years approaching 2000 head. The Beckwiths, like the rest of the Seven Rivers boys, got their herds by rustling from Chisum's giant herd of 80,000 head. Again, this is insider information. When Billy first returned to New Mexico Territory from Arizona Territory in September of 1877, he stayed with the Jones family at Seven Rivers, and got to know the Beckwiths - with their sons, John and Robert, eventually fighting for the Ring in the Lincoln County War (in which Robert "Bob" Beckwith was killed by friendly fire).]

the male members of the family are Henry beckwith and John Beckwith Robert <u>Beckwith</u> was killed the time McSweens house was burned.

[AUTHOR'S NOTE: Billy not only elaborates on the Beckwith family members (he leaves a blank, possibly unsure that the patriarch's name was Hugh), but relates Robert's death (he is underlined for emphasis) to the most dramatic event of the Lincoln County War: the murder of Alexander McSween in the escape. Billy's reference to "*the time McSween's house was burned*" implies his assumption that Wallace already knows he is referring to that arson; and even that they had discussed the event either at the "Squire" Wilson house meeting on March 17th or at his interview with Wallace on the 23rd. The quality of understatement comes through in the "*was killed,*" since Billy does not elaborate that it was friendly fire when he was serving arrest warrants on McSween, and the Ring partisans began shooting at McSween.]

Charles   Robert Olinger and Wallace Olinger are of the same gang. their cattle ranch is situated at Rock Corral twelve miles below Seven Rivers on the Pecos.

[AUTHOR'S NOTE: Billy, unsure of an uncertain "Charles's" last name, is very clear on the Olinger brothers, Robert and Wallace; referring to their being in "*the same gang,*" meaning the Seven Rivers boys. Robert Olinger, as the man Billy most hated, would become his last murder victim - in his great escape jailbreak. The ranch Billy locates presumably has the brothers' stock rustled from John Chisum.].

Paxton and Pierce are Still below them forty miles from Seven Rivers there are four of them Paxton: Pierce: Jim Raymen, and Buck Powel. they had when I seen them last about one thousand head of cattle:

[AUTHOR'S NOTE: Billy is here reporting on another rustler gang.]

at Rocky Arroya there is another Ranch belonging to Smith who Operated on the Penasco last year with the Jesse Evans gang

[AUTHOR'S NOTE: Billy here links a rustler to Jessie Evans, and consequently to possible Ring-related rustling.]

those and the places I mentioned

[AUTHOR'S NOTE: Intriguing is the statement "*and the places I mentioned.*" It implies a past conversation between Billy and Wallace. And I take it to mean a follow-up to the places mentioned in their interview of March 23, 1879, for which Wallace wrote his notes on "*Statements by Kid.*"]

are all I know of this man

[AUTHOR'S NOTE: Here it can be observed that Billy, as well as providing other information, seems to be answering, via this letter, a specific question about Chris Moten - whose name follows next.]

Chris Moten at the time they stole those Cattle was in the employ of J.J. Dolan an Co.

[AUTHOR'S NOTE: Since the letter fragment began with the Dolan outfit and with Jessie Evans gang rustlers' named along with Cris Moten, Billy may here be linking Moten to the rustling enterprise of James Dolan. Most important, however, is that this statement is a lead-in to the fragment's most important sentence for authentication as being Billy Bonney's.]

I afterwards Seen Some of the cattle at the Rinconada Bonita on the reservation those were the men we were in search of when we went to the Agency.

[AUTHOR'S NOTE: MOST IMPORTANT STATEMENT!
1) **Important because of insider information**: Billy here is describing, first hand, going as a posseman with Deputy Constable Dick Brewer's posse, on April 4, 1878, to the Mescalero Indian Reservation in search of murdered John Tunstall's stolen stock, and for his murderers - for whom they had Justice of the Peace "Squire" Wilson's arrest warrants. And the location is not just the reservation, but the specific place they went: the "*Agency*" way station and home of the Indian Agent, Frederick Godfroy. That makes the word "*Agency*" so dramatic. Only Billy would know this insider information; and he can even recognize the cattle! (When killed, Tunstall had only 600 head.) Note also the implication that Billy is following up, by way of explanation, on an earlier statement to Wallace, possibly at the interview, by saying: "*those were the men we were in search of when we went to the Agency.*"
2) **Important because the references here are connected to the Lincoln County War indictments for which Billy was negotiating his pardon deal**: This stop-over at the Indian Agency led to the Regulators accidental meeting with Andrew "Buckshot" Roberts, a Tunstall murderer. Roberts's resisting arrest led to his being killed. And Billy was one of the Regulators indicted for that in the April 1878 Grand Jury. Billy's other two murder indictments for the pardon deal were for Sheriff Brady and Deputy Hindman. So this follow-up reference is an apparent link to an earlier discussion between Billy and Wallace about the indictments for the pardon deal: occurring either at their March 17th meeting at Wilson's, or the March 23rd Billy-Wallace interview.]

the Beckwith family were attending to their own Business when this War started but G.W. Peppin told them that this was John Chisums War and so they took a hand thinking they would loose their Cattle in case that he Chisum won the fight.

[AUTHOR'S NOTE: Billy again demonstrates insider information about what made the Pecos River area ranchers join the fight on the Ring side. Billy spoke from knowing personally the people involved, as well as knowing the pre-War tensions between Chisum and the rustling Seven Rivers boys. As to personal contacts, besides the Beckwiths, from whom he soon became estranged in 1878, there was John Jones of the Ma'am Jones family, with whom Billy stayed close, until John Jones's murder by Robert Olinger (which was revenge for John Jones's killing of John Beckwith) - a murder which Billy allegedly promised the Jones family he would avenge (and did in his great escape by killing Robert Olinger).]

326

this is all the information I can give you on this point

[AUTHOR'S NOTE: Billy's precise concluding statement is almost identical to one he would use in his testimony in the Dudley Court of inquiry in which he stated on May 28, 1879, in answer to his observations on troops in Lincoln on July 19, 1878: *"When I escaped from the house three soldiers fired at me from the Tunstall store, outside corner of the store. That's all I know in regards to it."*]

Yours Respectfully Billie

[AUTHOR'S NOTE: The use of "Billie" is interesting beyond its unexpected spelling; though his reference to a "Billie Wilson" in his December 12, 1880 letter to Governor Lew Wallace indicates that he might have always spelled the name "Billy" as "Billie". And, as already discussed, Billy was free and easy with his names, having accumulated a variety autobiographically and by personal creation. In his known writings, he does not use the informal "Billy." In his recorded words, he does only in an answer from his May 28th Dudley Court of Inquiry testimony questioning about his aliases: *"Q. by Recorder. What is your name and place of residence? Answer. My name is William Bonney. I reside in Lincoln. Q. by Recorder. Are you known or called Billy Kidd, also Antrim? Answer. Yes Sir."* And in all Billy's other letters to Lew Wallace he uses a formal signature having for last name *"Bonney;"* and, for first name, either his *W.H.* initials for *"William Henry"* or just *William* or *W^m*. So it may be guessed that this communication represented something special to Billy, reflecting how he felt in relation to Governor Wallace at the time of its writing. There is only one other example of his name ending in *"ie."* And it was for wooing. In her diary, Sallie Chisum, the pretty blond niece of John Chisum wrote that *"Willie Bonney"* had given her two candy hearts. Presumably she got that spelling from an attached note, or from other notes reflecting his ardor. He failed to win Sallie, but the clue remains that Billy seems to have thought that the diminutive ending was endearing. So the big question is: When this letter was written, was Billy "courting" Lew Wallace, not just for annulling of indictments, but for affectionate acceptance? And more poignantly, was the use of that signature a sign of Billy's growing trust that they were indeed developing a real relationship with real and mutual goals of bringing to an end "outlawry" in Lincoln County? That reasonable possibility is of importance to determining a probable date for the "Billie" letter fragment's writing. And, as will be discussed, that window of opportunity was small, because what Billy meant by "outlawry" were the Ring realities discussed in this letter; and "outlawry" to Lew Wallace would very soon mean condemning and betraying Billy himself.]

AUTHENTICATION SUMMARY CHART

- Handwriting matches that in Bonney's signed letters.

- "Billie" signature, in particular, matches the name "Billie" [Wilson] written in Bonney's signed letter of December 12, 1879.

- Stylistic idiosyncrasy of no capitalizations for a new sentence matches that in all Bonney's signed letters.

- Stylistic idiosyncrasy of capitalization for word emphasis matches that in all Bonney's signed letters.

- Grammatical error of "seen" for "saw" matches that in Bonney's Dudley Court of Inquiry testimony given on May 28, 1879.

- Folio stationery with "Lady Liberty" stamp matches that of Bonney's signed letters of March 20, 1879 to Justice of the Peace "Squire" Wilson and to Governor Lew Wallace.

- Stationery with "Lady Liberty" stamp matches that in signed letters of Bonney allies in Lincoln in 1879 period.

- "Lady Liberty" stationery of the "Billie" fragment is from the same pulp batch as used by his jailor Juan Patrón for his own two letters written March 29, 1879.

- Stationery with "Lady Liberty" stamp is special; used only from March 1879 to June 1879 in Lincoln.

- Content is compatible with that in Lew Wallace's "*Statements by Kid*" interview notes of March 23, 1879.

- Content has information unique to Billy Bonney's Lincoln County War period knowledge.

HISTORICAL EXTRAPOLATIONS

There is literary aptness, given that the Lincoln County War was a freedom fight, that "Lady Liberty's" symbol was present in Lincoln among anti-Ring opponents - including Billy Bonney. That revolutionary sign stamping the "Billie" letter fragment, seems a fitting directional through Billy's time as a Tunstall Regulator, Lincoln County War fighter, guerrilla rustler, astounding jail breaker before hanging; and rebel to the end, dying yards from sleeping beloved Paulita Maxwell.

One can even surmise - and hope - that this international symbol's embossure was hand pressed in 1878 by idealistic John Henry Tunstall himself, at his Lincoln store; while musing, not coincidentally, on his own emancipating of local citizens, who had renamed their little town from La Placita del Rio Bonito, to Lincoln, after shock at that emancipating president's assassination - to be repeated by shock again thirteen years later at Tunstall's own assassination.

Irrespective of actual embossing by Tunstall, "Lady Liberty" folio stationery was likely limited to Lincoln town itself, as the only locale for miles around with big enough all-purpose stores like the House and Tunstall's.

But by early 1879, the House was bankrupt, and dead Tunstall's store was only haphazardly managed by traumatized widow, Susan McSween; and, by that year's end, was purchased by James Dolan for his own mercantile revival.

So it is likely that by early 1879 - the March through June 1st of known "Lady Liberty" stationery use - Lincolnites had dwindling paper supplies from their unstable stores. Even Governor Lew Wallace himself, when in town, resorted to scavenging dead Tunstall's left-over letterhead.

And fancy "Lady Liberty" paper appears parsed out among public official cohorts - as well as to the boy hero of the Lincoln County War secretly in their midst. And, I would hypothesize that Billy Bonney was being secretly assisted by those very men in gaining a gubernatorial pardon.

So "Lady Liberty" fittingly yields a key, not only to authenticating the "Billie" fragment, but to postulating an intrigue of Billy Bonney's friends, to help him attain his own freedom in the lost Lincoln County War's aftermath.

DATING THE "BILLIE" LETTER FRAGMENT

The "Billie" letter fragment's date can be derived by its handwriting, by dates of Billy Bonney's known letters on that same stationery, by dates of letters written by other "Lady Liberty" stationery users, and by its content.

BY HANDWRITING

The fragment's handwriting, which is in Billy Bonney's best Spencerian style, matches that in his three signed letters from March of 1879, two on that same stationery. Since quality of Spencerian penmanship is affected by desk and pen, matching implies also that Billy wrote all four letters at the same location, or in similar circumstances. That keeps the time span for writing the "Billie" fragment to that month of March.

BY BILLY'S DATED LETTERS

Two of Billy's three March of 1879 letters, with matching Spencerian handwriting, use the "Billie" letter fragment's "Lady Liberty" stationery, implying that he wrote them all in a close time-frame.

BY OTHER STATIONERY USERS

The other users of the "Lady Liberty" stationery imply that its source was Lincoln, either by their being residents or by their being in town: Juan Patrón, Justice of the Peace John "Squire" Wilson, Lincoln County Deputy Robert M. Gilbert, and George Taylor. In addition, all were anti-Ring as public officials or associated with an anti-Ring professional - like George Taylor being legal assistant to Attorney Ira Leonard.

As to the place of purchase, since Tunstall's store stayed operational after his death, even if he was not its original stationer, the paper, seen only locally, may have come from there. But its scarcity, available only in the period of March through June 1st of 1879, gives credence to dwindling supplies that could place its original availability back to late 1877 or early 1878 and to Tunstall's lifetime.

The other implication of scarcity is sharing among the stationery's users; and all of them readily had contact with each other in small Lincoln town in the timeframe of use. And their dated letters aid triangulation of the fragment's date.

Before Billy Bonney entered his sham incarceration, he used "Lady Liberty" stationery for his two signed letters of March 20, 1879; after having been right in stationery-user "Squire" Wilson's house three days earlier when meeting with Governor Wallace.

And, after Billy's jailing, on March 21st, at Juan Patrón's home, the "Billie" letter fragment was from the same "Lady Liberty" paper batch Patrón used himself on March 29th.

Additional "Lady Liberty" stationery users set the likely end of that paper's availability to Deputy Robert M. Gilbert's letter of June 1, 1879.

BY STATIONERY NON-USERS

Lincoln visitor, Lew Wallace, pointed to paper scarcity in town by using John Tunstall's old letterhead. Juan Patrón and "Squire" Wilson switched to different paper by April of 1879, indicating their supply of "Lady Liberty" paper was gone also.

BY CONTENT

The fragment's subject matter builds on Lew Wallace's interview notes titled "*Statements by Kid,*" dated March 23, 1879. The "Billie" letter fragment even states "*mentioned,*" as if referring to a prior conversation. The fragment also appears to answer questions, possibly posed at that interview; and, like it, omits Billy's actual outlaw friends. And, with Wallace staying just west of Juan Patrón's house, delivery was easy.

DECIDING ON THE DATE

I derived the date for the "Billie" letter fragment by its handwriting, by dates of other "Lady Liberty" stationery users, and by its apparent immediate follow-up to Billy Bonney's Lew Wallace interview of March 23rd, yielding its probable day of writing as March 24, 1879.

HISTORICAL ANALYSIS

Once I had authenticated the "Billie" letter fragment as by Billy Bonney and to Governor Lew Wallace, its "Lady Liberty" stationery, used also by other Lincolnites, enabled rethinking the March 1879 pardon deal by raising radical questions.

What if that testimony-for-clemency plan was devised not just by Billy, but with cooperation of his Lincoln area friends?

What if Billy's first letter of March 13(?), 1879 to Lew Wallace, proposing the bargain on fancy national capitol building embossed stationery, but omitting its place of writing, was created in San Patricio, in the office of McSween-side friend, Probate Judge Florencio Gonzales?

What if Billy's having written "*San Patricio*" as his location on his "Lady Liberty" stationery letter to Wallace seven days later, teasingly referenced his actual first location of March 13th, but now was self-protectively false?

What if Billy's hide-out that March of 1879 was least expected: Lincoln itself? By May, in his Court of Inquiry testimony, Billy said: "*I reside in Lincoln.*" In his Angel Deposition the year before, he was also living in "*said county.*"

What if that hide-out was, at the time of the first letter writings, the house of Billy's "*Friend Wilson;*" who, incognito and afraid of reprisals, still wanted to help him attain clemency? "Squire" Wilson's house was so set back from the single street that Wallace considered it ideal for his eventual "secret" meeting with Billy. And no one would have been suspicious of visits there to Billy by other helping public officials: like Billy's friend, jailor Juan Patrón, or friendly Sheriff George Kimbrell's deputy, Robert Gilbert.

What if the killing of Attorney Huston Chapman, the people's new hope for protection and justice against the Ring, made Lincoln officials devise or support revenge by eye-witness testimony against murdering local boss, James Dolan - without exposing themselves?

What if their chosen eye-witness was risk-taking Billy Bonney, scheming with these Lincoln County friends and past victims of the Lincoln County War to formulate his gubernatorial amnesty gamble to win a future on the right side of the law; and to win his own anti-Ring retribution?

This new pardon deal scenario can be constructed around the fact that the "Lady Liberty" stationery users were primarily Lincoln County public officials with legal knowledge; were all Billy's anti-Ring friends; and were all traumatized and enraged by murders which left them helpless for retribution - Tunstall's, McSween's, and Chapman's. Possibly, earlier that March, they first hid their boy hero of the Lincoln County War after Wallace placed the $1000 reward on his head.

Betting on Billy having loyal partisans is not far-fetched. Sheriff Pat Garrett was forced to use Texan possemen to hunting down Billy, because New Mexicans refused. The Ring feared those same partisans enough to hold Billy three extra months in the Santa Fe jail to await railroad completion for his transport to his Mesilla trial, to avoid his rescue on the road.

Billy knew he had backers. In his March 4, 1881 letter from the Santa Fe jail, he threatened Wallace with a rescue: *"I guess they mean to Send me up without giving me any Show but they will have a nice time doing it. I am not entirely without friends."*

Anti-loyalist precautions were again made to transport Billy back to Lincoln for hanging, with newspapers helpfully announcing that he would be shot if rescue was attempted.

And when Billy made his courthouse-jail escape on April 28, 1881, the Lincolnites waited inactively for hours while he broke his leg-chain with a pick-ax. Among the watchers would likely have been the users of the "Lady Liberty" stationery two years before. There were different ways to win the Lincoln County War: passive resistance was one.

So it is not far-fetched to postulate that in March of 1879 Billy had Lincoln area backers wanting his indictments voided. Probate Judge Florencio Gonzales and Justice of the Peace "Squire" Wilson could have devised the clemency plan with Billy to present to the new governor, already housed in Lincoln. Those officials were angry men. Gonzales remembered Sheriff Peppin's July 3, 1878 massacre at his town. Wilson had been victimized both by Governor Axtell and Commander Dudley.

Evidence of their collusion may be in Billy's first letter to Wallace, of March 13th. It has Billy's own wit and bravado, but also has technical legalese, implying assistance: using the correct word "annul" (his "annuly") for eliminating his indictments, instead of "pardon" (which is for convictions).

That it was written in San Patricio at Probate Judge Florencio Gonzales's office can be guessed first from its stationery: that official's national capital building embossed stationery, conceivably given Billy to make the best impression on the governor. Just four months earlier, Gonzalez himself had used that same good paper to write a letter to newly arrived Governor Wallace about local problems.

Billy, carrying a huge bounty, of course, did not reveal his location on that letter of March 13th. But a week later, he disingenuously wrote "San Patricio" as his place of writing his "Lady Liberty" letter to Wallace - when arguably at another safe haven: Lincoln itself and at the source of that paper.

The plot of partisans may have thickened when Lew Wallace decided to question a logical person - Justice of the Peace Wilson - about Billy's March 13th letter's bargain; never imagining that Wilson's offer of his own house for a meeting with the boy on the 17th coincided with a larger plan.

The next steps - planning a sham arrest and incarceration, which were likely Billy's survivalist idea - involved more friends: Deputy Sheriff Robert Gilbert and jailor Juan Patrón, in addition to "Squire" Wilson; all with "Lady Liberty" stationery to give Billy; who, on March 20th, wrote to Wilson on it, while, I would guess, hiding in Lincoln, but bluffing Wallace that same day by using "San Patricio" for writing location.

After arrest by Sheriff George Kimbrell, "jailed" Billy had access to Juan Patrón's dwindling "Lady Liberty" paper; possibly being shared with "Squire" Wilson - up the street - and with Attorney Ira Leonard's assistant, George Taylor; both men in town for the April Grand Jury and Dudley Court of Inquiry.

The plot with Billy may have grown as those public officials realized Lew Wallace was nonsensically focused on "outlawry." Wilson or Patrón could have encouraged Wallace to interview Billy for real issues. He did, on March 23rd.

The next day, the 24th, Billy apparently asked Patrón for stationery for a follow-up to Lew Wallace. So Patrón gave him his best: "Lady Liberty" stationery: likely two folios; one which Billy tore in half for his fifth page, signed "Billie." Left over was a half-folio page; and whatever else remained in the house.

As to deeper meaning, that letter's signature said it all: "*Billie.*" Within eleven days of contacting Lew Wallace, Billy had abandoned his first letter's formal "*W.H. Bonney.*" "*Billie*" came within three days of their meeting at "Squire" Wilson's, where Wallace, marveling at the remote night-time romance of a frontier town and bloodthirsty bandit king, must have misleadingly appeared to Billy as enthralled by his unexpected cleverness, knowledge, youth, and fine firearms.

"*Billie*" tumbled out after merely their second meeting, that Sunday evening interview, repeating the great and elegant man's rapt interest, and culminating in Billy's trust, never to be experienced again in his life. "*Billie*" was his most intimate name: the name a loving father could use; the name offered as so boyish that it would engender protectiveness. But the wise information shared would belie immaturity and engender paternal respect as they forged a common bond for justice.

Anticipating clemency, anticipating a life in which his intelligence allowed any profession - even becoming an attorney like Lew Wallace - Billy struggled to enter that new world.

And Billy, given that deserved amnesty, succeeding in the secret plan of his friends, winning for them the Lincoln County War differently and later, intended to marry Paulita Maxwell. Writing "*Billie,*" possibly first pausing at intimacy stimulating bottomless longing, was probably his most vulnerable moment: dropping his rough façade to be the child he never was.

Only if one could someday find Billy Bonney's love letters to Paulita Maxwell, would one see such a baring of his soul as is implied in the "Billie" letter fragment.

The unused, folio half of the "Billie" letter's last page became, on March 29th, one of Patrón's two letters to "His Excellency" Lew Wallace; and, of course, is an exact match to the paper pulp of that "Billie" letter fragment: Billy's last known letter from Lincoln.

And, acquisitive Lew Wallace, living there in Lincoln out of his suitcase, saved the letters on "Lady Liberty" stationary; though losing, in his jumbled papers then, or after his death two decades later, the front pages of that March 24th "Lady Liberty" letter signed "Billie" - and possibly never read - but still a valued memento from his adventure with "the Kid."

Wallace's Ominous Letter to Carl Schurz

ELITIST SCORN REVEALED

By March 31, 1879, the fourteenth day of their relationship, Billy Bonney's future betrayal in the pardon bargain was writing on the wall in the form of Lew Wallace's progress report sent to Secretary of the Interior Carl Schurz: Wallace's Washington, D.C. liaison to President Rutherford B. Hayes.

Wallace was irritable, with a task more time-consuming, and a populace more recalcitrant than anticipated. Wallace's draft, with small-lettered postscript, also exposed elitist scorn of Billy, trustingly housed yards away in their mutual plan. Wallace wrote: *"A precious specimen nick-named 'The Kid,' whom the Sheriff is holding here in the Plaza, as it is called, is an object of tender regard. I heard singing and music the other night; going to the door, I found the minstrels of the village actually serenading the fellow in his prison."* The letter stated:

Lincoln, N.M., March 31, 1879
Hon. Carl Schurz,
Sec'y Dept. Interior
Sir:
Today I forward a telegram to you, with another to the President, requesting him to proceed under his October proclamation and place this county and Doña Ana under martial law.

That step is induced by several reasons; chiefly, first, because it is apparent to me that the military do not enter heartily into the work requested of them. The work itself is evidently distasteful, and then they are really acting under direction of civilians.

In the next place, my expectation of a revival of courage and confidence on the part of the better people of the county is far from realized. The escape of Campbell and Evans shook their faith in the soldiers. As jurors and witnesses they are singularly unreliable on account of their fear of retaliation, if those whom they may be called upon to try or against whom they may testify should go free - and that, they say, is the assured event of trial in court. To add to their difficulties, no one of them seems to know who the other is serving. There is no such thing amongst them as real confidence in each other. Should the county court open next Monday week in the regular session, the liberation of the twelve prisoners now in custody - six for murder, six for horse and cattle stealing - would, in my opinion, be assured. And what that would end in you can readily perceive.

To still further weaken my confidence in juries as instruments of the law in this county, I have been forced to take into account of the fact that everybody of any force or character has in some way been committed to one side or other in the recent war, and is yet all alive with prejudices and partialities. **A precious specimen nick-named "The Kid," whom the Sheriff is holding here in the Plaza, as it is called, is an object of tender regard. I heard singing and music the other night; going to the door, I found the minstrels of the village actually serenading the fellow in his prison.** [Author's boldface] So, speaking generally the prisoners are good brave boys according to the side on which they have been fighting ~~and killing if the fighting and killing have been on the side of the persons with whom I talk~~. These prejudices and partialities are as certain to follow jurors into the box the day of the empanelling as that the day will come.

There is no penitentiary in the Territory, if peradventure a verdict of hard labor should be obtained; neither is there any law authorizing me or any other official to contract elsewhere for the keeping a convict. So, too, there is but one lawyer in the county [Sidney Wilson]. I offered him employment on behalf of the Territory. He did not dare accept the offer. As attorney for the prisoners he is moving in the matter of habeas corpus writs, and will succeed in setting at liberty seven of my most important prisoners, unless I decline to *obey the order of the court - the seven are in arrest without warrants. Only a military commission can bring them to punishment.*

Enough is disclosed to put you in possession of the reasons underlying my clear conviction that coming session of the court will in the present situation be useful only to the wrong-doers; leaving, as I see now after nearly one months study and patient exertion upon the very ground, nothing to be hoped except from martial law. The desperados include some of the most noted of their class in the United States, and they cannot be made quit except by actual war - by guns and pistols, not writs and lectures and then only by co-operative action between the military of New Mexico, Texas, and Arizona. Please give one glance at the County of Lincoln as it is defined on the map and note its extent and local advantages for operations like theirs, and you will see the force of these latter words.

I hope the President will act upon my request. The expeditions to which I have alluded have not been entirely barren of good results; one is certain, the enemy have been driven to their hiding places, and will not re-appear before the preliminary measures essential to the proposed new regime can be taken.

I have the honor to be,
Very respectfully,
Your friend & servant,
Lew Wallace
Gov. New Mexico

Judge Bristol has been notified of my opinion as to the advisability of holding his court, and my intention to ask a declaration of martial law. His views coincide with mine.

To enable the inhabitants of the town to defend themselves and property, of which latter they have very little left, on the farms not enough to put in their crops, I authorized a military organization of thirty two men - all who had arms and horses.

The instructions given the regular troops, copies of which were furnished you in my last letter, are continuous in their operation and will be carried out as the officers are more or less zealous. Not being able to do more, I will return to Santa Fe the last of this week or the first of next.

CHANGED CIRCUMSTANCES AGAIN

Circumstances would worsen for Billy and Wallace in two weeks. By April 13, 1879, the Ring acted to protect their own. To Fort Stanton, they sent major attorneys, Simon Newcomb, Sidney Wilson, and Albert Jennings Fountain, along with Ringman judge, Warren Bristol (ultimately Billy's hanging judge), to free all of Lew Wallace's prisoners there by filing writs of *habeas corpus* - claiming there was no legal justification to hold them any longer before the Grand Jury that month. (Billy, on the other hand, would be kept in jail from late December of 1880 to late March of 1881 for transport to trial in Mesilla, while the Ring awaited completion of the railroad to Mesilla, to thwart rescue attempts). So over twenty men - including James Dolan, indicted killer of Tunstall and chief suspect for Huston Chapman's slaughter - were freed.

That day, Billy Bonney's risk went up tremendously. His murderous enemies were back on the lose. And Lew Wallace, seeing his grand solution unraveling in mockery, experienced his own interest in local "troubles" becoming inversely proportional to his injured pride.

Also, as Billy sat trapped in Juan Patrón's house with the April Grand Jury fast approaching, Ringman District Attorney William Rynerson could simply walk him the short distance to the courthouse, where Ringman Judge Warren Bristol could act on Billy's 1878 murder indictments by declaring Lincoln County too partisan for a trial, and by having him transported immediately to Doña Ana County - that meant Mesilla - for a hanging trial he himself would preside over. Only Wallace's annulling of those indictments could prevent all that.

So after the Fort Stanton freeing, Billy awaited the Grand Jury where he unrealistically believed his testimony would free him. And Lew Wallace busied himself about town interviewing people preposterously about random outlaws and rustlers; and preparing for his Dudley Court of Inquiry testimony the following month, thinking unrealistically that the certain conviction of Commander Dudley would end the Lincoln County "troubles." Realistic only was Billy's developing of a friendship with Attorney Ira Leonard, in town for prosecuting.

Billy's Lost
Grand Jury Testimony

Fulfilling the "Anully" Deal

Billy Bonney fulfilled his side of his supposed Lew Wallace pardon deal by testifying against Attorney Huston Chapman's murderers - James Dolan, Billy Campbell, and Jessie Evans - in the April 1879 Lincoln County Grand Jury. He achieved those men's murder indictments: Dolan and Campbell for first degree murder; Jessie Evans for accessory to murder.

LOST TESTIMONY OF BILLY BONNEY

Billy Bonney's April 1879 Grand Jury testimony transcript is lost by a likely Ring expurgation. But it was confirmed in newspapers. On May 10, 1879, the Grant County *Herald* reprinted the article from the Mesilla *Thirty Four*.

It stated:

> At the recent term of court in Lincoln, about 200 indictments were found. Among them, Col. Dudley and George W. Peppin for burning McSween's house, **Dolan and Campbell for the Chapman murder, in which the Kid is the principal witness**; [Author's boldface] about 25 persons for the murder of MacNab; Tom O'Folliard for stealing Fritz's horses. But two criminal cases were tried - that of Lucas Gallagos for the murder of his nephew. He was found guilty and sentenced to one year; and a case of assault in which the accused was acquitted. No civil case was tried. In nearly all of them, one or the other party was dead. O'Folliard, Jack Long, Marion Turner, and others, plead the governors pardon and were discharged. Peppin, Dolan and Matthews took a change of venue to Socorro, and Dudley took a change of venue to Dona Ana

county. **The District Attorney would not consent to the release of the Kid for turning State's evidence. His case comes to Dona Ana county**. [Author's boldface] The greater portion of persons indicted will probably come forward and plead the governor's pardon. Dolan and Matthews, indicted in the last term for the Tunstall murder, also go to Socorro on change of venue. Opinion is divided as to what the result will be. Some think a fresh outbreak is imminent, and others that the trouble is over. The two opposing factions have about exhausted themselves and future troubles will only arise from bands passing through and plundering. Jesse Evans and Campbell have not been rearrested.

GRAND JURY JUDGE SPEAKS

A document that does exist is Ringman Judge Warren Bristol's prejudicial instructions to the jurymen, which attempted to counteract their knowledge that Lincoln County War issues were connected to the murder of Attorney Huston Chapman, a champion come to finally get justice. So his instruction can be read as his Santa Fe Ring threat to them:

> *We are all aware that partisan feeling has run very high; that it has been very intense and bitter; and for this reason I warn and admonish you that you cannot permit this partisan feeling to influence your action as grand jurors without violating the solemn oath you have taken as grand jurors that you will present no person by indictment through malice, hatred or ill will nor leave any unpresented through favor or affection.*

Two years later, in April of 1881, Judge Warren Bristol, repeating the same malicious intent of perverting justice, gave a Mesilla jury instructions which left them no other option but to declare a verdict of first degree murder against William Bonney, so that Bristol, at last, could sentence him to hanging - having missed that chance in June of 1879 when the boy had departed his sham imprisonment in Lincoln before Bristol and his Ring cronies could achieve that same result.

ATTORNEY LEONARD'S FEEDBACK TO WALLACE

Also confirming existence of Billy Bonney's Grand Jury testimony is Attorney Ira Leonard's letter of Sunday, April 20, 1879 to Governor Lew Wallace. It portrays graphically the harassment Billy endured from Ringman District Attorney William Rynerson. Evident also is Leonard's awareness of the corrupt politics behind it. And Leonard's outrage by that early date demonstrates his protective respect for Billy, to whom he would stay loyal into 1881. Leonard wrote:

> *I tell you, Governor, the District Attorney here is no friend to law enforcement. He is bent on going after the Kid. He proposes to destroy his evidence and influence and is bent on pushing him to the wall. He is a Dolan man and is defending him in every manner possible.*

Doubtless, Billy had courageously fulfilled his pardon bargain with the governor - if it had been real. While awaiting his planned Dudley Court of Inquiry testimony, Billy must have impatiently awaited notification that he was a free man.

Wallace Claims Credit

With brave efforts of Billy Bonney and other Lincoln County citizens, the Lincoln County Grand Jury of April 1879 achieved two hundred indictments, primarily of Ring-faction criminals. The result was satisfied quiet among the people as all expected justice to be achieved in upcoming trials. Of course, none realized that by changing the venues to Doña Ana County's Mesilla, Judge Warren Bristol removed likelihood of witnesses coming there all the way from Lincoln; ultimately enabling his dismissal of all those Ringmen cases by October).

Meanwhile, Billy expected nullification of his own murder indictments; possibly having even testified in other cases besides that of Huston Chapman's killing - like the civil case by Attorney Ira Leonard for Susan McSween against Commander N.A.M. Dudley, which had yielded his indictments for murder and arson - before the military Court of Inquiry would consider those same charges the following month.

But Governor Lew Wallace preempted that Grand Jury's achievement, claiming personal credit in a June 11, 1879 letter to Secretary of the Interior Carl Schurz. Even though Wallace mentions the Chapman murder, Billy Bonney would never be given credit by him for the indictments; in fact, as Wallace's newspaper articles of 1900 and 1902 showed, he perfidiously denied that Billy had given testimony at all.

Adding credence to Wallace's having intentionally tricked Billy by misleading wording in his original response, rather than really promising pardon (as in: *"I have the authority to exempt you from prosecution, if you will testify to what you say you know"*), is his blithe confiding to Schurz, in this letter of June 11, 1879, that his November 1878 Amnesty Proclamation never even made prior indictments an impassable obstacle to pardon (as Billy - and even Attorney Ira Leonard - believed)!

In fact, Wallace states in that letter that anyone indicted merely required a court appearance requesting a pardon (which Ringmen, represented by Thomas Benton Catron, used successfully). Though Billy Bonney never understood this loophole, it is the explanation behind his bewailing, after his conviction in 1881: *"I think it hard that I should be the only one to suffer the extreme penalty of the law."* The reason was that his Ring-protected War opponents were long off the hook.

About that loophole Wallace, boasted to Carl Schurz: *"As it was most of the indicted appeared in court and plead the amnesty in bar [of prosecution]."* Wallace's rationalization was unburdening courts from having trials for so many cases. He added to Schurz: *"Hereafter the labors of grand juries will be confined strictly to offences subsequent to my proclamation."*

So Billy, with his "pardon deal" must have seemed to Wallace just a dupe.

That Wallace felt no guilt pangs at cheating Billy is seen by his lying to Carl Schurz, in that same June 11th letter, that the disrest he had been sent to quell in New Mexico Territory had been caused by a *"confederacy of outlaws and their friends."* Certainly, Wallace counted the *"precious specimen," "the Kid,"* among them. And Wallace's request to President Hayes, through Schurz, was for martial law: meaning easier hangings.

Wallace's letter to Schurz of June 11, 1879 stated:

Executive Office,
Santa Fe, N.M.,
June 11, 1879.

Hon. C. Schurz,
Sec'y Dept. Interior.
Sir:

Enclosed please find a copy of the report of the commandant at Fort Stanton. As the statement of Capt. Purington is fully sustained by intelligence received privately, I think myself justified in informing you of a continuance in Lincoln county of the peace reported in my last letter. And in the connection, you will pardon me, I think, for calling your attention and the President's to the fact, that for quite eight months now there has been but one murder – Mr. Chapman's – with reference to which you know my procedure.

[AUTHOR'S NOTE: Wallace here claims all credit, as well as minimizing Chapman's killing, which was part of the reason for the "peace": terror at Ring retribution by the silenced citizens.]

This leaves me at liberty to repeat for your better understanding of the present situation there, that the old factions known respectively as the "Murphy-Dolan" and the "McSween" are as dead organizations;

[AUTHOR'S NOTE: Wallace is here misstating the results of his intervention: the quelling of citizens' protests against Ring domination. He should have been aware of the Santa Fe Ring from Attorneys Frank Warner Angel and Ira Leonard. And it was his policy of indifference to the real issues of the "troubles," that inadvertently worked to long-term Ring advantage. The "Murphy-Dolans" were alive and well – merely biding their time for the regrouping and recrudescence which occurred.]

to which may be added now, that my amnesty proclamation has had exactly the effect intended; which was to shear the past off, and make present and future all questions which might require official action, pertinent to civil affairs in the locality.

[AUTHOR'S NOTE: The month before, Wallace had been ridiculed in the Dudley Court of Inquiry for his Amnesty Proclamation's having been foolish. Here he uses it to claim credit for success.]

To illustrate, the grand jury empanelled for the recent county court was, with one or two exceptions, composed of men accounted of the McSween or anti-Dolan party, for it is undeniable that nearly all citizens eligible as grand-jurors are of that persuasion. They found nearly 200 indictments, the whole, with a few exceptions, against the Dolan people. Nearly 200 indictments in a county of a voting population of 150 total!

[AUTHOR'S NOTE: Wallace's callous indifference leaves him blind to the horrific impact of the war on the Lincoln County citizens. And it should not be forgotten that he began his March 1879 stay there by interviewing citizens for their grievances. He heard first-hand. But did he listen? Did he care? Apparently no.]

You cannot fail to see what would have come of trial of the accused – how long they would have lasted – the expenses to a county which has nothing in its treasury – the heart-burnings, disputes, revivals of old feuds, fights, shootings, bush-wackings, and general turmoil, ending, in probability, in the recall of the thieves now for the most part driven out.

[AUTHOR'S NOTE: Wallace was actually observing initial hope for justice, followed by helpless apathy of the people that continues to present day New Mexico, still ruled by a Ring system – which was Lew Wallace's legacy from its Territorial days.]

As it was most of the indicted appeared in court and plead the amnesty in bar. [Author's boldface] <u>Hereafter the labors of grand juries will be confined strictly to offences subsequent to my proclamation</u>.

[AUTHOR'S NOTE: This option – to "*plead amnesty in bar*" - was not made clear to Billy, or, apparently to Attorney Ira Leonard. But it appears that Wallace assumed his pardons would be claimed by those indicted – and would be granted! So, Billy appears to have been duped in his Wallace clemency deal by taking seriously the Amnesty Proclamation's denial of pardon to the indicted. What it really meant, however, was that anyone indicted, but with a Ring lawyer, received a pardon anyway. But Billy was the only person to take Wallace at his Amnesty Proclamation word, and attempt to negotiate a way of qualifying for a special exception. That was how Wallace was able to betray Billy - and those who may have naively assisted Billy in that plan.]

Now, from my saying that the old factions are dead, that peace is prevailing, and for eight months there has been but one murder in the county, you should not understand me as saying that the people are relieved of fears of further trouble. On the contrary there is great disquiet amongst them, and with reason. They know very well that the outlaws who so harried them are reacting in expectation of recall.

[AUTHOR'S NOTE: One can consider this as Wallace's self-serving turnabout from the real political causes of the people's uprising, to his suppression of it, by blaming "outlaws." Clearly, he had ignored the "Billie" letter and his citizen interviews. Because Wallace merely wanted "peace" - meaning quiet - he was actually suppressing the last of the Ring opposition.]

They go up to Fort Stanton witnesses on one side or the other of the Dudley court of inquiry, and see strange sights; they see Dolan, admittedly the leader of the fiercest refractories, at large and busy in Col. Dudley's behalf, although he is under two indictments for murder, one a murder in the first degree:

[AUTHOR'S NOTE: The first degree murder indictment for James Dolan was from Billy's testimony, as Wallace was well aware. The measure of Wallace's callousness is, thus, here well illustrated as taking the credit himself and abandoning Billy.]

they know he is not at large by consent or connivance of the Sheriff; they know the commandant of the Fort has my official request in writing to keep Dolan in close confinement; knowing this, and seeing what they see – Dolan free to go and come, a boarder at the Trader's store, attended by a gang well known as ready to do his bidding to any extreme – they are further met by threats of bloody things intended when Col. Dudley is acquitted by his court and restored to command of the post, and very naturally they are afraid, and so constantly alarmed as to find it impossible to settle down regularly to their pursuits.

[AUTHOR'S NOTE: This is another switching of blame, this time to Colonel Dudley, in whose biased Court of Inquiry, Wallace was, the month before, humiliated. But Wallace is again omitting that disrest connected to Dudley was connected to his Ring-sided military intervention in the Lincoln County War.]

You will see from this description that the only disturbing element remaining to be grappled with is the <u>confederacy of outlaws and their friends.</u> That done effectively, I believe a permanently healthful condition can be promised.

[AUTHOR'S NOTE: This is Wallace's switch from the real political and military villains to "outlaws" in general.]

The question is, how to best proceed.
The method which seems to have met with most favor in the Territory is martial law.

[AUTHOR'S NOTE: With his elitist and authoritarian bent from his Civil War days, Wallace gravitated to martial law. It had been his persistent request after arriving in the Territory; but he had been refused by President Hayes. The rest of his letter rationalizes not using martial law, but strengthening the local military at Fort Stanton against "outlaws." So intermingled with Wallace's statements is theorizing about the scope of "outlawry." Interestingly, the Ring would build on that view when, the following year, they brought in the Secret Service to hunt down Billy.]

And I confess at one time I thought it the best and only method. Two months upon the ground, however, and much study and reflection there where the advantages and disadvantages, forecasting probabilities, were directly under eye, have changed my opinion.
In the first place, martial law is after all but a temporary expedient. Next, it must in this instance be of limited application; to extend it to the whole of the Territory would be unjustifiable, while if applied to the counties of Lincoln and Doña Anà solely, it would certainly fail its immediate object; that is to say, it would fail to bring offenders to quick trial and certain punishment, since they would only have to cross certain near boundary lines to be safe. Yet further, military commissions under modern laws of war are governable by fixed procedures, and their findings must be according to rules of evidence, not the will of a captain, leaving it difficult as ever to overcome perjurious combinations. Finally, admitting it would be effective while in force – a point to which I am by no means assured, since as much would depend upon the officer charged with its execution and the number and zeal of the

subordinates and troops helping him – yet it must have an end; - and then what? The restoration of civil authority, it is to be feared, would, in this case at least, be the signal for the outlaws, over in Mexico, Texas, the Staked Plains, and for that matter, the contiguous counties of New Mexico, to return and renew their operations, with the additional incentive of fresh victims to prey upon.

[AUTHOR'S NOTE: This is Wallace's focus on "outlawry."]

To these objections, I have heard but one point in answer – that under military protection, the county would become settled, and able to take care of itself. Possibly so, though I doubt it, for the reason that, as a rule, people looking out for new homes find very little attraction in martial law;   the strongest ground for a belief is that its prevalence would be almost universally accepted as a warning to stay away. Under martial law contractors would multiply and flourish; men with families would look elsewhere.

To make application of these remarks – The time is come, in my judgment, to move radically that the present status in Lincoln County be assured permanently. Instead of martial law, I recommend simply a transfer of all troops now at Fort Stanton, except Captain Carroll and Lieut. Dawson and their companies; substituting, in place of the transferred, officers and troops wholly disconnected with the past troubles and without bias one way or the other – the command to be given an officer himself a stranger to parties involved, who has no hates or friendships in the locality, is above intimidation, and will execute present existing orders. Such orders, if enforced zealously and according to their plain letter, really give the civil authorities in very kind the strength attaching to martial law, bating only the military commissions – in fact, executed as the should be, they make martial law inexpedient.

I beg not to be required to support this recommendation with charges against anybody. They get me into personal quarrels for which life is too short; which in nineteen cases out of twenty, "the game is not worth the candle." Besides that, they are followed by investigations which have the effect to weaken me by convincing the opposition that I have not the confidence of the President. Respectfully but frankly, it is very desirable to know nearly as possible if the support heretofore given me will be continued – **_for now I can retire without loss of credit_***.* [Author's boldface]

[AUTHOR'S NOTE: Wallace appears to here be unconsciously revealing effects of his trouncing by Colonel Dudley's attorney at the Court of Inquiry the month before; and his expectation that Dudley will be exonerated. He now rejects aggravation of "*charges against anybody.*" He has checked out mentally and physically from Lincoln County "troubles;" and only wants no "*loss of credit.*" After all, he can afford no Washington dissatisfaction with his performance to interfere with his hope of leaving the Territory as soon as possible as Ambassador to Turkey.]

Not improbably the Honorable Secretary of War and General Sherman, to whom my recommendation will be referred, will be satisfied to take the opinion of Gen. Hatch, commanding the District of New Mexico. It gives me pleasure to say General H. has not only aided me promptly and with great intelligence, regardful of his orders; in fact he is the only person with whom I have constantly and freely advised. He knows the situation perfectly. If, however, the President thinks better to resort to martial law, his decision will be cheerfully accepted.

Passing from Lincoln county, it gives me great satisfaction to report the Territory elsewhere in a prosperous state. The recent mineral discoveries and the resolution of the railroad companies (the Denver and Rio Grande and the Atchison, Topeka and Santa Fe) to extend their lines immediately, are at last drawing to New Mexico the attention she really deserves, and already we are feeling the effects. The hotels in this city are crowded, and a stream of miners is pouring along the roads from the east.

[AUTHOR'S NOTE: This prosperity from mines, land, and railroads was the Santa Fe Ring's motivation for hegemony - and they were now prospering in those endeavors.]

I have the honor to be
Very respectfully
Your friend,
Lew. Wallace
Governor New Mexico

BILLY'S TRUSTING WAIT

By late April 1879, following his successful Grand Jury testimony, captive Billy Bonney had been brought westward up the street from Juan Patrón's home to Lincoln's courthouse by demand of District Attorney William Rynerson.

Before Judge Warren Bristol, Billy was handed down a change of venue for his murder indictments for Andrew "Buckshot" Roberts, Sheriff William Brady, and Deputy George Hindman, to take him from obviously knowledgeable and sympathetic future jurors in Lincoln County, to distant Doña County; so that Judge Bristol could guarantee himself a jury ignorant of the War issues and achieve his Ringman dictate: hanging of the troublemaking boy.

After that venue change, Billy, aware of possible imminent and fatal transfer, nevertheless, stayed in his Juan Patrón house arrest, testifying the next month, in May, in the Dudley Court of Inquiry; but surely awaiting, any day, for Governor Lew Wallace's pardon promise to be fulfilled.

Billy could not have conceived that, after having been used by Lew Wallace, after having been duped, after having a life deemed worthless by that egomaniacal selfish patrician, he had already been discarded as no longer useful - except as literary inspiration for a possible future romanticized fiction of a bloodthirsty frontier desperado.

Billy's Court of
Inquiry Testimony

`

A Boy Against the Ring

Billy Bonney's testifying against hated Commander Nathan Augustus Monroe Dudley - direct cause of the Lincoln County War's lost freedom fight and the killing of many men whom Billy loved - was Billy's own agenda; not part of his pardon deal; though Governor Lew Wallace may have been informed about Billy's courtroom participation by that Court's assisting prosecutor: Attorney Ira Leonard.

Billy's participating in that May to July of 1879, Fort Stanton, Court of Inquiry was more daring than his Frank Warner Angel deposition the year before. Billy had already revealed his awareness of Fort danger; writing to Lew Wallace on March 20, 1879: *"all I am afraid of is that in the Fort We might be poisoned or killed through a Window at night."*

Billy's testimony to come was as devastating as his eye-witness account of the Chapman murder, just given at the Lincoln County Grand Jury. When escaping the burning McSween house with others, Billy had seen Dudley's soldiers fire at least one volley at them: that meant in unison and under orders. Billy also saw law intern Harvey Morris shot down; and others killed also. So Dudley should have been Court Martialed and hanged for treason for murdering American citizens.

Braving assassination, on May 28th and 29th of 1879, Billy, still in the mock jailing at Juan Patrón's house, was transported the nine miles from Lincoln to the Fort Stanton courtroom, where the three Judges were Colonel Galusha Pennypacker, Captain Henry Brinkerhoff, and Major Nathan Osborne; the prosecutor was Captain Henry Humphreys with co-counsel Ira Leonard; and the defense attorney was Thomas Benton Catron's friend, famous trial lawyer, Henry Waldo.

Billy's Testimony

The transcript of Billy's two day testimony in the Fort Stanton Court of Inquiry for Commander N.A.M. Dudley reveals his precise mind. His questioning focused on the July 19, 1878 turning point in the Lincoln County War Battle when Dudley, in violation of the Posse Comitatus Act, forbidding military intervention in civil strife, brought to Lincoln his cavalry and infantry, a howitzer cannon, and a Gatling gun to aid Ring-partisan sheriff, George Peppin, who was losing the fight. In balance hung Ring power over Lincoln County - and potentially over the rest of New Mexico Territory.

Billy's location was inside the besieged, and eventually burning, house of Alexander McSween, along with that man; other freedom fighters; McSween's wife, Susan; her sister, Elizabeth Shield; and Elizabeth's five young children. Noteworthy is that McSween respected Billy enough to share with him his important letters to and from Dudley.

The prosecution, representing Susan McSween, charged Commander Dudley with the murder of her husband and the arson of her house. When Billy testified at that Court, Dudley had, the month before, already received civil indictments at the Lincoln County Grand Jury for those same crimes. It is possible that Billy also testified against Dudley then.

Unbeknownst to the prosecution side, however, the Court was rigged for certain victory for Dudley; with Chief Judge Galusha Pennypacker being Dudley's good friend, and Attorney Henry Waldo's skill far outstripping the abilities of Captain Henry Humphries and Attorney Ira Leonard.

That Court's decision would result in uncontested Santa Fe Ring dominance in the Territory, Lew Wallace's abandonment of Lincoln County issues and Billy Bonney, and Ring determination to end the career of that boy making a habit of giving devastating testimony against their members.

In the transcript below, the *"Recorder"* is the military prosecutor. *"By Col. Dudley"* refers to Dudley's attorney, Henry Waldo. One should also be aware that Attorney Ira Leonard, present throughout as advisor, would have heard Billy's testimony - possibly cementing his loyalty to the brilliant boy.

In his first day of testimony, on May 28, 1879, Billy responded as follows:

May 28, 1879
Present:
Col. G. Pennypacker 16th Infantry
Major N.W. Osborne 15th Infantry
Captain H.R. Brinkerhoff 15th Infantry
Captain H.H. Humphreys 15th Infantry, Recorder
Lieut. Col. Dudley and his Counsel, Mr. Ira E. Leonard and William Bonney were present.

WILLIAM BONNEY, a witness being duly sworn, testified as follows.

Q. by Recorder. What is your name and place of residence?

Answer. My name is William Bonney. I reside in Lincoln.

Q. by Recorder. Are you known or called Billy Kidd, also Antrim?

Answer. Yes Sir.

Q. by Recorder. Where were you on the 19th day of July last and what, if anything, did you see of the movements and actions of the troops in that city, state fully?

Answer. I was in the McSween house in Lincoln, and I saw soldiers come from the post with sheriff's party, that is the sheriff's posse joined them a short distance below there, the McSween house. Soldiers passed on by and the men dropped off and surrounded the house, the sheriff's party. Shortly after, the soldiers came back with Peppin, passed the house twice afterwards. Three soldiers came and stood in front of the house, in front of the windows. Mr. McSween wrote a note to the officer in charge asking what the soldiers were placed there for. He replied saying that they had business there, that if a shot was fired over his camp, or at Peppin, or at any of his men, that he had no objection to blowing up, if he wanted, his own house. I read the note myself, he handed it to me to read. I saw nothing further of the soldiers until night. I was in the back part of the house. When I escaped from the house three soldiers fired at me from the Tunstall store, outside corner of the store. That's all I know in regards to it.

[AUTHOR'S NOTE: This is an excellent example of Billy Bonney's precise mind. In addition, its meticulous conclusion - "*That's all I know in regards to it*"- mirrors the concluding statement used in the "Billie" letter fragment.]

Q. by Recorder. Did the soldiers that stood in front of the windows have guns with them while there?

Answer. Yes Sir.

Q. by Recorder. Who escaped from the house with you and who was killed at the time, if you know, while attempting to make their escape?

Answer. Jose Chavez escaped with me, Vincente Romero, Francisco Zamora and McSween.

Q. by Recorder. How many persons were killed in that fight that day, if you know, and who killed them, if you know?

Answer. I seen five killed, I could not swear to who killed them, I seen some of them that fired.

[AUTHOR'S NOTE: "Seen" for "saw" is Billy's characteristic and rare grammatical error.]

Q. by Recorder. Who did you see that fired?

Answer. Robt. Beckwith, John Hurley, John Jones, those three soldiers, I don't know their names.

[AUTHOR'S NOTE: This is the testimony that arguably sealed Billy's ultimate fate of Secret Service assisted murder: "*three soldiers.*" Billy was willing to risk saying that dangerous truth to bring down the Santa Fe Ring.]

Q. by Recorder. Did you see any persons setting fire to the McSween house that day, if so, state who it was, if you know?

Answer. I did, Jack Long, and there was another man I did not recognize.

Recorder stated he had finished with the witness.

Cross examination.

Q. By Col. Dudley. What were you, and the others there with you, doing in McSween's house that day?

Answer. We came here with McSween.

Q. By Col. Dudley. Did you know, or had you not heard, that the sheriff was endeavoring to arrest yourself and others there with you at the time?

Answer. Yes Sir. I had heard so, I did not know.

[AUTHOR'S NOTE: Billy is precise with having "*heard*," rather than to "*know*" with certainty. Also, he is unintimidated by aggressive and accusatory Attorney Henry Waldo. One should remember the context of this questioning: Judge Bristol in the Lincoln Grand Jury the month before had already changed Billy's murder indictments' venue to Doña Ana County. And Lew Wallace had not granted their annulment. Theoretically, Billy could have been transported right from Fort Stanton to Mesilla for his hanging trial.]

Q. By Col. Dudley. Then were you not engaged in resisting the sheriff at the time you were in the house?

Objected to by Recorder. The Court has already ruled that nothing extraneous from the actual occurrence that took place, and Col. Dudley's actions in connection therewith, should be further inquired into and nothing has been called out to the witness to authorize this mode of cross examination, it cannot be a matter of defense of Col. Dudley or justify his actions however much the parties may have been resisting the sheriff or civil authorities.

Lt. Col. Dudley, by his Counsel, states he does not deem it necessary to make reply to the objection.

Objection sustained.

Q. By Col. Dudley. In addition to the names you have given, are you also known as the "Kid?"

Answer. I have already answered that question, Yes Sir, I am, but not "Billy Kid" that I know of.

[AUTHOR'S NOTE: Billy first refers back to earlier questioning, and corrects that answer: he is not known as "Billy Kid."]

Q. By Col. Dudley. Were you not and were not the parties with you in the McSween house on the 19th day of July last and the days immediately preceding, engaged in firing at the sheriff's posse?

Court objects to the question. Lt. Col. Dudley, by his Counsel, ask, does the Court intend to rule here, that after once gone into this matter of firing into the McSween house by the testimony of this witness, it is not permissible to show all the circumstances under which this firing took place, as a part of the res gestae, and to leave it so far as this witness is concerned as though the firing into the house was without cause or excuse.

It is asked for information in order to guide us in the further examination of this witness.

Court cleared and closed.

Court opened and its decision announced.

Lt. Col. Dudley, and his Counsel, and Mr. Ira E. Leonard and witness being present.

The Court directs the case to proceed calling attention to its previous rulings which were deemed sufficient by explicit.

Q. By Col. Dudley. Whose name was signed to the note received by McSween in reply to the one previously sent by him to Col. Dudley?

[AUTHOR'S NOTE: This makes clear that McSween was sharing with Billy his communications with Dudley. One, thus, gets a glimpse of the respect this boy, then 18, engendered; McSween being an attorney and well able to deal with such legally fraught communications himself.]

Answer. Signed N.A.M. Dudley, did not say what rank, he received two notes, one had no name signed to it.

[AUTHOR'S NOTE: This answer demonstrates Billy's astounding memory and precision regarding the year before: he recalls Dudley's exact signature, missing rank, number of notes received, and lack of signature on one of them.]

Q. By Col. Dudley. Are you as certain of everything else you have sworn to as you are to what you have sworn to in answer to the last proceeding question?

Answer. Yes Sir.

[AUTHOR'S NOTE: Famous trial lawyer Henry Waldo cannot faze Billy. In addition, one should not miss Billy's presence of mind demonstrated here, by remembering that the other besieged occupants of the McSween house were likely panicked at this intervention of military might. It was so terrifying that all the other McSween-side fighters, in other locations throughout Lincoln, fled when Dudley entered the town with troops, Gatling gun, and howitzer cannon. Nevertheless, Billy had coolly been observing and remembering all the activities of their opponents from the besieged McSween house's windows.]

Q. By Col. Dudley. From which direction did Peppin come the first time the soldiers passed with him?

Answer. Passed up from the direction of where the soldiers camped, the first time I saw him.

[AUTHOR'S NOTE: Billy was prepared to give each Peppin walk-by; so he begins with the qualifying "*first.*"]

Q. By Col. Dudley. What direction did he come from the second time?

Answer. From the direction of the hotel from the McSween house.

[AUTHOR'S NOTE: This means Wortley Hotel, and from the west.]

Q. By Col. Dudley. In what direction did you go upon your escape from the McSween house?

Answer. Ran towards the Tunstall store, was fired at, and there turned towards the river.

Q. By Col. Dudley. From what part of the McSween house did you make your escape?

Answer. The Northeast corner of the house.

[AUTHOR'S NOTE: Billy does not say "kitchen." Part of his unusual survival skill might be this constantly precise orientation.]

Q. By Col. Dudley. How many soldiers fired at you?

Answer. Three.

Q. By Col. Dudley. How many soldiers were with Peppin when he passed the McSween house each time, as you say?

Answer. Three.

Q. By Col. Dudley. The soldiers appeared to go in company of threes that day, did they not?

Answer. All that I ever saw appeared to be three in a crowd at a time after they passed the first time.

[AUTHOR'S NOTE: Billy cannot be shaken by Attorney Waldo; though one can imagine Waldo perspiring at the dangerous implications of his testimony of soldiers illegally firing on civilians and illegally taking a side in the conflict - under defendant Dudley.]

Q. By Col. Dudley. Who was killed first that day, Bob Beckwith or McSween men?

Answer. Harvey Morris, McSween man, was killed first.

Q. By Col. Dudley. How far is the Tunstall building from the McSween house?

Answer. I could not say how far, I never measured the distance. I should judge it to be 40 yards, between 30 and 40 yards.

[AUTHOR'S NOTE: Again appears Billy's meticulous precision. He is willing to estimate distance, but qualifies that by denying his having done formal measurement. One wonders if he is toying audaciously with Waldo; having realized that he is probably more clever and more in control than is this man.]

Q. By Col. Dudley. How many shots did those soldiers fire, that you say shot from the Tunstall building?

Answer. I could not swear to that on account of firing on all sides, I could not hear. I seen them fire one volley.

[AUTHOR'S NOTE: Waldo must not have expected this precise and devastating answer. Notice first that Billy qualifies his answer as to counting shots by denying <u>hearing</u> them (since there was "*firing on all sides*"). But he was "looking." So he saw the black power puffs coming in unison from the muzzles of the soldiers' rifles. Since he was among their targets, and he had to cover about 40 yards to safety, one can marvel at his near superhuman self-control under duress. Billy's observation should have led to Dudley's proceeding to Court Martial and hanging for treason. Waldo knew this, and in his closing argument would spend an inordinate amount of time trying to debunk Billy's likelihood of making such a precise observation. But this answer alone shows just how dangerous a gadfly Billy could be.]

Q. By Col. Dudley. What did they fire at?

Answer. Myself and Jose Chavez.

Q. By Col. Dudley. Did you not just now state in answer to the question who killed Zamora, Romero, Morris, and McSween that you did not know who killed them, but you saw Beckwith , John Jones, and three soldiers fire at them?

Answer. Yes Sir. I did.

Q. By Col. Dudley. Were these men, the McSween men, there with you when the volley was fired at you and Chavez by the soldiers?

Answer. Just a short ways behind us.

Q. By Col. Dudley. Were you looking back at them?

Answer. No Sir.

Q. By Col. Dudley. How then do you know they were just behind you then, or that they were in range of the volley?

[AUTHOR'S NOTE: Waldo thinks he can trip Billy up by confusing questions.]

Answer. Because there was a high fence behind, and a good many guns to keep them there. I could hear them speak.

[AUTHOR'S NOTE: Billy is untouchable.]

Q. By Col. Dudley. How far were you from the soldiers when you saw them?

Answer. I could not swear exactly, between 30 and 40 yards.

[AUTHOR'S NOTE: Waldo repeated his distance question for trip-up; but Billy simply stuck to his original answer.]

Q. By Col. Dudley. Did you know either of the soldiers that were in front of the window of McSween's house that day? If so, give it.

Answer. No Sir, I am not acquainted with them.

Redirect.

Q. by Recorder. Explain whether all the men that were in the McSween house came out at the same time when McSween and the others were killed and the firing came from the soldiers and others?

Answer. Yes Sir, all came out at the same time. The firing was done by the soldiers until some had escaped.

Recorder stated that he had finished with the witness.

[AUTHOR'S NOTE: Captain Humphries is unable to make any use of Billy Bonney's brilliance. One is left dismayed at all the questions that Billy should have been asked by him to further solidify Commander Dudley's crimes. But throughout the trial, this pattern of the prosecution's inadequacy persisted.]

Q. by Col. Dudley. How do you know if you were making your escape at the time and the men Zamora, Morris and McSween were behind you that they were killed at that time, is it not true that you did not know of their death or the death of either of them until afterwards?

Answer. I knew of the death of some of them, I did know of the death of one of them. I saw him lying down there.

[AUTHOR'S NOTE: Waldo tries in vain to make Billy overstate - thus putting in doubt the precision of his answers. Billy, however, cannot be trapped since he is telling the truth *and* has total recall.]

Q. by Col. Dudley. Did you see any of the men last mentioned killed?

Answer. Yes Sir, I did, I seen Harvey Morris killed first, he was out in front of me.

Q. by Col. Dudley. Did you not then a moment ago swear that he was among those who were behind you and Jose Chavez when you saw the soldiers deliver the volley?

Answer. No Sir, I didn't think I did. I misunderstood the question if I did. I said he was among them that was killed not behind me.

[AUTHOR'S NOTE: Billy cannot be swayed; and coolly gives himself leeway of "*I misunderstood*" for any incorrect answer he might have given earlier.]

Witness then withdrew.

* * * * * * *

The Court reconvened the next day, Thursday, May 29, 1879 at 10 AM. Billy Bonney's testimony continued as follows:

Proceedings of May 28, 1879 were read and approved.

Q. by Court. Were the soldiers which you say fired at you as you escaped from the McSween house on the evening of July 19th last, colored or white?

Answer. White troops.

[AUTHOR'S NOTE: This is a prosecution success in clarifying "*white troops*," since that meant officers - further establishing under orders of Commander Dudley.]

Q. by Court. Was it light enough so you could distinctly see the soldiers when they fired?

Answer. The house was burning. Made it almost light as day for a short distance all around.

[AUTHOR'S NOTE: This is also devastating testimony as to excellent visibility being available. Waldo and Dudley must have been enraged.]

Witness then retired.

TROUBLE FOR BILLY

The Santa Fe Ring did not forgive Billy Bonney's incriminating, 1879 court testimonies against their minions: James Dolan and Commander N.A.M. Dudley.

Against Billy, Attorney Henry Waldo defensively vented that cabal's vindictive fury in his Court of Inquiry closing argument on behalf of Colonel Dudley on July 5, 1879. He crystallized Ring propaganda branding Billy as an outlaw.

Waldo had the critical need to debunk Billy's dangerously precise statements: a demonstration of the 19 year old boy's power. Waldo had to dissimulate that Billy lied and that the detail he observed was impossible. Furthermore, Waldo prevaricated that the firelight of the burning building could not have illuminated the attackers enough to identify them.

Waldo's dishonest words set the stage for Judge Warren Bristol's jury instructions and death sentence for Billy in April of 1881; and for Governor Lew Wallace's death warrant sent to Sheriff Pat Garrett soon after.

On the 49th and last day of Dudley's trial, Waldo stated:

Then was brought forward William Bonney, alias "Antrim," alias "the Kid," a known criminal of the worst type although hardly up to his majority, murderer by profession, as records of this Court connect him with two atrocious murders, that of Roberts and the other of Sheriff Brady. Both of them are cowardly and atrocious assassinations.

[AUTHOR'S NOTE: This rendition is double pronged in its damage to Billy. For this Court, it is intended to undermine his credibility as a witness to seeing shooting soldiers. Less obvious is its checkmate for Lew Wallace, creating a humiliating impossibility of any future pardon for the boy as a lawman-killing outlaw; thus, leaving open Ring intent to hang him for these indictments).]

There were warrants enough for him to the 19th of July last to have plastered him from his head to his feet, yet he was engaged to do service as a witness and his testimony showed that his qualifications did not terminate with blood guiltiness. His testimony was brief, yet he signalized his opening sentences with a lie. He swears that members of the sheriff's posse fell in with the troops and came up to the McSween house, but I will quote his words. "I was in the McSween house in Lincoln, and I saw the soldiers come down from the fort with the sheriff's party, that is, the sheriff's posse joined them a short distance above there, the McSween house, soldiers passed on by, the men dropped right off and surrounded the house." It has been proven by competent and unimpeachable witnesses that this statement is without any foundation in fact. Sheriff Peppin, his Deputy Sheriff Powell, Deputy Sheriff Marion Turner, Milo Pierce, Robert Olinger, Joseph Nash, Andrew Boyle, J.B. Matthews,

[AUTHOR'S NOTE: Those "*unimpeachable witnesses*" are all Ring partisans. Turner and Matthews received Wallace pardons by Attorney Thomas Benton Catron's representation.]

Lt. Goodwin, Captain Purington and Corporal Bugold, who brought up the rear of the column all swear that none of the posse was anywhere near the troops as they passed the Wortley Hotel and came up to the McSween house. It is plainly known that at least half an hour passed before any of the sheriff's posse went up to the McSween house ...

[AUTHOR'S NOTE: This mutually protective lying testimony by Ring partisans characterized the whole Court of Inquiry.]

He also testified as to the note received by McSween in answer to one sent by Col. Dudley. He swears that the note was signed N.A.M. Dudley, "did not say what rank." About this he might have been mistaken, but it shows him to be a willing and reckless witness. But what is of importance is that he swears that letter contained the following, he is positive about it because he says he read it, he volunteers that statement. His testimony stated three soldiers came down and stood in front of McSween's building and McSween's wife wants to know why they are there ... and Col. Dudley replied saying, "They had business there, and if a shot was fired over his camp, or at Peppin or any of his men, that he had no objection to his blowing up, if he wanted to, his own house." That this note contained nothing about firing upon Peppin or any of his men is clear enough ... to say nothing of the contradiction given by Lt. Goodwin, who wrote the note and signed it.

He also swears that three soldiers fired at him when he was escaping from the McSween building. Attention will also be called to this part of the testimony further on. It is sufficient to say of this part of the testimony now that if he swears falsely about so material a fact as to the manner of the sheriff's posse surrounded the house, that is to say under cover by means of protection of the troops as they marched by, he would not hesitate to swear falsely about soldiers firing at him that night as he was escaping. "A liar once is a liar all the time."

As to seeing the soldiers about the Tunstall building, at the time of the escape of the men from the McSween house the evening of the 19th of July last, Jose Chavez was also called. He was with the "Kid" according to both of them. "Kid" says that the soldiers stood at the outside corner of the Tunstall building ... Now this story comes with its own reputation. In the first place, in the intense excitement of the moment, these men could not have had the coolness to select from a number of shots delivered at them, the firing of certain particular shots, to fix it in their minds, the men who did the firing. Besides, in the deceptive glare of the fire, it is very doubtful if any of the parties who were looking upon the space between those two houses could identify with any degree of certainty, particularly at such a time, the kind of clothes anybody wore. This difficulty would be enhanced in the case of the "Kid" and Chavez because they were looking from the center of the light out against the darkness, which is a circumstance of the greatest importance. While from the darkness to the wall objects are plainly discernable, the direct opposite follows when the conditions are changed.

[AUTHOR'S NOTE: Waldo's preposterous lie about illumination being in only one direction is intended to discredit Billy's meticulous and damning observations; but shows the lengths of absurdity Waldo went to give excuses to the judges who had no intention of convicting Dudley.]

There is a considerable discrepancy between the two witnesses also as to the distance they say the three soldiers were from where they fired. "Kid" said 30 to forty yards, Chavez makes it only ten yards.

Another conclusive argument against the presence of soldiers there at the time is the extreme danger, the almost certain danger of death from such an exposed position, the witnesses testify that it would have been between cross fire at a time when everybody else was seeking and keeping cover. It is to be supposed for a moment that three soldiers, who had no interest in the contest would have been in such a place, for if they were at all they slipped out against orders and came there of their own choice.

[AUTHOR'S NOTE: Attacking Billy's testimony, Waldo misstates cross-fire position, and conceals that volley means under orders.]

Besides, it is clear the soldiers were not then present, the evidence of the Sergeant who testified that late roll call for the night was at dusk, or near as he can judge, about a quarter past eight, and that the men were then all there. This escape being among their first that was made must have been about that time ... In addition to all this we have the evidence of Boyle, or Nash, or Olinger or of Hurley all who say they had a distinct view of the space between the McSween house and the Tunstall building, and as the firing had come from the Tunstall building all that day, their attention at the time would have been drawn as much to one house as the other,

[AUTHOR'S NOTE: Waldo' omits that roll call was before the three officers left to shoot at the McSween house's escaping men. Also he lies about shooting from the Tunstall house, since its occupants had fled when Dudley entered the town. And, as usual, defense witnesses were lying Ring-biased Seven Rivers boys.]

and they all say ... that there was nobody at the corner of the Tunstall building, where these soldiers were located. The evidence of Olinger and Hurley is especially valuable, each of them had distinct views of this particular corner. One, Olinger being to the southwest in the Stanley house, and the other, Hurley, to the southeast of it in the Wilson house ...

Besides, we must take into consideration that some of these men were of the sheriff's posse, Boyle for one and the man "Dummy" who were right at the McSween house at the time, were dressed with soldier jackets and the "Dummy" in soldier pants, and it was easy enough for these frightened fleeing men, when they try to remember the events of that night to mis-locate the men they say shot at them. To all probability as they fled they may have seen some of these men who had soldiers' jackets and thought they were soldiers. It is more charitable to suppose this, than that they have come here and deliberately lied, although they must fear from the lying character of the testimony throughout.

[AUTHOR'S NOTE: One can almost hear Waldo's post-trial laugh with his cohorts about his comic fabrication of possemen wearing soldiers' uniforms - to further debunk Billy's observation of seeing "soldiers." This is what unchecked Santa Fe Ring evil looks like.]

INSULT FOR WALLACE

Lew Wallace, arriving in Lincoln County as a fawned-upon savior in March of 1879, began to realize by June that his testimony in the Dudley Court of Inquiry was likely to leave him more martyr than miracle-worker. On June 6th, Attorney Ira Leonard wrote to him, already returned to Santa Fe:

They mean to whitewash and excuse [Dudley's] *glaring conduct. They have transcended all rules of evidence to allow hearsay coming through other channels than direct parties, and are allowing liberally to Dudley what they peremptorily refused us. I am thoroughly and completely disgusted with these proceedings ... I had a good notion to show my disgust by abandoning the case and let them have it their own way. There is nothing to be looked or hoped for from the tribunal. It is a farce on judicial investigation and ought to be called and designated "The Mutual Admiration Inquiry."*

Lew Wallace, as placating Ira Leonard had seen, had been on Attorney Henry Waldo's hot seat before Billy Bonney that May of 1879; and, unlike Billy, had fared poorly.

That fiasco's aftermath must have been Wallace's outrage at the demeaning questioning of someone of his stature - since he was unaware that the Santa Fe Ring saw him as expendable and temporary, being poised to regroup as soon as he left the Territory. Waiting in the wings, in fact, was his replacement as Governor: Ring partisan, Lionel Sheldon. And past corrupt governor, Samuel Beach Axtell (whom the Ring's Washington co-boss, Stephen Benton Elkins, had tried to re-instate after Wallace), would be made Territorial Chief Justice.

So the scorn expressed toward Lew Wallace (and Attorney Ira Leonard by association) by Attorney Henry Waldo in his closing argument on the Court of Inquiry's forty-ninth and last day of July 5, 1879 should be seen in its context of Ringmen's arrogant belief in their immunity from prosecution. But for Wallace, the insults would be salt in a wound, not only from this Court, but from the battle of Shiloh.

Waldo stated:

Nothing has been accomplished in the least that connects Col. Dudley with anything which transpired in the town of Lincoln on the occasion of his presence there on the 19th and 20th day of July last, and all that has been truthfully told of his motives and actions reflects the highest credit upon him, as a man and as a soldier. Notwithstanding all this, motives the most laudable have been traduced, conduct the most praiseworthy distorted into great crimes. He has been libeled and vilified, insults have been heaped on him. He has been heralded forth as a house burner and a murderer from one end of the territory to the other. He has been branded as a conspirator, a robber and a thief by no less a person than Governor Wallace, whose lips have blistered to a crisp and pealed to the bone when they uttered the foul malicious accusation. False and slanderous charges have been preferred by the crafty and designing old lawyer, Ira E. Leonard, to the Secretary of war, and by the wily and unscrupulous politician Governor Wallace, to the Commander of the District.

Look at this for a moment, here was this man Leonard when he made these charges and had never even been in Lincoln county. He resided in Las Vegas, two hundred miles away, and never had an opportunity of seeing any of the witnesses, or making an investigation into the truth of the charges formulated by him. Governor Wallace had been in the county of Lincoln but one day, took no sworn or written testimony, never even inquired of the officers who were present with Col. Dudley, when he was in Lincoln at the time mentioned.

Language strong enough and severe enough cannot be employed in denunciation of the hideous and monstrous wickedness of these bad men who united in their efforts to disgrace and ruin a man who had never harmed either of them, in thought, word, or deed, and that man an officer of high rank, and long and distinguished service in the Army of this country. Here, has Col. Dudley been forced to submit to the humiliation and mortification of knowing that such charges had been lodged against him with the Department of War in Washington, and that he was the subject of comment and discussion of his superiors and among brother officers, besides the publicity which they necessarily obtained throughout the country, to the effect of *which can never be obliterated, and compelled to seek the vindication of himself, and able to obtain only the poor and meager and inadequate redress, which this Court of Inquiry can afford, hemmed in as it is by the limited scope of its duties and powers as defined in the orders by which it was convened. Lew Wallace and Ira E. Leonard are alone responsible for this annoyance trouble and harassing case. By their act, this disgrace has been brought upon a pure, humane, and just man. By their act has the luster of a bright and honorable career been dimmed. Time does not remain to Col. Dudley to clear away the stain, by them placed upon his name and character. The best years of his life are passed and gone, spent in the service of his country ...*

He [Wallace] did not come [to Lincoln] to learn the truth. He came bent on finding for which he could use to injure Col. Dudley. He came to accomplish the removal of Col. Dudley even if he had to manufacture the testimony which it would be necessary to have, in order to do it. To succeed, even if he had to write as evil and malicious a letter as that upon which the removal was effected. Did Gov. Wallace seek true knowledge of Col. Dudley's relations to Lincoln County matters? Why did he not come to officers of the post? Why did he not seek his information from all the parties, but no, he never came to the post, but went directly to Lincoln, and talked with a few rabid and malignant partisans, took a one sided version from prejudiced and irresponsible parties he knew he could get what he wanted from, and then tries to make it appear from the witness stand that this information was derived from persons who came from all parts of the county ...

For five days he attitudinized before this Court in a labored effort betwix an harangue and a narrative, the object of which was plainly manifest to be an exculpation of, or apology for the errors and follies of his course in dealing with Lincoln County matters ...

[Wallace] tries to make it appear from the witness stand that his information was derived from ... the public meeting at which he spoke ... It was after this purposely one sided investigation he comes to the post and wrote his letter of request, filling it with lying statements, which, with an hypocritical attempt at an apology, he states, he was cautious to say, were given upon information merely, and after he

had accomplished, in this unjust and infamous manner, the removal of Col. Dudley ... he places on it the flippant and insolent endorsement, "Colonel Dudley will excuse me if I decline to give him any advice." As if anybody had asked, or needed, the advice of Governor Wallace ...

He [Wallace] wants somebody to lay the blame upon. It [Amnesty Proclamation] was a weak and ridiculous idea in the first place. What the villains who had made a hell of Lincoln County needed was a gallows, not a pardon. The whole truth about that proclamation, as we look at it, is that just about the time the Governor was in great alarm about the awful "bug bear" the "Santa Fe Ring" preventing his confirmation. He wanted to manufacture some political thunder whose reverberation would resound in the halls of the Senate chamber in Washington ... He had been sent specifically to pacify the troubles in New Mexico. To this, his official announcement of the complete success of his efforts to pacification in Lincoln County is promulgated ...

At 4:30 PM that same July 5, 1879 day, Chief Judge Galusha Pennypacker, Colonel Dudley's close friend, delivered the three judges' decision. Pennypacker stated:

In view of the evidence adduced, Colonel N. A. M. Dudley is not guilty of any violation of law or of orders. And his act of proceeding to the town of Lincoln was prompted by the most humane and worthy motives and by good military judgment under exceptional circumstances. Proceedings before a Court Martial are therefore unnecessary.

BILLY'S SHAM ESCAPE

On June 17, 1879, nineteen days before this corrupt exoneration of N.A.M. Dudley, Billy departed his sham arrest, acknowledging with his Lincoln friends that his transport to Mesilla for a hanging trial was inevitable. Unaware that he had forever lost Lew Wallace's backing, Billy must have nursed hope of his pardon as he returned to professional gambling and gadfly rustling. But his Lincoln friends, more realistic, settled on a fearful silence, and never again defended him.

Hunted Billy's Letter to Wallace

THE HUNT IS ON

On December 12, 1880, a year and a half after his sham arrest and testimony for the pardon bargain, Billy Bonney next wrote a letter to Governor Lew Wallace [APPENDIX 7].

It came because Billy was being hunted for lack of Wallace's clemency; though Billy clung to that hope. Meanwhile, the Santa Fe Ring was relentlessly advertising his outlawry, preempting any action by Wallace - if any had been intended - by making clemency seem unjustified. The Ring's goal was extermination of Billy as their last opposition.

Billy had probably amazed these adversaries by remaining in the Territory after his supposed jail escape in 1879, and then by continuing his petty stock theft against them. His non-Ring outlets were counterfeiter, Dan Dedrick; Dedrick's two brothers with a White Oaks livery; and Pat Coghlan, Ring rustling competitor for fort and Indian reservation beef contracts.

By that December 12, 1880 day, Billy's brazenness or foolhardiness had also yielded Secret Service pursuit, another lost pardon opportunity, a double ambush by a White Oaks posse, and a new accusation of murder. Possibly his lover, Paulita Maxwell, finalized his hot-headed choice of residence. For his letter, "*Fort Sumner*" was given as his location.

Seven days later, Pat Garrett's posse would ambush his group there, killing Tom O'Folliard. Ten days away was Billy's capture at Stinking Springs by that posse. There, at dawn, Charlie Bowdre was shot dead by Garrett, mistaken for him.

But even by that December 12th, and throughout 1881, Billy's writing showed that, even hunted relentlessly, even jailed after capture, even sentenced to hang, even held shackled and continuously guarded, he had no doubt of escaping; and he had no diminution of his rebellious spirit.

SECRET SERVICE PURSUIT

When Billy wrote his December 12, 1880 letter to Governor Lew Wallace, he knew he was being pursued by a Washington-based organization: the Secret Service. He knew because his loyal attorney, Ira Leonard, told him. And Billy confirmed that for himself by robbing the mail coach and reading Special Operative Azariah Wild's reports to his Chief. Those reports featured Billy with criminal glamour.

His rebel glory would, however, have been dimmed by sadness - if Billy permitted that emotion - since lost was his second chance for pardon: Wild's exchange for his testimony about counterfeiting by Dan Dedrick. And that second bargain improved on Wallace's, being brokered by trusted Ira Leonard.

Azariah Wild described that possible pardon in his report of October 6, 1880, to his Chief, James Brooks, stating:

> I left Fort Stanton at 7 o'clock A.M. on the stage and reached Lincoln the County seat at 8:30 A.M. ... The object of my visit to Lincoln was to see Judge Ira Leonard ... In my report of October 5th ... I spoke of an outlaw whose name was Antrom alias Billy Bonney. During the Lincoln Co. War he killed men on the Indian Reservation for which he has been indicted in the territorial and the United States Court. Gov. Wallace has issued a proclamation granting immunity to those not indicted but as Antrom has been indicted the proclamation did not cover his (Antrom's) case and he (Antrom) has been in the mountains as an outlaw ever since a space of about two years time.
>
> Governor Wallace has since written Antrom's attorney on the subject saying he should be let go but has failed to put it on shape that satisfied Judge Leonard Antrom's attorney.
>
> It is believed and in fact is almost known that he (Antrom) is one of the leading members of this gang.
>
> **Antrom has recently written a letter to Judge Leonard which has been shown to me in confidence that leads me to believe that we can use Antrom in these cases provided Gov. Wallace will make good**

his written promises and the U.S. Attorney will allow the case pending in the U.S. Court to slumber and give him (Antrom) one more chance to reform. [Author's boldface]

I have promised nothing and will not except to receive any propositions he Leonard and his client see fit to make and submit them to U.S. Attorney Barnes.

Judge Leonard has written Antrom to meet him (Leonard) at once for consultation.

The chances are that the conversation will take place within the next week when I will report fully to you **and submit whatever propositions they see fit to make** [Author's boldface] *to US. Attorney Barnes for such action as he deems proper to take.*

That negotiation with Wild was sabotaged by James Dolan's telling Wild that Billy was that gang's leader. So gullible Wild planned to arrest Billy at any meeting. Learning that intent from the stolen report, Billy avoided meeting, losing that second pardon chance. Billy again, as he declared during his great escape, was "standing pat against the world."

Noteworthy, also is that this Wild report also confirms a lost letter or letters by Billy Bonney concerning the pardon agreement; as to his willingness to testify, and possibly his specific knowledge of the counterfeiting operation. The fact that Wild first scheduled a meeting with Attorney Leonard and Billy implies his satisfaction with that communication.

AMBUSHES BY POSSES

By November of 1880, blood was being shed in Billy Bonney's pursuit. Azariah Wild had facilitated election, on the second of that month, of Ring-compliant Lincoln County Sheriff Pat Garrett, whom he also appointed as Deputy U.S. Marshal to continue Billy's pursuit anywhere in the Territory.

A White Oaks posse next ambushed Billy and his companions at Coyote Spring on November 22, 1880. Two of their horses were shot; but Billy and the rest escaped.

That posse next surrounded, on November 28, 1880, Billy's group's stop-over at the ranch of "Whiskey Jim" Greathouse. The outcome was dire. Greathouse was taken hostage, and the possemen's community leader, Jim Carlyle, was held by Billy's group inside the house. But Carlyle, panicking, hurled himself outside through a large window, and was killed by his firing fellows, thinking he was Billy escaping; and confirming, for Billy, the posse's determination to kill him.

LURID PRESS

The Ring's press campaign against Billy Bonney also made him fair game for any gunman.

On December 3, 1880, the Las Vegas *Gazette* published an editorial titled "Powerful Gang of Outlaws Harassing the Stockmen." Nine days later, Billy's letter of December 12th, to Lew Wallace, would be his response to its accusations.

That editorial is noteworthy because, by apparently using Azariah Wild's supposedly secret, description of a "gang" led by Billy, it implies information being fed to its editor-owner, J.H. Koogler. And, as Wild's reports to Chief James Brooks had stated, that fantasized "gang," of up to sixty men was the largest counterfeiting and rustling consortium in the country! That was what the Ring wanted people to believe about Billy.

Billy's logical response should have been to high-tail it out of the Territory. He chose instead to write his corrective letter to the governor. The article had stated:

> The gang includes forty to fifty men, all hard characters, the off scouring of society, fugitives from justice, and desperados by profession. Among them are men, with whose names and deeds the people of Las Vegas are perfectly familiar, such as "Billy the Kid," Dave Rudabaugh, Charles Bowdre, and others of equally unsavory reputation ...
>
> The gang is under the leadership of "Billy the Kid," a desperate cuss, who is eligible for the post of captain in any crowd, no matter how mean and lawless. They spend considerable time in enjoying themselves at the Portales, keeping guards out and scouting the country for miles around before turning in for the night. Whenever there is

a good opportunity to make a haul they split up in gangs and scour the country ...

They run stock from the Panhandle country into the White Oaks and from the Pecos country into the Panhandle ...

Are the people of San Miguel county to stand this any longer? Shall we suffer this hoard of outcasts and the scum of society, who are outlawed by a multitude of crimes, to continue their way to the very border of our county?

We believe the citizens of San Miguel County to be order loving people, and call upon them to unite in forever wiping out this band to the east of us.

BILLY WRITES TO WALLACE ON DECEMBER 12, 1880

Billy Bonney's letter of December 12, 1880 is his fourth letter to Lew Wallace - counting the "Billie" letter fragment. It was also Billy's sixth communication with him: adding to their Lincoln meeting at "Squire" Wilson's house and Wallace's interview of him at Juan Patrón's house-jail.

The letter, sent as a rebuttal of the accusatory Las Vegas *Gazette* article nine days before, marks Billy's transformation: hardened by living daily with threat of being killed, and raging at injustice, he is now famous; even bestowed with a flashy sobriquet, "Billy the Kid," soon nationally known; and he is obviously reading his own press.

Writing in more upright, thick script reflecting non-ideal seating or pen, and on ruled paper with makeshift red ink, Billy was on the run, but tauntingly providing to Lew Wallace his home base as Fort Sumner - possibly Hargrove's Saloon; where, the year before, he had killed, in self defense, and with an incredible shot through the head, bounty-hunter Joe Grant.

To Lew Wallace, Billy now writes with new familiarity, though they were not known to have communicated since March of 1879; though there may be lost letters. Billy later wrote to Wallace, on March 2, 1881, about *"letters in his possession"* - implying that they documented their bargain.

Also, by that December 12th, Billy knew he had backing: Attorney Ira Leonard continued pardon attempts from Wallace or the Secret Service. Billy wrote:

Fort Sumner

Dec. 12th 1880

Gov. Lew Wallace

Dear Sir

I noticed in the Las Vegas Gazette a piece which stated that, Billy "the" Kid, the name by which I am known in the Country was the captain of a Band of Outlaws who hold Forth at the Portales. There is no such Organization in Existence. So the Gentleman must have drawn very heavily on his Imagination. My business at the White Oaks at the time I was waylaid and my horse killed was to See Judge Leonard who has my case in hand. he had written me to come up, that he thought he could get Everything Straightened up I did not find him at the Oaks & Should have gone to Lincoln if I had met with no accident. After mine and Billie Wilsons horses were killed we both made our way to a Station, forty miles from the Oaks kept by Mr Greathouse. When I got up the next morning The house was Surrounded by an outfit led by one Carlyle, Who had come into the house and Demanded a Surrender. I asked for their Papers and they had none. So I concluded that it amounted to nothing more than a mob and told Carlyle that he would have to Stay in the house and lead the way out that night. Soon after a note was brought in Stating that if Carlyle did not come out inside of five minutes they would Kill the Station Keeper)Greathouse) who had left the house and was with them. in a Short time a Shot was fired on the outside and Carlyle thinking Greathouse was Killed jumped through the window. breaking the Sash as he went and was killed by his own Party they think it was me trying to make my Escape. the Party then withdrew.

they returned the next day and burned an old man named Spencer's house and Greatrhouses also

I made my way to this Place afoot and During my absence Deputy Sheriff Garrett Acting under Chisum's orders went to the Portales and found Nothing. on his way back he went by Mr Yerby's ranch and took a pair of mules of mine which I had left with Mr Bowdre who is in Charge of mr Yerby's cattle.

he (Garrett) claimed that they were stolen and even if they were not he had no right to Confiscate any Outlaws property.

I had been at Sumner Since I left Lincoln making my living Gambling the mules were bought by me the truth of which I can prove by the best citizens around Sumner. J.S. Chisum is the man who got me into Trouble and was benefited Thousands by it and is now doing all he can against me There is no Doubt but what there is a great deal of Stealing going on in the Territory. and a great deal of the Property is taken across the [Staked] Plains as it is a good outlet but so far as my being at the head of a Band there is nothing of it in Several Instances I have recovered Stolen Property when there was no chance to get an Officer to do it.

one instance for Hugo Zuber Postoffice Puerto de Luna. another for Pablo Analla Same Place.

if Some impartial Party were to investigate this matter they would find it far Different from the impression put out by Chisum and his Tools.

Yours Respect

William Bonney

ANALYSIS OF THE LETTER

Billy Bonney's December 12, 1880 letter's over-riding theme is justice; inspired by injustices beginning with his return to New Mexico Territory; and echoing voices of disenfranchised Hispanic residents of Lincoln County and of its Homestead farmers, bled by the usurious Murphy-Dolan House. Billy had lived through the legal harassment of Tunstall and McSween by the Fritz insurance policy attachment and its excuse for murder. He had lived through Governor S.B. Axtell's corrupt proclamations against the Regulators: blocking arrest of real murderers and outlawing good men. He had lived through the Lincoln County War; in lead-up, in week's siege, in coerced warrants from Justice of the Peace Wilson, in military violation of the Posse Comitatus Act, and in murder and arson. He had lived through obstruction of justice, seeing the April 1879 Grand Jury indictments against Ringmen nullified by corruption, and Colonel Dudley exonerated at his corrupt Court of Inquiry. Now he himself was being unjustly accused of murdering his most recent attacker, Jim Carlyle, who was part of a mob, first at Coyote Spring, then at the Greathouse Ranch.

And, by then, Billy had accumulated knowledge of law: from Attorney Alexander McSween, intern Harvey Morris, Justice of the Peace "Squire" Wilson, community leader and jailor Juan Patrón, Attorneys Huston Chapman and Ira Leonard, and by his own deposing and testifying.

Billy now is no longer pleading, not deal-making, but taking a stand, on his own behalf, for his legal rights and the truth.

Fort Sumner
Dec. 12ᵗʰ 1880
Gov. Lew Wallace
Dear Sir
I noticed in the Las Vegas Gazette

[AUTHOR'S NOTE: Billy reads his own press.]

a piece which stated that, Billy "the" Kid, the name by which I am known in the Country

[AUTHOR'S NOTE: Billy is aware of his moniker.]

was the captain of a Band of Outlaws who hold Forth at the Portales. There is no such Organization in Existence. So the Gentleman must have drawn very heavily on his Imagination.

[AUTHOR'S NOTE: This is a meticulous correction typical of Billy, and accompanied by his ironic joke about "*imagination.*"]

My business at the White Oaks at the time I was waylaid and my horse killed,

[AUTHOR'S NOTE: Billy here portrays himself as businessman, like in Hoyt Bill of Sale. Introduced is injustice: his horse being killed, and obviously getting no recompense.]

was to See Judge Leonard who has my case in hand. he had written me to Come up. that he thought he could get Everything Straightened up I did not find him at the Oaks & Should have gone to Lincoln if I had met with no accident.

[AUTHOR'S NOTE: Inexplicably, Billy, usually so precise, does not elucidate the pardon deal with Azariah Wild that he would still have considered possible. Maybe he thought it confidential. Nevertheless, in all his letters to follow, as in his past ones, except for the first, he unfortunately never uses a word to confirm annulling, clemency, or pardon - possibly avoiding presumption - to the detriment of pressuring Wallace, or assisting any who now mull his getting a posthumous pardon.]

After mine and Billie Wilsons horses were killed we both made our way to a Station, forty miles from the Oaks kept by Mr Greathouse. When I got up the next morning The house was Surrounded by an outfit led by one Carlyle. Who had come into the house and Demanded a Surrender. I asked for their Papers and they had none. So I concluded that it amounted to nothing more than a mob

[AUTHOR'S NOTE: Billy is a stickler for legality. Here he checked for appropriate warrants ("*papers*"), well aware that the McSweens had possessed legal warrants through Justice of the Peace Wilson for the arrest of Tunstall's killers.]

and told Carlyle that he would have to Stay in the house and lead the way out that night.

[AUTHOR'S NOTE: Others were also trapped, but Billy with natural leadership, formulated a plan to leave without bloodshed; especially since the posse was illegal and dangerous.]

Soon after a note was brought in Stating that if Carlyle did not come out inside of five minutes they would Kill the Station Keeper)Greathouse) who had left the house and was with them.

[AUTHOR'S NOTE: Billy places blame for the ensuing fiasco squarely on the murderous illegal mob posse.]

in a Short time a Shot was fired on the outside and Carlyle thinking Greathouse was Killed jumped through the window. breaking the Sash as he went and was killed by his own Party they think it was me trying to make my Escape. the Party then withdrew.

[AUTHOR'S NOTE: This confirmation of Jim Carlyle's death by friendly fire, and not by Billy's hand, is the purpose of this letter. Did Billy think that would stimulate Wallace to help him? Was he hoping Wallace would finally act to save him from injustice? Billy certainly communicates the posse's intent to kill him by stating they believed that Carlyle was "*me trying to make my Escape.*"]

they returned the next day and burned an old man named Spencer's house and Greathouses also

[AUTHOR'S NOTE: Further demonstration that the White Oaks posse were a violent mob.]

I made my way to this Place afoot and During my absence Deputy Sheriff Garrett Acting under Chisums orders went to the Portales and found Nothing. on his way back he went by Mr Yerby's ranch and took a pair of mules of mine which I had left with Mr Bowdre who is in Charge of mr Yerby's cattle. he (Garrett) claimed they were stolen and even if they were not he had no right to Confiscate any Outlaws property.

[AUTHOR'S NOTE: Billy presents another legal technicality: accusations of his outlawry did not justify taking his property.]

I had been in Sumner Since I left Lincoln making my living Gambling the mules were bought by me the truth of which I can prove by the best citizens around Sumner

[AUTHOR'S NOTE: As with the Hoyt Bill of Sale, Billy documented stock ownership. He cites his home base and gambling profession to refute outlawry; gives references as "*best citizens*" who were town residents and probably the Maxwell family itself.]

J.S. Chisum is the man who got me into Trouble and was benefited Thousands by it and is now doing all he can against me

[AUTHOR'S NOTE: Though aware of the Ring politics, Billy had most animosity toward Chisum; possibly because he turned traitor to the Regulator side. Chisum, in fact, did attempt to implicate Billy to Azariah Wild; and probably was himself a victim of Billy's "*guerilla rustling.*" "*Benefited Thousands*" may mean Billy believed Chisum kept Tunstall's bank's money or was paid off by the Ring.]

There is no Doubt but what there is a great deal of Stealing going on in the Territory and a great deal of the Property is taken across the [Staked] *Plains as it is a good outlet*

[AUTHOR'S NOTE: Billy himself crossed the Staked Plains (Llano Estacado) to sell stock on the Panhandle at Tascosa. He appears also to be attempting ingratiatingly to renew his role of informing on outlaws, as with his Wallace interview and "Billie" letter.]

but so far as my being at the head of a Band there is nothing of it

[AUTHOR'S NOTE: Billy may have been confessing his petty outlawry by admitting that he knew Texas was a good "*outlet*;" but that is to show insignificance, and not his being a gang leader - as he knew the *Gazette* article and Azariah Wild called him.]

in Several Instances I have recovered stolen property when there was no chance to get an Officer to do it. One instance for Hugo Zuber Postoffice Puerto de Luna. another for Pablo Analla Same Place.

[AUTHOR'S NOTE: Besides giving references, Billy acknowledges his "Robin Hood" reputation of counteracting real outlawry.]

if Some impartial Party were to investigate this matter they would find it far Different from the impression put out by Chisum and his Tools.

[AUTHOR'S NOTE: This may refer to Billy's past experience with "impartial investigation" of Frank Warner Angel in 1878. Billy, unaware of the Wild-Garrett dragnet, blames traitorous Tunstall ally, John Chisum, for the "*impression*" of outlawry.]

Yours Respect

William Bonney

[AUTHOR'S NOTE: Gone is the trusting signature of the letter before this: "*Billie*." Without abbreviation, this is Billy's most formal and cold signature on all his writings. If anything, he is any man's equal in dignity; even the governor's. And, possibly unconsciously, he cannot bring himself to write out fully "respectfully" - nor would he in any of his future letters to Lew Wallace.]

WHERE WALLACE WAS

Lew Wallace never answered Billy Bonney, though he kept that December 12, 1880 letter. Physically, he was still in Santa Fe's Palace of the Governors. Mentally, he was planning departure for the New York release of his novel *Ben-Hur: A Tale of the Christ*. Within months, it would be his second best-seller; and he would also fulfill his attraction to the Near East: departing to Constantinople as new President James Abram Garfield's Ambassador to Turkey on May 30, 1881.

On December 14th, Wallace requested a leave of absence.

Executive Office,

SANTA FE, N.M.
Dec. 14. 1880.

Hon. C. Schurz,
Sec. Dept. Interior
Sir:
I have private business urgently requiring my business in New York City; on account of which I have the honor to ask a leave of absence not exceeding twenty days.

[AUTHOR'S NOTE: This leave was for the publisher's release of 5,000 copies of Wallace's *Ben Hur: A Tale of the Christ*.]

The suggestion that I made in my letter of 7th inst., to the repeal, as respects New Mexico, of the law prohibiting the use of troops in aid of civil authorities,

[AUTHOR'S NOTE: This is Wallace's attempted block of the Posse Comitatus Act, the only hope anti-Ring fighters had in the Lincoln County War. In other words, a future intervention to suppress citizens - like Commander Dudley's - would be legal.]

is of such importance that I desire to appear before the senate and House Committees on Territories, and urge immediate action in the matter. If that be not properly done, it looks as if, for a time at least, the thieves and murderers quartered in the pocket of Grant County south-west, and on the line of old Mexico, cannot be taken care of as they should be. Ranchmen and miners are harassed by raids to such an extent that, in instances, they have been driven from their property.

I have intelligence today from Lincoln county. The citizens are yet in the fields under an active and very energetic deputy-sheriff, who has had several skirmishes, and made five important arrests;

[AUTHOR'S NOTE: Empowered by Secret Service Operative Azariah Wild, Pat Garrett was acting for Ring interests – though Wallace omits this; making it seem part of his "war on outlawry."]

so that the authorities there are confident that they can take care of themselves. To stimulate them, I have made proclamation of $500 reward for the capture and delivery of the leader of the outlaws.

[AUTHOR'S NOTE: This "leader of the outlaws" is obviously Billy Bonney. His letter of December 12, 1880 had been scorned.]

If the leave is granted, be good enough to telegraph me.
I have the honor to be &c.
Lew Wallace
Gov. N.M.

A PRICE ON BILLY'S HEAD

Lew Wallace's $500 reward notice for Billy the Kid appeared as a column advertisement in the December 22, 1880 Las Vegas *Gazette*. It was Wallace's personal blood money.

BILLY THE KID

$500 REWARD

I will pay $500 reward to any person or persons who will capture William Bonney, alias The Kid, and deliver him to any sheriff of New Mexico. Satisfactory proofs of identity will be required.
LEW. WALLACE,
Governor of New Mexico

MORE LURID PRESS

On the same day as Lew Wallace's $500 Territorial reward notice for him appeared, Billy Bonney gained national fame - along with his bay racing mare and "outlaw gang" - in the December 22, 1880 New York *Sun*. One can wonder if New Yorker, Frank Warner Angel, read this outcome of his betrayal of Billy Bonney and the rest of the anti-Ring freedom fighters.

The article is pure dime-novel fabrication, with likely input from Lew Wallace, Santa Fe Ring journalists, and leaked Secret Service reports of Azariah Wild. Along with utter distortion of the Lincoln County War, were mythologized tales of "Billy the Kid" which would become Billy Bonney's history.

At this point, Billy had no hope of salvation - from Lew Wallace or Ring-propelled lawmen. But Billy never accepted that, even to the moment of escaping the inescapable jail before hanging, or stepping into darkness of Peter Maxwell's bedroom shortly before midnight a little less than seven months later.

The New York *Sun* article stated:

OUTLAWS OF NEW MEXICO.
THE EXPLOITS OF A BAND HEADED BY
A NEW YORK YOUTH.

The Mountain fastness of the Kid and his Followers— War against a Gang of Cattle Thieves and Murderers —The Frontier Confederates of Brockway, the Counterfeiter.

LAS VEGAS, New Mexico, Dec. 20.—One hundred and twenty-seven miles southeast of Las Vegas, New Mexico, is Fort Sumner, once the base of operations against the Indians who committed depredations against the stockmen. The fort was abandoned some ten or twelve years ago, owing to the removal of troops further south, toward the border of Mexico. The property was condemned and sold to Pete Maxwell, a well-known ranchman of the section. Since then it has been a depot of supplies for stockmen and a stage station on the postal route to the Pecos Valley and Panhandle, Texas.

Until recently, on almost any fair day, there might have been seen lounging about the store or engaged in target practice four men, all of them young, neatly dressed, and of good appearance. A stranger riding in the little hamlet would have taken them to be a party of Eastern gentlemen who had come into that sparsely settled region in search of sport. Many who have gone into that country have struck up an acquaintance with these men and found them agreeable fellows. These men are the worst desperadoes in the West, and large parties of armed men are now scouring the country in pursuit of them.

For a number of years the people of eastern New Mexico and Panhandle, Texas, have been harassed by a gang who have run off stock, burned ranches, and committed acts of violence and murder. It was only recently that the leaders and organization of the band were discovered. The leaders are Billy the Kid, so called from his youth; Dave Rudabaugh, Billy Wilson, and Tom O'Phallier, the four loungers about Fort Sumner. The Kid is the captain of the gang. Their fastness is about thirty-five miles nearly due east from Fort Sumner, on the edge of the great Staked Plain. In that region there is a small lake called Las Portales. It is surrounded by steep hills, from which flow numerous streams that feed the little lake. This place the robbers selected for their resort partly on account of its hiding places, but mainly on account of the opportunities it afforded them for stock thieving. No matter from what direction the storm came, it drove to the lake the herds of cattle which roam at large in the rich grazing country. There the band built for themselves one of those rude dugouts so common on the Western frontier, two sides formed by the side of the hill, the other two constructed of sod and dirt plastered together, and the whole covered by a thatched roof. Stockades or corrals were built near by in which to put stolen stock. During pleasant weather the members of the gang lounged about Fort Sumner or other stations in that section. When the storm sent cattle scudding over the plains to the haven afforded by the hill-protected lake basin, the gang would hurry to their rendezvous and cut out from the herds the best cattle, driving them into their corral, whence they were later sent to market. Their booty was large, for they had a vast stock to select from, the whole country for a distance of one hundred and fifty miles either way being a rich, continuous pasture. Besides the active members of the band, there were many who had apparently some settled occupation and made themselves useful in disposing of the stolen cattle. In every town of any size within a radius of 150 miles there were butchers who dealt regularly in this stolen stock. When supplies from roving herds ran short the desperadoes would make a raid on herds that were guarded, attacking ranches and killing or diving off the inmates. Besides their station at Las Portales, they had one at Bosque Grande, fifty miles to the southwest, and another at Greathouse's rancho, fifty miles to the north. Whenever they were pursued when running of stock, they had the choice of three places to which to resort.

The people of the surrounding country finally found the existence of this band unendurable. After repeated searches, which failed, owing to the smallness of the pursuing parties, it was resolved to organize several bands, who should cooperate in a campaign, which should end only when the outlaws were driven out of the country, or their capture, dead or alive, was effected. The authorities of the several counties which bordered on the country ranged over by the Kid's gang had been repeatedly petitioned to send out a posse of men to hunt them down, but, as Las Portales was on disputed territory, the authorities were never able to settle upon any plan of action. At last the ranchmen took the matter into their own hands, and the first party they sent out succeeded in getting on the track of a detachment of the gang who were hauling material to Las Portales, where they were building large stock yards. Although the party was not successful in capturing the outlaws, they made the outlaws flit about the country in a more lively manner than had been their wont. This showed that nothing could be done by a small force. A guard was always kept out on the numerous peaks about Las Portales, from which outlook; the country for twenty miles either way could be scanned by the outlaws, so that they could easily elude a small party!

The Panhandle Transportation Company, an association of stockmen of western Texas, banded together for mutual protection, commissioned their superintendent, Frank Stewart, a brave fellow, who was just the man for such work, to organize an expedition against the outlaws. The White Oaks, a flourishing mining camp, organized a band of rangers. Still another party of picked men, under the lead of Sheriff Pat Garrett of Lincoln County, who is considered one of the bravest and coolest men in the whole region, joined in the campaign. In the latter part of November Garrett, with a force of fourteen men, made a dash for Bosque Grande, riding all night, and there succeeded in capturing five of the outlaws. One of them was a condemned murderer who had escaped from jail; another of them was a murderer for whose arrest $1,500 had been offered. These are the sort of men who reinforce the band. Las Portales has long been an asylum for fugitives from justice. Bosque Grande (Great Forest) is situated in one of the most fertile regions of the West, and as the rich lands bordering on the Pecos River are the objective point of many who intend to settle in the Territory, it was thought best to rid that region of the outlaws first, in order that none might be deterred from settling there. Precautions have been taken which will prevent this refuge of the band from ever sheltering them again.

It was expected that the two other parties would work with Garrett's band, but the Panhandle party were delayed, owing to scarcity of feed, and the White Oaks Rangers had their hands full in another quarter. The latter party had a brush—with the Kid, Rudabaugh, Wilson, and several others at Coyote Spring, near the Oaks camp, and the outlaws succeeded in escaping, although two had their horses shot from under them. The rangers started back for reinforcements and supplies, and then pressed on after the outlaws, coming upon them at their other station at Greathouse's ranch. It was night when the rangers reached the ranch. They threw up earthworks a few hundred yards from the stockade of the ranch, and when the outlaws rose up in the morning they found themselves hemmed in. The rangers sent a messenger to Jim Greathouse, the owner of this ranch, demanding the surrender of the outlaws.

Greathouse replied in person. He came out to the camp of the rangers and stoutly asserted that the outlaws had taken possession of his ranch and that he had no power over them nor anything to do with them. It was considered best to hold Greathouse as a hostage, while Jim Carlyle, the leader of the rangers, heeded to the Kid's request for a conference. A long time elapsed and Carlyle did not return. His men began to feel uneasy about him, and dispatched a note to the renegade chief saying that unless Carlyle was given up in less than five minutes they would kill Greathouse. No reply was received. Soon after the rangers saw Carlyle leap from the window and dash down the hill toward their entrenchments. He had not gone far, however, when they saw the Kid throw half his body through the window, and, taking deliberate aim, brought down poor Carlyle, killing him instantly. A sharp fight followed, but the outlaws succeeded in making their escape, Greathouse also getting away during the confusion. Before leaving for home with the dead body of their leader, the rangers fired everything about the place, and Greathouse concealed some miles away, saw the smoke of his burning property.

The three parties are now engaged in scouting the country, and will not give up the chase till the country is rid of every one of the outlaws. Money and outfits have been freely offered by men who have large interests in that section. Government officials are now interested in the campaign, for, in addition to their other crimes, the outlaws have put in circulation a large quantity of the counterfeit money manufactured by William Brockway, the forger. The bills were obtained by one of the gang named Doyle who formerly operated in Chicago, and counterfeit $100 bills in large numbers have been put in circulation among the stockmen and merchants in all that region. The information that enabled the Government officers to discover the handling of counterfeit money by the Kid's gang came from a freighter named Smith. Soon afterward, while Smith was on his way from Las Vegas to Fort Sumner with a load of freight, he was waylaid and murdered by some of the gang.

William Bonney, alias the Kid, the leader of the band, is scarcely over 20 years of age. He is handsome and dresses well. He has a fair complexion, smooth face, blue eyes, and light brown hair. He is about six feet tall and deceptively handsome. A beautiful bay mare, that he has carefully trained, is all that he seems to care for, unless he reserves some affection for his brace of six-shooters and Winchester rifle, which have helped him out of many a tight place. His care of the beautiful mare is well deserved, for many a time has her fleetness which surpasses that of any other horse in the Territory, saved his life. The Kid is an admirable rider, and as he is always expected to be obliged to take flight, he usually rides another horse, leading his pet behind, in order to make the best time possible on a fresh horse. He is considered a dead shot and much of his time is spent in target practice. He was born in New York State, but his parents removed to Indiana when he was quite small, and thence to Arizona. There in the Tombstone District the Kid killed his first man when he was only 17 years old, and was obliged to leave the country. He came to New Mexico, where he has since lived.

About three years ago a difficulty arose in Lincoln County, New Mexico, between the stockmen and the Indian agent on the reservation. The trouble arose in regard to some cattle that had been purchased for the Indians. Nearly every man in the county was under arms, and the troops were called out by Gov. Wallace to quell the disturbance. The Kid was mixed up in the affair, and had some narrow escapes. On one occasion he was hotly pursued and was obliged to take refuge in a house in Lincoln, which was surrounded by sixty solders. To the demand to surrender, he only laughed and shot down a soldier just to show that he was game. The house was set on fire, when the Kid, after loading up his Winchester Rifle, leaped from the burning building and made a dash for liberty. All the while he was running he kept firing from his Winchester, bringing down a number of his pursuers. Bullets whistled over his head, but he made his escape, and leaping on a horse was soon laughing at his pursuers. There is no telling how many men he has killed. He sets no value on human life, and has never hesitated at murder when it would serve his purpose. Gov. Wallace a few days ago offered a reward of $500 for his capture, and prominent citizens would make up a handsome purse in addition.

Billy Wilson is much the same sort of good looking fellow as his chief. He is about the same build, with dark hair and a slight moustache. He left the Ohio home where his people, who are all highly esteemed, still reside, several years ago. After being engaged in the cattle business in Texas for some time, he came to New Mexico. When the excitement broke out over the new camp at White Oaks, he went there and was engaged in the butchering business. He was always considered a smart, energetic fellow, and was well thought of. In some way the Kid persuaded him to join his party, and it was by him that much of the forged paper was put into circulation.

Tom O'Phallier is a Texan and is also a man of good appearance. He has a ruddy, face, and can be an exceedingly agreeable companion. He has been with the band from the first, and has committed many crimes.

Dave Rudabaugh is 36 years old, and was born in New York city, where he lived until about eight years ago. He has raided over southern Kansas, the Indian nations, Texas, southern Colorado, and New Mexico. It would not be difficult to establish charges of murder against him in any or all of those States and Territories. In Colorado, a few years ago he ran off some Government stock, and, while pursued by a detachment of soldiers, he killed a Sergeant and two privates. He once headed an attack on the Las Vegas jail, in order to liberate one of his friends, and shot down a guard who interfered. He is a thorough desperado in look, word, and action, ready at all times for a fight. He thinks no more of putting a bullet through a human brain than through the bull's eyes of the target before which he is continually practicing. He is 5 feet 8 inches tall, and weighs about 180 pounds. He has a swarthy complexion, black hair and beard, and hazel eyes, whose cruel, defiant expression has often been noted.

The career of the band is about run, for they are hotly pursued, and the chances are that before long they will be killed or captured. It is not expected that the Kid or Rudabaugh will be taken alive, as they will fight to the last.

Jailed Billy's
Letters to Lew Wallace

WRITTEN PLEAS FOR JUSTICE

Governor Lew Wallace ignored Billy Bonney's December 12, 1880 letter to him. By December 19th, Deputy Sheriff Pat Garrett fatally shot Tom O'Folliard. By December 22nd, was Stinking Springs and Charlie Bowdre's killing. Captured were Billy, Billy Wilson, Tom Pickett, and "Dirty Dave" Rudabaugh.

From Stinking Springs, they were transported to Fort Sumner, where Billy bid farewell to Paulita Maxwell, her mother Luz, and family servant Deluvina.

Overnight jailing was in Las Vegas, New Mexico; followed by railroad transport to Santa Fe and its jail. From there, aware that the jail was only a few blocks from the Palace of the Governors, Billy would write four more letters of appeal to Lew Wallace: Billy's last known to that man.

Those four jail letters retained the more upright penmanship of Billy's December 12, 1880 letter to Wallace; and, like it, reflected lack of adequate writing conditions for proper Spencerian penmanship.

By April 15, 1881, ever the perfectionist and unbroken in spirit, Billy would offer his own explanation of that aesthetic failure to his attorney, Edgar Caypless, writing to him: *"excuse bad writing. I have my handcuffs on."*

Billy was in the Santa Fe jail from December 27, 1880 to March 28, 1881, awaiting completion of railroad tracks to his hanging trial. From February 28, 1881 to his departure, he was in solitary confinement after a jailbreak attempt.

Lew Wallace never answered Billy's jail letters. But calculatingly and pitilessly, he saved them with Billy's other letters, and took them all back to his Crawfordsville, Indiana, home in May of 1881, on his way to the next happy chapter of his life as ambassador in Constantinople.

First Santa Fe Jail Letter:
January 1, 1881

Billy Bonney's first letter to Lew Wallace [APPENDIX 8], written from the Santa Fe jail, by reputation a "terrible place," was on his fifth day there: January 1, 1881, a harsh new year. Hope of Wallace's propinquity seemingly made Billy invitingly polite; but his stance of equality was unbowed by adversity. Unaware that Wallace was not then in Santa Fe, Billy wrote:

> *Santa Fe*
> *Jan." 1ˢᵗ*
> *1881*
>
> *Gov." Lew Wallace*
> *Dear Sir*
> *I would like to see you for a few moments if You can spare the time.*
> *Yours Respect."*
> *W.H.Bonney*

Second Santa Fe Jail Letter:
March 2, 1881

Billy was in solitary confinement after his failed tunneling-out jailbreak of February 28th, when he wrote Lew Wallace, now returned to Santa Fe, on March 2, 1881 [APPENDIX 9]. It rankled, since Billy challenged him, writing: "*I have some letters which date back two years and there are Parties who are very anxious to get them but I will not dispose of them until I see you. that is if you come immediately.*"

Two decades later, still stung, Wallace wrote a long lying concoction for *New York World Magazine* of June 8, 1902, titled "General Lew Wallace Writes a Romance of 'Billy the Kid' Most Famous Bandit of the Plains: Thrilling Story of the Midnight Meeting Between Gen Wallace, Then Governor of New Mexico, and the Notorious Outlaw, in a Lonesome Hut in Santa Fe." With smarmy accusations of Billy's effeminacy, cowardice, and bad aim, Wallace re-wrote to re-work Billy's damning words.

The article does prove Lew Wallace's receiving and ignoring Billy's pleas; and, more importantly, confirms the existence of Billy's referenced letters of pardon proof - though they are now lost. As to Wallace's newspaper version of events, they are as fabricated as is the Lincoln pardon meeting being in a "Lonesome Hut in Santa Fe."

Lew Wallace's article stated:

The desperado's freedom, however, was not long-lived. He was arrested soon afterward for a series of murders, and was brought again to the Lincoln County Jail ... At any rate he must have considered himself in desperate straits. He sent for Gen. Wallace. The General refused to respond. Then the outlaw sent him a note. The note said:

"Come to the jail. I have some papers you would not want to see displayed."

"I knew what he meant," said Gen. Wallace, reminiscently. "He referred to the note he received from me in response to which he appeared in the hut on the mesa. He was threatening to publish it if I refused to see him. I thwarted his purpose by giving a copy of the latter and a narrative of the circumstances connected with it to the paper published in the town. It was duly printed and upon its appearance a copy was sent to "Billy" in his cell. He had nothing further to say."

Billy Bonney's actual second jail letter stated:

Santa Fe Jail New Mex
March 2d̲ 18<u>8</u>1

Gov." Lew Wallace
Dear Sir
I wish you would come down to the jail to see me. it will be to your interest to come and see me. I have Some letters, which date back two years. and there are Parties who are very anxious to get them. but I shall not dispose of them untill I see you. that is if you come immediately.
Yours respect -
Wm̲ H Bonney

THIRD SANTA FE JAIL LETTER: MARCH 4, 1881

Billy Bonney's third letter, two days later, on March 4, 1881 [APPENDIX 10], and still from solitary confinement, switched to threat of a leader of a possible freedom uprising of follower friends. He wrote: *"I guess they mean to Send me up without giving me any Show but they will have a nice time doing it. I am not entirely without friends."*

Audience is demanded with fired bullets of capitals: *"I shall Expect to See you Some time today."* The letter stated:

Santa Fe, In jail

March 4th 1881
Gov" Lew Wallace

Dear Sir

I wrote you a little note the day before yesterday, but have received no annser. I Expect you have forgotten what you promised me, this Month two Years ago. but I have not. and I think You had ought to have come and seen me as I requested you to. I have done Everything that I promised you I would, and You have done nothing that You promised me.

I think when You think the matter over, you will come down and See me. and I can then Explain Everything to you.

Judge Leonard, Passed through here on his way East, in January, and promised to come and see me on his way back, but he did not fulfill his Promise. it looks to me like I am getting left in the Cold. I am not treated right by [sic - U.S. Marshal] Sherman. he lets Every Stranger that comes to See me through Curiosity in to see me, but will not let a Single one of my friends in, not Even an Attorney.

I guess they mean to Send me up without giving me any Show. but they will have a nice time doing it I am not entirely without friends

I shall Expect to See you Sometime today
Patiently Waiting
I am Very truly Yours, Respt -
Wm H. Bonney

FURTHER ANALYSIS OF MARCH 4, 1881 LETTER

Santa Fe, In jail

[AUTHOR'S NOTE: Billy now truculently emphasizes that he is in jail by giving it as his location.]

March 4ᵗʰ 1881

[AUTHOR'S NOTE: Billy would know that this is just two days after his blackmail-like threat. Lack of Wallace's answer apparently left uncertainty about that tactic.]

Gov" Lew Wallace
Dear Sir
I wrote You a little note the day before yesterday but have received no answer.

[AUTHOR'S NOTE: Billy's appeal here is to Wallace's moral obligation, starting with Wallace's non-response to his letter.]

I Expect you have forgotten what you promised me, this Month two Years ago. but I have not. and I think You had ought to have come and seen me as I requested you to. I have done everything that I promised you I would, and You have done nothing that You promised me.

[AUTHOR'S NOTE: Though omitting the word "pardon," Billy for the first time eloquently puts words to betrayal as a *"promise"* that each of them made; but only he kept. He circumvents Wallace's self-deluding and possible trick of wording by framing non-compliance as comparable to lying under oath: "*I have done everything that I promised you I would, and You have done nothing that You promised me.*"]

I think when You think The Matter over, You will come down and See me,

[AUTHOR'S NOTE: Billy again presents Wallace with a moral choice. Though Wallace failed the test, he chewed his cud of guilt for the rest of his life - but by reworking the truth 20 years later.]

and I can then Explain Everything to you.

[AUTHOR'S NOTE: Billy may again be evoking the sham arrest in Lincoln, when he explained realities to a receptive Wallace.]

Judge Leonard, Passed through here on his way East, in January, and promised to come and see me on his way back, but he did not fulfill his Promise. it looks to me like I am getting left in the Cold. I am not treated right by Sherman. he lets Every Stranger that comes to See me through Curiosity in to see me. but will not let a Single one of my friends in, not Even an Attorney.

[AUTHOR'S NOTE: Billy' brings to mind their mutual friend, Ira Leonard, his primary champion to Wallace for his pardon.]

I guess they mean to Send me up without giving me any Show. but they will have a nice time doing it I am not entirely without friends.

[AUTHOR'S NOTE: Billy carefully avoids accusing Wallace of committing injustice, but uses "*they*," before challenging with his most ominous rendition yet of his "*friends.*"]

I shall Expect to See you Sometime today.

[AUTHOR'S NOTE: Billy's again creates a moral imperative, making failure to meet with him a moral failure - which it was.]

Patiently Waiting

[AUTHOR'S NOTE: Billy's tone changes from the blackmail-style prior letter; now evoking Wallace's own conscience.]

I am Very truly Yours Respt -

[AUTHOR'S NOTE: Billy concludes with openness like in the "Billie" letter by "Very truly yours." And there is some respect still.]

W$^{\underline{m}}$ H. Bonney

[AUTHOR'S NOTE: Billy uses his selected "jail name" - "*W$^{\underline{m}}$ H. Bonney*" - used only in some of the jail letters for reserved and formal dignity.]

FOURTH SANTA FE JAIL LETTER: MARCH 27, 1881

Billy Bonney's last known letter written to Lew Wallace is dated March 27, 1881 [APPENDIX 11]; still from solitary confinement, and a day before his railroad transport to Mesilla for the trial he knew would sentence him to hanging.

With self-possession he would have maintained on the gallows - and did maintain when he refused to say a word in Judge Bristol's Court after hanging sentencing - Billy, about to depart after the three month incarceration, put the moral choice and obligation to save him squarely on Lew Wallace.

And Billy's signature is his most minimal - almost an afterthought as he prepares to enter destiny's current - just "*WBonney.*"

One should not miss the letter's implication of a secret "*friend,*" even while he was in jail; because his four letters have apparently all been transported by Wallace by a "*bearer.*"

Of course, Lew Wallace did not respond.

Santa *Fe New. Mexico*

March27ᵘ/81

Gov. Lew Wallace
Dear Sir
                    for the last time I ask.
Will you keep Your promise. I start below tomorrow Send Annser by bearer
                    Yours Respt
                    WBonney

Billy's Mesilla
Hanging Trial

THE RING AND THE NOOSE

By March 28, 1881, the Santa Fe Ring was eagerly poised to eliminate Billy Bonney. In Mesilla, under puppet Judge Warren Bristol, far from knowledgeable Lincoln County jurors or witnesses, hanging was certain. And Billy's indictments did sound horrifying out of context: murders of two lawmen - Sheriff William Brady and Deputy George Hindman - and of a man crippled in one arm: Andrew "Buckshot" Roberts.

But the Ring had three obstacles. First was Billy's loyal anti-Ring attorney, Ira Leonard; Ring assassination of him in Lincoln on April 25, 1879 having failed. Leonard even succeeded in quashing the "Buckshot" Roberts indictment on March 30, 1881 on a technicality. So the Ring, probably by death threat, made him withdraw; leaving Billy with court-appointed, blasé, local attorney, Albert Jennings Fountain.

The second obstacle was needing a sentence of first degree murder for hanging. But all the killings occurred in Regulator groups, without proof Billy even fired. That was second-degree murder. In fact, in August of 1880, Jessie Evans, imprisoned in Fort Davis, Texas, for killing a Texas Ranger with his gang, even had the District Attorney arguing second-degree. (Jessie got twenty years at Huntsville prison; but escaped in under two years.) So Judge Bristol selected an Hispanic, non-English-speaking jury, gave no translator except for his instructions, and made those instructions biased for a first degree verdict.

The third obstacle was Billy's possible appeal of his sentence. And the lack of a translator gave grounds. So Bristol set the hanging date thirty days away, to make finding an attorney almost impossible. Furthermore, Billy had no money to hire one. The Ring had a fail-safe noose - or so they thought.

JUDGE BRISTOL'S JURY INSTRUCTIONS

After Attorney Ira Leonard's successful quashing of the "Buckshot" Roberts case, came Billy Bonney's murder trial on April 8th to 9th for Sheriff William Brady, with representation by court-appointed Albert Jennings Fountain and John D. Bail.

Billy had no defense witnesses; and James Dolan himself testified for the prosecution. Judge Warren Bristol provided a translator for his jury instructions. And, though the trial transcripts appear expurgated like those of the 1879 Lincoln Grand Jury, those instructions still exist. Bristol essentially ordered jurymen to ignore first degree criteria: the suspect's premeditated and provable killing of the victim. Instead, he made presence alone guilt in the first degree, and stated:

Territory of New Mexico
District Court 3d Judicial
District Doña Ana County
April Term A.D. 1881

In the Third Judicial
District Court April Term / 1879

Territory of New Mexico	)
vs	)
	) *Murder*
William Bonney alias Kid	) *1st Degree*
Alias William Antrim	)

Gentlemen of the Jury:
The defendant in this case William Bonney alias Kid alias William Antrim is charged in and by the indictment against him which has been laid before you with having committed in connection with certain other persona the crime of murder in the County of Lincoln in the 3d Judicial District of the Territory of New Mexico in the month of April of the year 1878 by then and there unlawfully killing one William Brady by inflicting upon his body certain fatal gunshot wounds from a premeditated design to effect his death.

The case is here for trial by a change of venue from the said County of Lincoln.

The facts alleged in the indictment if true constitute Murder in the 1ˢᵗ and highest degree and whether these allegations are true or not true are for you to determine from the evidence which you have heard and which is now submitted to you for your careful consideration.

In the matter of determining what your verdict shall be it will be improper for you to consider anything except the evidence before you.

You as Jurors are the exclusive judges of the weight of the evidence. You are the exclusive judges of the credibility of the witnesses. It is for you to determine whether the testimony of any witnesses whom you have heard is to be believed or not. You are also the exclusive judges whether the evidence is sufficiently clear and strong to satisfy your minds that the defendant is guilty.

There is no evidence tending to show that the killing of Brady was either justifiable or excusable by law. As a matter of law therefore such killing was unlawful and whoever committed the deed or was present and advised or aided or abetted and consented to such killing committed the crime of murder in some one of the degrees of murder.

There is no evidence before you showing that the killing of Brady is murder in any degree than the first.

Your verdict therefore should be either that the defendant is guilty of the murder in the 1ˢᵗ degree or that he is not guilty at all under this indictment.

Murder in the 1ˢᵗ degree consists in the killing of one human being by another without authority of law and from a premeditated design to affect the death of the person killed.

Every killing of one human being by another that is not justifiable or excusable should be necessarily a killing without authority of law.

As I have already instructed you to consider murder in the 1ˢᵗ degree it is necessary that the killing should have been perpetrated from a premeditated design to effect the death of the person killed.

As to this premeditated design I charge you that to render design to kill premeditated it is not necessary that such design to kill should exist in the mind for any considerable length of time before the killing.

If the design to kill is completely formed in the mind but for a moment before inflicting the fatal wounds it would be premeditated and in law the effect would be the same as though the design to kill had existed for a long time.

In this case in order to justify you in finding this defendant guilty of murder in the 1st degree under the peculiar circumstances as presented by the indictment and the evidence you should be satisfied and believe from the evidence to the exclusion of every Reasonable doubt of the truth of several propositions.

1st That the defendant either inflicted one or more of the fatal wounds causing Brady's death or that he was present at the time and place of the killing and encouraged – incited – aided in – abetted – advised or commanded such killing.

2d That such killing was without justification or excuse.

3d That such killing of Brady was caused by inflicting upon his body a fatal gunshot wound.

And 4th that such fatal wound was either inflicted by the defendant upon a premeditated design to effect Brady's death or that he was present at the time and place of the killing of Brady and from a premeditated design to effect his death he then and there encouraged – incited – aided in – abetted – advised or commanded such killing.

If he was so present – encouraging – inciting – aiding in – abetting – advising – or commanding the killing of Brady he is as much guilty as though he fired the fatal shot.

I have charged you that to justify you in finding the defendant guilty of murder in the 1st degree you should be satisfied from the evidence to the exclusion of every reasonable doubt that the defendant is actually guilty.

As to what would be or would not be reasonable doubt of guilt I charge you that belief in the guilt of the defendant to the exclusion of every reasonable doubt does not require you to so believe absolutely and to mathematical certainty – That is to justify a verdict of guilty it is not necessary for you to be as certain that the defendant is guilty as you are that two and two are four or that two and three are five.

Merely a vague conjecture or bare possibility that the defendant my be innocent is not sufficient to raise reasonable doubt of his guilt.

If all the evidence before you which you believe to be true convinces and directs your understanding and satisfies your reason and judgment while acting upon it conscientiously under your oath as jurors and if this evidence leaves in your minds an abiding conviction to a moral certainty that the defendant is guilty of the crime charged against him: then this would be proof of guilt to the exclusion of every reasonable doubt and would justify you in finding the defendant guilty.

You will apply the evidence to this case according to the instructions I have given you and determine whether the defendant is guilty of murder in the 1ˢᵗ degree or not guilty.

Murder in the 1ˢᵗ degree is the greatest crime known to our laws. The legislature of this Territory has enacted a law prescribing that the punishment for murder in the 1ˢᵗ degree shall be death.

This then is the law: No other punishment than death can be imposed – for murder in the 1ˢᵗ degree.

If you believe and are satisfied therefore from the evidence before you to the exclusion of every reasonable doubt that the defendant is guilty of murder in the 1ˢᵗ degree then it will be your duty to find a verdict that the defendant is guilty of murder in that degree naming murder in the 1ˢᵗ degree in your verdict and also saying in your verdict that the defendant shall suffer the punishment of death.

If from the evidence you do not believe to the exclusion of every reasonable doubt that the defendant is guilty of murder in the 1ˢᵗ degree or if you entertain a reasonable doubt as to the guilt of the defendant, then in that case your verdict should be not guilty.

532

Territory
  Vs.   ) Murder
William Bonney
Alias "Kid" alias
William Antrim

Filed in my office this 9th day of April A.D. 1881.
George R. Bowman
Clerk

BILLY BONNEY'S ABANDONMENT

Billy Bonney lacked adequate representation at his Brady murder trial. His lead attorney, Albert Jennings Fountain, an opponent of outlawry and indifferent to Lincoln County's anti-Ring fight, had only repugnance for him; as reflected in his lackadaisical jury instructions, which merely vouched for Judge Warren Bristol's convicting agenda. So, of course, Billy received a verdict of first degree murder from the jurymen.

ATTORNEY ALBERT JENNINGS FOUNTAIN'S INSTRUCTIONS ASKED BY DEFENDANT

> *Territory of New Mexico*
> *vs   ) Murder*
> *William Bonney alias Kid alias William Antrim*

> *In the District Court of Doña County March 1881 term.*

Instructions asked for by Defendants counsel. The Court is asked to instruct the Jury as follows: to wit:

1st Instructions asked –
Under the evidence the Jury must either find the defendant guilty of Murder in the 1st degree, or acquit him.
2nd Instruction asked –
The jury will not be justified in finding the defendant guilty of Murder in the 1st degree unless they are satisfied, from the evidence, to the exclusion of all reasonable doubt, that the defendant actually fired the shot that caused the death of the deceased Brady, and that such shot was fired by the defendant with the premeditated design to effect the death of the deceased, or that the defendant was present and actually assisted in firing the fatal shot or shots that caused the death of the deceased, and that he was present in a position to render such assistance and actually rendered assistance from a premeditated design to effect the death of the deceased.

Instruction asked –

If the Jury are satisfied from the evidence to the exclusion of all reasonable doubt that the defendant was present at the time of the firing of the shot or shots that caused the death of the deceased Brady, yet, before they will be justified in finding the defendant guilty, they must be further satisfied from the evidence and the evidence alone, to the exclusion of all reasonable doubt, that the defendant either fired the shots that killed the deceased, or some one of them, or that he assisted in firing said shot or shots, and that he assisted in firing said shot or shots, or assisted in firing the same, or assisted the parties who fired the same either by his advice, encouragement pr procurement or command, from a premeditated design to effect the death of Brady. If the Jury entertains any reasonable doubt upon any of these points they must find a verdict of acquittal.

A.J. Fountain
J.D. Bail

WALLACE'S PARDON INTERVIEW

Lew Wallace gave no pardon for Billy Bonney's conviction; and apparently still nursed resentment from Billy's jail letter citing letters proving its promise. On April 28, 1881, coincidentally Billy's jailbreak day, Wallace, unaware of that, gave the owner-editor of the Las Vegas *Gazette*, J.H. Koogler, his "Interview with Governor Lew Wallace on 'The Kid.' "

The conversation drifted into the sentence of "the Kid." "It looks as though he would hang, Governor." "Yes, the chances seem good that the 13th of May would finish him." "He appears to look to you to save his neck." "Yes," said Governor Wallace smiling, "but I can't see how a fellow like him should expect any clemency from me." Although not committing himself, the general tenor of the governor's remarks indicated that he would resolutely refuse to grant "The Kid" a pardon. It would seem as though "the Kid" had undertaken to bulldoze the governor, which has not helped his chances in the slightest.

WALLACE WRITES THE DEATH WARRANT

Lew Wallace wanted Billy Bonney dead. On April 30, 1881, he produced the boy's official death warrant for Sheriff Pat Garrett. Wanting the corpse confirmed, he stated: *"And make due return of your acts hereunder."* Maybe Wallace's hope was that killing the gadfly could kill reality of his own evil.

To the Sheriff of Lincoln County, New Mexico, Greeting:

At the March term, A.D. 1881 of the District Court for the Third Judicial District of New Mexico, held at La Mesilla in the County of Doña Ana, William Bonney alias Kid, alias William Antrim, was duly convicted of the crime of murder in the First Degree; and on the fifteenth day of said term, the same being the thirteenth day of April, A.D. 1881, the judgment and sentence of said court were pronounced against the said William Bonney, alias Kid, alias William Antrim, upon said conviction according to law: whereby the said William Bonney, alias Kid, alias William Antrim, was adjudged and sentenced to be hanged by the neck until dead, by the Sheriff of the said County of Lincoln, within said county.

Therefore, you the Sheriff of the said county of Lincoln, are hereby commanded that on Friday, the thirteenth day of May, A.D. 1881, pursuant to the said judgment and sentence of the said court, you take the said William Bonney, alias Kid, alias William Antrim, from the county jail of the county of Lincoln where he is now confined, to some safe and convenient place within the said county, and there, between the hours of ten o'clock, A.M. and three o'clock, P.M., of said day, you hang the said William Bonney, alias Kid, alias William Antrim, by the neck until he is dead. And make due return of your acts hereunder:

> *Done at Santa Fe in the Territory of New Mexico, this 30th day of April, A.D. 1881. Witness my hand and the great seal of the Territory.*
>
> *Lew Wallace*
> *Governor New Mexico*

Billy's Jail Letter to Edgar Caypless

NEVER GIVING UP

On Friday April 15, 1881, two days after receiving his first degree murder sentence, with its hanging just twenty-eight days away, Billy Bonney wrote to an attorney named Edgar Caypless, whom he had engaged on contingency when jailed in Santa Fe; and likely met because Caypless was representing his fellow inmates from their Stinking Springs capture: Billy Wilson and "Dirty Dave" Rudabaugh.

During that Santa Fe incarceration - from December 27, 1880 to March 28, 1881 - Billy used Attorney Caypless to file a replevin, or recovery of property, case, against Pat Garrett's Texan posseman, Frank Stewart, for the theft of his bay racing mare, confiscated at his Stinking Springs capture.

Earlier communication with Caypless must be missing, because Billy's letter to him demonstrates his knowledge of the mare's fate. Frank Stewart had sold her to a Winfred Scott Moore, the owner of Moore's Hotsprings Hotel in Las Vegas; who gifted her to his wife, Minnie. Minnie Moore, in turn, had boldly named the mare Kid Stewart Moore. So Billy knew his horse had to be repossessed from the Moores.

Possibly, at the Santa Fe jail, Edgar Caypless or Ira Leonard gave Billy the Las Vegas *Gazette* article of March 12, 1881 about his case for his famous mare. It stated: "The suit will be warmly contested." By April 15th, Billy knew the mare was his only money source for appealing his hanging sentence.

That day's letter proves Billy's tenacity in fighting impossible odds. It also explains the altered penmanship of his jail letters. Ever the perfectionist, Billy apologizes to Attorney Caypless for its appearance by stating: "*excuse bad writing. I have my handcuffs on.*"

Billy's Letter to Edgar Caypless
of April 15, 1881

Billy Bonney's April 15, 1881 letter to his attorney, Edgar Caypless, is his last known writing; and the original is lost. No response from Caypless is known.

The original letter was owned by a George Griggs, who had a Billy the Kid Museum in Mesilla. Griggs reprinted it in his 1930 book titled *History of the Mesilla Valley*, as follows:

Dear Sir. I would have written before this but could get no paper. My United States case was thrown out of court and I was rushed to trial on my Territorial charge. was convicted of murder in the first degree and am to be hanged on the 13th day of May. Mr. A.J. Fountain was appointed to defend me and has done the best he could for me. He is willing to carry the case further if I can raise the money to bear his expense. The mare is about all I can depend on at present so hope you will settle the case right away and give him the money you get for her. If you do not settle the matter with Scott Moore and have to go to court about it either give him [Fountain] the mare or sell her at auction and give him the money. please do as he wishes in the matter. I know you will do the best you can for me in this. I shall be taken to Lincoln tomorrow. Please write and direct care of Garrett, sheriff. excuse bad writing. I have my handcuffs on. I remain as ever

Yours respectfully,
W.H. Bonney

Analysis of Billy's Letter

Aloneness is the sad subtext of this Billy Bonney letter to Attorney Edgar Caypless. Billy had no trial witnesses on his behalf. Even his "friends" now offered no money for his appeal. And neither Susan McSween nor Attorney Ira Leonard rallied. Lastly, this letter, to save his own life, was almost impossible to write for lack of paper; and is analyzed below.

Dear Sir. I would have written before this but could get no paper. My United States case was thrown out of court and I was rushed to trial on my Territorial charge.

[AUTHOR'S NOTE: Billy here refers to Attorney Ira Leonard's quashing of the "Buckshot" Roberts case based on improper jurisdiction of the federal court of the United States over the Territorial crime of a murder on the private property of Blazer's Mill. The *"Territorial charge"* that followed was the murder of Sheriff William Brady.]

was convicted of murder in the first degree and am to be hanged on the 13th day of May.

[AUTHOR'S NOTE: Billy, clearly pressured, leaves out "I," but dispassionately gives his hanging date by quoting the judge perfectly. All emotions connected to the injustice are blocked. But the letter itself - an attempt to appeal the verdict - demonstrates his awareness of it; and one can extrapolate his rage.]

Mr. A.J. Fountain was appointed to defend me and has done the best he could for me. He is willing to carry the case further if I can raise the money to bear his expense.

[AUTHOR'S NOTE: Billy seems either unaware of Fountain's paltry representation; or that man was his only option. It does appear that Billy and Fountain had discussed his further representation contingent on his being paid.]

The mare is about all I can depend on at present

[AUTHOR'S NOTE: Remarkable or tragic is that Billy does not mention Lew Wallace, and that the ultimate moment for his pardon has come. He does not even request assistance of Attorney Ira Leonard. These eleven words are Billy's letting go of any faith in them. He accepts that he is entirely on his own.]

so hope you will settle the case right away and give him the money you get for her. If you do not settle the matter with Scott Moore and have to go to court about it either give him [Fountain] *the mare or sell her at auction and give him the money. please do as he wishes in the matter.*

[AUTHOR'S NOTE: Billy takes no chances here, and is directing Attorney Caypless. By this point, he has little reason to trust lawyers; and he is using his legal knowledge to strategize his options.]

I know you will do the best you can for me in this.

[AUTHOR'S NOTE: Billy, with no money to pay Attorney Caypless either, is cautiously placating to get his services.]

I shall be taken to Lincoln tomorrow. Please write and direct care of Garrett, sheriff.

[AUTHOR'S NOTE: Billy is announcing his transport for hanging. Pathetic is his forced reliance on Pat Garrett, who captured him and is to hang him. Even sadder is that Garrett, as an older man and vague father figure, may have ultimately inhibited Billy's self-defense shooting at him in the Peter Maxwell bedroom ambush. But here, Billy foregoes maudlin emotions, and is only business-like in the midst of his life-or-death crisis.]

excuse bad writing. I have my handcuffs on.

[AUTHOR'S NOTE: Billy cannot be broken. Even here, even now at death's door, he remembers his penmanship; and deep-down, possibly, the affection of his silver City teacher, Mary Richards.]

I remain as ever

                     Yours respectfully,

[AUTHOR'S NOTE: Billy returns to "*respectfully*," even though he had tersely abbreviated it as "*respect*" in all his jail letters to Lew Wallace; as if full respect had run out for that man.]

                     W.H. Bonney

[AUTHOR'S NOTE: This signature is the same as the one he used for his deposition with Investigator Frank Warner Angel. It takes Billy's signings to an inadvertent full circle, marking his three years of attempts to achieve justice.]

Billy's
Balcony Speech

LAST LINCOLN COUNTY WAR

On April 21, 1881, Billy Bonney arrived from Mesilla's jail at Lincoln's new jail, which was on the second floor of the refurbished Murphy-Dolan House. The House had been helpfully mortgaged by Thomas Benton Catron after James Dolan's bankruptcy; then sold to the county for conversion.

Lincoln County Sheriff Pat Garrett was responsible for Billy's hanging, scheduled for May 13, 1881. To insure that death, Garrett had Billy hand and leg shackled, chained to a floor-ring, and given twenty-four hour guard under his deputies, James Bell and Robert Olinger. But Garrett was ignorant of Lincoln County War history and of Billy's Lincoln friends. Billy, of course, was not. So one can guess that although he was masking emotion, as evidenced by his April 15, 1881 letter to Attorney Edgar Caypless, hope must have been smoldering along with fury.

Seven days later, Billy's opportunity for escape came. Likely he had accomplices, though, obviously, they remained forever secret. But he did get a revolver. Then he was on his own to achieve a legendary jailbreak.

That great escape proved more than Billy Bonney's nerve and stamina. It tested the Lincolnites. It presented their chance to win the Lincoln County War a few months short of its third anniversary of defeat. All they needed to do was nothing. They gathered. They watched; presumably Juan Patrón and John "Squire" Wilson among them. Also watching were five fellow prisoners from the Tularosa Ditch War, who had been across the street with Deputy Robert Olinger having lunch at the Wortley Hotel.

Lost Balcony Speech

The remodeled courthouse-jail had retained the Murphy-Dolan House's second-story front balcony, reached only from its upstairs hallway. Facing Lincoln's single unpaved street, it had no external stairs. That balcony became Billy's stage for uttering the most important words of his life.

All by himself, after killing his deputy guards, he had to prevent townspeople's stopping his escape; which took hours because of difficulty breaking his leg chain so he could ride.

What he said was recalled, rather than recorded. But his warning against interference was defiant, lethal, and grand: "I'm standing pat against the world."

FICTIONALIZING THE GREAT ESCAPE SPEECH

Below is the *Billy and Paulita* fictionalized great escape with its hypothetical balcony speech.

APRIL 28, 1881   11:54 AM   THURSDAY

After having dealt James Bell another tempting hand only to have him fold, Billy said it seemed he played a cautious game. Bell answered that his mother, who'd raised him after his father died, was a religious Methodist, who felt gambling led to other vices. Billy said, "I can see how a Ma could worry. But seems to me poker's like living: how you play the hand you're dealt." He was riffle shuffling to minimize movement of the left manacle. The sleeve of his long underwear was now glued to his lacerated skin by dried blood.

At the same time, Bob Olinger, in the hall and at the stairway, saw Gottfried Gauss coming up, but sent down the five prisoners anyway, trapping him against the wall. "Vere you tink you komm mit all dat rush?" asked the old man, uncharacteristically obstreperous. He watched the group turn left on the landing, disappearing to exit the side door.

Billy and Bell heard knocking. Their door opened. Gauss held his broom; a dust rag hung from his pocket. He said, "Guten day. I komm to tell dat Deputy Olinger took de Tularosa men to de Vortley."

Bell rotated, and winced at pain radiating down one leg. "Why tell me?" He opened his tin-lidded pocket watch. "He does that every day around this time."

"Javoll." Flustered, Gauss glanced at the watching blue eyes. "Zo, Herr Deputy, I komm to clean de Sheriff's office. Und den I do ... here." The door closed.

Inside Garrett's office, Gauss saw only one key. The rag reentered the pocket. The key was gone. With agitation, he pushed papers aside and opened drawers. "Mein Gott," he thought, "wo ist der andere Schlüssel?" Finally he abandoned the search for the second key.

He returned, sweeping in forceful exaggeration. Bell was considering his cards. Gauss said, "It iz varm today. But dere iz big vind. Zo I vill leave de front vindow closed zo no dust vill come in."

Next he pushed up the large lower casement of the east window, met Billy's eyes, and said, *"Dis* iz de *good* vindow."

Gauss continued talking to Bell, who was unaware the loquaciousness was odd. "Deputy Bell, I vas tinking, maybe tell you a vunny story von de old days. Vone day, der vas much shooten here - like a vor. Zo everybody runs und hides. Dummy und anoder - Herr Jack Long - dey jumps inside an outhouse hole."

Gauss forced a laugh. "Two." He repeated, *"Two,"* eyes flicking to Billy's. "Understand, *two* vas hidden dere in de hole ... vor der escape ... von death." Bell chuckled.

"Life iz vunny. Maybe it iz all big yoke zo Gott can laugh mit his kinder he loves. His childs dat he ... loves." Gauss's cheeks colored. His voice became insistent. "Now I make de horse ready vor Herr Burt. He iz in der oder courthouse. Zo I vill hitch him here. I even check de shoes vor long ride." He rushed out.

Billy smiled. "Sorry to bring this up, Deputy Bell, but that outhouse story inspired me. Think I'll pay ours a visit. Let's leave our cards." Billy smiled again. "When we come back, maybe luck will change."

Crouching painfully at the boy's feet, James Bell said, "Must be rheumatism. All this sitting and bending's hard on my back. My mother had it bad before she went."

"Sorry to hear that," said the boy, whose heart pounded as he looked down on the narrow back and lowered head with scalp showing through sparse dark hair. When Bell was upright, Billy asked, "What time's it?"

One, two, three ... seven seconds, the watch dragged out on its imitation silver chain. Eight, nine, when opening the lid. Ten, eleven. Checking. Twelve. Thirteen. "It's twelve sixteen."

Billy lifted his leg chain, stopping at the door. "Can I go through now?" he asked in the ritual dictated by Garrett, noting the Whitney shotgun still at its right side.

In the hallway, Billy's back was to Bell, who could not see his eyes dazzling with arousal. Twenty-seven to the top of the sixteen steps. Sixty-eight: down to the landing. "Wait up," called Bell. By seventy-six, the man was at his side. "Go on now," Bell said. Seventy-nine. A stop as Bell opens the side door. Over the threshold. Eighty-six. A minute and a third.

Thirty-four strides across the property to the outhouse. After entering the door to the right, Billy groped inside the seat hole with shackled hands. At the rear, where a horizontal cross-board supported the platform seat, his fingers touched cold metal. It was a Colt .44, hanging from a nail by its trigger guard. Seizing it, his caressing thumb felt a pattern in its walnut grip.

It was an upside down U. He smiled. Masking sound by coughing, he opened its gate, half-cocked the hammer, and spun the cylinder with six, dull golden flashes before the weapon was concealed in his waistband and under the vest. One.

Billy reached back into the hole. On a second nail was a screw key. When it would not open the leg shackles, he visualized Olinger putting that one in his pocket. "Goddamn," his lips mouthed fiercely.

He screwed opened the wrist cuffs, but re-engaged their claw tops. Into newsprint, he balled the key, dropped it into the depths, and stepped out.

"That was fast," said Bell.

"Some things that give a man great pleasure happen *real* fast." Bell laughed.

As Billy walked, he glanced toward the stable where Gauss was beside a saddled and bridled white pony. Giving no sign of noticing, the man thought, "Nun est alles in seinen handen, Gott. In your hands," he whispered, as ill-tempered little Collie laid back his ears and impatiently pawed.

It was 12:36 PM. Billy was aware only of the gun's rigid mass with each stride. At the entry door, he stopped as the deputy opened it.

"Bell," he murmured. The man turned to him questioningly. Billy smiled strangely, and took the two strides to the landing, the one step onto it, the two across, and mounted the stairs.

At the top, Billy looked back. Pain slowed James Bell. Billy disappeared to the left: the correct direction toward Garrett's office. The fingers of Bell's left hand, thumb downward, curled around the edge of the wall, pulling himself up the last step to the hall.

The boy's voice asked, "Sorry to bother you. The time?"

As James Bell watched his emerging watch, a dark form passed. He looked up. The boy was between him and the stairwell. Then he saw the Colt .44. Billy said, "I don't want to hurt you. Get those hands high." He wore no wristcuffs.

"Don't kill me, Kid," Bell gasped, eyes darting wildly.

Billy said, "There's rope in Garrett's office. I'll tie you.

They'll find you after I'm gone."

Bell exclaimed, "I'll tell the truth about Carlyle." As the boy took his revolver, Bell bolted for the stairs. Billy blocked him, striking a glancing blow to his head with the gun barrel, hoping to stun him.

Clutching the bleeding gash, Bell leapt into the stairwell, stumbling with gory hand against the wall to his right, while running down.

Billy fired just as Bell tripped and almost fell, the bullet passing over him and exploding a crater in the wall at the base of the landing. At the last step, turning leftward, Bell again lost balance, arms flinging upward.

Billy fired, this bullet passing thorough Bell's chest sideways, and splattering the blasted whitewash red.

James Bell staggered toward the exit, but the boy did not wait. With lifted leg chain, he ran into the armory and grabbed a holstered cartridge belt which he strapped on over Bell's revolver, and put Yginio Salazar's Colt in it. With a Winchester carbine from the gun rack, Billy smashed one of the glass cases, and took another Colt .44, which he slipped into the cartridge belt. From an ammunition crate, he poured cartridges into each vest pocket.

Next he ran through Garrett's office, grabbed the Whitney shotgun, and raced to the east window, propping the Winchester, and climbing inside the deep recess.

With back pressed to its right side, boot soles braced against the opposite one, he depressed the Whitney's first trigger and released the barrels to check the loads. A cartridge was in each.

Downstairs, Bell saw the door open. A man was leading him out behind the building. Gauss looked down at the exsanguinating man without pity. Then he ran toward the Wortley Hotel.

As Gottfried Gauss came into view, the boy whispered, "Good," his high-perched panther body, waiting panther-eyed. "Goood," he purred, feline and lethal.

Gauss's agitated behavior attracted passersby. Inside, he found Bob Olinger and gasped, "Herr Deputy ... Bell iz shot. Go qvick. De *eazt* zide."

Olinger sprinted, followed by the five Tularosa Ditch War prisoners, who halted in confusion at the street. Charles Wall said, "Let's make a run for it." Augustin Davales objected that it was loco to think of escaping with leg chains. Alexander Nunnelly, John Copel, and Marejildo Torres agreed.

Olinger's thudding boots made intoxicating rhythm for one waiting with lips so tight that teeth were fully exposed. Olinger slowed, holding his Colt .44. When he was the end of a trajectory twenty-six feet long, the other end being the muzzles of his own shotgun, he heard, "Look up," sounding so calm that he squinted uncertainly into the sun, almost directly overhead. Billy leaned, lowering his right leg down the outside.

"Kid!" Olinger cried out.

The right barrel blasted. The exploding swarm of pellets ripped open his chest, ricocheting destruction within. The boy yelled, "Olinger!" as he fired the second barrel into the supine body, which then contained three ounces of buckshot.

Men were running as the news was shouted: "The Kid's shot Bell! Shot Olinger!" Like a crystal precipitating a supersaturated solution, the original nidus of Tularosa prisoners became the gathering point.

Unaware, Billy was in murderous frenzy. "Olinger!" he screamed at the body, "goddamn cocksucker, die!" The killing already achieved.

Grasping the heavy weapon by its barrels as he would an ax, and with the tremendous strength of rabid paroxysms, he swung it over his head as if slashing the Celtic sword of Cú Chulainn. Its butt struck the windowsill, shattering off at its waist. Berserk, Billy hurled the severed barrels and frame like a spear, striking the corpse.

Shrieking, "Die, die, you cocksucker," he hit the corpse again with the buttstock. Leaning far out, he said, "You're dead, Olinger. Dead," finally satiated.

Noticing the cluster at the Wortley Hotel for the first time, Billy saw Gottfried Gauss and remembered the shackles. Lifting his chain, he ran into the hallway, glanced at the manacles on the floor beside its west wall, flung open both doors to the balcony so wildly that their glass panels shattered, and rushed to the balustrade high above the street.

Waving Yginio's Colt, he shouted, "You, Mister Gauss, get me that miner's pick in the storeroom. But don't go near the back stairs. I'll kill anyone who comes near me. Hand it up to me here." The people watched with fascination.

Billy saw "Squire" Wilson, Sam Wortley, Juan Patrón, John Newcomb, and George Washington approaching with José Montaño and Ike Stockton. There was Sam Corbett, Isaac Ellis, Steve Stanley, and Harry Schon. Beside Martin Chávez was the boy he did not know: Miguelito Luna.

Billy yelled, "I didn't want to kill Bell. He wouldn't let me tie him. I had to. It's just me now. I'm standing pat against the world."

Soon, there was movement to the left. Billy swung around and aimed. Gauss stopped on the porch at the front edge the balcony and, holding the miner's pick by the center of its double pointed arc, extended upward its three-and-a-half foot wooden handle.

Billy shouted, "I've got to go back in, you people. Got to break this chain. But I can see through the windows. I'll shoot any man that comes closer."

Holding the chain, he ran to the steel fastening ring and lay the pick beside it. As in the dark Santa Fe jail, he chose one oval link. He slid its end through the steel ring.

The pick was then passed through that protruding link, held by its two rear mates.

Leaning because of the short handle, Billy pulled back to make the hook-like point rise with the head pivoting on the anchoring ring. The ring held firmly.

Again and again, Billy hauled back the handle as the tip rocked upward, impacting the link. Twenty times. Forty times. Soaked in perspiration, he continued to wrench, oblivious to blood running from his reopened wrist wounds.

But when he checked, the link seemed unchanged. Billy licked his finger and touched. The link was burning hot. Trying even harder, he used his entire body. Suddenly the pick point snapped. He careened backward, howling in rage.

Back on the balcony, Billy shouted to the crowd, "This will take longer. Mister Gauss, get me a horse. Put a blanket around the saddle. 'Cause of the chains."

Dummy, exiting the Wortley Hotel, called, "Hello, Billy!" waving and laughing.

Billy suddenly realized that, if the people had wanted, they could have prevented his escape. It was more than waiting. He called to them, "We're going to win this War in Lincoln! There are different ways to fight." Miguelito Luna lifted his fist as if stretching. Billy saw it and knew he was connected to Yginio.

With renewed energy, he put his hands on the railing, leaning closer to his people, his soldiers. He shouted, "They didn't dare have my trial here 'cause you good citizens know the truth."

"A...men," murmured George Washington as he watched the boy running back inside.

Now, repositioning the link and using the remaining point, Billy yanked the miner's pick again. This time, however, he yelled, "The War! The Lincoln County War!" pumping and slamming his metal against the enemy metal: his curved horns of the giant bull of

Cú Chulainn, goring enemy flesh as each impact of metal on metal became thrilling: a thrusting and thrusting of the point.

The pick was soaring upward as his legs were backward stumbling. Almost at the north wall, he stopped. There were two trailing lengths of chain.

On the balcony again, Billy yelled to the people, "Victory! Freedom!"

Hitched at the post below was the white pony with Gauss's red blanket tied over the saddle. Joining the crowd, County Clerk Billy Burt called to Billy, "That's my horse."

Billy panted, "I'll send him back ... I've got to ride. To ride!"

Racing back inside and leaping as the trailing chains tried to trip him, he laughed at their game. At the east window, he seized the Winchester carbine and noticed the distant pick. "It's all silver and gold!" he called to it.

Setting the carbine on the floor, he wound each chain around its ankle, ran to the hallway, and bounded down the stairway, hundreds of bells sounding at his feet.

Outside, he saw James Bell's body and said, "You didn't have to kill and you didn't have to die;" before racing to the street, sun throwing his long shadow on its red earth skimmed by strong wind coursing eastward. Gauss was leading the white pony to him.

As Billy slid the Winchester into the scabbard, the crimson blanket blew wildly. He sprang up, seeking the stirrups.

Collie knew the clattering and red flapping were an attack. Terrified, he bucked. With no traction, Billy slid off, landing on his rear. Laughing, he jumped up. But his audience was silent, watching with grim enthrallment.

Gauss caught the small animal. Billy asked his name. His life depended on this being. He took the reins and said, "It's the wind, Collie. Easy, Collie." He turned him sideways, so the blanket merely flattened. Collie looked back, frightened eyes examining, relaxing. "We're going to ride, boy. Ride to freedom."

Then the white pony's trot became a gallop, and the racing air carried back to the people the words the boy was half singing and half shouting: "Glory, glory hallelujah! Glory, glory, hallelujah! His truth is marching on. Glory, glory, hallel ..." And they were left with only the sound of wind and the vision of sun-spangled dust.

But the crowd waited, looking at the House: monument to greed, corruption, hubris, and oppression, conquered in hours and transformed into a symbol of freedom. George Washington, tears in his eyes, murmured, "So David prevailed over Goliath. And no jail could hold him, no hand of man could shackle him. Billy of Lincoln town."

PARDON TWO DECADES TOO LATE

As already noted, on that April 28, 1881 day, unaware of Billy's escape, Governor Lew Wallace gave his supercilious newspaper interview about never pardoning Billy. Two decades later, Wallace would, as quoted earlier, shamelessly confirm their pardon deal, while lying that Billy had reneged on it.

Fittingly for Billy's triumph over Lew Wallace, shamed Sheriff Pat Garrett used Wallace's own death warrant on April 30th as paper to write the news:

I certify that I rec'd the within named William Bonny into my custody on the 21st day of April 1881. And I further certify that on April 28th he made his escape by killing his guards James Bell and Robert Olinger in Lincoln Co. N. M.

It ended with Garrett's incorrectly calculated fees:

Boarding Prisoner and two Guards 8 days - $40.00. Guarding and transporting from Fort Stanton - $69.00. Returning Writ - $.50. Total: $109.00.

Billy's Ironic Wit

A Legend in His Time

Billy Bonney stood out among his contemporaries for many reasons; one was his jaunty and ironic wit. That wit, with insoucient nonchalance, masked a lifetime of traumatic losses; it hid pain and rage. It amused his cohorts enough to be recounted in their old age. It was his weapon when captive, blasting truth through reporters' haze. It added to his drama as the last freedom fighter; and punctuated his dialogue from the high balcony of his great escape to his Lincoln audience.

By his Stinking Springs capture, on December 22, 1880, Billy was famous, locally, among his partisans, as a bi-cultural freedom fighter; and nationally, via Santa Fe Ring propaganda, as a rustler, counterfeiter, and mythic murderer. Even earlier that year, Billy was a coast-to-coast media star, and referenced his own press in a pre-capture letter to Governor Lew Wallace.

Facing his Mesilla hanging trials, then faced by his unjust sentence, Billy gave newspaper interviews in the shadow of a noose, but defiant with lively humor as well as truth.

Wit permeated Billy's courage, so cavalier that, escaping jail just two weeks from hanging, he chose to ride 150 miles north to Fort Sumner and his lover and death, instead of 150 miles south to Old Mexico and life. "The laugh's on me this time" - his interview response after capture - was his inside joke with the grim reaper.

With irony he would have savored, the press recorded his post-escape sightings as all around the country - when he was really in Fort Sumner and in Paulita Maxwell's arms.

And, with final macabre jest, the press kept him alive with post-death sightings, equally geographically varied, and for more years than twice his actual lifespan.

FIRST MEDIA STAR

Billy Bonney was a media star whose words were preserved by newspapers. His wit is highlighted below in boldface.

Billy read his own press, as shown in his December 12, 1880 letter to Governor Wallace, saying: *"I noticed in the Las Vegas Gazette a piece which stated that Billy 'the' Kid, the name by which I am known in the Country was the captain of a Band of Outlaws who hold Forth at the Portales."*

THE JOE GRANT KILLING

By January of 1880, Billy had sufficient "reputation," by publicity of mouth and press, to tempt a Texas cowboy, and possible bounty-hunter, named Joe Grant, to aim for his back in Hargrove's Saloon. Grant's borrowed pistol misfired. And the Las Vegas *Daily Optic* quoted Billy's wry comment after his own split-second bullet exploded Grant's brain:

It was a game of two and I got there first.

LEAVING THE LAS VEGAS JAIL

By December 28, 1880, six days post-Stinking Springs, after being locked up for a day in the Las Vegas jail along with Billy Wilson and Tom Pickett, before proceeding on to the one in Santa Fe, Billy spoke to Lucius "Lute" Wilcox, city editor for J.H. Koogler's Las Vegas *Gazette*, for an article to be called "The Kid. Interview with Billy Bonney The Best Known Man in New Mexico." Billy simply teased and taunted any future hangman and his own fate. The reporter recorded:

Wilson scarcely raised his eyes, and spoke but once or twice to his compadres. **Bonney on the other hand was light and chipper, and was very communicative, laughing, joking and chatting with bystanders.**

"You appear to take it easy," the reporter said.

"Yes! What's the use of looking on the gloomy side of everything. The laugh's on me this time," he said.

Billy used reporter "Lute" Wilcox to ridicule sarcastically his Santa Fe Ring propaganda by commenting on the gathered onlookers. Billy was quoted:

"There was a big crowd gazing at me, wasn't there?" he exclaimed, smiling. **"Well, perhaps some of them will think me half man now; everyone seems to think I was some sort of animal."**

In entirety, that Las Vegas *Gazette* article of December 28, 1880, "The Kid. Interview with Billy Bonney The Best Known Man in New Mexico" is below.

Though "Billy the Kid" is negatively editorialized by prejudicial reporter Wilcox, the real Billy Bonney, nevertheless, comes through in playful and seductive glory; charming his big audience of locals, gathered outside the jail because of his celebrity presence.

The article stated:

With its customary enterprise, the *Gazette* was the first paper to give the story of the capture of Billy Bonney, who has risen to notoriety under the sobriquet of "the Kid," Billy Wilson, Dave Rudabaugh and Tom Pickett. Just at this time everything of interest about the men is especially interesting, and after damning the men in general and "the Kid" in particular through the columns of this paper we considered it the correct thing to give them a show.

Through the kindness of Sheriff Romero, a representative of the *Gazette* was admitted to the jail yesterday morning.

Mike Cosgrove, the obliging mail contractor, who has met the boys frequently while on business down the Pecos, had just gone in with four large bundles. The doors at the entrance stood open, and the large crowd strained their necks to get a glimpse of the prisoners, who stood in the passageway like children waiting for a Christmas tree distribution. One by one the bundles were unpacked disclosing a good suit of clothes for each man. Mr. Cosgrove remarked that he wanted "to see the boys go away in style."

"Billy the Kid," and Billy Wilson who were shackled together stood patiently while a blacksmith took off their shackles and bracelets to allow them an opportunity to make a change of clothing. Both prisoners watched the operation which was to set them free for a short while, but Wilson scarcely raised his eyes, and spoke but once or twice to his compadres. **Bonney on the other hand, was light and chipper, and was very communicative, laughing, joking and chatting with the bystanders.**

"You appear to take it easy," the reporter said.

"Yes! What's the use of looking at the gloomy side of everything. The laugh's on me this time," he said. Then looking about the placita, he asked: "Is the jail at Santa Fe any better than this?"

This seemed to trouble him considerably, for as he explained, "this is a terrible place to put a fellow in." He put the same question to every one who came near him and **when he learned that there was nothing better in store for him, he shrugged his shoulders and said something about putting up with what he had to.**

He was the attraction of the show, and as he stood there, lightly kicking the toes of his boots on the stone pavement to keep his feet warm, one would scarcely mistrust that he was the hero of "Forty Thieves," romance which this paper has been running in serial form for six weeks or more.

"There was a big crowd gazing at me wasn't there?" he exclaimed, and then smiling continued: "Well perhaps some of them will think me half a man now; everyone seems to think I was some kind of an animal."

He did look human, indeed, but there was nothing very mannish about him in appearance, for he looked and acted like a mere boy. He is about five feet, eight or nine inches tall, slightly built and lithe, weighing about 140; a frank and open countenance, looking like a school boy, with the traditional silky fuzz on his upper lip, **clear blue eyes, with a roguish snap about them,** light hair and complexion. He is, in all, quite a handsome looking fellow, the only imperfection being two prominent front teeth, slightly protruding like a squirrels' teeth, and he has agreeable and winning ways.

INSIDE THE TRAIN TO SANTA FE JAIL

Also on December 28, 1880, still in Las Vegas, but already in the train at the depot, Billy was interviewed a second time by editor "Lute" Wilcox or owner J.H. Koogler, for the Las Vegas *Gazette*, while awaiting departure to Santa Fe and jail.

Billy's nonchalant banter adds grim irony when one realizes that his interview was being conducted while the train was being detained by a shouting mob on the tracks, whose intent was either lynching or rescuing him. Billy's teasing words were punctuated by flashing his handcuff.

"They wouldn't let me settle down; if they had I wouldn't be here today." And he held up his right arm on which was the bracelet.

Billy also joked to the reporter about his Stinking Springs capture - concealing his raw wound of Charlie Bowdre's killing, mistaken for him - and merely floated a silly dime novel escape fantasy about jumping his famous bay mare out of the rock-walled, line cabin's doorway, which was obstructed by a dead horse, already shot by Pat Garrett. Billy was quoted:

If it had not been for the dead horse in the doorway I wouldn't be here in Las Vegas. I would have ridden out on my bay mare and taken my chances of escaping. But I couldn't ride over that for she would have jumped back **and I would have got it in the head**.

Departing, Billy avoided morbidity by another jaunty joke. Recorded by the reporter was:

As the train rolled out, he lifted his hat and invited us to call and see him in Santa Fe, calling out "*adios*."

Below is the entire article of that train depot interview:

We saw him again at the depot when the crowd presented a really war like appearance. Standing by the car, out of one of the windows from which he was leaning, he talked freely with us of the whole affair:

"I don't blame you for writing of me as you have. You have had to believe others' stories, but then I don't know as anyone would believe anything good of me, anyway," he said. "I really wasn't the leader of any gang. I was for Billy all the time. About that Portales business, I owned the ranch with Charlie Bowdre. I took it up and was holding it because I knew that at some time a stage line would run there, and I wanted to keep it for a station. **But I found that there were certain men who wouldn't let me live in the country and so I was going to leave.**

[AUTHOR'S NOTE: Billy ironically omits that his plan *"to leave"* because *"certain men wouldn't let me live in the country"* had largely been influenced by Pat Garrett's posse blasting away Tom O'Folliard nine days before that decision to exit the Territory!]

We had all our grub in the house when they took us in, and we were going to a place six miles away in the morning to cook it and then light out. I haven't stolen any stock. I made my living by gambling, but that was the only way I could live. **They wouldn't let me settle down; if they had I wouldn't be here today," and he held up his right arm on which was the bracelet.**

"Chisum got me into all this trouble and then wouldn't help me out. I went up to Lincoln to stand my trial on the warrant that was out for me, but the Territory took a change of venue to Dona Ana, and I knew I had no show, and so I skinned out ...

If it had not been for the dead horse in the doorway I wouldn't be here in Las Vegas. I would have ridden out on my bay mare and taken my chances of escaping. But I couldn't ride over that for she would have jumped back **and I would have got it in the head**. We could have stayed in the house but there wouldn't have been anything gained by that for they would have starved us out. **I thought it was better to come out and get a square meal - don't you?"**

The prospects of a fight exhilarated him, and he bitterly bemoaned being chained. "If I only had my Winchester, I'd lick the whole crowd" was his confident comment on the strength of the attacking party. He sighed and sighed again for the chance to take a hand in the fight and the burden of his desire was to be set free to fight on the side of his captors as soon as he should smell powder.

As the train rolled out, he lifted his hat and invited us to call and see him in Santa Fe, calling out "*adios.*"

ARRIVING IN DOÑA ANA COUNTY FOR TRIAL

On March 29, 1881, after three months in the Santa Fe jail, and railroad transport to the Rincón depot - as far as the southward tracks had been built by then - Billy's group, traveling by coach, finally stopped at Las Cruces, where a crowd of the curious awaited. With Billy were fellow captive Billy Wilson, Attorney, Ira Leonard - who had accompanied Billy from Santa Fe - and their guards.

A spectator named W.S. Fletcher from Mesilla either asked, or witnessed someone else ask, the group which was Billy the Kid. Billy's cheeky response was reported in the April 3, 1881 Santa Fe *Daily New Mexican* in its article: "Something About the Kid." Indicating his balding, nothing-like-a-kid companion, Ira Leonard, Billy said, "This is the man!"

That same article, with hyperbole about Billy's crimes, misinformation about specifics, and reporting on his starting trial, also gave his quip: "At least two hundred men have been killed in Lincoln County during the past three years, but I did not kill all of them."

The entire article stated:

Something about the Kid.

An extract of a letter written by W.S. Fletcher from Mesilla to a gentleman in the city reads about as follows: Tony Neis and Francisco Chaves, deputy U.S. Marshals, arrived Thursday night with Billy, the Kid, and Billy Wilson. They met an ugly crowd at Rincon, where some threats were made, but Tony's crowd were too much for them. **At Las Cruces an impulsive mob gathered around the coach and someone asked which is "Billy the Kid." The Kid himself answered by placing his hand on Judge Leonard's shoulder and saying "this is the man."** The Kid weakened somewhat at Las Cruces, where he found quite a number of Lincoln

County men, who were to appear against him as witnesses.

[AUTHOR'S NOTE: Billy had no witnesses for his defense in his trials. The "Lincoln men," as witnesses for the prosecution, were Ringmen like James Dolan, Saturnino Baca, and past William Brady deputy, Billy Matthews.]

He says at least two hundred men have been killed in Lincoln County during the past three years, but that he did not kill all of them. I think twenty murders can be charged against him. He was arraigned yesterday (Wednesday) before the United States court for the murder of Roberts, on the Mescalero Apache reservation, in 1878. Judge Leonard was assigned to his defense. Judge Newcomb gave notice that he had three other indictments for murder against him, and it looks as if he had no show to get off. His counsel asked today for time to send to Lincoln, which was granted, so that his trial will not commence for at least ten days. Billy Wilson's case is before the grand jury. He is charged with passing counterfeit money. He has retained Judge Thornton as his counsel. He seems to have friends here while the Kid has none.

No mails between Rincon and Doña Ana for the past week. Mosquitoes and flies abound and weather hot as blazes.

AFTER THE HANGING SENTENCE

In Mesilla, on April 15, 1881, two days after his hanging sentence, and the same day as writing his desperate letter to Attorney Edgar Caypless about selling his bay mare for appeal money, Billy was interviewed by a *Mesilla News* reporter. The article appeared the next day.

After recounting injustices of his trial; misstatements by Simon Newman, editor of the *Semi-Weekly* (demonstrating that Billy was still keeping up with his press); he made wry comments about "mob law;" but topped them off with usual double entendre of "personal advice." Billy was quoted:

"If mob law is going to rule, better dismiss judge and sheriff and let all take chances alike. I expect to be lynched in going to Lincoln. **Advise persons never to engage in killing.**"

And Billy ironically worded his own tragi-comedy:

I think it hard that I should be the only one to suffer the extreme penalty of the law.

In full, that *Mesilla News* article of April 16, 1881 stated:

Well I had intended at one time not to say a word on my own behalf because persons would say, "Oh he lied." Newman, editor of the *Semi-Weekly*, gave me a rough deal; he created prejudice against me, and is trying to incite a mob to lynch me. He sent me a paper which showed it; I think it a dirty mean advantage to take of me, **considering my situation and knowing that I could not defend myself by word or act. But I suppose he thought he would give me a kick down hill.** Newman came to see me the other day. I refused to talk to him or tell him anything. But I believe the *News* is always willing to give its readers both sides of a question. **If mob law is going to rule, better dismiss judge and sheriff and let all take chances alike.** I expect to be lynched going to Lincoln. **Advise persons never to engage in killing.**

In it, Billy also commented sourly about Wallace and the pardon with a terse understatement - "Don't know that he will do it." With philosophical perspective, and with much truth about their bargain, he stated:

Considering the active part Governor Wallace took on our side and the friendly relations that existed between him and me, and the promise he made me, I think he ought to pardon me. **Don't know that he will do it.** When I was arrested for that murder he let me out and gave me freedom of the town, and let me go about with my arms. When I got ready to leave Lincoln in June, 1879, I left. **I think it hard that I should be the only one to suffer the extreme penalty of the law.**

SECRET TRANSPORT FROM MESILLA

In darkness, on April 17, 1881, Billy was secretly taken by wagon from the Mesilla jail to prevent rescue attempts on his way to the Lincoln jail and to hanging. Newman's *Semi-Weekly* reported his departure, with Billy, as usual, joking:

> On Saturday night about 10 o'clock Deputy U.S. Marshal Robt. Ollinger with Deputy Sheriff David Woods and a posse of five men ... started for Lincoln with Henry Antrim alias the Kid. The fact that they intended to leave at that time had been purposely concealed and the report circulated that they would not leave before the middle of the week in order to avoid any possibility of trouble, it having been rumored that the Kid's band would attempt a rescue. They stopped in front of the Semi-Weekly office while we talked to them, and we handed the Kid an addressed envelope with some paper and he said he would write some things he wanted to make public. **He appeared quite cheerful and remarked that he wanted to stay until their whiskey gave out, anyway.** Said he was sure that his guard would not hurt him unless a rescue should be attempted and he was certain that it would not be done unless perhaps "those fellows at White Oaks come out to take me," meaning to kill him. **It was, he said, about a stand-off whether he was hanged or killed in the wagon.**

Billy's Wit Fondly Remembered

Billy, usually frenetically exuberant and an inveterate prankster, was fondly remembered by his Lincoln County War cohorts whose spirits he lifted frequently by his wit in the midst of their tension from opposing daunting Santa Fe Ring enemies.

George Coe, on page 90 of his 1934 *Frontier Fighter, The Autobiography of George Coe Who Fought and Rode With Billy the Kid* presented a telling anecdote of Billy's teasing bravado occurring around April 3, 1878:

We made a big bonfire, and sat around swapping lies and bragging ... Then we talked about riding into Lincoln and setting in short order all the difficulties that were troubling the people there. We were a brave band as we told it.

Our guns, which formed the most important part of our possessions, had been placed carelessly around against nearby trees. Billy sized up the situation and, looking for a little fun and excitement with an inexperienced bunch of greenhorns, he slipped about five or six cartridges out of his belt and tossed them into the fire. In less than a minute they began to go off, and such a mad dash for tall timber you have never seen ... I looked back as I ran, and there stood the Kid with his arms folded, perfectly unconcerned ...

"Well, you're a damn fine bunch of soldiers. Run like a bunch of coyotes and forget to take your guns. I just wanted to break you in a little before we met the enemy, and, boys, I'm sure proud of your nerve."

After Billy's great escape, Billy's friend, John Meadows, was at his Peñasco River ranch when he arrived; and though the most hunted person in the nation, was still just joking.

Old Man Salazar let the Kid have a little sorrel horse and a good one, and also a saddle. He hung around for a day or so under cover in the hills and one night, after dark he showed up at Tom Norris' and my ranch, on the Peñasco about four miles below where Elk now stands ...

I remember how he made his appearance at the place. Tom Norris and I was in the cabin cooking some supper. Kid come up to the corner of the house and seeing there was nobody there but us two, whom he could trust, he stepped to the door and said, "Well, I've got you, haven't I?"

I said, "Well, you have. So what are you going to do with us?"

He said, "I'm going to eat supper with you."

WIT WRITTEN TO WALLACE

Billy Bonney's wit flashed in his letters to Governor Lew Wallace and "Squire" Wilson, as presented below in boldface.

Billy's March 13(?), 1879, first letter to Wallace, bristles with cockiness bolstered by his allies' respect and his possible secret support by Lincoln officials. To the lofty governor's inauspicious dead-or-alive reward of a $1000 on his head, Billy flippantly reinterprets: "*I have heard that You will give one thousand $ dollars for my body* **which as I can understand it means alive as a Witness. I know it is as a witness against those that murdered Mr. Chapman.**" Tackling his dire indictments - murders of two lawmen and a civilian - he simply understates them: "*indictments against me* **for things that happened** *in the late Lincoln County War.*"

On March 20, 1879, in his letter arranging "sham arrest" for his Wallace pardon deal, Billy wrote tongue-in-cheek to "**Friend Wilson**" - likely his secret "friend" convincing the governor of this plan, as well providing its fine stationery. The letter to "Squire" Wilson even playfully omits Wallace's name - a take-off on Wallace's naively telling Billy to keep their meeting "secret" - and says: "**Please tell You know who** *that I do not know what to do now ...*"

That same March 20th, Billy teases Lew Wallace by a letter, saying: "*it is not my place to advise you, but I am anxious to have them caught,* **and perhaps know how men hide from Soldiers better than you.**"

By Billy's December 12, 1880 letter and no pardon, his wit becomes testy to Lew Wallace: "*I noticed in the Las Vegas Gazette a piece which stated that Billy "the" Kid, the name by which I am known in the Country was the captain of a Band of Outlaws who hold Forth at the Portales.* **There is no such Organization in Existence. So the Gentleman must have drawn very heavily on his Imagination.**"

In his March 4, 1881 letter from the Santa Fe jail, Billy's wit became snide to Wallace with "*patiently waiting*" meaning its opposite; and stating: "**I guess they mean to Send me up without giving me any Show but they will have a nice time doing it. I am not entirely without friends.** *I shall expect to see you sometime today.* **Patiently waiting ....**"

Aftermath

BURYING BILLY BONNEY

After Billy Bonney, with heart successfully pierced by Pat Garrett's bullet, was buried, on July 15, 1881, in Fort Sumner's Maxwell family cemetery, his words and his reality were buried by Santa Fe Ring propaganda; then by its translation into movie Westerns. Buried was his freedom fight; replaced by a fabricated outlaw and gunslinger - an illiterate, wanton murderer, killing a man for each of his twenty-one years.

Burying Billy were also his 20th century historians, as if lulled by New Mexico's state motto, "the Land of Enchantment." Bewitched by Billy's desperado myth or haunted by his frightening Ringmen ghosts, they clung to misinformation; blinded to Billy's writings, deaf to his words.

WALTER NOBLE BURNS

Walter Noble Burns was Billy Bonney's first historian; with his 1926 *The Saga of Billy the Kid* bridging dime novel style of Pat Garrett's *Authentic life of Billy the Kid* and his own journalistically florid drama. To Burns, Billy was a terrifying mix of outlaw and Satan's seductiveness. Burns wrote:

> He placed no value on human life, least of all upon his own. He killed a man as nonchalantly as he smoked a cigarette. Murder did not impress Billy the Kid as tragedy; it was merely a physical process of pressing a trigger ... He put a bullet through a man's heart as coolly as he perforated a tin can set upon a fence post. He had no remorse.

Walter Noble Burns was unaware of Billy Bonney's literacy, letters, or testimonies; but presented a pardon agreement, possibly gleaned from Lew Wallace's 1900 and 1902 newspaper articles. Burns, however, created his own bizarre version of it with Billy the Kid's ignoring Governor Lew Wallace's "proclamation of amnesty;" and single-handedly continuing "in arms" to such dramatic effect that Wallace was "determined to have a personal interview ... and use his powers of persuasion to induce him to settle down to useful citizenship."

So, in Burns's cartoon, they meet in Lincoln - along with an oddball crowd of General Hatch, Juan Patrón, and army officers - at a random resident's porch, after Billy simply rides up! Burns saw only incompatibility: "It was a meeting, not so much of two men, as of two worlds ... The governor was an intellect; the Kid a trigger finger." Burns's Wallace presents the pardon deal; but bad-boy Billy refuses it. Wallace intones:

> "I want to see peace again in these mountains. You can help me bring it about. I want you to surrender ... and stand trial on whatever charges may be brought against you. ... I will pardon you if the verdict goes against you. But I want you first to stand trial like a man" ...
>
> "No, Governor," he said. "I can't do it ... I've got to go on as I am, and when the time comes, die with my boots on ... Good-bye, Governor," said the Kid.
>
> "Good-bye, my boy," said the governor.

In Walter Noble Burns's day, Billy's old-timer pretenders still lived, and used his book to form their confabulations as "outlaws." Burns had defined Billy's image as follows:

> His destructive and seemingly futile career served a constructive purpose: it drove home the lesson that New Mexico's prosperity could be built only upon a basis of stability and peace. After him came the great change for which he involuntarily had cleared the way. Law and order came in on the flash and smoke of the six-shooter that with one bullet put an end to the outlaw and to outlawry.

WILLIAM KELEHER

After three more decades and research in the Lew Wallace Collection and elsewhere, historian William Keleher retained Walter Noble Burns's impression of Billy Bonney. Keleher's 1957 book, *Violence in Lincoln County*, titles the Wallace-Bonney meeting chapter: "The Governor and the Outlaw."

Class-conscious as was Walter Noble Burns, William Keleher declares the Wallace-Bonney communication "an extraordinary correspondence between two men of extreme contrasts in character, personality and disposition." He writes:

> One correspondent was a man of great prestige; the governor of a Territory; a man of acknowledged pre-eminence in letters and literature; a gallant soldier, who had been privileged to wear with honor and distinction the shoulder straps of a major general in the army of his country in time of war; a man accepted as a celebrity in the national capital and elsewhere throughout the country. The other party to the correspondence was scarcely of legal voting age; **almost illiterate** [Author's boldface]; acquainted with comparatively few people; a desperado, gunman and outlaw; a man who had not hesitated to take human life on more than one occasion ...

Though calling Billy "almost illiterate," William Keleher, nonetheless, dutifully reproduces in *Violence in Lincoln County* Billy's very literate letters to Governor Lew Wallace.

A psychological quirk called "operational set" - expectation distorting perceptions - seems at play. Keleher believed Billy was an ignorant outlaw. No information could change that.

Prejudice notwithstanding, William Keleher's Wallace-Bonney pardon meeting improves a bit on Walter Noble Burns's fantasized one. Correctly in "Squire" Wilson's house, it still has Billy "ready to pull the trigger at an instant's notice." There is no pardon linked to Chapman testimony (and there is a fictionalized caveat of reporting on "cattle stealing"). Keleher's version has Wallace merely promising "protection under the law," "simulated arrest," and explaining to Billy how he "could take advantage of the amnesty proclamation" (though that method is not given). Keleher apparently sees the pardon exercise as merely Wallace's "plan to bring about Bonney's arrest and imprisonment." The unsavory matter of Wallace's possible betrayal of an actual promise is disposed of later, by Keleher's claim that "Governor Wallace had considered pardoning Bonney for his offenses, but had decided not to do so." As proof, Keleher merely quotes Wallace's supercilious, anti-clemency, Las Vegas *Gazette* interview of April 28, 1881.

As to Billy's devastating Dudley Court of Inquiry testimony, Keleher misstates: "Unfortunately, his testimony was brief and failed to throw much light during the period July 14 to July 20;" even though he even reproduces Billy's devastating testimony: "Three soldiers fired at me."

More subtlely misleading is William Keleher's description of Lincolnites inaction during Billy's great escape as some form of "exciting drama"- presumably as respite from boring, pre-television lives. Keleher wrote:

> A crowd quickly gathered about the courthouse following the shooting. Bonney's coolness and demonstration of generalship proved most impressive. Onlookers witnessed with amazement the unfolding of an exciting drama. No man in the crowd said one word in opposition to the proceeding or raised a hand in an attempt to prevent Bonney's escape.

Missed is the people's revelation that one man could defeat a juggernaut; that the Lincoln County War could be won by not stopping Billy; as portrayed in my *Billy and Paulita* as follows:

> But the crowd waited, looking at the House: monument to greed, corruption, hubris, and oppression, conquered in hours and transformed into a symbol of freedom. George Washington, tears in his eyes, murmured, "So David prevailed over Goliath. And no jail could hold him, no hand of man could shackle him. Billy of Lincoln town."

FREDERICK NOLAN

Thirty-five years after William Keleher's *Violence in Lincoln County*, and sixty-six years after Walter Noble Burns's *The Saga of Billy the Kid*, came a tome by the greatest historian the Lincoln County War period: Frederick Nolan. It was his 1992 *The Lincoln County War: A Documentary History*. With his other related publications, it influenced a generation of Billy the Kid popularizers. But perplexingly, in it, Nolan expressed greater distaste for Billy Bonney than had Keleher.

The Lincoln County War's assumption appears to be that Billy Bonney was a "callow youngster," a bit player caught up in events and accidentally became mythologized. Delayed, thus, into the 21st century, was Billy's revisionist history.

And the Santa Fe Ring only drifts through that book like an occasional dark cloud having uncertain effects. Nolan wrote:

> With Republican presidents occupying the White House since 1860, a well-entrenched Republican machine, feeding on the beneficence of Washington, controlled New Mexico. At its head was Thomas Benton Catron, U.S. district attorney [sic-U.S. Attorney] ...

John Tunstall, John Chisum, Alexander McSween, and "Squire" Wilson are named as anti-Ring; in contrast to James Dolan with "the Santa Fe Ring behind him." And Governor Axtell delivers "all legal power into the hands of the minions of the Santa Fe Ring." But the over-riding impact of that Ring on the history is missing. Thus, after Tunstall's murder, when Billy rides with those "calling themselves 'the Regulators;' " its Revolutionary War meaning as freedom fighters is lost.

As to their motivation, Nolan states vaguely on page 219:

> What prompted the men to take up arms? There can be little doubt that they were motivated by the complex mixture of emotion and rationalization that military historian John Keegan calls "the will to combat," a mixture made up in varying degrees of personal loyalties and resentments, the pressure of unavoidable

compulsion, the prospect of personal enrichment, the endorsement of religion (making killing lawful in time of "war") and not at all the least, drink, which we have already seen as a major factor in the violence of the times. Fueled in greater or lesser part by "the will to combat," inured by upbringing and experience to the commonplace character of violence in frontier life, decent men could - and would - justify to themselves actions they would - and did - condemn outright in other circumstances.

Instead of Regulators fighting the Ring, one gets drunken hooligans with bad backgrounds and "will to combat;" and none of the motivation and idealism that would shape Billy's life.

At the end of *The Lincoln County War*, Frederick Nolan, after 439 fact-packed pages, states, unmoved:

> Fueled by greed, propelled by religious and racial prejudice, by liquor, by firearms, and by some powerful American misbeliefs, the Lincoln County War was based on a whole catalog of self-deceptions. Each side believed it was "us" against "them" ... The Lincoln County War was a false premise pursued to an illogical conclusion.

Lacking framework of the struggle against the Santa Fe Ring, Frederick Nolan is left merely with "outlaw" Billy; and uses a Procrustean bed to truncate facts to that image.

An example is Frederick Nolan's attributing Santa Fe Ring motivation to simply protecting Lincoln town's James Dolan. So page 387 states:

> Rynerson went on to secure a conviction for murder and a change of venue to Doña Ana County, which must have given the Kid plenty of food for thought. He had no illusions about his fate if he was tried there. The Santa Fe Ring looked after his own, and Rynerson would see him hanged long before Jimmy Dolan's case ever came to court.

Beyond omitting Billy Bonney's anti-Ring motives for testifying in that April 1879 Grand Jury, is deeper hostility. Nolan seems disinclined to take seriously the high-minded purpose of lower class rabble which largely constituted the freedom fighters - and that rabble included Billy. The first page of *The Lincoln County War* comments with bemusement:

> Indeed, those who savor the ironies of history may find a certain sweet justice in the fact that today, of all the powerful, rich, and famous men of his era, it is the Kid who is remembered best - and at that, for the things he never did.

Comparable class snobbery slips also into Nolan's analysis of a letter by a Territorial visitor, Montague Leverson, to Secretary of the Interior Carl Schurz. In truth, it portrays the Regulators motive in killing Sheriff Brady as attempting to protect Alexander McSween from murder by him. Opposing corrupt Ring politics, Leverson was, at the time, aspiring to seek Territorial governorship. But Nolan's page 246 states:

> Leverson's *faux naif* description of Billy the Kid, Jim, French, Charlie Bowdre, Frank MacNab, Henry Brown, and John Middleton as "being among the best citizens in the county" does not inspire confidence in his account.

Reprinting Billy's earliest letters to Governor Lew Wallace - as had William Keleher - Frederick Nolan, unmoved by their statements, motives, courage, or context, states on page 382:

> These two letters were the beginning of a correspondence unique in the **annals of outlawry.** [Author's boldface]

To justify the Secret Service's and Pat Garrett's 1880 hunting of Billy, Nolan attests, on page 397, that utterly unreliable, dime-novel journalist Ash Upson's rendition of Billy's outlawry was actually reliable:

Upson's catalogue of the Kid's thievery is likely to be accurate as any other. It paints a believable picture of his activities, and confirms why he and his *compadres* were soon to be considered as big a menace as the original gang whose name they now bore - the Rustlers ...

But the times at last were changing, and a cold new wind of law and order was beginning to blow.

For the November 1880 sheriff's election of incumbent George Kimbrell against Pat Garrett, Nolan states that Kimbrell was "paralyzed by fear of the outlaws" - meaning Billy; though Billy considered Kimbrell such a reliable friend that he had chosen him for his sham arrest for Lew Wallace.

Billy's alleged outlawry is used to scoff at his letter of December 12, 1880 to Governor Wallace, denying being *"captain of a Band of Outlaws"* or killing Jim Carlyle. So Nolan states on page 401:

Governor Wallace's reaction to this catalog of half-truths and self-justification was one of indifference; he had already decided that there was only one way to get rid of the Kid. It was simple, brutal, and unequivocal.

BILLY THE KID
$500 REWARD

For Billy's Stinking Springs capture, Nolan insults Billy's intelligence: "The Kid had forgotten that Garrett knew his hideouts as well as he knew them himself." In actuality, Pat Garrett likely followed tracks in deep snow to that rock line cabin from the group's hide-out in the Wilcox-Brazil Ranch.

Presenting post-capture newspaper interviews of Billy's professing innocence, Nolan discounts him as a hero of the resistance, cruelly stating on page 409:

The Kid told his side of the story one more time for the reporter. Perhaps he was still naïve enough to believe there was someone in New Mexico Territory who would believe it.

Having defined Billy Bonney as a universally reviled criminal, having discounted Pat Garrett's need for Texan possemen to hunt Billy because New Mexicans refused, and having ignored months of Ring precautions against his rescue by compatriots, Nolan is left surprised by Lincolnites inactivity during Billy's great escape. He states on page 414:

> The astonishing fact of the matter is that though apparently everyone in Lincoln saw what happened, not one soul lifted a finger to stop the Kid.

When Billy is finally killed, Frederick Nolan eradicates even the boy's likely moral choice, stating on page 425,:

> He never even knew who killed him.

Pat Garrett himself contemplated otherwise in his *Authentic Life of Billy the Kid*. In what were probably his own words, rather than ghost-writer Ash Upson's, Garrett said:

> It will never be known whether the Kid recognized me or not ... He had also said that he knew, should we meet, he would have to choose between the several alternatives of surrendering, or killing me, or getting killed himself.

One is left to wonder why a competent historian like Frederick Nolan missed the clue to Ring terrorism by the generation of silence that followed Billy Bonney's killing; though Billy's fame was national. In Nolan's chapter "Finale," on page 427 of *The Lincoln County War*, he states:

> With the death of Billy the Kid it was as if every one of the men who had participated in the years of bloodshed took a vow of silence. Thus, nowhere in the literature of the Lincoln County troubles is there any article, any memoir, any reminiscence of the times written between 1882 and the middle 1920's by someone who was actually there.

RESURRECTING BILLY THE KID

History, lived forwards, is better comprehended backwards. That "vow of silence," noted by historian, Frederick Nolan, as extending from "1882 to the middle 1920's," by the generation knowing Billy Bonney, is a clue to rediscovering Billy the Kid.

That generation startled Nolan by violating his historian's wisdom that people record their memorable events. That generation did not, because that generation lived in abject terror of truths they dared not give to outsiders - including historians. Those truths did silence their generation.

They had witnessed the holocaust birth of the Santa Fe Ring in its robbery of the Maxwell and other land grants; its slaughter of hundreds; its crushed rebellions in Grant County, Colfax County, and Lincoln County; its murders of John Tunstall and Alexander McSween; its massacre at San Patricio; its illegal march of Commander N.A.M. Dudley's troops with howitzer and Gatling gun crushing their Lincoln County War freedom fight; its assassination of Attorney Huston Chapman and near-assassination of Attorney Ira Leonard, both there to prosecute Ring criminals; and its illegal killings of Tom O'Folliard and Charlie Bowdre. That generation of silence had seen all crimes against justice go unpunished and all criminals prospering wildly; and that generation knew the possibility of death or retribution if opposition to the Santa Fe Ring was visible.

Finally - and that was when the "vow of silence" began - the Ring killed Billy Bonney. Finally the assassin crept into a bedroom where you felt most safe and fired your death bullet in darkness of a plot you never suspected and was never revealed. If you opposed the Ring, like Billy, there would be no friend to save you, no attorney to defend you, no place to hide.

And if you were an Hispanic hero of the Lincoln County War - an Yginio Salazar, living with opium for pain of war bullets in his back; a Francisco Zamora killed then; a Vincente Romero killed then; a Juan Patrón murdered three years after Billy - you were unsung and forgotten.

If you rode with Billy, like him, you would be remembered only by vilification as a reprehensible outlaw-desperado.

The Santa Fe Ring and historians, however, were left with an unanticipated problem: the silent people did not forget.

RECONSTITUTED SANTA FE RING

After his Mesilla hanging sentence, Billy Bonney gave to a reporter a true and prescient quote: "I think it hard that I should be the only one to suffer the extreme penalty of the law." In the Lincoln County War period, and its aftermath - epitomized by Billy's capture, hanging trial, and killing - not one Ring criminal was prosecuted; and all Ringmen profited.

Killing Billy Bonney unleashed the Santa Fe Ring. Its members repositioned. A month and a half before Garrett's fired fatal bullet, on May 30, 1881, Lew Wallace, with relief, left for Constantinople; replaced as governor, to Ring relief, by their partisan, Lionel Sheldon, recommended to President James Abram Garfield by Thomas Benton Catron and Steven Benton Elkins. Briefly disgraced, Ringman, ex-governor, Samuel Beach Axtell, rose again as Territorial Chief Justice. James Dolan, indicted for Tunstall's and Chapman's murders, was cleared by Judge Warren Bristol; purchased Tunstall's store; and became rich after marrying Charles Fritz's daughter and inheriting, through her, a stake in Jack Winter's North Homestake gold mine. Catron, with his six million acres, had accumulated more land than any American before or after. By 1912, he was appointed one of the first two senators for New Mexico's new statehood (paying out $1 million in apparent bribes). His partner, Elkins, became so rich with land, railroads, mines, banks, and coal deposits in West Virginia, that he and his wife ate from solid gold dinnerware in their Newport Beach-style, West Virginia mansion, Halliehurst.

President Rutherford B. Hayes, arguably Santa Fe Ring complicit, remained unscathed by any exposé up to the present. Hayes's Secretary of State, William Evarts, having been the Washington-positioned attorney assisting Catron and Elkins in acquiring the Maxwell Land Grant, later politically blocked the Tunstall family's monetary reparations for their son's murder and theft of his property - because of their linking his death to complicit United States officials. President Hayes's successor, James Abram Garfield, continued the policy of concealing the Santa Fe Ring. After all, Garfield's Secretary of State, James Blaine, had been backed in his own presidential bid by his own good friend, Stephen Benton Elkins.

By the 1900's, Ring-biased historians wrote sanitized hagiographies for Catron - Victor Westphall's 1973 *Thomas Benton Catron and His Era* - and Elkins - Oscar Lambert's 1955, *Stephen Benton Elkins: American Foursquare*. Influential New Mexican historian, Ralph Emerson Twitchell, in his 1912, two volume *The Leading Facts of New Mexican History*, avoided any focus on the Santa Fe Ring. The message for the 1900's was that the Santa Fe Ring had never existed at all.

But Billy the Kid's fame had an unexpected side-effect. It yielded 20th century pretenders, whose hoaxes would, ironically, defeat Santa Fe Ring opportunists by the 21st.

ILLITERATE BILLY THE KID PRETENDERS

Billy the Kid's writings, coupled with his freedom fighter role, undid his 20th century, old-timer pretenders. Those illiterate eccentrics based confabulated identities on his outlaw image. With tall tales about surviving Pat Garrett's shooting, a few got hoaxing authors relying on public ignorance from paltry publications and early Western films. My book, *Billy the Kid's Pretenders: Brushy Bill and John Miller,* debunked them.

The most successful pretender was a Texan named Oliver Pleasant Roberts, calling himself "Bushy Bill," and having been one month shy of two years old when Billy Bonney was killed. But his author, William V. Morrison, saw "Brushy's" potential for lucre, and used a minor historian named Charles Leland Sonnichsen to add flash as co-author for their book titled *Alias Billy the Kid*. That creation relied on their huckster claim that "Brushy Bill" Roberts knew things "never printed" - and, being illiterate, could not have "studied-up."

As to real Billy Bonney's very literate letters, Morrison - and subsequent "Brushy Bill" authors - were forced to invent a "friend" who wrote them. (That friend had to be Billy's shadow, even in solitary confinement in the Santa Fe jail!)

Illiteracy did not rule out coaching! Transparently used by William Morrison were Billy's letters (giving "Brushy" near-verbatim quotes 70 years post-writing); Pat Garrett's *Authentic Life of Billy the Kid;* Walter Noble Burns's *The Saga of Billy the Kid*; works by historians Robert Mullin and Maurice Garland Fulton; and other books by Billy's contemporaries like

Charlie Siringo, Jim East, and George Coe. Added were a few archival documents, Morrison's 1949 interviews with Lincoln residents, and taking "Brushy" on a tour of that town.

Tellingly, when historical sources ran out, so did "Brushy's" "memory" - or his confabulations took over. Not only did he lack special knowledge, he lacked all period details - including the Lincoln County War, the Santa Fe Ring, and true-love Paulita Maxwell. And, like prevalent Billy the Kid myths, "Brushy" called himself an "outlaw; not a "fighter."

But William Morrison, using Billy Bonney's March 4, 1881 jail letter to Governor Lew Wallace about the pardon bargain, has "Brushy" parrot: "I done everything I promised him to do." Their real Billy prompt-letter, however, said beautifully and unattainably: *I have done everything that I promised you I would, and you have done nothing that you promised me.* So the Morrison-Sonnichsen-"Brushy Bill" hoax only proves a pig's ear cannot make a silk purse.

But by 1950, William Morrison, seeking fame and profit, tried for the ultimate publicity coup: getting "Brushy Bill" Roberts a belated gubernatorial pardon as Billy the Kid. Their day's New Mexico governor, Thomas Jewett Mabry, fortunately was no fool. After interviewing "Brushy," and getting input from descendants and historians, he concluded: "I am taking no action, now or ever, on this application for a Pardon for Billy the Kid because I do not believe this man is Billy the Kid."

Nevertheless, "Brushy Bill" Roberts, to this day, has true-believer authors and conspiracy theorist followers; and a Hamilton, Texas, gravesite fitted-out with a modern tombstone inscribed with real Billy Bonney's approximate birthdate!

A less successful, illiterate pretender was an Arizona madman named John Miller; who, at ten years older than the actual Billy Bonney, was no kid - and would have been older than most Lincoln County War participants, including Billy's boss, John Tunstall. But John Miller, who merely chatted to neighbors about being Billy, did get an author, Helen Airy, whose slim book, *Whatever Happened to Billy the Kid*, shows as little legwork as did Miller in formulating that hoaxlet.

Oliver "Brushy Bill" Roberts and John Miller would have languished as jokes appended to real Billy Bonney's history, had it not been for the 21st century Santa Fe Ring.

MODERN SANTA FE RING AND BILLY THE KID

Billy Bonney's fame exposed the old Santa Fe Ring. It also tempted the modern Santa Fe Ring to collude in law enforcement fraud which brought it closer to defeat than had the original Lincoln County War freedom fight.

In 2003, New Mexico public officials decided to hijack Billy's history for profit, political fodder, and publicity. They declared that Pat Garrett had not killed Billy the Kid; naming that "investigation" "the Billy the Kid Case." Imperiled was actual Billy Bonney's iconic history and its tourist sites.

The historic/forensic/legal hoax replicated antique Santa Fe Ring players: the governor, the Attorney General (like the Territorial U.S. Attorney), sheriffs, deputies, district judges, and lawyers. Their goal was likewise a throw-back: to "prove" that Oliver "Brushy Bill" Roberts *was* Billy the Kid; and to grant *him*, posthumously, Lew Wallace's gubernatorial pardon.

For taxpayer funding and court standing for exhumation petitions, they filed a real, cold-case, murder investigation as Lincoln County Sheriff's Department Case No. 2003-274. The suspect was Sheriff Pat Garrett. His alleged victim, on July 14, 1881, was a random youth he killed to enable Billy's escape. Garrett was also faked as providing Billy's jailbreak gun; thus, being accessory to murdering his own two deputies.

Garrett's "crimes" (making him the most evil lawman in American history) were to be solved by the hoaxers by "forensic DNA": matching DNA from Billy the Kid's grave with his mother's in Silver City to prove, by mismatch, that the "unknown cowboy" lay in Fort Sumner. Omitted was that uncertain location of both graves caused the New Mexico Office of the Medical Investigator to refuse exhumation permits. Omitted was that Billy's killing by Garrett was irrefutable. Omitted was that the hoaxers had no contrary evidence.

But for the Santa Fe Ring, corrupt power trumps truth. The hoax's backer was New Mexico Governor Bill Richardson, using it as a publicity stunt for his presidential bid and as pay-to-play for a big political donor: apparently a "Brushy Bill" Roberts fan, who also acted as "Billy the Kid's" attorney in court, proclaiming that "Brushy," *as Billy*, deserved that pardon for having led "a long and law-abiding life!"

That Billy the Kid Case hoax used two Lincoln County Sheriffs, deputies, and a De Baca County Sheriff. Richardson-appointed judges heard the lawmen's exhumation petitions, and ignored dead Billy in court as their co-petitioner for digging up himself and his mother! Arizona officials got involved in exhuming John Miller - as Billy! Taxpayers also paid, from 2007 to 2014, for the hoaxers' attorneys blocking my open records violation case against them.

In New Mexico to write *Billy and Paulita* when the Billy the Kid Case hoax broke, I led all its opposition; first legally blocking digging up the gravesites of Billy and his mother.

So the hoaxers rewrote their "innocent victim" scam, claiming Billy as shot, but *playing dead* while bleeding on an old carpenter's workbench. (Supposedly Garrett, back then, at the townspeople's vigil, slipped in his "innocent victim," as Billy painfully rode off). A forensic expert, paid by a TV producer faked getting "Billy's blood DNA" from that bench; though proving neither blood nor link to Billy. Unfazed, the hoaxers lied that they had "Billy's DNA" to exhume John Miller for its matching - a warm-up for its rerun with "Brushy Bill." But Texas officials blocked them. Thus, "Brushy Bill" Roberts lost the "I am Billy" stakes by bogus DNA in this hoax rerun.

Throughout this travesty, the hoaxing law enforcement officers concealed their fake forensic reports by evading all my open records requests; even under court order for turn-over.

Meanwhile, they profited with a front page *New York Times* article, History Channel program, and a Cannes Film Festival movie; while remaining legally untouchable in Santa Fe Ring tradition of protective "friends" in high places.

My book *MegaHoax: The Strange Plot to Exhume Billy the Kid and Become President* tells the story of my fight against that Santa Fe Ring gambit. It helped me to appreciate Billy Bonney's courage - and to see humor in Ring politics where winning at any cost includes making a fool of yourself.

And, at stake in the Billy the Kid Case hoax, was Billy Bonney's literacy. Had the hoax succeeded, lost would have been brilliant Billy Bonney - replaced by an illiterate lunatic: "Oliver "Brushy Bill" Roberts. One could say that everything came down to my cherishing Billy's writings, words and wit.

THE MEMORY OF THE PEOPLE

Fate's revenge on Lew Wallace was being forgotten - even as *Ben-Hur's* author - while Billy Bonney's fame is world-wide.

And I believe that Billy knew his fight, and that of his compatriots, was grand. In *Billy and Paulita*, I give him words that people may finally appreciate as Ring-style greed and arrogance of power are eroding democracy into plutocracy.

MAY 30, 1881   6:38 PM   MONDAY

In the vegetable garden to the south of the mansion, Deluvina picked the season's first squash. Periodically, she glanced westward to high tangled vegetation, and gazed at the low orange sun thrusting crepuscular rays in soaring display.

She said to the boy, who had thought he was unnoticed, "There is great beauty in life. You come often and with danger of death." Into rustling leaves, he said not to Paulita. "To her heart. If you are killed." Friends would warn him, he said.

"You know the true danger, but you stay."

Billy's voice said, "There's no place safe for anyone with me. Not in the Territories. Not in the States. Not in Old Mexico. You know what happened to Victorio. Not just him, everyone with him. And to Charlie and Tom for being with me.

"I can't put her at that risk. With time, things may change."

He knew they would not, Deluvina said, and asked if this was enough. She heard, "It's the hand we're dealt. Life."

Again there was silence as sky colored the land red. The wind became stronger. His voice rode it. "We won because I won. And the memory of people is stronger than death."

"Then it is as it should be. It is your path, Billy Bonney. A good path. A blessed path."

References and Resources

APPENDICES OF ORIGINAL
BILLY THE KID WRITINGS

APPENDIX 1: June 8, 1878. Signature for transcribed deposition to Investigator for the Departments of Justice and the Interior, Frank Warner Angel [Reprinted from the Angel Report. *In the Matter of the Examination of the Causes and Circumstances of the Death of John H. Tunstall a British Subject.* October 4, 1878. Microfilm File Case Number 44-4-8-3. Record Group 060. Microfilm No. M750. Roll 1. National Archives and Records Administration. U.S. Department of Justice. Washington, D.C. (Deposition of William H. Bonney. pp. 314-319.)] - See Page 475.

APPENDIX 2: October 28, 1878. Bill of Sale for a horse to Dr. Henry Hoyt [Printed with permission of: Panhandle-Plains Historical Museum, Canyon, Texas, for Item Number X1974-98/1] - See Page 479.

APPENDIX 3: March 13, 1879. Letter to Governor Lew Wallace to request a pardon [Printed with permission of: Lincoln County Heritage Trust Collection (AC 481), Fray Angélico Chávez History Library, NMHM, Santa Fe, New Mexico] - See Page 483.

APPENDIX 4: March 20, 1879. Letter to Lincoln County Justice of the Peace John "Squire" Wilson about meeting with Governor Lew Wallace [Printed with permission of: Indiana Historical Society, Indianapolis, Indiana; from the Lew Wallace Collection, Number M0292] - See Page 487.

APPENDIX 5: March 20, 1879. Letter to Governor Lew Wallace to arrange the feigned arrest for the pardon agreement [Printed with permission of: Indiana Historical Society, Indianapolis, Indiana; from the Lew Wallace Collection, Number M0292] - See Page 491.

APPENDIX 6: March 24 (?), 1879. The "Billie" Fragment Letter, probably to Governor Lew Wallace, giving information about Territorial outlawry, with Lincoln County War references [Printed with permission of: Indiana Historical Society, Indianapolis, Indiana; from the Lew Wallace Collection, Number M0292] - See Page 495.

APPENDIX 7: December 12, 1880. Letter to Governor Lew Wallace denying personal outlawry and the murder of Jim Carlyle [Printed with permission of: Indiana Historical Society, Indianapolis, Indiana; from the Lew Wallace Collection, Number M0292] - See Page 499.

APPENDIX 8: January 1, 1881. First Santa Fe jail letter to Governor Lew Wallace requesting a meeting about the pardon [Printed with permission of: Indiana Historical Society, Indianapolis, Indiana; from the Lew Wallace Collection, Number M0292] - See Page 505.

APPENDIX 9: March 2, 1881. Second Santa Fe jail letter to Governor Lew Wallace about a meeting for the pardon [Printed with permission of: Lincoln County Heritage Trust Collection (AC 481), Fray Angélico Chávez History Library, NMHM, Santa Fe, New Mexico] - See Page 509.

APPENDIX 10: March 4, 1881. Third Santa Fe jail letter to Governor Lew Wallace requesting a meeting about the pardon [Printed with permission of: Indiana Historical Society, Indianapolis, Indiana; from the Lew Wallace Collection, Number M0292] - See Page 513.

APPENDIX 11: March 27, 1881. Fourth Santa Fe jail letter to Governor Lew Wallace requesting a meeting about the pardon [Printed with permission of: Indiana Historical Society, Indianapolis, Indiana; from the Lew Wallace Collection, Number M0292] - See Page 517.

APPENDIX 1: June 8, 1878. Signature at end of court reporter transcribed deposition to Investigator for the Departments of Justice and the Interior Frank Warner Angel, with witnessing by Justice of the Peace John Wilson; about the murder of John Henry Tunstall

in the meantime joined deponent and Widenmann and Brewer. Deponent then made the best of his way to Lincoln in company with Robt. A. Widenmann, Brewer, Waite and Biddleton stopping on the Rio Ruidoso in order to get men to look for the body of W. H. Tunstall —

Deponent further says that neither he nor any of the party fired off either rifle or pistol and that neither he nor the parties with him fired a shot.

William. H. Bonney

Sworn and subscribed to before me this eighth day of June A.D. 1878.

John B. Wilson

Justice of the Peace

APPENDIX 2: October 28, 1878. Bill of Sale for horse to Dr. Henry Hoyt

Toscoso Texas
Thursday Oct 4th
1878

Know all persons by these presents
that I do hereby Sell and deliver
to Henry F. Hoyt one Sorrel
Horse Branded **BB** on left hip
and other indistinct Brands on
Shoulders. for the Sum of Seventy five
Dollars. in hand received

W H Bonney

Witness
Jas McMasters
Geo. Howard

The above is The handwriting of the
outlaw known as "Billy the Kid"
H.F.H.

APPENDIX 3: March 13, 1879. Letter to Governor Lew
Wallace to request a pardon

To his Excellency the Governor.
General Lew. Wallace

Dear Sir I have
heard that You Will give one thousand
dollars for my body which as I can
understand it means alive as a Witness.
I know it is as a Witness against those
that Murdered Mr Chapman. if it was so
as that I could appear at Court I could
give the desired information. but I have
indictments against me for things that
happened in the late Lincoln County War
and am afraid to give up because my
Eniميs would kill me, the day Mr Chapman
Was Murdered I Was in Lincoln, at the request
of good Citizens to meet Mr J. J. Dolan
to meet as Friends, So as to be able to lay
aside our arms and go to Work, I was present
When Mr Chapman Was Murdered and know
who did it and if it were not for those
indictments I would have made it clear before now

if it is in your power to annully
those indictments I hope you will do so
so a to give me a chance to explain.
please send me an answer telling me what
you can do You can send answer by bearer
  I have no Wish to fight any more indeed
I have not raised an arm since your proclamation
as to my Charactar I refer to any of
the Citizens. for the majority of them are
my Friends and have been helping me
all they could. I am called Kid Antrim
but Antrim is my stepfathers name.
  Writing an answer I remain
Your Obedient Servant
  W. H. Bonney

APPENDIX 4: March 20, 1879. "Lady Liberty" stationery letter to Lincoln County Justice of the Peace John "Squire" Wilson about the planned meeting with Governor Lew Wallace

San Patricio

Thursday 20th
18-72

Friend Wilson.
        Please tell
You know who that I do not
know what to do, now as those
Prisoners have escaped. to send word
by bearer. a note through You
it may be that he has made different
Arragements if not and he still wants
it the same to Send: William Hudgins:
as Deputy. to the Junction tomorrow
at three Oclock with Some men you know
to be all right. Send a note telling
me what to do   W H Bomey

P. S. do not Send Soldiers

"Billy the Kid"

APPENDIX 5: March 20, 1879. "Lady Liberty" stationery letter to Governor Lew Wallace to arrange the feigned arrest for the pardon agreement. Its "Lady Liberty" seal is reversed on the first page and correctly located on the second, because writing on the single folio sheet began on its "back."

San Patricio
Lincoln County
Thursday 20th 1879

General Lew Wallace;

Sir I will keep
the appointment I made
but be sure and have men come
that you can depend on I am not
afraid to die like a man fighting
but I would not like to be killed
like a dog unarmed, tell Kimbal
to let his men be placed around
the house. and for him to come in
alone; and he can arrest us. all I am
afraid of is that in the Fort we
might be poinined, or killed through
a Window at night, but you can
arrange that all right. tell the
Comanding Officer to Watch) Lt Goodwin
he would not hesitate to do anything
there Will be danger on the road of
Somebody Waylaying us to kill us on the
road to the Fort.

You Will never catch those
fellows on the road Watch
Fritzes. Captain Bacas. ranch
and the Brewerys they Will either
go to Seven Rivers or to Jicarillo
Montañas they Will stay around close
untill the scouting parties come in
give a Spy a pair of glasses and let
him get on the Mountain back of Fritzes and
Watch and if they are there ther will be provisons
carried to them, it is not My place
to advise you, but I am anxious
to have them Caught, and perhaps
know how men hide from Soldiers, better
^{than} you, please Excuse me for having so much to say
and I still remain Yours Truly

P.S,   W. H. Bonney

I have changed my mind Send Kimbal to
Gutieres. just below San Patricio one mile. because
Sanger and Ballard are or were great friends of Corruls
Ballard told me <del>today</del> Yesterday tt leave for you were doing
every thing to catch me. it was a blind to get me to leave

for I may not be thare before to come before daylook or
tell Kimbal not to leave

APPENDIX 6: March 24, 1879 (Author's attribution). The "Billie" letter fragment on "Lady Liberty" stationery; probably to Governor Lew Wallace, giving information about Territorial outlawry and Lincoln County War issues

On the Pecos. all that I can remember
are the so called Dolan Outfit but they
are all up here now: and on Rio Grande
this Man Cris Moten I believe his name is
he drove a herd of 780 head one Year ago
last December in Company with Frank Wheeler
Frank Baker deceased Jesse Evans George Davis
alia Tom Jones. Tom Hill. his name in Texas being
Tom Chelson also deceased they drove the Cattle to
the Indian Reservation and sold them to John Riley
and J J Dolan. and were this cattle turned in for Beef for the
Indians the Beckwith family Made their boasts that they
came to Seven Rivers a little over four Years ago
with one Milch Cow borrowed from John Chisum
they had when I was there Year ago one thousand six
hundred head of cattle. the Male members of the family are is Henry
beckwith and John Beckwith Robert Beckwith was killed
the time McSweens house was Burned.
Charles   Robert Olinger and Wallace Olinger
are of the same gang. their cattle ranch is
situated at Rock Corral twelve Miles below Seven Rivers
on the Pecos. Paxton and Pierce are still below
them forty Miles from Seven Rivers there are four

of them Paxton: Pierce: Jim Raymes, and Buck Powel.
they had when I seen them last about one thousand
head of cattle: at Rocky Arroya there is another Ranch
belonging to Smith who Operated on the Penaco
last year with the Jesse Evans gang there and
the places I mentioned are all I know of
this man Cris Moten at the time they stole those
Cattle was in the employ of J. J. Dolan, an Co
I afterwards seen some of the Cattle at the
Rinconada Bonita on the Reservation those were
the men we were in search of when we went to
the agency. the Beckwith family were attending
to their own business when this war started but
G. W. Peppin told them that this was
John Chisums war and so they took a hand
thinking they would lose their Cattle in case
that he Chisum won the fight. this is all the
information I can give you on this point

Yours Respectfully Billie

APPENDIX 7: December 12, 1880. Letter to Governor Lew Wallace denying the murder of Jim Carlyle

Fort Sumner

Dec 12th 1880

Gov— Lew Wallace

Dear Sir

I noticed in the Las Vegas Gazette a
preice which stated that, Billy" the " Kid, the
name by which I am Known in the Country
was the Captian of a Band of Outlaws who
hold Forth at the Portales. There is no
such Organization in Existence. So the Gentlemen
must have Krawn very heavily on his Imagination,
My bussinoess at the White Oaks the time I was
waylard and my horse killed, was to See
Judge Leonard who has my Case in hand.
he had written to me to Come up, that he thought
he could get Everything Straightend up
I did not find him at the Oaks & should
have gone to Lincoln if I had met with no
accident; After mine and Billie Wilsons horses

2

were Killed we both made our way to a
Station, forty miles from the Oaks kept by
Mr Greathouse. When I got up next morning
The house was Surrounded by an outfit led
by one Carlyle, who came into the house and
demanded a Surrender. I asked for their
Papers and they had none. So I Concluded
it Amounted to nothing more than a mob
and told Carlyle that he would have to
Stay in the house and lead the way out
that night. Soon after a note was brought
in Stating that if Carlyle did not come out
inside of five minutes they would kill the
Station keeper (Greathouse) who had left the
house and was with them, in a short time a
Shot was fired on the outside and Carlyle thinking
Greathouse was killed jumped through the
window, breaking the Sash as he went
and was killed by his own Party they thinking
it was me trying to make my Escape.
the Party then withdrew.

they returned the next day and burned an old
Man named Spencer's house and Greathouses, also

3

I made my way to this Place afoot and
During my absence Deftuty Sheriff Garrett
Acting under Chisums Orders went to the Portales
and found Nothing. on his way back he went
by Mr Yerbys ranch and took a pair of mules
of mine which I had left with Mr Bowdre
who is in Charge of mr Yerbys Cattle.
he (Garrett) Claimed that they were stolen
and Even if they were not he had a right
to Confiscate any Outlaws property.
I have been at Summer Since I left
Lincoln making my living Gambling
the mules were bought by me the truth of which
I can prove by the best Citizens around Summer
J. S. Chisum is the man who got me into
Trouble. and was. benifited Thousands by it
and is now doing all he can against me
There is no Doubt but what there is a great deal
of Stealing going on in the Territory. and a great
deal of the Property is taken across the Plains as
it is a good outlet but so far as my being

4

at the head of a Band there is nothing of it
in Several Instances I have recovered Stolen
Property when there was no Chance to get an
Officer to do it—

        one Instance for Hugo Zuber
Postoffice Puerto De Luna. another for
Pablo Analla Same Place.

if Some impartial Party were to investigate
this matter they would find it for Different
from the impression put out by Chissum and his
Tools.

      Yours Respec
          William Bonney

APPENDIX 8: January 1, 1881. First Santa Fe jail letter to Governor Lew Wallace requesting a meeting about the pardon

Santa Fe
Jan." 1st
1881

Gov." Lew Wallace
        Dear Sir
    I would like to see you
for a few moments if you can
spare time
        Yours Respect."
            W. H. Bonney

APPENDIX 9: March 2, 1881. Second Santa Fe jail letter to Governor Lew Wallace requesting a meeting about the pardon

Santa Fe Jail New Mex
March 2d 1881

Gov. Lew Wallace
         Dear Sir

    I wish you would come down to
the Jail and see me. it will be to
Your interest to come and see me, I have
some letters which date back two
Years, and there are Parties who
are very anxious to get them
, but I shall not dispose of them
untill I see You. that is if you
will come imediatly
             Yours Respect—
             Wm H Bonney

"Billy the Kit"

APPENDIX 10: March 4, 1881. Third Santa Fe jail letter to Governor Lew Wallace requesting a meeting about the pardon

Santa Fe, In Jail
March 4th 1881

Gov. Lew Wallace

Dear Sir

I wrote you a little note
the day before yesterday, but have
received no answer, I Expect you have forgot
ten, what you promised me, this Month two
Years ago, but I have not, and I think You
had ought to have come and see me as I
requested you to. I have done Everything that
I promised you I would, and you have done
nothing that you promised me,
I think when you, think the matter over, you
will come down and see me, and I can then
Explain Everything to you.
Judge Leonard, Passed through here on
his way East, in January and promised to
come and see me on his way back but he did
not fulfill his Promise, it looks to me like I am
getting left in the Cold. I am not treated right

by Sherman, he lets Every Stranger
that comes to see me through Curiosity
in to see me, but will not let a single one of
my friends in, not Even an Attorney
I guess they mean to send me up without giving me
any show, but they will have a nice time doing it
I am not intirely without friends

   I shall Expect to See you Sometime today
       Patiently waiting
       I am very Truly Yours Respect=

           Wm H. Bonney

APPENDIX 11: March 27, 1881. Fourth Santa Fe jail letter to Governor Lew Wallace requesting a meeting about the pardon

Santa Fe New Mexico
March 2ᵈ/81

Gov: Lew Wallace
Dear Sir
                    for the last
time I ask, Will You keep
Your promise. I start below
tomorrow Send Aunser by bearer
            Yours Respt
                    W Bonney

ANNOTATED BIBLIOGRAPHY

GLOBAL HISTORICAL REFERENCES FOR BILLY THE KID AND THE LINCOLN COUNTY WAR

Nolan, Frederick. *The Lincoln County War: A Documentary History.* Norman: University of Oklahoma Press. 1992.
_____. *The West of Billy the Kid.* Norman: University of Oklahoma Press. 1998.

GLOBAL HISTORICAL REFERENCES FOR WILLIAM HENRY BONNEY ("BILLY THE KID")

AUTHORSHIP / TESTIMONY / INTERVIEWS

BILL OF SALE

Bonney, W H. "Know all persons by these presents ..." (Hoyt Bill of Sale). Thursday, October 24, 1878. Collection of Panhandle-Plains Historical Museum, Canyon, Texas. (Item No. X1974-98/1)

LETTERS TO LEW WALLACE

Bonney, W H. "I have heard you will give one thousand $ dollars for my body which as I see it means alive ..." March 13 (?), 1879. Fray Angélico Chávez Historical Library, Santa Fe, New Mexico. Lincoln County Heritage Trust Collection. (AC481).
_____. "I will keep the keep the appointment ..." March 20, 1879. Indiana Historical Society. M0292.
_____. "... on the Pecos." ("Billie" letter fragment). March 24 (?), 1879. Indiana Historical Society. M0292. **(Typed copy denying its being written by Billy Bonney, made May 15, 1947 by Herman Weisner, is in the Herman B. Weisner Papers, Circa 1957-1992. Ms 0249. New Mexico State University Library at Las Cruces, Archives and Special Collections Department. Box 13, W - Folder 3, S. The same copy is in the Midland, Texas Haley Library's Robert Mullin Collection, and annotated as possibly by Bonney.)**

522

_____. "I noticed in the Las Vegas Gazette a piece which stated that 'Billy the Kid' ..." December 12, 1880. Indiana Historical Society. Lew Wallace Collection. M0292.

_____. "I would like to see you ..." January 1, 1881. Indiana Historical Society. Lew Wallace Collection. M0292.

_____. "I wish you would come down to the jail and see me ..." March 2, 1881. Fray Angélico Chávez Historical Library, Santa Fe, New Mexico. Lincoln County Heritage Trust Collection. (AC481).

_____. "I wrote you a little note day before yesterday ..." March 4, 1881. Indiana Historical Society. Lew Wallace Collection. M0292.

_____. "For the last time I ask ..." March 27, 1881. Indiana Historical Society. Lew Wallace Collection. M0292.

LETTER TO SQUIRE WILSON

Bonney, W H. "Friend Wilson ..." March 18, 1879. Robert N. Mullin Collection. File RNM, IV, NM, 43. Nita Stewart Haley Memorial Museum. Haley Library. Midland, Texas. (Original in Indiana Historical Society.)

LETTER TO EDGAR CAYPLESS

Bonney, W H. "I would have written before ..." April 15, 1881. Copy in William Keleher's *Violence in Lincoln County;* originally reproduced in Griggs *History of the Mesilla Valley.* (**Original is lost.**)

LETTER (POSSIBLY DICTATED) FOR EDGAR WALZ

Regulator. "Mr. Walz. Sir ..." Letter to Edgar Walz. July 13, 1878. Adjutant General's Office. File 1405 AGO 1878. (Quoted in Maurice Garland Fulton, *History of the Lincoln County War.* Tucson: University of Arizona Press. 1975. pages 246-247, and Frederick Nolan, *The Lincoln County War: A Documentary History*, page 310.)

NEWSPAPER INTERVIEWS (CHRONOLOGICAL)

Wilcox, Lucius "Lute" M. (city editor, owner, J.H. Koogler). "The Kid. Interview with Billy Bonney The Best Known Man in New Mexico." Las Vegas *Gazette.* December 28, 1880. (**Has quote about "the laugh's on me this time"**)

_____. Interview, at train depot. Las Vegas *Gazette.* December 28, 1880. (**Has "adios" quote.**)

No Author. "At least two hundred men have been killed in Lincoln County during the past three years ..." Santa Fe *Daily New Mexican.* March 28, 1881.

No Author. "Something About the Kid." Santa Fe *Daily New Mexican.* April 3, 1881. **(With quotes "this is the man" and "two hundred men have been killed ... he did not kill all of them.")**

No Author. "I got a rough deal ..." *Mesilla News.* April 15, 1881.

Newman, Simon N. Ed. Interview with "The Kid." *Newman's Semi-Weekly.* April 15, 1881.

_____ . Departure from Mesilla. *Newman's Semi-Weekly.* April 15, 1881.

No Author. "Advise persons never to engage in killing." *Mesilla News.* April 16, 1881.

TESTIMONY

Angel, Frank Warner. *In the Matter of the Examination of the Causes and Circumstances of the Death of John H. Tunstall a British Subject.* Report filed October 4, 1878. Angel Report. Microfilm File Case Number 44-4-8-3. Record Group 060. Microfilm No. M750. Roll 1. National Archives and Records Administration. U. S. Department of Justice. Washington, D.C. **(Deposition of William H. Bonney. June 8, 1878. pp. 314-319.)**

No Author. *Dudley Court of Inquiry. (May 2, 1879 - July 5, 1879).* 16W3/16/28/6. Boxes 1923-1923A. File Number QQ1284. National Archives and Records Administration. Old Military and Civil Branch. Records of the Office of the Judge Advocate General. Washington, D.C. **(Testimony of William H. Bonney. May 28 and 29, 1879.)**

WILLIAM BONNEY BIOGRAPHICAL BOOKS

Abbott, E.C. ("Teddy Blue") and Helena Huntington Smith. *We Pointed Them North: Recollections of a Cowpuncher.* Norman, Oklahoma: University of Oklahoma Press. 1955. **(Billy the Kid's multiculturalism, page 47.)**

Anaya, Paco. *I Buried Billy.* College Station, Texas: Creative Publishing Company. 1991.

Ball, Eve. *Ma'am Jones of the Pecos.* Tucson, Arizona: The University of Arizona Press. 1969.

Bell, Bob Boze. *The Illustrated Life and Times of Billy the Kid.* Cave Creek, Arizona: Boze Books. 1992. (Frank Coe quote about the Kid's cartridge use, page 45.)

Bell, Bob Boze. *The Illustrated Life and Times of Billy the Kid.* Second Edition. Phoenix, Arizona: Tri Star-Boze Publications, Inc. 1996.

Burns, Walter Noble. *The Saga of Billy the Kid.* Stamford, Connecticut: Longmeadow Press. 1992. (Original printing: 1926, Doubleday.) **(About Billy's outlawry: pages 54, 57; about pardon: page 152)** _____. *"I also know that the Kid and Paulita were sweethearts."* Unpublished letter to Jim East. June 3, 1926. Robert N. Mullin Collection. File RNM, IV, NM, 116-117. Nita Stewart Haley Memorial Museum, Haley Library. Midland, Texas.

Coroner's Jury Report for William Bonney. July 15, 1881. (Copy) Herman Weisner Collection. Lincoln County Papers. New Mexico State University Library at Las Cruces. Rio Grande Historical Society Collection. Box No. 1. Folder Name: Billy the Kid Legal Documents. Folder No. 14C. 26.

Garrett, Pat F. *The Authentic Life of Billy the Kid The Noted Desperado of the Southwest, Whose Deeds of Daring and Blood Made His Name a Terror in New Mexico, Arizona, and Northern Mexico.* Santa Fe, New Mexico: New Mexico Printing and Publishing Co. 1882. (Reprint used: New York: Indian Head Books. 1994.) **(About the kid's devil, page xxvii; about Garrett's possible guilty feelings, pages 218-219.)**

Hendron, J. W. *The Story of Billy the Kid. New Mexico's Number One Desperado.* New York: Indian Head Books. 1994.

Jacobsen, Joel. *Such Men as Billy the Kid. The Lincoln County War Reconsidered.* Lincoln and London: University of Nebraska Press. 1994.

Kadlec, Robert F. *They "Knew" Billy the Kid. Interviews with Old-Time New Mexicans.* Santa Fe, New Mexico: Ancient City Press. 1987.

Keleher, William A. *Violence in Lincoln County 1869-1881.* Albuquerque, New Mexico: University of New Mexico Press. 1957. **(Pardon agreement: pages 212, 216, 335; comparison with Wallace: page 221; Court of Inquiry testimony: page 233; Las Vegas *Gazette* article of December 28, 1880, "The Kid. Interview with Billy Bonney The Best Known Man in New Mexico": pages 293-295; Las Vegas *Gazette* article of December 28, 1880. Untitled - at train station. Pages 296-297; great escape: page 333;)**

McFarland, David F. Reverend. *Ledger: Session Records 1867-1874. Marriages in Santa Fe New Mexico. "Mr. William H. Antrim and Mrs. Catherine McCarty." March 1, 1873.* (Unpublished). Santa Fe, New Mexico: First Presbyterian Church of Santa Fe.

Meadows, John P., Ed. John P. Wilson. *Pat Garrett and Billy the Kid as I Knew Them: Reminiscences of John P. Meadows.* Albuquerque: University of New Mexico Press. 2004.

Mullin, Robert N. *The Boyhood of Billy the Kid.* Monograph 17, Southwestern Studies 5(1). El Paso, Texas: Texas Western Press. University of Texas at El Paso. 1967.

Poe, John W. *The Death of Billy the Kid.* (Introduction by Maurice Garland Fulton). Boston and New York: Houghton Mifflin Company. 1933.

_____. "The Killing of Billy the Kid." (a personal letter written at Roswell, New Mexico to Mr. Charles Goodnight, Goodnight P.C., Texas) July 10, 1917. Earle Vandale Collection. 1813-946. No. 2H475. Center for American History. University of Texas at Austin.

Rakocy, Bill. *Billy the Kid.* El Paso, Texas: Bravo Press. 1985.

Rasch, Phillip J. *Trailing Billy the Kid.* Laramie, Wyoming: National Association for Outlaw and Lawman History, Inc. with University of Wyoming. 1995.

Russell, Randy. *Billy the Kid. The Story - The Trial.* Lincoln, New Mexico: The Crystal Press. 1994.

Siringo, Charles A. *The History of Billy the Kid.* Santa Fe: New Mexico. Privately Printed. 1920.

Tuska, Jon. *Billy the Kid. His Life and Legend.* Westport, Connecticut: Greenwood Press. 1983.

Utley, Robert M. *Billy the Kid. A Short and Violent Life.* Lincoln and London: University of Nebraska Press. 1989.

Weddle, Jerry. *Antrim is My Stepfather's Name. The Boyhood of Billy the Kid.* Monograph 9, Globe, Arizona: Arizona Historical Society. 1993. (**Quotes from Mary Richards about Billy on pages 19-20.**)

Wild, Azariah F. "Daily Reports of U. S. Secret Service Agents, Azariah F. Wild." Microfilm T-915. Record Group 87. Rolls 306 (June 15, 1877 - December 31, 1877), 307 (January 1,1878 - June 30, 1879), 308 (July 1, 1879 - June 30, 1881), 309 ((July 1, 1881 - September 30, 1883), 310 (October 1, 1883 - July 31, 1886). National Archives and Records Department. Department of the Treasury. United States Secret Service. Washington, D. C.

No Author. "The Prisoners Who Saw the Kid Kill Olinger." Herman Weisner Collection. Accession No. MS249. Lincoln County Papers. New Mexico State University Library at Las Cruces. Rio Grande Historical Collections. Box No. 30. Folder Name: The Prisoners who saw the Kid Kill Olinger. Box No. T-8.

WILLIAM BONNEY BIOGRAPHICAL
NEWSPAPER ARTICLES (CHRONOLOGICAL)

No Author. Grant County *Herald.* May 10, 1879. Results of the Lincoln County Grand Jury. (**Also published in the Mesilla *Thirty Four.* Confirmation of the William Bonney testimony and James Dolan and Billy Campbell murder indictments, from page 224 of William Keleher, *Violence in Lincoln County.*)**

No Author. Editorial. "Powerful Gang of Outlaws Harassing the Stockman." Las Vegas *Gazette.* December 3, 1880. (**Condemnation of William Bonney as an outlaw leader; and resulting, according to William Keleher, who quotes it in his**

Violence in Lincoln County, on pages 286-288, as motivating Bonney's response letter of December 12, 1880 to Governor Lew Wallace.)

Wallace, Lew. "Billy the Kid: $500 Reward." December 22, 1880. Las Vegas *Gazette*.

No Author. "A Big Haul! Billy Kid, Dave Rudabaugh, Billy Wilson and Tom Pickett in the Clutches of the Law." *The Las Vegas Daily Optic*. Monday, December 27, 1880. Vol. 2, No. 45. Page 4, Column 2.

No Author. "Outlaws of New Mexico. The Exploits of a Band Headed by a New York Youth. The Mountain Fastness of the Kid and His Followers - War Against a Gang of Cattle Thieves and Murderers - The Frontier Confederates of Brockway, the Counterfeiter." *The Sun*. New York. December 22, 1880. Vol. XLVIII, No. 118, Page 3, Columns 1-2.

No Author. " 'The Kid.' The greatest excitement prevailed yesterday when the news was abroad that Pat Garrett and Frank Stewart had arrived in town bringing with them Billy 'the Kid.' " Las Vegas *Gazette*. December 27, 1880.

Wilcox, Lucius "Lute" M. "Interview With The Kid." *Las Vegas Gazette*. December 28, 1880.(From "Billy the Kid: Las Vegas Newspaper Accounts of His Career, 1880-1881." W.M. Morrison – Books, Waco, Texas. 1958.) **(With "laugh's on me" quote, and mention of the dead horse blocking escape at Stinking Springs.)**

No Author. "A Bay-Mare. Everyone who has heard of Billy 'the kid' has heard of his beautiful bay mare." *Las Vegas Morning Gazette*. Tuesday, January 4, 1881.

No Author. "The Kid. Billy 'the Kid' and Billy Wilson were on Monday taken to Mesilla for Trial." *Las Vegas Morning Gazette*. Tuesday, March 15, 1881.

Newman, Simon. "In the Name of Justice! In the Case of Billy Kid." *Newman's Semi-Weekly*. Saturday, April 2, 1881.

No Author. "Billy the Kid. Seems to be having a stormy journey on his trip Southward." *Las Vegas Morning Gazette*. Tuesday, April 5, 1881.

Koogler, J. H. "Interview with Governor Lew Wallace on 'The Kid.'" *Las Vegas Gazette*. April 28, 1881.

No Author. "The Kid." *Santa Fe Daily New Mexican*. May 1, 1881. Vol. X, No. 32, Page 1, Column 2.

No Author. "Billy Bonney. Advices from Lincoln bring the intelligence of the escape of 'Billy the Kid.' " *Las Vegas Daily Optic*. Monday, May 2, 1881.

No Author. "The Kid's Escape." *Santa Fe Daily New Mexican*. Tuesday Morning, May 3, 1881. Vol. X, No. 33, Page 1, Column 2.

Wallace, Lew. "Billy the Kid. $500 Reward." *Daily New Mexican*. May 3, 1881. Vol. X, No. 33, Page 1, Column 3.

No Author. "Dare Devil Desperado. Pursuit of 'Billy the Kid' has been abandoned." *Las Vegas Daily Optic*. May 4, 1881.

No Author. "More Killing by Kid." Editorial. *Santa Fe Daily New Mexican*. Wednesday Morning, May 4, 1881. Vol. X, No. 34, Page 1, Column 2.

No Author. "Kid was then in Albuquerque ..." *Santa Fe Daily New Mexican*. May 5, 1881. p.4. c. 1.

No Author. "The question if how to deal with desperados who commit murder has but one solution - kill them." *Las Vegas Daily Optic*. Tuesday, May 10, 1881.

No Author. "Billy 'the Kid.' " Las Vegas *Gazette*. Thursday, May 12, 1881.

No Author. "The Kid was in Chloride City ..." *Santa Fe Daily New Mexican*. May 13, 1881. p.4. c. 3.

No Author. "Billy 'the Kid' is in the vicinity of Sumner." Las Vegas *Gazette*. Sunday, May 15, 1881.

No Author. "The Kid is believed to be in the Black Range ..." *Santa Fe Daily New Mexican*. May 19, 1881. p.4. c. 1.

No Author. "Billy the Kid was last seen in Lincoln County ..." *Santa Fe Daily New Mexican*. May 19, 1881. p.4. c. 1.

No Author. " 'Billy the Kid' has been heard from again." *Las Vegas Daily Optic*. Friday, June 10, 1881.

No Author. " 'Billy the Kid.' He is Reported to Have Been Seen on Our Streets Saturday Night." *Las Vegas Daily Optic*. Monday Evening, June 13, 1881. Vol. 2, No. 188, Page 4, Column 2.

Wilcox, Lute, Ed. "Billy the Kid would make an ideal newspaper-man in that he always endeavors to 'get even' with his enemies." *Las Vegas Daily Optic*. Monday Evening, June 13, 1881. Vol. 2, No. 188, Page 4, Column 1.

No Author. "Land of the Petulant Pistol. 'Billy the Kid' as a Killer." *Las Vegas Daily Optic*. Wednesday Evening, June 15, 1881. Vol. 2, No. 190.

No Author. "Barney Mason at Fort Sumner states the 'Kid' is in Local Sheep Camps." *Las Vegas Morning Gazette*. June 16, 1881.

No Author. "The Kid." *Santa Fe Daily New Mexican*. June 16, 1881. Vol. X, No. 90, Page 4, Column 2.

No Author. "Billy the Kid." *Las Vegas Daily Optic*. Thursday, June 28, 1881.

No Author. " 'The Kid' Killed." *Las Vegas Daily Optic*. July 18. 1881.

Wallace, Lew. "Old Incident Recalled," *The* (Crawfordsville) *Weekly News-Review*, December 20, 1901. Lew Wallace Collection. Indiana Historical Society. MO292.

_____. "General Lew Wallace Writes a Romance of 'Billy the Kid' Most Famous Bandit of the Plains: Thrilling Story of the Midnight Meeting Between Gen Wallace, Then Governor of New Mexico, and the Notorious Outlaw, in a Lonesome Hut in Santa Fe." *New York World Magazine*. Sunday, June 8, 1902. Lew Wallace Collection. Indiana Historical Society. MO292.

LEW WALLACE WRITINGS ABOUT/TO WILLIAM BONNEY

LETTERS (CHRONOLOGICAL)

Wallace, Lew. Letter to W H. Bonney. "Come to the house of Squire Wilson ..." March 15, 1879. Indiana Historical Society.Lew Wallace Collection. MO292. Box 4. Folder 6.

_____. Letter to W. H. Bonney. "The escape makes no difference in arrangements ..." March 20, 1879. Indiana Historical Society. Lew Wallace Collection. MO292. Box 4. Folder 6.

_____. Letter to Carl Schurz. "A precious specimen named 'The Kid,' whom the sheriff is holding ..." March 28, 1879. Letters to Carl Schurz. Herman Weisner Collection. Lincoln County Papers. New Mexico State University Library at Las Cruces. Rio Grande Historical Collections. Box No. 7. Folder Name: Interior Dept. 1851 1914. Folder No. L2. From Department of the Interior, Washington, D. C. Territorial Papers, M-364. Group 48. Roll 8.

_____. Letter to Carl Schurz. "A precious specimen nicknamed 'The Kid'." March 31, 1879. Indiana Historical Society. Lew Wallace Collection. MO292. Box 4. Folder 1.

_____. Request for draft of "Billy the Kid" $500 Reward Proclamation. December 13, 1880. Herman Weisner Collection. Lincoln County Papers. New Mexico State University Library at Las Cruces. Rio Grande Historical Collections. Box No. 13. Folder Name: Wallace, Gov. N. M. Box No. W3. From Lew Wallace Papers. New Mexico State Records Center. Santa Fe, New Mexico.

NOTES

Wallace, Lew. "Statements by Kid, made Sunday night March 23, 1879." March 23, 1879. Indiana Historical Society. Lew Wallace Collection. M0292. Box 4. Folder 7.

DEATH WARRANT FOR WILLIAM BONNEY

Wallace, Lew. "To the Sheriff of Lincoln County, Greeting ..." April 30, 1881. Indiana Historical Society. Lew Wallace Collection. M0292. Box 9, Folder 11.

REWARD NOTICES

Wallace, Lew. "Billy the Kid: $500 Reward." Las Vegas *Gazette*. December 22, 1880.

_____. "Billy the Kid. $500 Reward." May 3, 1881. *Daily New Mexican*. Vol. X, No. 33. p. 1, c. 3.

REWARD POSTERS

Greene, Chas. W. "To the New Mexican Printing and Publishing Company." May 20, 1881. (Bill to Lew Wallace for Reward posters for "Kid"). Indiana Historical Society. Lew Wallace Collection. M0292. Box 4, Folder 18.

_____. "I enclose a bill ..." Letter to Lew Wallace for "Kid" wanted posters. June 2, 1881. Indiana Historical Society. Lew Wallace Collection. M0292. Box 4, Folder 18.

Indiana Historical Society. Lew Wallace Collection. M0292. Box 4, Folder 18.

ARTICLES (CHRONOLOGICAL)

"Wallace's Words ..." (interview with Lew Wallace conducted in Washington, D.C. on January 3, 1881), Chicago *The Daily Inter Ocean*, January 4, 1881, p. 2, c. 4.

(Richard Dunham's May 2, 1881 encounter with Billy the Kid), *Santa Fe Daily New Mexican,* May 5, 1881, p.4, c. 3.

(O.L. Houghton's Conversation with Lew Wallace, before May 26, 1881), *The Las Vegas Daily Optic*, May 26, 1881, p.4, c.4.

"Billy the Kid ..." (Lew Wallace interviewed on June 13, 1881), Crawfordsville (Indiana) *Saturday Evening Journal*, June 18, 1881. Indiana Historical Society. Lew Wallace Collection. MO292.

"Street Pickings," *Crawfordsville* (Weekly) *Review – Saturday Edition*, January 6, 1894. Lew Wallace Collection. Indiana Historical Society.

Wallace, Lew. "Old Incident Recalled," *The* (Crawfordsville) *Weekly News-Review*, December 20, 1901. Indiana Historical Society. Lew Wallace Collection. MO292.

_____. "General Lew Wallace Writes a Romance of 'Billy the Kid' Most Famous Bandit of the Plains: Thrilling Story of the Midnight Meeting Between Gen Wallace, Then Governor of New Mexico, and the Notorious Outlaw, in a Lonesome Hut in Santa Fe." *New York World Magazine*. Sunday, June 8, 1902. Page 4. Indiana Historical Society. Lew Wallace Collection. MO292.

HISTORICAL FIGURES (PERIOD)

ANGEL, FRANK WARNER

PRESIDENT HAYES MEETING

Mullin, Robert N. Re: Frank Warner Angel Meeting With President Hayes August, 1878. Binder RNM, VI, M. (Unpublished). Nita Stewart Haley Memorial Museum. Haley Library. Midland, Texas. (Undated).

LETTER

Angel, Frank Warner. "I am in receipt of a copy of a letter sent you by one Wm McMullen ..." Letter to Carl Schurz. September 9, 1878. The Papers of Carl Schurz 1842 - 1906 in 165 Volumes. Library of Congress 1935. General Correspondence July 26, 1878 - October 7, 1878. Shelf Accession No. 14,803. Container 45.

PAPERS

McMullen, William. "In view of the existing troubles in our territory   I appeal ..." Letter to Carl Schurz. August 24, 1878. The Papers of Carl Schurz 1842 - 1906 in 165 Volumes. Library of Congress 1935. General Correspondence. July 26, 1878 - October 7, 1878. Shelf Accession No. 14,803. Container 45.

McPherson, Mary E. Letters and Petitions to President Rutherford B. Hayes re: Removal Governor Axtell and the Santa Fe Ring. Frank Warner Angel File. Microfilm File Case Number 44-4-8-3. Record Group 060. Microfilm Roll M750. National Archives and Records Administration. U.S. Department of Justice. Washington, D. C.

REPORTS

Angel, Frank Warner. "Examination of charges against F. C. Godfroy, Indian Agent, Mescalero, N. M." October 2, 1878. (Report 1981, Inspector E. C. Watkins; Cited as Watkins Report). M 319-20 and L147, 44-4-8. Record Group 075. National Archives and Records Administration. U. S. Department of Justice. Washington, D. C.

_____. In the Matter of the Examination of the Causes and Circumstances of the Death of John H. Tunstall a British Subject. Report filed October 4, 1878. Angel Report. Microfilm File Case Number 44-4-8-3. Record Group 060. Microfilm No. M750. Roll 1. National Archives and Records Administration. U. S. Department of Justice. Washington, D.C.

_____. *In the Matter of the Investigation of the Charges Against S. B. Axtell Governor of New Mexico.* Report and Testimony.

October 3, 1878. Angel Report. Microfilm File No. 44-4-8-3. Record Group 060. Microfilm Roll M750. National Archives and Records Administration. U. S. Department of Interior. Washington, D.C.

_____. *In the Matter of the Lincoln County Troubles. To the Honorable Charles Devens, Attorney General.* October 4, 1878. Angel Report. Microfilm Case File No. 44-4-8-3. Record Group 060. Microfilm Roll M750. National Archives and Records Administration. U. S. Department of Justice. Washington, D. C.

Nolan, Frederick W. "A Sidelight on the Tunstall Murder. *New Mexico Historical Review.* 31 (3). July, 1956. Pages 206-222. (**Documenting his 1954 discovery of the Angel reports.**)

NOTEBOOK

Theisen, Lee Scott. "Frank Warner Angel's Notes on New Mexico Territory, 1878." *Arizona and the West,* 18 (4) (Winter 1976) 333-370.

AXTELL, SAMUEL BEACH

Angel, Frank Warner. *In the Matter of the Investigation of the Charges Against S. B. Axtell Governor of New Mexico.* Report and Testimony. October 3, 1878. Angel Report. Microfilm Case File No. 44-4-8-3. Record Group 060. Microfilm Roll M750. National Archives and Records Administration. U. S. Department of Interior. Washington, D.C.

_____. "The Honorable C. Schurz ... I enclose copies of letter received by me from Gov. Axtell (marked A) and my reply there to (marked B)." August 24, 1878. Microfilm Roll M750. National Archives and Records Administration Record Group 060. Microfilm Number 44-4-8-3. U. S. Department of Interior. Washington D. C.

_____. "The Hon. C. Schurz, Secretary of the Interior, Sir: I have just been favored by a call from W. L. Rynerson Territorial Dist. Attorney 3rd District New Mexico - in the interest of Gov. Axtell." (Letter) September 6, 1878. Microfilm M750. National Archives and Records Administration Record Group 060. Microfilm Number 44-4-8-3. U. S. Department of Interior. Washington D. C.

Axtell, Samuel B. "Hon. Carl Schurz. Sir: I have today mailed to you a reply to the charges on file in your Dept against me." (Letter regarding charges in Colfax County). Microfilm Roll M750. National Archives and Records Administration Record Group 060. Microfilm Case Number 44-4-8-3. U. S. Department of Interior. Washington , D. C.

_____. "To the President. I am unable to enforce the law ..." (Telegram). March 3, 1878. Microfilm Roll M750. National Archives and Records Administration Record Group 060. Microfilm Case File Number 44-4-8-3. U.S. Department of Interior. Washington D. C.

Bradstreet, George P. "Referring to the nomination of Sam'l B. Axtell of Ohio to be Chief Justice of the Supreme Court of New Mexico ... he is alleged to have been removed by President Hayes ..." (Presentation to the U. S. Senate Chamber). Microfilm Roll M750. National Archives and Records Administration Record Group 060. Microfilm Case Number 44-4-8-3. U. S. Department of Interior. Washington D. C.

Elkins, Stephen B. "To the President. Referring to a conversation had with you last week ... Hon S. Elkins favors appointment Axtell, Ex Gov. as Gov'r of New Mexico". (Letter) March 23, 1881. (Received Executive Mansion April 6, 1881). Microfilm Roll M750. National Archives and Records Administration Record Group 060. Microfilm Number 44-4-8-3. U. S. Department of Interior. Washington, D.C.

Springer, Frank. "Hon Carl Schurz, Secretary of the Interior. Sir: I endorse herewith, directed to the President charges against S. B. Axtell Governor of New Mexico ..." (Letter) June 10, 1878. Frank Warner Angel File. Microfilm Roll M750. National Archives and Records Administration Record Group 060. Microfilm Case Number 44-4-8-3. U. S. Department of Interior. Washington D. C.

BOWDRE, CHARLES

Regulator. "Mr. Walz. Sir ..." Letter to Edgar Walz. July 13, 1878. Adjutant General's Office. File 1405 AGO 1878. (Attributed to Charles Bowdre in Maurice Garland Fulton, *History of the Lincoln County War*. Tucson: University of Arizona Press. 1975. pages 246-247, and Frederick Nolan, *The Lincoln County War: A Documentary History*, page 310.)

BRADY, WILLIAM

Brady, William. Affidavit of July 2, 1876 concerning appointment as Administrator for the Emil Fritz Estate. Copied from the original District Court Record. In private collection.

_____. Affidavit of August 22, 1876 documenting business debts to L. G. Murphy and Co. pertaining to the Emil Fritz Estate. Copied from the original District Court Record. In private collection.

_____. Affidavit of July _, 1876 of Resignation as Emil Fritz Estate Administrator. Copied from the original District Court Record. In private collection.

_____. Affidavit of August 22, 1876 confirming giving Alexander McSween the books of the L.G. Murphy Company for the purpose of making business debt collections. Copied from the original District Court Record. In private collection.

_____. "List of Articles Inventoried by Wm Brady sheriff in the suit of Charles Fritz & Emilie Scholand vs A.A. McSween now in the dwelling house belonging to A.A. McSween." (undated) In private collection.

Bristol, Warren. "Action of Assumpsit to command Sheriff Brady of Lincoln County to attach goods of Alexander A. McSween." February 7, 1878. District Court Record. (Private Collection).

_____. Preprinted form for "Writ of Attachment" (Printed and sold at the office of the Mesilla News) filled out to command the Sheriff of Lincoln County to attach goods of Alexander McSween for a suit of damages for ten thousand dollars. February 7, 1878. District Court Record. (Private Collection).

Lavash, Donald R. *Sheriff William Brady. Tragic Hero of the Lincoln County War.* Santa Fe, New Mexico: Sunstone Press. 1986.

CASEY FAMILY

Klasner, Lilly. Eve Ball. Ed. *My Girlhood Among Outlaws.* Tucson, Arizona: The University of Arizona Press. 1988.

CATRON, THOMAS BENTON

Cleaveland, Norman, *A Synopsis of the Great New Mexico Cover-up.* Self-printed. 1989.

_____ . *The Great Santa Fe Cover-up. Based on a Talk given Before the Santa Fe Historical Society on November 1, 1978.* Self-printed. 1982.

_____. *The Morleys - Young Upstarts on the Southwest Frontier.* Albuquerque, New Mexico: Calvin Horn Publisher, Inc. 1971.

Dunham, Harold H. "New Mexican Land Grants with Special Reference to the Title Papers of the Maxwell Grant." *New Mexico Historical Review.* (January, 1955) Vol. 70. No. 1. pp. 1 - 23.

Hefferan, Vioalle Clark. *Thomas Benton Catron.* Albuquerque, New Mexico: University of New Mexico. Zimmerman Library. Unpublished Thesis for the Degree of Master of Arts. 1940.

Keleher, William A. *The Maxwell Land Grant. A New Mexico Item.* Albuquerque, New Mexico: University of New Mexico Press. 1964.

Lamar, Howard Robert N. *The Far Southwest 1846 - 1912. A Territorial History.* New Haven and London: Yale University Press. 1966.

Montoya, María E. *Translating Property. The Maxwell Land Grant and the Conflict Over Land in the American West, 1840-1900.* Berkeley and Los Angeles: University of California Press. 2002.

Mullin, Robert N. "A Specimen of Catron's Dirty Work. Sworn Affidavit of Samuel Davis." October 1, 1878. Binder RNM IV, EE. (Unpublished). Midland, Texas: Nita Stewart Nita Stewart Haley Memorial Museum. Haley Library. Midland, Texas.

_____. "Catron Embarrassed Throughout His Life by an Affliction." (Date Unknown). Binder RNM, IV, M. (Unpublished). Nita Stewart Haley Memorial Museum. Haley Library. Midland, Texas.

534

_____. Catron letter to Governor S. B. Axtell to intervene in
Lincoln County. May 30, 1878. Binder RNM IV, EE (Unpublished).
Nita Stewart Haley Memorial Museum. Haley Library. Midland,
Texas.

_____. "Prior to Lincoln County War Catron Had Defended
Colonel Dudley." (No Date). Notes from "Lincoln County War Cast of
Characters." Nita Stewart Haley Memorial Museum. Haley Library.
Midland, Texas.

Murphy, Lawrence R. *Lucien Bonaparte Maxwell. Napoleon of the
Southwest.* Norman: University of Oklahoma Press. 1983.

Pearson, Jim Berry. *The Maxwell Land Grant.* Norman: University of
Oklahoma Press. 1961.

Sluga, Mary Elizabeth. *Political Life of Thomas Benton Catron 1896-
1912.* Albuquerque, New Mexico: University of New Mexico.
Zimmerman Library. Unpublished Thesis for the Degree of Master of
Arts. 1941.

Taylor, Morris F. *O. P. McMains and the Maxwell Land Grant Conflict.*
Tucson, Arizona: The University of Arizona Press. 1979. (**Page 36,
Thomas Benton Catron as legal counsel for Maxwell Land
Grant Company.**)

Westphall, Victor. "Fraud and Implications of Fraud in the Land Grants
of New Mexico." *New Mexico Historical Review.* 1974. Vol. XLIX,
No. 3. 189 - 218.

_____. *Thomas Benton Catron and His Era.* Tucson, Arizona:
University of Arizona Press. 1973.

Wooden, John Paul. *Thomas Benton Catron and New Mexico Politics
1866-1921.* Albuquerque, New Mexico: University of New Mexico.
Zimmerman Library. Unpublished Thesis for the Degree of Master of
Arts. 1959.

No Author. Catron Files Statement of Sole ownership of Carrizozo Ranch
in Tax Dispute Case. Herman Weisner Collection. Lincoln County
Papers: New Mexico State University Library at Las Cruces. Rio
Grande Historical Collections. Box No. 2. Folder Name "T. B. Catron
Tax Troubles." Folder No. C-8.

CAYPLESS, EDGAR

Keleher, William A. *Violence in Lincoln County 1869-1881.* Albuquerque,
New Mexico: University of New Mexico Press. 1957. (**Pages 320-321,
the lost William Bonney letter of April 15, 1881 to Attorney
Edgar Caypless is presented; crediting the original letter to
the Billy the Kid Museum in Mesilla as published by its
founder, George Griggs, in *History of the Mesilla Valley*.
On page 320 is also the *Las Vegas Gazette* article of March 12,
1881 about Billy's replevin case with Caypless for his mare.**)

CHAPMAN, HUSTON

Chapman, Huston. Letter to Governor Lew. Wallace. November 29, 1878. Herman Weisner Collection. Lincoln County Papers: New Mexico State University Library at Las Cruces. Rio Grande Historical Collections. Box No. 2. Folder Name H. J. Chapman. Box No. C-9.

CHISUM, JOHN SIMPSON

Hinton, Harwood P., Jr. "John Simpson Chisum, 1877-84." *New Mexico Historical Review* 31(3) (July 1956): 177 - 205; 31(4) (October 1956): 310 - 337; 32(1) (January 1957): 53 - 65.

Klasner, Lilly. Eve Ball. Ed. *My Girlhood Among Outlaws.* Tucson, Arizona: The University of Arizona Press. 1988.

CHISUM, SALLIE

Chisum, Sallie. Diary 1878. Historical Center for Southwest New Mexico, Roswell. Archives. Sallie Chisum Diary. Page 142. (**Reference to "Willie Bonney."**)

Klasner, Lilly. Eve Ball. Ed. *My Girlhood Among Outlaws.* Tucson, Arizona: The University of Arizona Press. 1988.

COE FAMILY

Coe, George. Doyce B. Nunis, Jr. Ed. *Frontier Fighter. The Autobiography of George Coe Who Fought and Rode With Billy the Kid.* Chicago: R.R. Donnelley and Sons Company. 1984. (Original copyright, 1934.) (**Quote about Billy's seeming "college-bred" and singing and dancing, pages 49-50; bonfire scene, pages 90-91; "we'll die first" quote, page 163.**)

Coe, Frank. "He was brave and reliable ..." *El Paso Times* of September 16, 1923. (Excerpt in Frederick Nolan's *The West of Billy the Kid.* page 155.)

_____"He was a wonder ..." Letter to William Steele Dean. August 3, 1926. Museum of New Mexico History Library. Santa Fe. Unpublished. (Excerpt in Frederick Nolan's *The West of Billy the Kid.* page 135.)

Coe, Wilbur. *Ranch on the Ruidoso. The Story of a Pioneer Family in New Mexico, 1871 - 1968.* New York: Alfred A. Knopf. 1968.

DEDRICK BROTHERS

No Author. "Arrests of Dedricks. Legal Documents." Herman Weisner Collection. Lincoln County Papers. New Mexico State University Library at Las Cruces. Rio Grande Historical Collections. Box 1. Folder Name Lincoln County Bonds. Folder No. B-8.

Upham, Elizabeth. (Related by marriage to Daniel Dedrick). Personal interviews. 1998.

Upham, Marquita. (Relative by marriage to Daniel Dedrick). Personal interview. 1998.

DOLAN, JAMES J.

Angel, Frank Warner. *In the Matter of the Examination of the Causes and Circumstances of the Death of John H. Tunstall a British Subject.* Report filed October 4, 1878. Angel Report. Microfilm File Case Number 44-4-8-3. Record Group 060. Microfilm No. M750. Roll 1. National Archives and Records Administration. U.S. Department of Justice. Washington, D.C. (James J. Dolan Deposition. June 20, 1878. pp. 235-247.)

Dolan, James. "Confidential Letter to Lew Wallace." December 31, 1878. Herman Weisner Collection. Lincoln County Papers: New Mexico State University Library at Las Cruces. Rio Grande Historical Collections. Box No. 4. Folder Name. Fulton's File. Folder No. F3.

Murphy, Lawrence G. "Will of Lawrence G. Murphy." Herman Weisner Collection. Lincoln County Papers. Accession No. MS 249. New Mexico State University Library at Las Cruces. Rio Grande Historical Collections. Box No. 11. Folder Name: Murphy, Lawrence G. No. P15.

Nolan, Frederick. Biographical information on James Dolan. Unpublished. Personal communication 2005.

No Author. *Proceedings of a Court of Inquiry in the Case of Col. N.A.M. Dudley (May 2, 1879-July 5, 1879).* File Number QQ1284. (Boxes 3304, 3305, 3305A). Court Martial Case Files 1809-1894. Records of the Office of the Judge Advocate General – Army. Record Group 153. National Archives and Records Administration. Old Military and Civil Branch. Washington, D.C. (James J. Dolan Testimony. June 5, 1879.)

Wild, Azariah F. "Daily Reports of U. S. Secret Service Agents, Azariah F. Wild." Microfilm T-915. Record Group 87. Rolls 307 (January 1,1878 - June 30, 1879) and 308 (July 1, 1879 - June 30, 1881). National Archives and Records Department. Department of the Treasury. United States Secret Service. Washington, D. C.

DUDLEY, NATHAN AUGUSTUS MONROE

Kaye, E. Donald. *Nathan Augustus Monroe Dudley: Rogue, Hero, or Both?* Parker, Colorado: Outskirts Press, Inc. 2007.

No Author. *Dudley Court of Inquiry. (May 2, 1879 - July 5, 1879).* Record No. 16W3/16/28/6. Boxes 1923 - 1923A. File No. QQ1284. National Archives and Records Administration. Old Military and Civil Branch. Records of the Office of the Judge Advocate General. Washington, D. C.

ELKINS, STEPHEN BENTON

BIOGRAPHY

Cleaveland, Norman, *A Synopsis of the Great New Mexico Cover-up*. Self-printed. 1989.

_____ . *The Great Santa Fe Cover-up. Based on a Talk given Before the Santa Fe Historical Society on November 1, 1978*. Self-printed. 1982.

_____. *The Morleys - Young Upstarts on the Southwest Frontier*. Albuquerque, New Mexico: Calvin Horn Publisher, Inc. 1971.

Lambert, Oscar Doane. *Stephen Benton Elkins. American Foursquare*. Pittsburgh, Pennsylvania: University of Pittsburg Press. 1955.

Montoya, María E. *Translating Property. The Maxwell Land Grant and the Conflict Over Land in the American West, 1840-1900*. Berkeley and Los Angeles: University of California Press. 2002.

Taylor, Morris F. *O. P. McMains and the Maxwell Land Grant Conflict*. Tucson, Arizona: The University of Arizona Press. 1979. (**Page 36, Stephen Benton Elkins as president of the Maxwell Land Grant Company.**)

Westphall, Victor. *Thomas Benton Catron and His Era*. Tucson, Arizona: University of Arizona Press. 1973.

LETTERS

Devens, Charles. "To honorable S. B. Elkins re. T. B. Catron continuing to act as U. S. Attorney." November 12, 1878. Angel Report. Microfilm File Case No. 44-4-8-3. Record Group 060. National Records and Archives Administration. Microfilm No. M750. Roll 1. U. S. Department of Justice. Washington, D. C.

Elkins, Stephen B. "Asking delay of action upon charges against U.S. Atty. Catron ..." September 24, 1878. Angel Report. Microfilm File Case No. 44-4-8-3. Record Group 060. National Records and Archives Administration. Microfilm No. M750. Roll 1. U.S. Department of Justice. Washington, D. C.

_____. "Regarding Attorney General's decision on T.B. Catron." Letter. September___, 1878. Angel Report. Microfilm File Case No. 44-4-8-3. Record Group 060. National Records and Archives Administration. Microfilm No. M750. Roll 1. U.S. Department of Justice. Washington, D. C.

_____. "Relative to resignation of T. B. Catron U. S. Attorney." Letter. November 10, 1878. Angel Report. Microfilm File Case No. 44-4-8-3. Record Group 060. National Records and Archives Administration. Microfilm No. M750. Roll 1. U.S. Department of Justice. Washington, D. C.

_____. "To the President. Referring to a conversation had with you last week ... Hon. S. B. Elkins favors appointment Axtell, ExGov. as Gov'r of New Mexico." (Letter) March 23, 1881. (Received Executive Mansion April 6, 1881). Microfilm Roll M750. National Archives and Records Administration. Record Group 060. Microfilm File No. 44-4-8-3. U.S. Department of Interior. Washington, D. C.

EVANS, JESSIE

McCright, Grady E. and James H. Powell. _Jessie Evans: Lincoln County Badman._ College Station, Texas: Creative Publishing Company. 1983.

No Author. "Charges against Jessie Evans and John Kinney." Doña Ana County Criminal Docket Book. August 18, 1875 to November 7, 1878. Herman Weisner Collection. Accession No. MS249. Lincoln County Papers: New Mexico State University Library at Las Cruces. Rio Grande Historical Collections. Box No. 13. Folder Name: Venue, Change of. Folder No. V3.

FOUNTAIN, ALBERT JENNINGS

Gibson, A. M. _The Life and Death of Colonel Albert Jennings Fountain._ Norman: University of Oklahoma Press. 1965.

FRITZ FAMILY (CHARLES FRITZ AND EMILIE SCHOLAND)

Fritz, Charles. Affidavit of September 18, 1876 claiming that Emil Fritz had a will. Probate Court Record. In private collection.

_____. Affidavit of September 26, 1876 Authorizing Alexander McSween to Receive Payments for the Emil Fritz Estate. Probate Court Record. In private collection.

_____. Affidavit of December 7, 1877 to order Alexander McSween to pay the Emil Fritz insurance policy money. Probate Court Record. In private collection.

_____. Affidavit sworn before John Crouch, Clerk of Doña Ana District Court, for Writ of Attachment issued against property of Alexander A. McSween. Probate Court Record. February 6, 1878. In private collection.

_____ and Emilie Scholand. Attachment Bond sworn before John Crouch, Clerk of Doña Ana District Court, against Alexander A. McSween for indebtedness to them. February 6, 1878. (Private Collection).

Scholand, Emilie and Charles Fritz. Affidavit of September 26, 1876 appointing McSween to collect debts for the Emil Fritz Estate. Copied from the original District Court Record. In private collection.

Scholand, Emilie. Affidavit of December 21, 1877 Accusing Alexander McSween of Embezzlement. Copied from the original District Court Record. In private collection.

No Author. Diagram showing parcels of land to each of the heirs of Emil Fritz. Herman Weisner Collection. Accession No. MS249. Lincoln County Papers: New Mexico State University Library at Las Cruces. Rio Grande Historical Collections. Box No. 11. Folder Name. Charles Fritz Estate. Box No. P1

GARRETT, PATRICK FLOYD

Garrett, Pat F. *The Authentic Life of Billy the Kid The Noted Desperado of the Southwest, Whose Deeds of Daring and Blood Made His Name a Terror in New Mexico, Arizona, and Northern Mexico.* Santa Fe, New Mexico: New Mexico Printing and Publishing Co. 1882.

Metz, Leon C. *Pat Garrett. The Story of a Western Lawman.* Norman: University of Oklahoma Press. 1974.

Mullin, Robert N. "Killing of Joe Briscoe." Letter to Eve Ball. January 31, 1964. (Unpublished). Binder RNM, VI, H. Nita Stewart Haley Memorial Museum. Haley Library. Midland, Texas.

_____. "Pat Garrett. Two Forgotten Killings." *Password.* X(2) (Summer 1965). pp. 57 - 65.

_____. "Skelton Glen's Manuscript Entitled 'Pat Garrett As I Knew Him on the Buffalo Ranges.'" (Unpublished). Binder RNM, III B, 20. Nita Stewart Haley Memorial Museum. Haley Library. Midland, Texas.

Upson, Ash. Letter from Garrett's Ranch to Upson's Nephew, Frank S. Downs, Esq. re. "His Drawers and pigeon holes of his desk were full of letters, deeds, bills, notes, agreements, & C. I have burned bushels of them and am not through yet." October 20, 1888. (Unpublished). Binder RNM, V1-MM. Nita Stewart Haley Memorial Museum. Haley Library. Midland, Texas.

Wild, Azariah F. "Daily Reports of U. S. Secret Service Agents, Azariah F. Wild." Microfilm T-915. Record Group 87. Rolls 306 (June 15, 1877 - December 31, 1877), 307 (January 1,1878 - June 30, 1879), 308 (July 1, 1879 - June 30, 1881), 309 (July 1, 1881 - September 30, 1883), 310 (October 1, 1883 - July 31, 1886). National Archives and Records Department. Department of the Treasury. United States Secret Service. Washington, D. C.

ARTICLE (Lew Wallace Collection. Indiana Historical Society) "[Pat F. Garrett] Recommended by Gen. Wallace," *The* (Crawfordsville) *Weekly News-Review*, December 20, 1901. Collection Indiana Historical Society. Lew Wallace Collection. (M0292).

GILBERT, ROBERT M.

Gilbert, Robert M. Letter to Lew Wallace. June 1, 1879. Collection Indiana Historical Society. Lew Wallace Collection. M0292. Box 4, Folder 11. (**On Lady Liberty stationery.**)

GONZALES, FLORENCIO

Gonzales, Florencio. Letter to Governor Lew Wallace. October 8, 1878. Collection Indiana Historical Society. Lew Wallace Collection. M0292. Box 3, Folder 15. (**Lincoln County Probate Judge residing in San Patricio. His stationery's embossed seal is different from the lady's head seal on the "Billie" letter and the signed W.H. Bonney letter of March 20, 1879 from San Patricio.**)

HATCH, EDWARD

Hatch, Edward. Letter to Governor Lew Wallace. March 6, 1879. Indiana Historical Society. Lew Wallace Collection. M0292. Box 4, Folder 4. (**About tracking Bonney, but used as sample of excellent Spencerian penmanship.**)

HOOKER, HENRY CLAY

Bailey, Lynn R. *Henry Clay Hooker and the Sierra Bonita*. Tucson, Arizona: Westernlore Press. 1998.

HOYT, HENRY F.

Bonney, William H. Bill of Sale to Henry Hoyt. October 24, 1878. Collection of Panhandle-Plains Historical Museum. Canyon, Texas. (Item No. X1974-98/1)

Hoyt, Henry F. Handwritten note on back of Bill of Sale. 1927. Collection Indiana Historical Society. Lew Wallace Collection. M0292, Box 14, Folder 11.

_____ . Letter to Lew Wallace Jr. "This time it is me that is apologizing ..." April 27, 1929. (Unpublished). Collection Indiana Historical Society. Lew Wallace Collection. M0292, Box 14, Folder 11.

_____ . *A Frontier Doctor*. Boston and New York: Houghton Mifflin Company. 1929. (**Describes Billy's superior abilities, pp. 93-94.**)

JONES, BARBARA ("MA'AM") AND FAMILY

Ball, Eve. *Ma'am Jones of the Pecos*. Tucson: University of Arizona Press. 1969.

KINNEY, JOHN

Mullin, Robert N. "Here Lies John Kinney." *Journal of Arizona History.* 14 (Autumn 1973). pp. 223 - 242.

No Author. "Charges against Jessie Evans and John Kinney." Doña Ana County Criminal Docket Book. August 18, 1875 to November 7, 1878. Herman Weisner

Collection. Accession No. MS249. Lincoln County Papers: New Mexico State University Library at Las Cruces. Rio Grande Historical Collections. Box 13. Folder Name: File Name. Venue, Change of. Folder No. V-3.

No Author. "Obituary of John Kinney." *Prescott Courier.* August 30, 1919. Obituary Section.

No Author. Obituary. "Over the Range Goes Another Pioneer." *Journal Miner.* Tuesday Morning, August 26, 1919.

LEONARD, IRA

Nolan, Frederick. "Biography and Photograph of Ira Leonard." Unpublished. Personal communication 2005.

No Author. *Proceedings of a Court of Inquiry in the Case of Col. N.A.M. Dudley (May 2, 1879 - July 5, 1879).* File Number QQ1284. (Boxes 3304, 3305, 3305A). Court Martial Case Files 1809-1894. Records of the Office of the Judge Advocate General - Army. Record Group 153. National Archives and Records Administration. Old Military and Civil Branch. Washington, D.C.

See also: WALLACE, LEW for Ira Leonard letters

MATTHEWS, JACOB BASIL "BILLY"

Fleming, Elvis E. *J.B. Matthews. Biography of a Lincoln County Deputy.* Las Cruces, New Mexico: Yucca Tree Press. 1999.

MAXWELL FAMILY

Cleaveland, Norman. *The Morleys - Young Upstarts on the Southwest Frontier.* Albuquerque, New Mexico: Calvin Horn Publisher, Inc. 1971.

Dunham, Harold H. "New Mexican Land Grants with Special Reference to the Title Papers of the Maxwell Grant." *New Mexico Historical Review.* (January 1955) Vol. 30, No. 1. pp. 1 - 23.

Freiberger, Harriet. *Lucien Maxwell: Villain or Visionary.* Santa Fe, New Mexico: Sunstone Press. 1999.

Keleher, William A. *The Maxwell Land Grant. A New Mexico Item.* Albuquerque, New Mexico: University of New Mexico Press. 1964.

Lamar, Howard Roberts. *The Far Southwest 1846 - 1912. A Territorial History.* New Haven and London: Yale University Press. 1966.

Montoya, María E. *Translating Property. The Maxwell Land Grant and the Conflict Over Land in the American West, 1840-1900.* Berkeley and Los Angeles, California: University of California Press. 2002.

Murphy, Lawrence R. *Lucien Bonaparte Maxwell. Napoleon of the Southwest.* Norman: University of Oklahoma Press. 1983.

Pearson, Jim Berry. *The Maxwell Land Grant.* Norman: University of Oklahoma Press. 1961.

Poe, Sophie. *Buckboard Days.* Albuquerque, New Mexico: University of New Mexico Press. 1964.

Taylor, Morris F. *O. P. McMains and the Maxwell Land Grant Conflict.* Tucson, Arizona: The University of Arizona Press. 1979.

No Author. "Mrs. Paula M. Jaramillo, 65 Died Here Tuesday." *The Fort Sumner Leader.* Official Newspaper County of De Baca. December 20, 1929. No. 1158, Page 1, Column 1.

McKINNEY, THOMAS "KIP"

Grey, Frederick. W. *Seeking Fortune in America.* Chapter XIV. Pages 118-119. London: Smith, Elder & Co. 1912. (**McKinney's tale of Billy the Kid's killing occurring in Paulita Maxwell's bedroom rather than her brother's.**)

McPHERSON, MARY TIBBLES

Cleaveland, Norman, *A Synopsis of the Great New Mexico Cover-up.* Self-printed. 1989.

_____ . *The Great Santa Fe Cover-up.* Based on a Talk given Before the Santa Fe Historical Society on November 1, 1978. Self-printed. 1982.

_____. *The Morleys - Young Upstarts on the Southwest Frontier.* Albuquerque, New Mexico: Calvin Horn Publisher, Inc. 1971. (**Pages 132, 141, 145 document Mary McPherson's Washington, D.C. ally, Attorney W.B. Matchett.**)

McPherson, Mary E. Letters and Petitions to President Rutherford B. Hayes re: Removal Governor Axtell and the Santa Fe Ring. Frank Warner Angel File. Microfilm File Case Number 44-4-8-3. Record Group 060. Microfilm Roll M750. National Archives and Records Administration. U.S. Department of Justice. Washington, D. C.

Taylor, Morris F. *O. P. McMains and the Maxwell Land Grant Conflict.* Tucson, Arizona: The University of Arizona Press. 1979.

McSWEEN, ALEXANDER

Angel, Frank Warner. *In the Matter of the Examination of the Causes and Circumstances of the Death of John H. Tunstall a British Subject.* Report filed October 4, 1878. Angel Report. Microfilm File Case Number 44-4-8-3. Record Group 060. Microfilm No. M750. Roll 1. National Archives and Records Administration. U. S. Department of Justice. Washington, D.C. Deposition given June 6, 1878, pp. 5-183.

_____. *In the Matter of the Lincoln County Troubles. To the Honorable Charles Devens, Attorney General.* October 4, 1878. Angel Report. Microfilm File Case Number 44-4-8-3. Record Group 060. Microfilm No. M750. Roll 1. National Archives and Records Administration. U. S. Department of Justice. Washington, D. C.

Bristol, Warren. Action of Assumpsit to command Sheriff of Lincoln County to attach goods of Alexander A. McSween. February 7, 1878. District Court Record. (Private Collection).

_____. Preprinted form in his name for "Writ of Attachment" (Printed and sold at the office of the Mesilla News) filled out to command the Sheriff of Lincoln County to attach goods of Alexander McSween for a suit of damages for ten thousand dollars. February 7, 1878. (Private Collection).

Fritz, Charles. Affidavit sworn before John Crouch, Clerk of Doña Ana District Court, for Writ of Attachment issued against property of Alexander A. McSween. Probate Court Record. February 6, 1878. (Private Collection).

Fritz, Charles and Emilie Scholand. Attachment Bond sworn before John Crouch, Clerk of Doña Ana District Court, against Alexander A. McSween for indebtedness to them. February 6, 1878. (Private Collection).

McSween, Alexander, *Will. February 25, 1878.* Herman Weisner Collection. Accession No. MS249. Lincoln County Papers. New Mexico State University Library at Las Cruces. Rio Grande Historical Collections. Box No. 10. Folder Name: Will and Testament A. McSween. Box No. M15.

MEADOWS, JOHN P.

Meadows, John P. "Billy the Kid to John P. Meadows on the Peñasco, c. May 1-2, 1881." *Roswell Daily Record. February 16, 1931. Page 6.*

Meadows, John P. Ed. John P. Wilson. *Pat Garrett and Billy the Kid as I Knew Them: Reminiscences of John P. Meadows.* Albuquerque: University of New Mexico Press. 2004.

PATRÓN, JUAN

Patrón, Juan. First letter to Lew Wallace onMarch 29, 1879. Indiana Historical Society. Lew Wallace Collection. M0292. Box 4, Folder 7. (**On Lady Liberty stationery; best example of seal.**)
_____. Second letter to Lew Wallace onMarch 29, 1879. Indiana Historical Society. Lew Wallace Collection. M0292. Box 4, Folder 7. (**On Lady Liberty stationery; best example of seal.**)
_____. Letter to Rosa. April 12, 1879. Indiana Historical Society. Lew Wallace Collection. M0292. Box 4, Folder 9. (**On national capitol building stationery.**)

POE, JOHN WILLIAM

Poe, John W. "The Killing of Billy the Kid." (a personal letter written at Roswell, New Mexico to Mr. Charles Goodnight, Goodnight P.C., Texas) July 10, 1917.
_____. *The Death of Billy the Kid*. (Introduction by Maurice Garland Fulton). Boston and New York: Houghton Mifflin Company. 1933.
Poe, Sophie. *Buckboard Days*. Albuquerque, New Mexico: University of New Mexico Press. 1964.

SHERMAN, JOHN

Sherman, John. Letter to Governor Lew Wallace. October 4, 1878. Indiana Historical Society. Lew Wallace Collection. M0292. Box 3, Folder 15. (**First reference of "outlaw," Billy Bonney, to Governor Wallace.**)

SINGER, FRANK

Cleaveland, Norman, *A Synopsis of the Great New Mexico Cover-up*. Self-printed. 1989.
_____ . *The Great Santa Fe Cover-up. Based on a Talk given Before the Santa Fe Historical Society on November 1, 1978*. Self-printed. 1982.
_____. *The Morleys - Young Upstarts on the Southwest Frontier*. Albuquerque, New Mexico: Calvin Horn Publisher, Inc. 1971.
Taylor, Morris F. *O. P. McMains and the Maxwell Land Grant Conflict*. Tucson, Arizona: The University of Arizona Press. 1979.

TAYLOR, GEORGE

Taylor, George. Letter to Lew Wallace. April 25, 1879. Indiana Historical Society, Lew Wallace Collection. MO292. Box 4, Folder 9. (**On Lady Liberty stationery.**)

TUNSTALL, JOHN HENRY

Angel, Frank Warner. *In the Matter of the Examination of the Causes and Circumstances of the Death of John H. Tunstall a British Subject.* Report filed October 4, 1878. Angel Report. Microfilm File Case Number 44-4-8-3. Record Group 060. Microfilm Roll No. M750. Roll 1. National Archives and Records Administration. U. S. Department of Justice. Washington, D.C.

_____. *In the Matter of the Lincoln County Troubles. To the Honorable Charles Devens, Attorney General October 4, 1878.* Angel Report. Microfilm Case File No. 44-4-8-3. Record Group 060. Microfilm Roll No. M750. National Archives and Records Administration. U. S. Department of Justice. Washington, D. C.

Nolan, Frederick W. *The Life and Death of John Henry Tunstall.* Albuquerque, New Mexico: University of New Mexico Press. 1965.

Nolan, Frederick W. "A Sidelight on the Tunstall Murder. *New Mexico Historical Review.* 31 (3). July, 1956. Pages 206-222.

WALLACE, LEW

BOOKS - BIOGRAPHICAL

Jones, Oakah L. "Lew Wallace: Hoosier Governor of Territorial New Mexico. 1878-81." *New Mexico Historical Review. 59(1)* (January, 1984).

Morsberger, Robert E. and Katherine M. Morsberger. *Lew Wallace: Militant Romantic.* New York: McGraw - Hill Book Company. 1980.

Stephens, Gail. "Shadow of Shiloh: Major General Lew Wallace in the Civil War." Indianapolis: Indiana Historical Society Press. 2010.

Wallace, Lew. *An Autobiography. Vol. I.* New York and London: Harper and Brothers Publishers. 1997.

_____. *An Autobiography. Vol. II.* New York and London: Harper and Brothers Publishers. 1997.

PAPERS

Wallace, Lew. Collected Papers. Microfilm Project by the National Historical Publications Commission. Microfilm Roll No. 99. Santa Fe, New Mexico: New Mexico Records Center and Archives. 1974.

Wallace, Lew. Lew Wallace Collection. Indiana Historical Society. M0292.

Wallace, Lew. Wallace Collection. Bloomington, Indiana, University of Indiana Lilly Library. Mss.

NOTES

Wallace, Lew. "Statements by Kid, made Sunday night March 23, 1879." March 23, 1879. Indiana Historical Society. Lew Wallace Collection. M0922. Box 4. Folder 7.

LETTERS (See Bonney, William for that correspondence)

TO JOHN "SQUIRE" WILSON

Wallace, Lew. "I enclose a note for Bonney." March 20, 1879. Indiana Historical Society. Lew Wallace Collection. M0922. Box 4. Folder 6.

TO CARL SCHURZ

Wallace, Lew. "As to the basis of the request which I have to prefer ..." October 5, 1878. Indiana Historical Society. Lew Wallace Collection. M0292. Box 3, Folder 15.

_____ . "I have the honor to report that affairs of the Territory are moving on quietly ..." December 21, 1878. Letter to Carl Schurz. The Papers of Carl Schurz 1842 - 1906 in 165 Volumes. Library of Congress 1935. General Correspondence November 30, 1878. Shelf No. 14,803. Container 47.

_____. Letter to Carl Schurz. "A precious specimen nick-named 'The Kid'." March 31, 1879. Lew Wallace Collection. Indiana Historical Society. MO292. Box 4. Folder 1.

FROM AND TO EDWARD HATCH

Hatch, Edward. Letter to Lew Wallace. March 6, 1879. Indiana Historical Society. Lew Wallace Collection. M0292. Box 4, Folder 4.

Wallace, Lew. Letter to General Edward Hatch. March 6, 1879. Indiana Historical Society. Lew Wallace Collection. Box 9, Folder 10. (**Written on dead John Tunstall's letterhead stationery.**)

TO AND FROM IRA LEONARD:

Leonard, Ira. "... the assassination of H.I. Chapman ..." February 24, 1879. Indiana Historical Society. Lew Wallace Collection. MO292.

Wallace, Lew. "It is important to take steps to protect the coming court." April 6, 1879. Indiana Historical Society. Lew Wallace Collection. MO292.

_____. "To work trying to do a little good, but with the world against you, requires the will of a martyr. Indiana Historical Society. Lew Wallace Collection. MO292.

Leonard, Ira. "He is bent on going for the Kid ..." April 20, 1879. Indiana Historical Society. Lew Wallace Collection. MO292.

_____. "... the Santa Fe Ring that has been so long an incubus on the government of this territory." May 20, 1879. Indiana Historical Society. Lew Wallace Collection. MO292.

_____. "... we are pouring 'hot shot' into Dudley ..." May 23, 1879. Indiana Historical Society. Lew Wallace Collection. MO292.

_____. "I am thoroughly and completely disgusted with their proceedings." June 6, 1879. Indiana Historical Society. Lew Wallace Collection. MO292.

_____. "... they would not enter our objections ..." "... would not allow us to show the conspiracy formed with Dolan beforehand ..." "I tell you Governor as long as the present incumbent occupies the bench all that Grand Juries may do to bring to justice these men every effort will be thwarted by him and the sympathizers of that side." June 13, 1879. Indiana Historical Society. Lew Wallace Collection. MO292.

TESTIMONY

No Author. *Dudley Court of Inquiry. (May 2, 1879 - July 5, 1879).* Record No. 16W3/16/28/6. Boxes 1923-1923A. File Number QQ1284. National Archives and Records Administration. Old Military and Civil Branch. Records of the Office of the Judge Advocate General. Washington, D.C.

NOTEBOOK FOR WALLACE

Angel, Frank Warner. "To Gov. Lew Wallace, Santa Fe, N. M., 1878." (Cover of notebook written for Wallace reads "Gov. Lew Wallace, Santa Fe, N.M." Microfilm No. F372. From a document now missing in original form from the Indiana Historical Society. Lew Wallace Collection. MO292.

Theisen, Lee Scott. "Frank Warner Angel's Notes on New Mexico Territory, 1878." *Arizona and the West*, 18 (4) (Winter 1976) 333-370.

ARTICLES (CHRONOLOGICAL)

Wallace, Lew. "General Lew Wallace Writes a Romance of 'Billy the Kid,"
Most Famous Bandit of the Plains." June 8, 1902. *New York Sunday
World Magazine.* Page 4. Indiana Historical Society. Lew Wallace
Collection. MO292.

"Wallace's Words ..." (interview with Lew Wallace conducted in
Washington, D.C. on January 3, 1881), Chicago *The Daily Inter
Ocean.* January 4, 1881. p. 2, c. 4. Indiana Historical Society. Lew
Wallace Collection. MO292.

(Richard Dunham's May 2, 1881 encounter with Billy the Kid), Santa Fe
Daily New Mexican, May 5, 1881, p.4, c. 3. Indiana Historical
Society. Lew Wallace Collection. MO292.

(O.L. Houghton's Conversation with Lew Wallace, before May 26, 1881),
The Las Vegas Daily Optic, May 26, 1881, p.4, c.4. Indiana Historical
Society. Lew Wallace Collection. MO292.

"Billy the Kid ..." (Lew Wallace interviewed on June 13, 1881),
Crawfordsville (Indiana) *Saturday Evening Journal*, June 18, 1881.
Indiana Historical Society. Lew Wallace Collection. MO292.

"Street Pickings," *Crawfordsville* (Weekly) *Review – Saturday Edition*,
January 6, 1894. Indiana Historical Society. Lew Wallace Collection.
MO292.

"An Old Incident Recalled," *The* (Crawfordsville) *Weekly News-Review*,
December 20, 1901. Indiana Historical Society. Lew Wallace
Collection. MO292.

DEATH WARRANT FOR WILLIAM BONNEY

Wallace, Lew. "To the Sheriff of Lincoln County, Greeting ..."
April 30, 1881. Indiana Historical Society. Lew Wallace Collection.
M0292. Box 9, Folder 11.

REWARD NOTICES FOR WILLIAM BONNEY

Wallace, Lew. "Billy the Kid: $500 Reward." Las Vegas *Gazette.*
December 22, 1880.
_____. "Billy the Kid. $500 Reward." May 3, 1881. *Daily New
Mexican.* Vol. X, No. 33. p. 1, c. 3.

REWARD POSTERS FOR WILLIAM BONNEY

Greene, Chas. W. "To the New Mexican Printing and Publishing
Company." May 20, 1881. (Bill to Lew Wallace for Reward posters for
"Kid"). Indiana Historical Society. Lew Wallace Collection. M0292.
Box 4, Folder 18.

_____. "I enclose a bill ..." Letter to Lew Wallace for "Kid" wanted posters. June 2, 1881. Indiana Historical Society. Lew Wallace Collection. M0292. Box 4, Folder 18.

WILD, AZARIAH

Brooks, James J. *1877 Report on Secret Service Operatives.* (September 26, 1877). "On Azariah Wild." p.392. Department of the Treasury. United States Secret Service. Washington, D.C.

Nolan, Frederick. "Biography of Azariah Wild." Personal communication. 2005.

Wild, Azariah F. "Daily Reports of U. S. Secret Service Agents, Azariah F. Wild. Microfilm T-915. Record Group 87. Rolls 306 (June 15, 1877 - December 31, 1877), 307 (January 1, 1878 - June 30, 1879), 308 (July 1, 1879 - June 30, 1881), 309 (July 1, 1881 - September 30, 1883), and 310 (October 1, 1883 - July 31, 1886). National Archives and Records Department. Department of Treasury. United States Secret Service. Washington, D. C.

Wild, Azariah. Telegraph on counterfeit bills. January 4, 1881. Herman Weisner Collection. Lincoln County Papers. New Mexico State University Library at Las Cruces. Rio Grande Historical Collections. Box No. 11. Folder Name: Olinger, Robert and James W. Bell. Folder No. O-1.

WILSON, JOHN "SQUIRE"

Wilson, John. Letter to Lew Wallace. Unsigned but noted as from "Sqr. Wilson by Wallace. Undated, but likely March, 1879. Indiana Historical Society, Lew Wallace Collection. MO292. Box 4, Folder 7. **(On Lady Liberty stationery.)**

_____. Signed JBW. April 8, 1879. Indiana Historical Society, Lew Wallace Collection. MO292. Box 4, Folder 8. **(Matching Wilson's handwriting and on Lady Liberty stationery.)**

_____. Letter to Lew Wallace. May 18, 1879. Indiana Historical Society, Lew Wallace Collection. MO292. Box 4, Folder 5. **(On legal length stationery.)**

LETTER TO JOHN "SQUIRE" WILSON

Wallace, Lew. "I enclose a note for Bonney." March 20, 1879. Indiana Historical Society. Lew Wallace Collection. M0922. Box 4. Folder 6.

550

HISTORICAL ORGANIZATIONS (PERIOD)

SANTA FE RING

Angel, Frank Warner. *Examination of Charges Against F. C. Godfroy, Indian Agent, Mescalero, N. M. October 2, 1878.* (Report 1981, Inspector E. C. Watkins; Cited as Watkins Report). M 319-20 and L147-44-4-8. Record Group 075. National Archives and Records Administration. U. S. Department of Justice. Washington, D. C.
_____. "To Gov. Lew Wallace, Santa Fe, N. M., 1878." (Cover of notebook written for Wallace reads "Gov. Lew Wallace, Santa Fe, N.M." Microfilm No. F372. From a document now missing from the Lew Wallace Collection (M0292), Indiana Historical Society.
_____. *In the Matter of the Examination of the Causes and Circumstances of the Death of John H. Tunstall a British Subject.* Report filed October 4, 1878. Angel Report. Microfilm File Case Number 44-4-8-3. Record Group 060. Microfilm No. M750. Roll 1. National Archives and Records Administration. U S. Department of Justice. Washington, D.C.
_____. *In the Matter of the Investigation of the Charges Against S. B. Axtell Governor of New Mexico.* October 3, 1878. Angel Report. Microfilm File No. 44-4-8-3. Record Group 060. Roll M750. National Archives. U.S. Department of Interior. Washington, D.C.
_____. *In the Matter of the Lincoln County Troubles. To the Honorable Charles Devens, Attorney General. October 4, 1878.* Angel Report. Microfilm Case File No. 44-4-8-3. Record Group 060. Microfilm Roll M750. National Archives and Records Administration. U.S. Department of Justice. Washington,   D. C.
Cleaveland, Norman, *Colfax County's Chronic Murder Mystery.* Santa Fe: New Mexico. The Rydel Press. 1977.
_____ . *A Synopsis of the Great New Mexico Cover-up.* Self-printed. 1989.
_____ . *Some Comments Norman Cleveland May Make to the Huntington Westerners on Sept. 19, 1987.* Unpublished.
_____. *Some Highlights of William R. Morley's Contribution to the Pioneer Development of the Southwest.* Self-printed. No Date.
_____ . *The Great Santa Fe Cover-up.* Based on a Talk given Before the Santa Fe Historical Society on November 1, 1978. Self-printed. 1982.
Cleaveland, Norman and George Fitzpatrick. *The Morleys - Young Upstarts on the Southwest Frontier.* Albuquerque, New Mexico: Calvin Horn Publisher, Inc. 1971.

Keleher, William A. *The Maxwell Land Grant. A New Mexico Item.* Albuquerque, New Mexico: University of New Mexico Press. 1964.

Lamar, Howard Robert N. *The Far Southwest 1846 - 1912. A Territorial History.* New Haven and London: Yale University Press. 1966.

Leonard, Ira. Letters to Governor Lew Wallace. "... the Santa Fe ring that has been so long an incubus on the government of this territory." May 20, 1879. Indiana Historical Society. Lew Wallace Collection. MO292.

_____. "... they would not enter our objections ..." "... would not allow us to show the conspiracy formed with Dolan beforehand ..." "I tell you Governor as long as the present incumbent occupies the bench all that Grand Juries may do to bring to justice these men every effort will be thwarted by him and the sympathizers of that side." June 13, 1879. Indiana Historical Society. Lew Wallace Collection. MO292.

Meinig, D. W. *The Shaping of America. A Geographical Perspective on 500 Years of History. Vol. 3. Transcontinental America 1850 - 1915.* New Haven and London: Yale University Press. 1998. (**Pages 127 and 132 are on the Santa Fe Ring.**)

Milner, Clyde A. II, Carol A. O'Connor, Martha Sandweiss. Eds. *The Oxford History of the American West.* New York and Oxford: Oxford University Press. 1994.

Montoya, María E. *Translating Property. The Maxwell Land Grant and the Conflict Over Land in the American West, 1840-1900.* Berkeley and Los Angeles: University of California Press. 2002.

Naegle, Conrad Keeler. *The History of Silver City, New Mexico 1870-1886.* University of New Mexico Bachelor of Arts thesis. Pages 30-60. Unpublished. 1943. Collection of the Silver City Museum, Silver City, New Mexico.

Pearson, Jim Berry. *The Maxwell Land Grant.* Norman: University of Oklahoma Press. 1961.

Taylor, Morris F. *O. P. McMains and the Maxwell Land Grant Conflict.* Tucson, Arizona: The University of Arizona Press. 1979.

Theisen, Lee Scott. "Frank Warner Angel's Notes on New Mexico Territory, 1878." *Arizona and the West,* 18 (4) (Winter 1976) 333-370.

Twitchell, Ralph Emerson. *The Leading Facts of New Mexico History.* Vol. I-II. Santa Fe: Sunstone Press. 2007. (Reprinted from 1912 edition) (**Reputed Ringman and its cover-up historian**)

Westphall, Victor. *Thomas Benton Catron and His Era.* Tucson, Arizona: University of Arizona Press. 1973.

See Also: THOMAS BENTON CATRON

See Also: STEPHEN BENTON ELKINS

SECRET SERVICE

Bowen, Walter S. and Harry Edward Neal. *The United States Secret Service.* Philadelphia and New York: Chilton Company Publishers. 1960.

Brooks, James J. *1877 Report on Secret Service Operatives.* (September 26, 1877). "On Azariah Wild." p.392. Department of the Treasury. United States Secret Service. Washington, D.C.

Burnham, George P. *American Counterfeits. How Detected, And How Avoided. Comprising Sketches of Noted Counterfeiters, and Their Allies, Of Secret Agents, and Detectives; Authentic Accounts of the Capture of Forgers, Defaulters, and Swindlers; With Rules for Deciding Good and Counterfeit Notes, or United States Currency; A List of Terms and Phrases in Use Among This Fraternity of Offenders, &c., &c.* Springfield, Massachusetts: W. J. Holland. 1875.

_____. *Memoirs of the United States Secret Service With Accurate Portraits of Prominent Members of the Detective Force, Some of Their Most Notable Captures, and a Brie Account of the Life of Col. H. C. Whitley, Chief of the Division.* Boston: Lee, Shepard. 18??.

_____. *Three Years With Counterfeiters, Smugglers, and Boodle Carriers; With Accurate Portraits of the Prominent Members of the Detective Force in The Secret Service.* Boston: 560. John P. Dale & Co. 18??.

Johnson, David R. Illegal Tender. Counterfeiting and the Secret Service in Nineteenth Century America. Washington and London: Smithsonian Institution Press. 1995.

Wild, Azariah F. "Daily Reports of U. S. Secret Service Agents, Azariah F. Wild. Microfilm T-915. Record Group 87. Rolls 306 (June 15, 1877 - December 31, 1877), 307 (January 1, 1878 - June 30, 1879), 308 (July 1, 1879 - June 30, 1881), 309 (July 1, 1881 - September 30, 1883), and 310 (October 1, 1883 - July 31, 1886). National Archives and Records Department. Department of Treasury. United States Secret Service. Washington, D. C.

Wild, Azariah. Telegraph on counterfeit bills. January 4, 1881. Herman Weisner Collection. Lincoln County Papers. New Mexico State University Library at Las Cruces. Rio Grande Historical Collections. Box No. 11. Folder Name: Olinger, Robert and James W. Bell. Folder No. O-1.

NEW MEXICO TERRITORY REBELLIONS (PERIOD)

GRANT COUNTY REBELLION

Naegle, Conrad Keeler. *The History of Silver City, New Mexico 1870-1886.* University of New Mexico Bachelor of Arts thesis. Pages 30-60. Unpublished. 1943. Collection of the Silver City Museum, Silver City, New Mexico.

_____. "The Rebellion of Grant County, New Mexico in 1876." *Arizona and   the West* (published by *Journal of the Southwest*). Autumn, 1968. Volume 10. Number 2. Pages 225-240.

Sullivan, A.P., "Diario del Consejo der Territorio de Neuvo Mejico, Session de 1871-1872. Santa Fe: *Santa Fe New Mexican.* January 8, 1872. Pages 144-154. **[A Ring expurgated document, with a copy found in 1942 by historian Conrad Naegle; confirms troops to "preserve peace."**]

Vincent, Wilson, Jr. *The Book of Great American Documents.* Brookville, Maryland: American History Research Associates. 1993.

No author. "Diario del Consejo der Territorio de Neuvo Mejico, Session de 1871-1872. Las Cruces: *Borderer.* January 24, 1872. Pages 110-113. **[Don Diego Archuleta, President of the Council, gives speech objecting to troops in legislature.**]

_____. Grant County *Herald.* September 16, 1876. **[The intent to annex Grant County to Arizona was announced.**]

_____. Grant County *Herald.* September 23, 1876. **[Need for school system stressed.**]

_____. Grant County *Herald.* September 30, 1876. **["Annexation Meeting" announced.**]

_____. Grant County *Herald.* October 7, 1876. **["Grant County Declaration of Independence" published.**]

COLFAX COUNTY WAR

Caffey, David L. *Frank Springer and New Mexico: From the Colfax County War to the Emergence of Modern Santa Fe.* Texas A and M. University Press. 2007.

Cleaveland, Norman. *The Morleys - Young Upstarts on the Southwest Frontier.* Albuquerque, New Mexico: Calvin Horn Publisher, Inc. 1971.

Dunham, Harold H. "New Mexican Land Grants with Special Reference to the Title Papers of the Maxwell Grant." *New Mexico Historical Review.* (January 1955) Vol. 30, No. 1. pp. 1 - 23.

Keleher, William A. *The Maxwell Land Grant. A New Mexico Item.* Albuquerque, New Mexico: University of New Mexico Press. 1964.

554

Lamar, Howard Roberts. *The Far Southwest 1846 - 1912. A Territorial History.* New Haven and London: Yale University Press. 1966.

Montoya, María E. *Translating Property. The Maxwell Land Grant and the Conflict Over Land in the American West, 1840-1900.* Berkeley and Los Angeles, California: University of California Press. 2002.

Murphy, Lawrence R. *Lucien Bonaparte Maxwell. Napoleon of the Southwest.* Norman: University of Oklahoma Press. 1983.

Pearson, Jim Berry. *The Maxwell Land Grant.* Norman: University of Oklahoma Press. 1961.

Poe, Sophie. *Buckboard Days.* Albuquerque, New Mexico: University of New Mexico Press. 1964.

Taylor, Morris F. *O. P. McMains and the Maxwell Land Grant Conflict.* Tucson, Arizona: The University of Arizona Press. 1979.

No Author. "Mrs. Paula M. Jaramillo, 65 Died Here Tuesday." *The Fort Sumner Leader.* Official Newspaper County of De Baca. December 20, 1929. No. 1158, Page 1, Column 1.

COLFAX COUNTY WAR LETTERS (CHRONOLOGICAL)

Matchett, W.B. and Mary E. McPherson. "Make certain charges against the U.S. Officials in the Territory of New Mexico." To the President . April, 1877. Microfilm File Case Number 44-4-8-3. Record Group 060. Microfilm No. M750. Roll 1. National Archives and Records Administration. U. S. Department of Justice. Washington, D.C. (**Sent to President Rutherford B. Hayes and Secretary of the Interior Carl Schurz 141 pages of letters, affidavits, petitions, newspaper articles, itemized requests for removal of Governor Samuel Beach Axtell and District Judge Warren Bristol, documentation of use of the military against civilians, documentation of the Ring murder of Ring opponent Reverend F.J. Tolby, and identification of the Santa Fe Ring.**)

Springer, Frank. "I endorse herewith, directed to the President ..." To Secretary of the Interior Carl Schurz. June 10, 1878. Microfilm File Case Number 44-4-8-3. Record Group 060. Microfilm No. M750. Roll 1. National Archives and Records Administration. U. S. Department of Justice. Washington, D.C.

_____. "The undersigned, a citizen of the County of Colfax ..." To His Excellency, the President of the United States. Enclosed in letter to Secretary of the Interior Carl Schurz. June 10, 1878. Microfilm File Case Number 44-4-8-3. Record Group 060. Microfilm No. M750. Roll 1. National Archives and Records Administration. U. S. Department of Justice. Washington, D.C.

LINCOLN COUNTY WAR

Angel, Frank Warner. *Examination of charges against F. C. Godfroy, Indian Agent, Mescalero, N. M. October 2, 1878.* (Report 1981, Inspector E. C. Watkins; Cited as Watkins Report). M 319-20 and L147, 44-4-8. Record Group 075. National Archives and Records Administration. U. S. Department of Justice. Washington, D. C.

_____. *In the Matter of the Examination of the Causes and Circumstances of the Death of John H. Tunstall a British Subject.* Report filed October 4, 1878. Angel Report. Microfilm File Case Number 44-4-8-3. Record Group 060. Microfilm No. M750. Roll 1. National Archives and Records Administration. U. S. Department of Justice. Washington, D.C.

_____. *In the Matter of the Investigation of the Charges Against S. B. Axtell Governor of New Mexico. October 3, 1878.* Angel Report. Microfilm No. 44-4-8-3. Record Group 060.Roll M750. National Archives. U. S. Department of Interior. Washington, D.C.

_____. *In the Matter of the Lincoln County Troubles. To the Honorable Charles Devens, Attorney General. October 4, 1878.* Angel Report. Microfilm Case File No. 44-4-8-3. Record Group 060. Microfilm Roll M750. National Archives and Records Administration. U. S. Department of Justice. Washington, D. C.

Cramer, T. Dudley. *The Pecos Ranchers in the Lincoln County War.* Orinda, California: Branding Iron Press. 1996.

Fulton, Maurice Garland. Robert N. Mullin. Ed. *History of the Lincoln County War.* Tucson, Arizona: The University of Arizona Press. 1997.

Jacobson, Joel. *Such Men as Billy the Kid. The Lincoln County War Reconsidered.* Lincoln and London: University of Nebraska Press. 1994.

Keleher, William A. *Violence in Lincoln County 1869-1881.* Albuquerque, New Mexico: University of New Mexico Press. 1957.

Mullin, Robert N. Re: Frank Warner Angel Meeting with President Hayes. August, 1878. Binder RNM, VI, M. (Unpublished). Nita Stewart Haley Memorial Museum. Haley Library. Midland, Texas.

Nolan, Frederick W. *The Life and Death of John Henry Tunstall.* Albuquerque, New Mexico: The University of New Mexico Press. 1965.

Rasch, Philip J. *Gunsmoke in Lincoln County.* Laramie, Wyoming: National Association for Outlaw and Lawmen History, Inc. with University of Wyoming. 1997.

_____. Robert K. DeArment. Ed. *Warriors of Lincoln County.* Laramie: National Association for Outlaw and Lawmen History, Inc. with University of Wyoming. 1998.

Utley, Robert M. *High Noon in Lincoln. Violence on the Western Frontier.* Albuquerque, New Mexico: University of New Mexico Press. 1987.

Wilson, John P. *Merchants, Guns, and Money: The Story of Lincoln County and Its Wars.* Santa Fe, New Mexico: Museum of New Mexico Press. 1987.

No Author. "Amnesty for Matthews and Long in the Third Judicial Court April Term 1879." Herman Weisner Collection. Lincoln County Papers. New Mexico State University at Las Cruces. Rio Grande Historical Collections. Box No. 1. Folder: Amnesty. Folder No. 4.

No Author. "Brady Inventory McSween Property." Herman Weisner Collection. Lincoln County Papers. New Mexico State University Library at Las Cruces. Rio Grande Historical Collections. Box No. 10. Folder Name: Will and Testament A. McSween. Folder No. M15.

No Author. "Charges against Jessie Evans and John Kinney." Doña Ana County Civil and Criminal Docket Book. August 18, 1875 to November 7, 1878. Herman Weisner Collection. Accession No. MS249. Lincoln County Papers. New Mexico State University Library at Las Cruces. Rio Grande Historical Collections. Box No. 13. Folder Name. Venue, Change Of. Folder No. V3.

No Author. "Dismissal of Cases Against Dolan, Matthews, Peppin, October 1879 District Court." Herman Weisner Collection. Lincoln County Papers. New Mexico State University Library at Las Cruces. Rio Grande Historical Collections. Box No. 13. Folder Name: Venue, Change Of. Folder No. V3.

"Disturbances in the Territories, 1878 - 1894. Lawlessness in New Mexico." Senate Documents. 67th Congress. 2nd Session. December 5, 1921 - September 22, 1922. pp. 176 - 187. Washington, D.C.: Government Printing Office. 1922.

No Author. *Dudley Court of Inquiry. (May 2, 1879 - July 5, 1879).* Record No. 16W3/16/28/6. Boxes 1923-1923A. File Number QQ1284. National Archives and Records Administration. Old Military and Civil Branch. Records of the Office of the Judge Advocate General. Washington, D.C.

No Author. "Killers of Tunstall. February 18, 1879." Herman Weisner Collection. Lincoln County Papers. New Mexico State University Library at Las Cruces. Rio Grande Historical Collections. Box No. 12. Folder Name: Tunstall, John H. Folder No. T1.

No Author. "Lincoln County Indictments July 1872 – 1881." Herman Weisner Collections. Lincoln County Papers. New Mexico State University Library at Las Cruces. Rio Grande Historical Collections. Box No. 8. Folder Name. Lincoln Co. Indictments. Folder No. L11.

PRETENDERS AND HOAXERS (MODERN)

BOOKS

Airy, Helen L. *Whatever Happened to Billy the Kid?* Santa Fe, New Mexico: Sunstone Press. 1993. (**John Miller as Billy the Kid.**)

Cooper, Gale. *Billy the Kid's Pretenders: Brushy Bill and John Miller. Albuquerque, New Mexico.* Gelcour Books. 2010.

_____. *MegaHoax: The Strange Plot to Exhume Billy the Kid and Become President.* Albuquerque, New Mexico: Gelcour Books. 2010.

Jameson, W.C. and Frederic Bean. *The Return of the Outlaw Billy the Kid.* Plano, Texas: Republic of Texas Press. 1997. (**"Brushy Bill" Roberts as Billy the Kid.**)

Kaplan, Harold I, M.D. and Benjamin J. Sadock, M.D. *Synopsis of Psychiatry.* Philadelphia: Lippincott Williams & Wilkins. 1994. (**Confabulation: page 285.**)

Morrison, William V. and C.L. Sonnichsen. *Alias Billy the Kid.* Albuquerque: University of New Mexico Press. 1955. (**"Brushy Bill" Roberts as Billy the Kid.**)

Sonnichsen, C.L. and William V. Morrison. *Alias Billy the Kid.* Albuquerque, New Mexico: University of New Mexico Press. 1955. (**Oliver "Brushy Bill" Roberts as Billy the Kid.**)

PRESS RELEASE (GOVERNOR BILL RICHARDSON)

Richardson, Bill. "Governor Bill Richardson Announces State Support of Billy the Kid Investigation." June 10, 2003.

ARTICLES (CHRNOLOLOGICAL)

Janofsky, Michael. "122 Years Later, the Lawmen Are Still Chasing Billy the Kid." *The New York Times.* June 5, 2003. Vol. CLII, No. 52,505. Pages 1 and A31. (**First national announcement of the Billy the Kid Case by its hoaxers.**)

Bommersbach, Jana. "Digging Up Billy: If Pat Garrett didn't kill the Kid, who's buried in his grave?" *True West.* August/September 2003. Volume 50. Issue 7. Pages 42-45.

Bommersbach, Jana. "From Shovels to DNA: The inside story of digging up Billy." *True West.* October/November, 2003. Volume 50. Issue 7. Pages 42-45.

Fecteau, Loie. "No Kidding: Governor Taps Lawyer For Billy." *Albuquerque Journal.* November 19, 2003. Page 1, A6.

Jameson, W.C. and Leon Metz. "Was Brushy Bill Really Billy the Kid? Experts face off over new evidence." *True West.* November/December, 2003. Volume 50. Issue 10. Pages 32-33.

WRITING, PAPER, AND IMPLEMENTS (PERIOD)

REFERENCE BOOKS

Baker, Cathleen A. *From the Hand to the Machine: Nineteenth-century American paper and mediums: technologies, materials, and conservation.* Ann Arbor, Michigan: The Legacy Press. 2010.

Nickell, Joe. *Pen, Ink, & Evidence.* New Castle, Delaware: Oak Knoll Press. 2003.

Thornton, Tamara Plakins. *Handwriting in America: A Cultural History.* New Haven and London: Yale University Press. 1996.

SPENCERIAN PENMANSHIP

Spencer, Platt Rogers. *Spencerian Penmanship.* New York: Ivison, Phinney, Blakemont Co. 1857.

_____. *Spencerian System of Practical Penmanship.* (New York: Ivison, Phinney, Blakemont Co. 1864). Reprinted by Milford, Michigan: Mott Media, Inc. 1985.

Spencer, H.C. (Prepared for the "Spencerian Authors) *Spencerian Key to Practical Penmanship.* New York: Ivison, Phinney, Blakemont, Taylor & Co. 1874.

_____. (Prepared for the "Spencerian Authors) *Theory of Spencerian Penmanship for Schools and Private Learners Developed by Questions and Answers with Practical Illustrations: Designed to Be Used by Pupils in Connection With the Use of Spencerian Copybooks.* New York: Ivison, Phinney, Blakemont, Taylor & Co. 1874.

Spencerian Authors. *Theory of Spencerian Penmanship for Schools and Private Learners Developed by Questions and Answers with Practical Illustrations: Designed to Be Used by Pupils in Connection With the Use of Spencerian Copybooks.* (New York: Ivison, Phinney, Blakemont, Taylor & Co. 1874.) Reprinted and modified by Milford, Michigan: Mott Media, Inc. 1985. **(Page 30 describes forming "the capital stem;" pages 2-7 describe "position" and "hand-arm movements;" and page 45 describes the pen and "shading.")**

Sull, Michael, *Spencerian Script and Ornamental Penmanship.* Prairie Village: Kansas. (Unpublished, undated, modern manual).

ACKNOWLEDGMENTS

This roster of appreciation includes some contributing sources from my Billy Bonney novel, *Billy an Paulita*; and are also included in Annotated Bibliography. Responsibility for errors is my own. Overriding is my debt to William Bonney, whose cause, courage, brilliance, tenacity, and joie de vivre are my inspiration.

Historical bedrock came from books by Frederick Nolan on Billy the Kid, the Lincoln County War, and John Henry Tunstall. As valuable was Leon Metz's Pat Garrett biography and Jerry Weddle's book on Billy Bonney's adolescence. Period military consultation was by Steven Alley, curator at the Kansas Fort Leavenworth Army Museum; historians Jim Minor and Tim Smith at the Shiloh National Military Park; and Bill Gwaltney, a General Miles Marching and Chowder Society re-enactor.

National Archive specialists were Clarence Lyons, Wayne DeCesar, and Fred Romanski at the Civilian Records Branch; Dr. Milt Gustafson at the Civilian Records Branch Classification; Janice Wiggins at the Justice Department; Joseph Schwarz at the Department of Interior; Michael Sampson at the Secret Service Library Counterfeit Division; and Mike Meir at the Department of War, Old Military and Civil Branch.

Libraries and archivists assisting were the Las Cruces, New Mexico State University Library's Archives and Special Collection's Herman Weisner Collection with processing archivist Charles Stanford; the University of New Mexico Library's Southwestern Collections' Catron Papers; the Roswell, Chavez County Historical Center for Southeast New Mexico with curator Elvis Flemming; Midland, Texas Nita Stewart Haley Memorial Library with archivist Jim Bradshaw; the Santa Fe, New Mexico Fray Angélico Chávez Historical Library with archivist Tomas Jaehn; the Canyon, Texas Panhandle-Plains Historical Museum with archivist Warren Stricker; Ken Earle from the State of New Mexico Office of Cultural Affairs Historic Preservation Division; past New Mexico State Historian Estevan Rael-Galvez and current State Historian Rick Hendricks at the Office of the New Mexico State Historian; Susan Berry of the Silver City Museum and Library; and President Rutherford B. Hayes's Memorial Library in Fremont, Ohio with curator Nan Card.

Specific to collections with William Bonney's writings were the Indiana Historical Society's Lew Wallace Collection in Indianapolis with Doug Clanin, retired Chief Editor of the Lew Wallace Collections; Paul Brockman, Director of Manuscript and Visual Collections; Suzanne Hahn, Director of Reference Services; Susan Sutton, Coordinator Visual Reference Services; Susan Rogers, Paper Conservator; David Turk, technical photographer; and Steve Haller, Senior Director Collections and Library.

Assistance with the Lew Wallace Collection in the Lilly Library of the Bloomington campus of Indiana State University was provided by Erika Dowell, Public Services Librarian.

Spencerian penmanship was discussed with Mott Media; David Sull; and the Iowa, Ames Historical Society's curators, Dennis Wendell and Sarah Vouthilak.

Antique New Mexico newspaper archivists and experts who assisted were New Mexico Highland University's Cathleen Kroll for the Las Vegas *Daily Optic* and Las Vegas *Gazette*; Dennis Daily and Austin Hoover of the Rio Grande Historical Collections at the New Mexico State University Library at Las Cruces; Marilyn Fletcher at the Center For Southwestern Research at the University of New Mexico Library in Albuquerque; Jim Bowers of the *New Mexico Optic*; and Michael E. Pitel, retired Heritage Tourism Development Program Officer for the New Mexico Tourism Department and current President of TravelSource New Mexico.

Computer graphics were done by Samantha Morris, Seth Scott, and Bobbi Jo MacElroy.

Literary advice and encouragement came from author and composer Mark N. Grant and from my mother, Dr. Rose Cooper.

INDEX

CPSIA information can be obtained
at www.ICGtesting.com
Printed in the USA
BVHW030527271021
619953BV00001B/8